CANNIBALS of the HEART

CANNIBALS

of the

HEART

A Personal Biography of
Louisa Catherine and John Quincy Adams

JACK SHEPHERD

McGraw-Hill Book Company

New York   St. Louis   San Francisco
Hamburg   Mexico   Toronto

Copyright Acknowledgments

The author is grateful to the following publishers, journals, and individuals for permission to quote selections from previously copyrighted materials:

Alfred A. Knopf, Inc., for *John Quincy Adams and the Union* by Samuel Flagg Bemis, copyright © 1956 by Samuel Flagg Bemis.

Houghton Mifflin Company, for *New Letters of Abigail Adams*, edited by Stewart Mitchell, copyright 1947, © 1974 by the American Antiquarian Society.

Frederick Ungar Publishing Co., Inc., for the *Diary of John Quincy Adams, 1794–1845*, edited by Allan Nevins (American Classic Series.). Copyright 1928 by Longmans, Green and Co., Copyright 1951 by Allan Nevins.

The Belknap Press of Harvard University Press, for the following:

Diary and Autobiography of John Adams (4 vols.), edited by L. H. Butterfield. Copyright © 1961 by the Massachusetts Historical Society.

Diary of Charles Francis Adams (6 vols.), edited by Marc Friedlaender and L. H. Butterfield. Copyright © 1964, 1968, 1974 by the Massachusetts Historical Society.

Adams Family Correspondence (4 vols.), edited by L. H. Butterfield. Copyright © 1963, 1973 by the Massachusetts Historical Society.

1 2 3 4 5 6 7 8 9 D O D O 8 7 6 5 4 3 2 1

LIBRARY OF CONGRESS CATALOGING IN PUBLICATION DATA

Shepherd, Jack.
Cannibals of the heart.
Bibliography: p.
Includes index.
1. Adams, John Quincy, Pres. U.S., 1767–1848.
2. Adams, Louisa Catherine Johnson, 1775–1852.
3. Presidents — United States — Biography.
4. Presidents — United States — Wives — Biography.
I. Title.
E377.S53   973.5'5'0922 [B]   80–23578
ISBN 0–07–056730–1

Book design by Roberta Rezk.

To
Susanna Linda Goldman
August 2, 1955–May 29, 1976
and her parents
Martin and Marian Goldman

The mischievous consequences of vice and folly,
or irregular desires and predominant passions,
are best discovered by those relations which are
levelled with the general surface of life, which
tell not how any man became great, but how he was
made happy, not how he lost the favour of his
Prince, but how he became discontented with himself.

SAMUEL JOHNSON, *The Idler*

Acknowledgments

Putting together a book of this length and scope is never the work of a single person. Behind the author stand ranks of people who gave support in a variety of forms. Thanking them all individually is impossible, and this brief note will have to suffice.

I would like to thank Dr. Robert Taylor, editor-in-chief of The Adams Papers in Boston, both for his patient direction and help, and for his suggestions regarding research. The Adams Papers, on microfilm, are an invaluable asset for historical scholars.

Dr. Daniel J. Boorstin, the Librarian of Congress, also very kindly welcomed me into his splendid office in that national treasure, the Library of Congress. Dr. Boorstin introduced me to members of his staff and the research facilities of the Library, both of which proved exceptional. I wish particularly to thank Edward N. MacConomy for his guidance.

I have always maintained that an author is only as good as his libraries. I would like to thank three — and their staffs. My first cut through the research took place at Low Library, Columbia University, New York City, and the second at Bailey Library, University of Vermont, Burlington, Vermont. I especially want to thank Milton Crouch, the Assistant Director of the UVM library, for his patient assistance over a long period. The bulk of my research took place at Baker Library, Dartmouth College, Hanover, New Hampshire, near my home. The staff there cheered me through long winters of research. I especially wish to thank Lorraine Hunt, Supervisor of the Jones Microtext Center at Baker Library, who put up with my slowly plowing through the entire relevant Adams Papers on microfilm, a process that took some eighteen months of work, seven days a week, twelve hours a day. Thanks, also, to her assistants Charles Stone, Sara Jones, and Ulla Sonnerup. They each brightened seemingly endless hours.

A special thanks must also go to my editor, Curtis Kelly, for her skill, patience and — John Quincy Adams's favorite word — perseverance in guiding this manuscript to completion.

ACKNOWLEDGMENTS

There were, as well, friends who massaged my back and ego when the book seemed overwhelming. Good people like Lance and Neila Wyman and Jody and Arnold Spellun of New York City welcomed me into their comforting homes, during research excursions, and put up with my eccentricities. Jim Gold and Penny McConnell sent notes and calls of cheer, which carried me along. My two noisy, wonderful, enthusiastic, lovable kids, Kristen and Caleb, and my protective and nurturing "best friend," Kathy, deserve my eternal hugs and kisses for their tiptoes and whispers and innumerable sacrifices.

I cannot end this catalog without mentioning Martin and Marian Goldman, to whom this book is dedicated. At the worst instant, when the research was tougher than me, when my fingertips went numb from typing, when winter seemed without end, their warm love gave me the strength to continue — "and, dammit, finish." The book is dedicated to them, and their daughter Susanna, on whose funeral day I agreed to undertake this project. Their love renewed me.

Contents

[*Illustrations follow page 190*]

Foreword

Women, the old saying goes, are the forgotten men of history.

No woman has been more forgotten in the widely published history of the Adams family than Louisa Johnson Adams, the wife of John Quincy Adams. The Adams men felt the lot of women was to be passive spectators, subservient to their fame, controlled by them in every way. Louisa Adams refused to fit into this doctrine. She refused to remain silent about an Adams myth: that public service is built without private cost.

The purpose of this book, therefore, is to invert the historical viewpoint. It attempts to elevate Louisa Adams onto the pedestal with her lofty and accomplished husband. And it seeks to offer a fresh perspective on John Quincy Adams's formidable public career, by looking at it from within the family; that is, placing Louisa and her life close in the foreground, and moving John Quincy and his public accomplishments to the background.

The struggle, candidly, is not always successful. John Quincy Adams spent fifty-four years in the public service. He kept a diary that spanned sixty-seven years. He preserved most of his letters, and those written to him. His father and mother also preserved letters, and John Quincy's father also kept a diary, as did John Quincy's son, Charles. Further, this vast and rich record was not left untampered. Charles Francis Adams, John Quincy's son, burned his brother George's letters and cut paragraphs from the letters of others, including his mother, Louisa Adams. And when *his* son, Henry, was editing Louisa's letters, Charles warned: "I have been carefully over my mother's papers since my return, and have reduced their volume essentially, perhaps rather too much for your purpose."

Perhaps, as well, too much for ours. The result is a distortion: What is known about the Johnson side remains meager by comparison. The Adamses overwhelm. And here one proceeds with caution. John Quincy Adams calculated what history should know of him. He seldom put pen to paper without considering the historian or the next generation of Adamses reading over his shoulder. His diaries, written in the cold light of morning, are least spontaneous. It did not help that John Quincy caught his brother Charles reading his private diaries; the entries became, for a while, even more guarded.

Letters between family members formed the backbone of my research. They impressed me as being most spontaneous and, therefore, probably nearest the truth. Louisa's two major diary works — "Record of A Life, Or, My Story," and the revealingly titled "The Adventures of a Nobody" — also gave, with close reading, information corroborated elsewhere; both documents, however, were written as retrospectives, not diaries, and therefore flawed. I used John Quincy Adams's diaries as backup to his letters. Equally interesting were the family's financial ledgers, receipts, random newspaper accounts, letters from anonymous or unknown Americans, petitions received to abolish slavery. I urge every student of American history to read through these; a sharp sense of the American people emerges.

Although Louisa was well educated by comparison to other women of her time, she wrote without a sound knowledge of grammar and spelling. In all cases I have left her voice as I found it and added commas, or corrected spelling, only to keep the writing clear. John Quincy wrote very well, and correctly; his work is entirely untouched here. Finally, because John Quincy Adams has the same first name as his son and his father, and his full name is long, I have used, in places, his initials, JQA, as he sometimes signed his letters.

The book, then, examines two lives — Louisa's and JQA's — through their personal documents: letters, diaries, essays, ledgers. Looking out from inside this family, we see not merely the bright strokes of public accomplishment, but life as they lived it. The illnesses, journeys, love and abuse of their children, struggles with alcoholism and depression, persistent worry about money and housing, the education of their children are all fragments of a whole. The Adamses, like many of us, fought over money, fell into debt, argued with each other and their children; they even owned a dog. By examining these small puzzle pieces, we seek a new perspective, and discover a far more important place in history for the forgotten wife of this great public man.

Jack Shepherd
Norwich, Vermont

I
London

1797

1

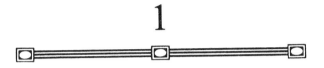

LOUISA JOHNSON loved spring best of all the seasons. It was a time of promise and a season of insistence, when all that had been dead was born again. During her life, Louisa measured the passing of winter and the rains, and welcomed the clouds of wild pigeons filling the spring sky, the flowering of the earth, the singing of birds, the rich smells of tree and vine. Louisa loved the heat, a characteristic that her grandsons later attributed to her Southern (Maryland) blood, and spring carried with it the never-failing promise of warmer weather. Like her favorite season, Louisa was a velvet-budding spirit who grew up as a welcomed, carefree, and spoiled child. She filled the air about her with music, and played the pianoforte and the harp; she wrote and recited poetry, and she sang, either alone or with one of her sisters, sometimes reaching such volumes of enthusiasm that men — always men — in neighboring hotel rooms harrumphed loudly or pounded the walls. Louisa loved the excitement of her impulses, and she indulged herself. She danced whenever asked, but never alone. She was all her life a pretty, almost beautiful woman. She was a punster, and became so expert at fortune-telling that her women friends often asked her to consult the cards. Louisa knew everyone's future but her own.

John Quincy Adams liked the snow and cold, as did his mother; heat troubled him. He was born in New England — a land of steady habits — and was as hard, cold, and purposeful as a stone wall. He was the first-born son of a Founding Father who had been the new nation's first Vice President and its second President. The Adams family was the first American political dynasty, and JQA was nurtured in its Massachusetts compound at Quincy by a father and mother who carefully planned his political life. Before he was seventeen, John Quincy Adams was an intense and ambitious young man who carried "a certain superiority about himself." He had served his father in Paris, Amsterdam, and The Hague, and traveled to and from Russia as private secretary to the United States Commissioner to St. Petersburg. Between 1800 and 1848, Adams would hold almost every important diplomatic and political position in the United States.

Adams enjoyed being precise. No, not enjoyed — JQA enjoyed little — rather he *made* it his duty to be precise. He measured, timed, observed, and recorded everything that occurred every day of his adult life. He started a diary, at his father's insistence, at fourteen and kept it faithfully each day for almost sixty-seven years. He deprived himself of pleasure, as Louisa knew before they wed, and welcomed misfortune as a means of improving character. He held grudges, and whatever real emotions Adams had he buried carefully and methodically in his diary, where he wrote of intense hatreds and loves, of humor and sorrow, and kept a neat list of his enemies. Throughout his life he would rise every day at four or five, build his own fire, read his Bible, then work a full day and lament the social events of evening that interfered with his privacy. He never lost sight of history: He had an overriding need to preserve his likeness, and sat for his portrait more than sixty times, often when too busy for anyone else. He viewed his portraits and diary in a historical sense, as a permanent record for the nation, part of its heritage — and a way of assuring that the next generations knew who he was and what he looked like. Adams exercised with equal intensity: fast walks, horseback rides, skinny-dips in the Potomac River; Louisa thought he bathed too much. JQA always maintained that there were three rules to living correctly: (1) Regularity, (2) Regularity, (3) Regularity.

On Wednesday, July 26, 1797, Louisa Johnson and John Quincy Adams walked together in the sunshine to the Church of All Hallows Barking, Tower Hill, London. Safely three thousand miles from his domineering mother, John Quincy had decided, at age thirty, to get married. Only his brother Thomas, serving as best man, was with him. Adams had knocked at the Johnson home on Tower Hill at exactly nine o'clock that morning, and the wedding party had walked slowly across Tower Hill to the church, and to this incongruous union. Beyond the double, thick oak doors, beyond row after row of empty pews, beyond the devotive candles flickering in the transept, only seven people gathered around the Reverend John Hewlett, B.D. There was no one else in the church. The slanting July sun made stained-glass patches on the dim stone floor. Louisa appeared, as always, delicate and small, with soft, dark-brown eyes and light-brown hair that curled out around her blue-ribboned hat. She radiated, an observer once said, "the most bewitching smile" a woman ever had. John Quincy wore a powdered wig, which made his deep, black eyes appear even darker. He was neither elegant nor commanding, but short, slightly plump, and, even in his early manhood, balding. Their low voices echoed among the ancient shadows: He vowed to love and cherish, she to honor and obey; both would struggle to keep these promises. For they entered the marriage not with the passion of love or even the joy of romance, but from a sense of duty. Louisa was twenty-two, and John Quincy eight years older; it was time for both to marry, and both had parted from earlier loves.

At the altar of All Hallows, Louisa Johnson and John Quincy Adams, the best generation of their well-known families, were opposites come together. Where she was kind, loving, and gentle, he was stern, gruff, and sometimes nasty. Where her love was spontaneous and wide, his was parceled out narrowly: first to God, then to Country, then to Duty, then to Family, and finally to individuals. Louisa cherished the "Johnson wit," and could buckle the stiffest guest with her humor and smile. Adams had difficulty appearing cheerful. "Gravity is natural to him," said one artist, "and a smile looks ill at home." Louisa lived her

[5]

childhood, free and expansive, in Europe, uninhibited by the claims of a New England conscience: "Though Boston is the land of learning," she said, "I never found it the land of wit." Adams smoked a pipe and cigars; Louisa abhorred the stench of "that poison tobacco." She was certain that snuff caused madness. While Louisa read history, volumes of poetry, French translations, and novels of the day, JQA gloried in his Bible and solid classical fare. Cicero, Louisa said ruefully, was his "passion." She, evidently, was not. He loved her most when they were apart.

Where she was an indulgent, gentle mother, he was a strict and demanding father. He believed in the continuity of children, but without sentimentality. He saved his kindnesses for people on the periphery of his life. JQA gave his family a harsh outer shell, a list of demands for excellence, and unattainable goals. He handed money to strangers and beggars, flattered artists, and spoiled his servants. Louisa had to discipline them. He tolerated a lazy coachman and a drunken houseman. But when his sons did not meet his relentless list of expectations, his wrath seared them.

John Quincy, later in life, admitted the many differences "of sentiment, of tastes, and of opinions in regard to domestic economy, and to the education of children, between us. There are frailties of temper in both of us; both being quick and irascible, and mine being sometimes harsh." But, he concluded, marriage was better than celibacy. Louisa, after fifty years, thought, with a gloom worthy of Keats, "that hanging and marriage were strongly assimilated."

Louisa had reason to feel that way. She entered this marriage aware of her husband's character and their conflicts, and, as a woman, facing a lifetime of subordination to him. Louisa lived in the transition between two eras. Where her mother-in-law had enjoyed some freedoms as a pre-Revolutionary American woman, and had given voice and tongue to issues of consequence, Louisa found herself silenced by a social age that relegated her to the role of mere ornament for her husband's glorification. Louisa never understood the institutional nature of discrimination against women. But she felt it.

On July 26, 1797, in the springtime of her springtime, Louisa Johnson Adams entered her womanhood full of promise. But hers was a marriage out of season: of light to shadow; of springtime to winter; of heart to cannibal.

2

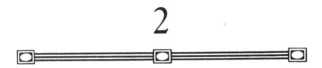

LOUISA CATHERINE JOHNSON was born in London on February 12, 1775. She was the second child of Joshua Johnson and Catherine Nuth, who gave birth to seven daughters and one son, every one of them "remarkable for beauty." Life was from the start serene and comfortable. The distant rumbling of the American Revolution scarcely intruded upon the Johnson family, and their lives during the harsh years of the war and turmoil contrasted sharply with those of John and Abigail Adams in Massachusetts. While the Adamses were frequently separated, and always in danger of being caught in skirmishes or seized by the British as traitors, the Johnsons settled easily into the luxurious pace and surroundings of wealth, and the security of being more than three thousand miles from the battlefields.

Louisa's father, Joshua, was an enterprising and well-connected man from a large Maryland family, who had been sent by his Annapolis trading partnership to England to learn and later manage the transatlantic affairs of his mercantile firm. Johnson proved clever at this, and soon, with charm and persistence, overcame the hostility of English merchants who complained, he wrote to his partners, of his "ambitiousness." Wisely, Johnson steered an apolitical course, seeming to take no sides in the emerging conflict between British crown and American colonies, and it became clear to him and to his partners that Johnson's skills included not coarse aggressiveness, but a certain willingness to cope with the British colonial system of trade, by joining it.

The odds against Joshua Johnson's success were high and risky. He was separated from his partners by an ocean that took months to cross in small, often undependable sailing ships. He was dependent on sea trade between two antagonists going to war. Johnson was a native-born son of the American colonies living in the capital of England. Worse, he was a member of an old and established colonial family, some of whose offspring now sat, along with John Adams, in Philadelphia, plotting the overthrow of the British King — who lived but a short carriage ride from Johnson's home. Moreover, Catherine Nuth Johnson was a British subject.

Joshua Johnson was descended from a sea captain who had traded from Liverpool to America, and from a political activist who had fled England for the more tolerant American colonies. In both the Johnson and Adams families, spoilage tended to seep down through the generations: In the late 1600s, Thomas Johnson had fallen in love with Mary Baker, a chancery ward, whom he was forbidden by law to marry because she was a maid and he an upper-class gentleman. Maids in every century have been sexual outlets for the men who kept them, and long after Thomas's dalliance, when both the Johnsons and the Adamses considered themselves and their nation aristocratic — and liked it that way — two of Louisa and John Quincy Adams's sons would sexually pursue lower-class women, and one of Louisa's nephews would elope with her womanservant. The outrage would be no louder in the nineteenth century than it had been in the seventeenth. But laws never conquered love in any age. Thomas and Mary eloped, sailing from Yarmouth, England, to settle in St. Leonard, Calvert County, Maryland Colony, around 1700. They opened a trading post near the mouth of Leonard's Creek and traded with Indians who canoed across the Chesapeake. Here, along the shores of the bay, on March 30, 1725, Thomas Johnson, Jr., married Dorcas Sedgewick, and they raised a large family that eventually spread north, along the bay, and inland, and included a prominent member of the first

Continental Congress, a doctor, Maryland's first elected governor, and Louisa Johnson's father.

In all, Thomas, Jr., and Dorcas had seven sons. Thomas, Baker, James, and Roger were the most prosperous. They were also smarter and, some said, of higher character than Benjamin, Dr. John, and Joshua. In 1774, Joshua's brother Thomas Johnson and John Adams served together in the Continental Congress in Philadelphia; they were both members of the "Great Committee," which, among other things, detailed the colonists' grievances against England. From the start, Adams admired this Johnson's "clear and cool head," and the two frequently walked or dined together. Later, in 1801, as John Adams closed out his Presidency, he would offer Thomas Johnson, who had already served as Maryland's first governor, the position of First Chief Justice of the Circuit Court of the District of Columbia. Johnson, however, declined because he was, he said, "crouching under the load of more than eighty years." That same year, President Adams appointed Joshua Johnson Superintendent of Stamps in Washington, and later Louisa and John Quincy would take in two Johnson nephews and a niece. Other Johnsons gladly accepted Adams largess, and the Johnson family early became dependent upon the Adams family for jobs, shelter, promotion, sustenance. This suspect unsteadiness permeated half the Johnson family, a condition the New England Adamses disapproved of; unfortunately, it was this side of the Johnsons that bonded with them. Unlike the intelligent and admired Thomas, his brother Joshua Johnson did not measure up to Adams standards. Although nothing was said from family to family, James Johnson, Jr., in a letter to his mother in 1843, described Joshua Johnson as "a weak, vain man, fond of great people, and impoverished by an ambitious and extravagant wife."

Early on, Joshua had been attracted by the fast life in Annapolis and the promise it dangled. By the mid-eighteenth century, Annapolis was the Maryland seat of government and an important trade center located on the Severn River, within easy sail of the Chesapeake and the Atlantic Ocean. A vigorous merchant community thrived there, and its theater, horse racing and "plenty of gaming," great homes, and glittering social life were enjoyed by wealthy merchants and the "grandees of government." Here Joshua Johnson, Charles Wallace, and John Davidson formed their mercantile partnership, which sent Johnson to London in 1771.

In England, Joshua soon met a young Englishwoman named Catherine Nuth. Little is known of her family, although Louisa recalled from conversations that her mother's father had been a "Writer" in the India Office "like that of Charles Lamb mentioned in his memoirs." She also knew that her grandmother, Mary Young, was an "extremely beautiful" daughter of a brewer in London, and that her mother had been one of twenty-two children.

The vain Joshua, filled with hope, and the lovely and ambitious Catherine, just sixteen and filled, it now appears, with child, were married sometime between November 1773 and February 1774. Birth control, not unknown, was not widely practiced; the only trustworthy method was *coitus interruptus*. Condoms were available in London, but the clumsy things were made from sheep gut and secured to the wearer at the base with a red ribbon, tied about the scrotum. Joshua disdained either method, and Nancy, the first-born, arrived in December 1773. Louisa followed in 1775, and then Carolina Virginia Marylanda, in July 1776, named to mark the vote of those colonies for independence by the Continental Congress. One son, Thomas Baker Johnson, and three more daughters followed.

Louisa Johnson's childhood world contained no terrors, no discomforts. It was well ordered, unthreatened. In its reassuring hierarchy, her father stood at the head: protector, master, unquestioned power. He symbolized the family, and when he was rich and successful, the family appeared good and right. But when he failed, as he would, the family failed with him and became something broken and wrong. Louisa loved her father more than she ever loved any other person, and thought him "the handsomest man I ever beheld." He was, she said, honest, kind, even-tempered, and affectionate, and his usual expression, she remembered, "was sweetness and benevolence." But Joshua could lose his temper, and when he did showed "a dazzling fixed severity that was absolutely aweful, and which seemed by its vivid scrutiny to drive into the very depths of the human heart." And so while she loved her father, Louisa feared him; she also inherited his temper.

Louisa's mother used both natural beauty and innate cunning to define her role. She was small and delicate-featured, exquisitely beautiful in her laces, silks, and ruffles. Catherine learned early how to make Joshua do as she wished, and was so spoiled that, whenever she fell ill, Joshua wrapped paper around the handles of the knives and forks and placed them before the fire to take the chill off before she was allowed to handle them. He also sat by her and cut her food, and fed it to her. Catherine, too, knew how to spend Joshua's money, and used their homes and social entertainments to exhibit her skills and her family's talents. "She was lively," Louisa said, "and her understanding highly cultivated, and her wit brilliant." Catherine charmed the male guests, and presented her daughters to them in the best light possible for the market. She used Joshua's money and his children to enhance his prospects; she was indeed ambitious for her husband's success. Every Sunday Louisa's mother dressed them in identical clothes, even little Thomas, and they marched in twos to church, strung out along the roadside by height, foot stride, and inclination. As long as life was good, it was very, very good: Louisa called her childhood a time when "even our sorrows are like rainbow clouds dispersed ere they are seen." The Johnsons lived richly, and on the very edge of their resources. It was a precarious position from which the fall would be swift and hard, and, to Louisa at least, a lifelong shame.

In early 1778, when Louisa was three and the Revolutionary War made life uncomfortable for Americans in England, the Johnsons sailed to France. They wished to book passage to Maryland, but with four children, the oldest only five, the long sea voyage in wartime was too risky. Instead, they settled in the port city of Nantes, where Johnson undertook commissions for Congress and Maryland, and became embroiled in the political intrigues and commercial schemes found in every French port during the war.

Nantes, near the mouth of the Loire River, connected Paris and its manufacturing with overseas commerce. The city was both ideally located and beautiful, scattered among fine meadows along either bank of the river and on several islands, which were connected to one another and the shore by arched bridges. The first island from the sea contained homes built of durable stone, like those in Paris, and here the Johnsons settled for the duration of the war, living "in a handsome style." Louisa remembered:

> The House was an immense building forming a hollow Square, and was called the Temple de Gout. The name itself was enough to turn the head of a beautiful and much admired young Woman like my Mother; new to the world, and probably engendered *tastes* and *ideas* perhaps calculated to lavish on her children a more expensive and higher order of education, than my Fathers station in life, or circumstances as a Commission Merchant prudently authorized.

The Johnsons entertained lavishly at the Temple de Gout, and their guests included Jonathan Williams, great-nephew of Benjamin Franklin (then one of the American ministers in Paris); John Paul Jones, in Nantes outfitting the *Bonhomme Richard* for its rendezvous with history in 1779; and John Adams, passing on his way from Paris to Boston with his awkward but precocious son, John Quincy Adams. He was but twelve years old, and Louisa only three, and there is no evidence that they met. John Quincy was far more interested in translating into English Cicero's first Philippic against Catiline, and Louisa preferred child's play among the islands and meadows. Her recollections, in fact, were not of this chance meeting, but of her home and culture.

Louisa and her sisters spoke only French, and she remained fluent in the language for the rest of her life. In a short time, she forgot every word of English, "and we were to all intents and purposes, in manners, language, and dress French children." She grew up with private tutors and servants — not unusual in this period when one-third of all American and British households contained living-in slaves, free slaves, or indentured or free servants. When Louisa reached school age, she and her sister Nancy went to the nearby Catholic convent school. Since her parents emphasized no religion over another, Louisa embraced during this time the Roman Catholic Church. Late in her adulthood she would recall the strong influence the church had upon her, "the heartfelt humility with which I knelt before the image of the tortured Jesus and the horror I felt at the thought of mixing with heretics." Louisa was a thoughtful and sometimes solemn child, and a "creature of ardent affections and strong impulse," she said. She and her sisters took dancing lessons, and they spent much of their childhood, while in France, "constantly exhibiting and performing in full dress at Childrens Balls" and being "perfectly ruined by adulation and flattery." Even so, Louisa later wrote, she much preferred attending Catholic Mass in the convent, and listening to music in the cathedrals, and kneeling "in adoration before the crucifix, in silent prayer and veneration," to dancing at the balls. She and her sisters and brother attended church every Sunday, a practice Louisa quit after her marriage.

3

JOHN QUINCY ADAMS was born on July 11, 1767, in a small upstairs bedchamber of the family's farmhouse in Massachusetts Bay Colony. The property dated back to 1639, and at one time had included immense reaches of land south and east of the village of Boston, in a farming area called Braintree and later Quincy. John Quincy Adams's ancestors on both sides of the family, the Adamses and the Smiths, had lived among these rolling hills near the sea for more than 150 years before his birth. His father, John Adams, had inherited 140 acres and two New England farmhouses, each typical two-story salt-boxes, from his father in 1761. John Adams himself had been born in one house in 1735, and on this day in 1767, John Quincy Adams drew first breath in the upper story of the house next to it. His birth was presided over by Elizabeth Quincy Smith, Abigail Adams's sister, who held in her heart the knowledge that on that same day in another candlelit room, in her father's house by the sea, a life was ebbing out. On July 13, John Quincy, age seventy-eight, the great-grandfather of this newborn boy, the venerated man of the colonial legislature, would die. So John Quincy Adams would be named for the great departing patriarch, and for three days, as one life entered and another departed this world, the treasured Adams name and heritage stretched back in the heart of the old man to 1688, the colony's earliest days, and rested in the newborn boy, who would carry them almost halfway into the nineteenth century. For a brief moment, in the passing of these namesakes, this American family, seen from the historian's perspective, spanned 160 years, from the colonial period to the age of steam and the edge of civil war.

John Quincy Adams was a son of the American Revolution. His father, John Adams, was a circuit lawyer who by 1767 had already attended meetings of the Sons of Liberty organized by the baby's uncle, Samuel Adams. His father moved the family several times between the Braintree farm and houses in Boston, where JQA and his older sister, Abigail, called Nabby by the family, heard the Sons of Liberty play violins and flutes under their windows as the children prepared for bed. Toddling one day with Uncle Samuel around Boston Common, little Johnny, as his parents called him, made the mistake of admiring the British redcoats at drill. His uncle, JQA recalled, gave him an early political lesson by shouting: "Haughty redcoats! Wicked redcoats! They must *go away!*"

John Quincy's mother, Abigail Smith Adams, had married John when she was not yet twenty. She gave birth five times between 1765 and 1772; the Continental Congresses became John and Abigail's birth control. Abigail bore two daughters, one of whom, Susanna, died before age two, and three sons: John Quincy, Charles, and Thomas Boylston Adams.

Abigail took charge of the Adams farm when her husband was in Philadelphia at the Continental Congresses. She gave the orders, hired and fired the workers, paid the wages, made clothing, and directed everything from meal preparation to planting. With John gone — Abigail complained that they were not together more than half of their first twelve years of marriage — she raised and educated John Quincy and his brothers and sister. Abigail Adams, however, had never gone to school. In her youth "it was fashionable to ridicule female learning," and she was sick much of the time. "Female education," she said, "in the best families, went no further than writing and arithmetic; in some few and rare instances music and dancing." Abigail's maternal grandmother had educated her; the old lady had been a tough and valued colonial woman, and Abigail became literate and even well-read. She quoted Shakespeare, the Bible, and such popular eighteenth-century authors as Swift, Sterne, and Burke in her letters. Throughout her life, Abigail conveyed a strong moral authority, and even as an old woman could reduce her teenage grandsons to tears with her reprovals for misconduct.

John Adams, to a remarkable degree for the time and his distance, took a deep interest in the day-to-day education of his children. During his long absences, he wrote Abigail that they must, together, apply themselves to the cultivation of their farm and children. "Let Frugality, And Industry, be our Virtues," he said. Abigail and John turned to Newton and Locke for childrearing advice, and stressed the importance of early years, habit forming, and set of the will. In August 1774, while attending the first Continental Congress, John Adams wrote Abigail that "The Education of our Children is never out of my Mind.

> Train them to Virtue, habituate them to industry, activity, and Spirit. Make them consider every Vice, as shameful and unmanly; fire them with Ambition to be useful — make them disdain to be destitute of any useful or ornamental Knowledge of Accomplishment. Fix their Ambition upon great and Solid Objects, and their Contempt upon little, frivolous, and useless ones. It is Time, my dear, for you to begin to teach

them French. Every Decency, Grace, and Honesty should be inculcated upon them."

The theme of John Quincy's life, then, was established: His mind would be fixed upon "great and Solid Objects."

John and Abigail insisted upon diligence, piety, industry. They taught their children that life was serious, that they must excel in all they did. And John Quincy reflected his parents' expectations in a letter to his father: "I hope I grow a better Boy and that you will have no occasion to be ashamed of me when you return. . . . I read my Books to Mama. We all long to see you; I am Sir your Dutiful Son."

By age ten, this dutiful son knew something of the English classics, Shakespeare, and Milton, and the King James translation of the Bible. Although *Paradise Lost*, his parents' favorite poem, proved difficult for him, he read it twice. He copied out in his own hand the Preceptor's *Elements of Logic*. Abigail read Dr. Watts's "Moral Songs for Children" to him, and, with the war swirling around their home, Rollin's *The Ancient History*. John Quincy read *The Arabian Nights*, and learned by heart the entire series, appropriately titled, of *The Renowned History of Giles Gingerbread, A Little Boy who Lived upon Learning*.

John Quincy Adams was Giles. A month before his tenth birthday he set himself the goal of reading the third volume of Smollett's *History of England* by the end of the week, and six days later proudly reported to his father that he had almost completed the volume by spending several hours a day at the book — this in June in Massachusetts.

Here was another theme of Adams's young life: Perseverence. Duty. Driving himself to fulfill his parents' ambition for him. In a letter to his father in June 1777, still nine, he wrote: "I Love to receive Letters very well much better than I love to write them, I make but a poor figure at Composition my head is much too fickle, my Thoughts are running after birds eggs play and trifles, till I get vexed with my Self, Mamma has a troublesome task to keep me Steady, and I own I am ashamed of myself. I Have but Just entered the 3d volume of Smollett tho I had designed to have got it Half through by this time." He asked his father to give him instruction on the proper use of time, how to proportion study and play, and he promised to keep his father's advice close at hand. He ended the letter with a postscript requesting a "Blank Book" so he could take notes from his reading of the most important sections "to fix them upon my mind." JQA and his father exchanged letters during 1777 about Bampfylde Moore Carew's popular book *Life and Adventures* and his *Apology*, and John Adams warned his son about the ill effects when great talent is misapplied, "and what Miseries, Dangers and Distresses Men bring themselves into when they depart from the Paths of Honour, Truth and Virtue." His father enclosed a long reading list that included *The History of the Wars of Flanders*, written in Italian. Later that summer, as his son turned ten, Adams suggested that JQA start reading Thucydides, in Greek, "the most perfect of all languages."

That same June, John wrote Abigail to be sure that their firstborn son was acquiring the best knowledge. "Let him know that the moral sentiments of his Heart, are more important than the Furniture of his Head. Let him be sure that he possess the great Virtues of Temperance, Justice, Magnanimity, Honour and Generosity, and with these added to his Parts he cannot fail to become a wise and great man." This, too, was what they wished for him: to be wise and great. The Adamses considered themselves America's aristocracy; it was up to them to lead, and to train their children to be leaders. Long before there was a Presidency, even before there was a United States, or independence, John and Abigail prayed and planned and toiled and directed their son toward leadership. They educated and guided him, and he obeyed their every command and direction. His life, at age nine, had already started the slow, careful ascent toward the nation's highest office. It was their dream, and his goal. In 1777, with the nation's destiny clear but its fulfillment uncertain, John Adams wrote his son suggesting that the lad study the Revolutionary War thundering around his home: read the newspapers, read history, make observations. This war, the father told the son, may in the future require other wars, as well as councils and negotiations, and he should turn his thoughts early to such studies that would give "solid Instruction and Improvement for the Part which may be allotted you to act on the Stage of Life."

In fact, the Revolutionary War was a daily, frightening

reality. In September 1774, a militia raiding party marched by the Adams farm to steal powder from the storage house in town and carry it to safety in another parish. The next spring, when General Gage ordered his British regulars out of Boston to seize other powder stores, the battles of Lexington and Concord made clear that war was inevitable, and would reach the farm. John Quincy Adams brought passing Minutemen water from the well, and Nabby served slices of salt meat. One day, a raggedy armed band stopped and asked if Abigail had any metal to spare to make bullets. She gathered the family's pewter dishes and put them into a large kettle to be melted down over the kitchen fire. When JQA squeezed through the cluster of Minutemen, he asked Elihu Adams: "Why, uncle, what are you doing? What strange soup."

"Bullet soup," Uncle Elihu replied.

"Do you wonder," Adams wrote sixty-eight years later, "that a boy of seven who witnessed this scene should be a patriot?"

Abigail and her children lived in constant fear. In "the space of twelve months," JQA later wrote, "my mother with her infant children dwelt, liable every hour of the day and of the night to be butchered in cold blood, or taken and carried into Boston as hostages." The British had sent out foraging parties searching for Samuel Adams and John Hancock, without success, and the Adamses knew that their husband and father, a member of the Congress now funding arms against England, was a traitor who would be hanged in the Tower of London if caught. But Abigail conveyed to her husband their resolution. "We now expect our seacoast ravaged. Perhaps the very next letter I write will inform you that I am driven away from our yet quiet cottage. Necessity will oblige Gage to take some desperate steps. We are told for truth that he is now eight thousand strong. We live in continual expectation of alarms. Courage, I know we have in abundance; conduct I hope we shall not want; but powder — where shall we get a sufficient supply?"

On Saturday morning, June 17, 1775, about three o'clock, Abigail and her children were awakened by what they first thought was a spring thunderstorm. The distant thunder was not rain coming for their thirsty crops, but cannon for the revolution. Like a mother of ancient Rome, Abigail thought it wise that her son witness war, although she, the daughter of a clergy-man, detested it. History was being hammered out upon the anvil before them, and her son would have an advantage seeing for himself what other sons would only read in history books. Abigail led John Quincy up Penn's Hill behind the Adams farm. They hurried through orchard and thickening meadow grass, over rock walls, until they reached the top, where, looking toward Boston, they could see the flashes of cannon and puffs of explosion, bright and gentle at such a distance. Charlestown, she later wrote her husband, "is laid in ashes." The British attack upon entrenchments at Breed's and Bunker's Hill brought can-nonading all Saturday and into Sunday. "The constant roar of the cannon," Abigail wrote, "is so distressing that we cannot eat, drink or sleep." John Quincy thought the battle was like those he had read about in the Bible, "the sword of the Lord and of Gideon," and he never forgot it. Late that Sunday afternoon, Abigail learned that their dear friend Dr. Joseph Warren had been killed at Bunker Hill, and that his body still lay behind British lines. John Quincy, too, was deeply grieved at Dr. War-ren's death, and seventy-one years later recalled that his mother, in the spring of 1775, had taught the boy daily to repeat before rising in the morning the Lord's Prayer and then William Col-lins's "Ode Written in the Beginning of the Year 1746," about the patriots who fell in the Jacobite rebellion of 1745. Dr. War-ren had loved the words John Quincy memorized: "How sleep the Brave who sink to rest / By all their Countrys wishes blest?" Those words took on special meaning for the Adamses huddled in their farmhouse in the middle of war, with a friend fallen in battle. John Quincy Adams could recite the poem until his death.

They needed the defense of poetry against cannon. In early March 1776, Gen. Washington's troops started bombarding the British in Boston to divert them from their fortification of the heights on Dorchester Neck. The cannonading was almost con-tinuous, and the episode offers a vivid picture of the terror and danger that were a constant part of young Adams's boyhood. On March 3, his mother wrote his father: "I went to bed after 12 but got no rest. The Cannon continued firing and my Heart

Beat pace with them all night." On Monday, JQA and his mother, sister, and brothers watched the local militia march toward Boston, every man carrying three days' rations and a blanket on his back. Their absence left the villages of Weymouth, Hingham, and Braintree defenseless. Once again, Abigail and the children climbed Penn's Hill and listened to "the amazing roar" of the twenty-four-pounders and watched bursting shells in the dusk. She went to bed at midnight, but slept only an hour. The windows rattled, the house shook, the bursting shells brightened the night sky and kept them in terror. The cannonading went on nightly for a week, and the farmhouse shuddered with every burst. "I sometimes think I cannot stand it," Abigail wrote John. "I wish myself with you, out of hearing as I cannot assist them."

Bad weather and rough water prevented the British from assaulting the American fortifications, which were strengthened and enlarged every day. After a second week of shelling, Abigail, Nabby, and Johnny made their daily climb up the hill, but what a sight they found: "Between seventy and eighty vessels of various sizes lie in a row in fair sight of this place," Abigail said. She thought it "the largest fleet ever seen in America." The children counted 170 ships, and thought the furled sails and bare masts looked like a forest across Boston harbor and the bay. The ships soon filled with British soldiers and American loyalists fleeing Boston, and within a day, fragments of excellent furniture washed to shore near the Adams home, furniture too heavy and too cumbersome to make the sea voyage to Nova Scotia. Some eleven hundred loyalist Americans who had taken refuge in Boston, confident of British arms and support, were ruined. They, too, climbed on board. Boston was free, and the town that Abigail feared might "cost a river of blood" was regained "without one drop shed!"

But the war was far from over, and soldiers and cannonading only part of the Adamses' fears. Disease cut through their family as no cannon ever did. Elihu Adams died of dysentery, a dreaded disease, while in the field commanding Continental troops at Cambridge. Abigail herself took violently sick with the disease, and came near death; Tommy and then Nabby fell ill, too. "Our House is an hospital in every part," Abigail wrote, and she washed the entire farmhouse with vinegar to halt the sickness. But when her mother arrived to help care for them, she, too, got dysentery, and died within six days.

One of the most terrifying and disfiguring diseases was smallpox. Until the first half of the eighteenth century, it struck all ages, and killed quickly and mysteriously; clergymen refused to bury anyone who died from it, lest they catch the disease. The ravages were so great that the beautiful were rendered hideous; fathers did not recognize their children after smallpox finished with them. In 1775, more than seven thousand people got smallpox in Massachusetts colony, and when Abigail saw the results, she wrote: "I should dread it more now than before I saw it. . . . Indeed this smallpox is no triffel." Oliver Goldsmith caught the ruin of it:

> Lo, the smallpox with horrid glare
> Levelled its terror at the fair;
> And, rifling every youthful grace,
> Left but the remnant of a face.

In 1776 the American medical profession — a cluster of barbers, magicians, charlatans, and dedicated physicians — was helpless before disease. Measles killed three hundred children in Boston in a single month. Little could be done: physicians had only meager knowledge of causes, symptoms, personal hygiene, or care. The standard treatment for any complaint was a violent cleansing of evil "humours" in the body through bloodletting, induced vomiting, and constant application of purges and enemas to clean out the stomach and bowels. Remedies were simplistic and primitive. To cure apoplexy, for example, the patient swallowed a glass of urine from a healthy person, mixed with salt, to induce vomiting. For gout, one applied live earthworms to the affected area until they began to swell. For cataracts, the afflicted had someone blow dried and powdered human excrement into the eye. By 1776, physicians understood three diseases and their remedies: fever, treated by quinine; dysentery, treated with ipecacuanna; and smallpox, treated by inoculation. Such remedies, tentative and still experimental, did not prevent these diseases, or their cures, from killing many people.

In the summer of 1776, after the British evacuation, Abigail packed up her children and set out for Boston to be inoculated against smallpox. She clearly understood, as did others, that inoculation was dangerous and painful, but it might prevent death or disfigurement. That year alone, some 5,292 people in and around Boston got smallpox. Of these, 304 cases were caused naturally and 29 died; but 4,988 cases were caused by the inoculation, and of that large number only 28 people died. Abigail knew that the process took a long time and was sometimes fatal, but the odds were clearly on her side.

On the twelfth, she and her four children — Nabby, John Quincy, Charles, and Thomas — began their smallpox inoculation. Special "hospitals" — really a cluster of buildings — had been established in Boston and outlying villages of Brookline, Watertown, Newton, and Redford, for a massive inoculation program. Entering patients were sent to the "cleansing house" where "cleansers" removed the patient's clothing, washed him or her in a solution of rum and vinegar, and fumigated both the patient and the clothes. Next, the patient started purging: usually thirty to forty grains of mercury and two or three purges every day for six or seven days, sufficient to remove "old obstructions."

The Adamses avoided this, largely because John Adams, in Philadelphia, anxiously wrote Dr. Cotton Tufts, Abigail's uncle, to oversee his family's inoculations, and sent Dr. Tufts copies of Dr. Benjamin Rush's opinions on the smallpox procedure. Where Dr. Rush called for the "entire Alteration of the Blood and Juices and the removal of inveterate obstruction" in order to "discharge from the Body all superfluous Juices and Fluids and especially to free the more open passages from Impurities," Dr. Tufts was a bit more gentle. He did not think an "entire Alteration" necessary. Instead, Abigail and her children took the popular method designed by Englishmen Adam Thompson and Robert Sutton. This included a light, "non-stimulating" diet, and "purging powders" of "Calix of antimony, ten drachms, Calomel [mercurous chloride], eight drachms." Usually this combination of mercury and antimony, with purging and sometimes bleeding, was followed for two weeks. For unknown but perhaps obvious reasons, Dr. Tufts prescribed for the Adamses a diet that lasted only two days.

The next step was inoculation. The physician cut the patient with a lancet, making an incision about one-eighth inch long, and inserted a small piece of lint moistened with pus from a person suffering a mild form of smallpox. Each patient got two incisions, either on the outside of the arm or the inside of the leg, which were covered with a simple plaster dressing. Then they waited until the disease occurred in a mild form, or they died. Using the Thompson/Sutton method, Dr. Tufts made a small puncture about two or three inches above Abigail's elbow. The incision hurt, and infection of the area was not unknown, and not treatable. Into the small wound, he inserted a thread that had been drawn through a ripe pustule of a diseased patient, and then covered the incision with a sticking plaster. Dr. Tufts repeated the method on each Adams, himself, his son Bill, and Mary Cranch, Abigail's sister.

After being inoculated just above their elbows, the children, Bill, Abigail, Mary, and Dr. Tufts retired to a special house and waited for the disease to erupt on their skin in a mild form, thus insuring immunity. Here, too, a regimen had to be followed. Air was thought beneficial, so they took walks or rode horseback, and slept on the floor — or anything hard — on carpets and straw beds, with the windows open. A special diet included puddings, gruel, sago, milk, fruits, and vegetables for nine or ten days. Their diet was kept free from "Spirit, Salt and Fats."

Not every inoculation "took." Mary Cranch and Dr. Tufts were inoculated four times without any sign of the disease. Dr. Tufts inoculated his son five times. At first, the four Adams children and their mother had few eruptions — Abigail produced but one — and only their sore arms attested that they had been inoculated at all. To be certain, Abigail had them all done a second time and Thomas a third. Nabby became "cold and shivery" followed by a "violent Heat" with eruptions upon her eyes, and took the symptoms "very severely . . . and small pox in plenty, she can reckon 500 allready." John Quincy was more fortunate. He took the inoculation well "and has it exactly as one would wish, enough to be well satisfied and yet not be troublesome."

By August 7, everyone had come through the inoculation well, and safely. After more than a month, the Adamses prepared to leave Boston. They were washed with soap and rubbed with vinegar and brandy (instead of rum). After putting on clean clothing, they were fumigated with sulphur in a smokehouse, and then released. During their inoculation period, the Declaration of Independence, newly written and signed in Philadelphia, had arrived in printed form in Boston. On July 18, Abigail, as part of her smallpox regimen, had walked to King Street to hear it read from a balcony of the State House. She was much pleased with Jefferson's (and Adams's) work. Troops appeared under arms, bells rang, gunships in Boston harbor and batteries in the forts fired salutes. The King's Coat of Arms was removed from the State House, "and every vestige of him burnt in King Street." Newly liberated from George III and the smallpox, the Adamses rode home to Braintree, fit and ready to serve their young nation.

4

IN APRIL 1783, the Johnsons left France and returned to England. Although his business fluctuated violently from postwar economic stresses, Joshua remained foolishly indulgent with his wife and family, and they continued to live extravagantly. He purchased a large house in Cooper's Row on Great Tower Hill, which overlooked the Tower of London and the Thames. He had the family's coat of arms painted on their carriages with "the Crest embroidered on the Hammer Cloth," and engraved on all the silverware. Joshua staffed the house with eleven servants, three of whom had been with him since he and Catherine had married; all were devoted, perhaps because he was, for the time, a rich man, or perhaps because he allowed them excesses with the kitchen provision, and one another. Catherine Nuth Johnson had to oversee the household, an upper-class woman's role, and hold the servants in line. Joshua prided himself on running the entire operation — staff, wife, children — "like clock work," and had the household "so perfectly regulated" that when he was at home the place, Louisa said, felt like a ship at sea with all hands moving smartly. Louisa and her sisters thought it all good fun, and loved being at home. One time, her father started a training program for his girls. Louisa, then fifteen, fell under the supervision of the cook, and learned all Louisa ever knew about food, especially an early devotion to chocolate. Each daughter, with Joshua's insistence, took turns supervising the household staff for a week at a time, which taught them, Louisa said, "all the labours and troubles of family economy."

Louisa admitted that her parents spoiled her. She was, she said, "the first object of attention at home, every fault pardoned, every virtue loved." Her mother and father filled Louisa's room with playthings, and Louisa tried to keep them to herself, away from her brother and sisters, who always wanted to play in her room. The spoiling and toys resulted from Louisa's recurring childhood illnesses, which always brought special attentions from parents and servants. These attentions were delicious, separating her from her sisters, cornering the love and pity of a busy father and a narcissistic mother, and Louisa interspersed real illness with feigned illness with such skill that, years later, even she could not tell the difference.

One real illness Louisa remembered with fondness occurred when she was nine. She went to bed with what was then described as "a one-and-twenty-day fever," whose alarming symptoms were similar to typhus. Her parents, not unexpectedly, watched her day and night, indulging her every whim, and father and mother vied with each other in surprising her with presents and spoiling her with succulent out-of-season fruits. Louisa remembered her mother sitting on her bed "anxiously noting every change." She sewed clothes for Louisa's favorite doll, and dressed her to Louisa's commands, trying to amuse the child. Louisa used the illness to dominate her sister Harriet, then a pesty three years old, who proved a quick and clever rival for her mother's attentions. Whenever Harriet entered her sickroom, Louisa screamed and thrashed in her bed. If her mother even spoke to Harriet, Louisa would faint — or pretend to. This achieved two desired results: the swift dismissal of Harriet from Louisa's room, and her mother's continued anxiety, with its rich attentions focused almost continuously upon Louisa. Such were the rainbow days at home.

Out of her house, however, Louisa found adjustment to England difficult. For one thing, the contrast between her family's wealth and London's poverty was vast. There were in the East End large areas of slum tenements where several families shared a single privy, and "a reservoir of putrid matter" collected in the basements, which were never drained. Unsanitary conditions and rotten food among the poor caused epidemics of dysentery and intestinal worms. The swift bacterial and viral infections visited frequently, as did the slow destructive power of tuberculosis, or "consumption," a common cause of death among young children. Isolated by wealth, diet, care, Louisa was also isolated by language. When she arrived in London, she spoke no English but "yes" and "no." Everything was foreign to her: the dirt, disease, poverty, sounds; even the plain English fashions of white frocks and pink sashes contrasted with the fine silk dresses with hoops that she and her sisters wore.

To ease her adjustment and, more directly, to prepare her for life as a woman, Joshua immediately placed Louisa and her two sisters Nancy and Carolina in a large English boarding school with forty young women, ages seven to twenty years old. This was a common practice among the upper-class, but here, the "pure and unadulterated French" that Louisa and her sisters spoke was laughed at and corrected, and their French clothes made them the focus of snickering and teasing.

Most painfully, Louisa had to resolve conflicts about her religious upbringing. As a child who had loved the music and ritual of the Catholic Church in France, and spent days admiring and being educated by nuns, Louisa found herself entering the Episcopal Church in England. The first time she was forced to attend Episcopal services with her classmates, Louisa was forced "to kneel down among what I had been taught in France to call the *hereticks*." She was then eight, and the scene so shocked her that she fainted. Led once more to the services, Louisa fainted again — and again. The trauma of her move, of the contrasts between France and England, came together in the pain of dissolving one strict religious training and substituting another. Joshua was summoned to the school, and rather than bring his daughter home, placed her with a kind Anglican clergyman named John Hewlett, who undertook the process of withdrawing the child from the Catholic faith and educating her to the Episcopal. The Johnsons trusted Hewlett with their precious daughter and attended his church on Tower Hill.

When Louisa returned to school, her parents instructed the headmistress that she not be "harried or urged too much upon the subject of going to church." She was accustomed gradually to the Episcopal services, but fainted several more times before feeling at ease. The episode was more bizarre because Joshua Johnson was neither Catholic nor Episcopal. He was a Unitarian, but never bothered to indoctrinate his children in his own faith. Instead, he placed them in the care of the church of the country in which they lived. Louisa, after decades of struggle with her personal beliefs, embraced the Episcopal church as her church of record, if not choice. She was not baptized in the church until she was sixty-three years old.

The faintings at chapel and the teasings of her classmates made Louisa melancholy and gloomy at her English boarding school, and for years her girlhood playmates cruelly nicknamed her "Miss Proud." The pain cut deeply: "Every feeling of my heart was roused against this unjust treatment and I fear my character was stamped from that moment." Louisa reacted, she said later, with "the haughtiness and pride of character which it has been impossible for me to subdue." She lived in "constant torment." After each vacation at home, when she reluctantly returned to school, Louisa immediately made a list of the months and days until she could return home again. Her greatest pleasure, she said, was each morning marking off another day which shortened the time in school and brought her closer to leaving. "Oh home! sweet home!" Louisa wrote. "Thou ever wert to me the joy of life."

There occurred during these years a series of small events that, linked together, created a major impact upon Louisa's later life. She was, by her social position, isolated from direct contact with — although not from observation of — other people in other social classes. Louisa was bright, alert, and had already traveled more than most women would in a lifetime. But she was naive about social conditions, about what was happening to her and how that compared to what was happening to other women. While in London, for example, Louisa received as a house guest a family friend, Kitty Carroll, from Maryland. Miss Carroll was accompanied by a young black slave girl, about Louisa's age, and for the first time, Louisa watched and thought about how a black slave woman was treated. The slave, Louisa said blandly, was "a novelty to us," but the black's subservience, the cruel language spoken toward her, the suppression of her *spirit* shocked Louisa. About the same time, in school, Louisa befriended a dark-skinned young woman her own age, an East Indian who was "as remarkable in her temper and manners as myself." They roomed together, read books and discussed ideas together, and "were almost inseparable." It was this exposure to slave and roommate that first lifted Louisa's consciousness. The juxtaposition of her own, inner pain at this time of her life, of her roommate, and of her observation of the slave girl, took root in Louisa's heart and led her, by ways now clear but then difficult to see, to the central purpose of her life.

At the boarding school, Louisa also admired a young teacher, a Miss Young, who was, she said, "a most extraordinary woman." Unlike most women of her day, Miss Young had been educated with boys and young men. She had worn boys' clothing and, far more important in Louisa's perception, she had acquired the classical education usually reserved only for young men. She knew Greek and Latin, and although "her person was masculine and her manners forbidding," Miss Young's heart was kind and her intellect exciting and full of things that fascinated Louisa. Here was an educated, comparatively free woman, who demanded that her favorite students — and Louisa was one of them — follow her example. Here was a woman who dared reveal her intelligence, which gave her superiority over most other women, and many men. Louisa was quick in her lessons and Miss Young, in the few years they shared, made Louisa question things and converse openly about books and ideas. This was radical stuff.

Louisa's education was considered excellent for this period; she spoke French, and she knew a little, from her travels, of what life held. She was also bright enough to know that it didn't hold, for women, any opportunities. Was she, in fact, much different from the slave girl? Women were taught not to think and question. "Polite education for ladies" centered upon the arts of housekeeping and conversation. "Genteel" and "fashionable" were the key words of the day. Louisa's curriculum consisted of reading, writing, enough math for running a house, dancing, French, drawing, singing with piano — just enough music to entertain men in a parlor. Her days were filled with paper-cutting, waxwork, painting on glass, patchwork, shellwork, mosswork, featherwork, embroidery and needlework, white-on-white stitchery and cross-stitch — and, when a lady got good at all this, fancywork, beadwork, silk on velvet, and other time-devouring trivia. Louisa received training in proper manners and conduct in company. The skills of school and home had one purpose for a woman: to entice a man to marry her. One headmistress said that "our great female boarding schools are so many seminaries of candidates for matrimony." The novitiates in the worship of man soon learned that heaven was marriage and the highest accolade was to be known as a superb coquette or gossip or card-player or stitcher or housewife. Many of these leisured and bored wives tended to lapse into melancholia, and within three decades the connection between female idleness and mental disease became increasingly clear.

Louisa, exposed to such teachers as Miss Young and alert to social differences (and parallels) between herself and others, was soon trapped by her intellect. Women, and men, were fearful of what they called the "learned ladies," and if a young woman like Louisa Johnson persisted, she had to hide her intellect, to conceal whatever learning she attained "with as much solitude as she would hide crookedness or lameness." Louisa soon lamented being a woman who loved books; she always regretted being a victim of "a happy but alas visionary education" that did not prepare her for "the disgusting realities of a heartless political life, a source of perpetual disappointment." She was awakening to so much. When her father gave Louisa a guinea one day, she bought two books, both of them revealing of this development:

Mason's *Self Knowledge* and Milton's *Paradise Lost*. She soon understood Milton far better than John Quincy Adams, although she never let him know it; more than that, Louisa grew to *feel* the words of that majestic work. She especially pondered Milton's thought that "all our knowledge was ourselves to know." Louisa was discovering a serious and contemplative world within herself which was already in conflict with the boundaries placed around her, and she later wondered: "How often since that time have I thought it injured me, by teaching me to scrutinize too closely into motives, and looking too closely at the truth. Much, much depends upon the reading of our early life."

Sadly, when Louisa was twelve, Miss Young left her school. Within two years, Joshua removed Louisa, Nancy, and Carolina from the boarding school. Three more daughters had been born into the Johnson family, and the expense of keeping females in private school was proving too great. Joshua instead engaged a French couple: the man as tutor for the Johnson's only son Thomas, and the woman as governess for the young ladies, who would continue learning things genteel and fashionable. Milton would wait; Louisa's formal education ended. She now discovered her own interpretation for these words from *Paradise Lost*:

> From the cheerful ways of men
> Cut off, and for the book of knowledge fair
> Presented with a universal blank
> Of nature's works to me expunged and razed,
> And wisdom at one entrance quite shut out.

In a few years, Joshua would send Thomas home to America for his education, which included instruction at Harvard, but his daughters would have to be content with trivialities.

5

THE EDUCATION of John Quincy Adams took an entirely different path. As the firstborn son, he stood at the forefront of his family; he was their hope. In 1777, when Congress appointed John Adams as a joint commissioner (with Benjamin Franklin and Arthur Lee) to represent the United States in France, John Quincy Adams, age ten, sailed with his father to Europe. They returned home after an abortive year, passing through Nantes and visiting the Johnsons in May 1779, only reaching Boston to turn around and sail again through the British fleet to a second appointment in Paris.

In all, John Quincy Adams lived eight years in Europe with his father. He put the time to excellent purpose. He spent his voyages learning the names of all the sails and the use of the mariner's compass. He started school at Passy, then a suburb of Paris, where he rose at six and studied until eight-thirty in the evening. When his father went to the Netherlands as a private citizen to negotiate a Dutch loan for the United States, JQA went to school at the University of Leiden. He learned French, Latin, and Dutch.

Abigail sent her son instructions on his behavior and learning. She urged him to "govern and control" his temper, to observe, listen, report, and use the "superior advantages" of traveling with his father. Her ambition for him was boundless, and her letters sounded a litany of expectations. It was not enough to travel and enjoy leisure and idleness, she warned; he must prepare himself. "Justice, humanity and benevolence are the duties you owe to society in general." To your country, Abigail told her son, he should pay a price, "sacrificing ease, pleasure, wealth, and life itself for its defence and security. To your parents you owe love, reverence, and obedience to all just and equitable demands."

In July 1781, John Quincy Adams, then just fourteen, left his studies in the Netherlands and traveled as secretary to Francis

Dana, who had been appointed minister without portfolio to St. Petersburg, Russia. Here, again, JQA's parents used the experience as a way to make their son enrich his mind, develop his powers of observation, learn. His father wrote the boy and urged him to report on the state of education, the construction of the houses, the styles of the people, the religions, and the public buildings, and John Quincy reported in detail, much to his father's pleasure. The son learned well from his mother and father. His desire to please them was obsessive. He was the empty crucible into which they poured and ground their ideas and morality. Their lessons, their dreams, took shape in him. Unlike Louisa, John Quincy from boyhood carried a sense of purpose, of destiny. He later wrote his brother Charles: "We are Sent into this World for Some end. It is our duty to discover by Close Study what this end is & when we discover it to pursue it with unconquerable perseverance." This theme always separated Louisa and John Quincy: He was convinced that his life had a purpose, and he searched for it; she thought her life meaningless, and its purpose came searching for her.

On September 3, 1783, the American and British concluded a Definitive Treaty of Peace, ending the Revolutionary War, but not the conflict between the two nations. John Quincy and his father toured England together, visited Parliament, and soothed themselves at Bath. In June 1784, Abigail and Nabby sailed for England to join them — leaving Charles and Thomas behind with relatives — and in June 1785, after a sojourn in Paris, the Adamses took a house in Grosvenor Square, one of London's fashionable districts, while John Adams served as the first U.S. Ambassador to Great Britain.

At this time, John Quincy Adams and his parents made a decision about his education. He had savored the delicacies of Europe, both diplomatic and social, and found them to his taste. He had studied German, Latin, Greek, Dutch, and French. He had traveled, sometimes on his own, to the major cities: Paris, London, St. Petersburg, The Hague, Amsterdam. He had met and dined with many of the leading men of the day, and his diary was filled with the names of Vergennes, Franklin, Pitt, Lafayette, Jay. One entry recorded: "Spent the evening with Mr. Jefferson whom I love to be with." In 1825, his father would remind Thomas Jefferson that "when you was at Cul de sac at Paris he [John Quincy Adams] appeared to me to be almost as much your boy as mine." Europe, obviously, held many attractions.

But early in 1783, Abigail had written to her son: "I have a desire that you might finish your education at our University, and I see no chance for it unless you return in the course of the year." In the fall of 1784, John Adams wrote President Joseph Willard of Harvard to ask that John Quincy be admitted. Willard replied that the young man could join whatever class an examination showed him qualified to enter. In languages and literature, John Quincy was admirably prepared for Harvard; the classics were part of his daily reading, and remained so throughout his life. But the young man's knowledge of mathematics was deficient, even though his father had spent the entire previous year — "Instead of playing Cards, like the fashionable world" — struggling with his son over geometry, trigonometry, conic sections, and differential calculus. The elder Adams concluded that his son was "as yet but a Smatterer like his Father." JQA needed more tutoring and preparation, and it was arranged that he would return and stay with Aunt Elizabeth and Uncle John Shaw in Haverhill. He sailed for America on May 12, 1785. Abigail wrote: "I feel very loth to part with my son. . . . I shall miss him more than I can express, but I am convinced that it will be very much to his advantage to spend one year at Harvard. . . . He will find there companions and associates. Besides, America is the theatre for a young fellow who has any ambition to distinguish himself."

John Quincy and his sister exchanged a regular journal and letters during their separation after Paris. He wrote about the simple household of the Shaws, while she described the London scene. He told Nabby he felt overwhelmed by the work for his entrance examination:

"I am told I have much more to do than I had any idea of. . . . In the Greek I have to go from the beginning to learn the grammar, which is by no means an agreeable task; to study the New Testament nearly or quite through, between three or four books in Xenophon's Cyropaedia, and five or six books in Homer's Iliad. On Latin I have but little else to go through but Horace, part of which I have already done. In English, I have to study Watt's Logic, Locke on the Human Understanding, and something in Astronomy.

During the previous fall and winter, while preparing for his entrance examination, he never left the Shaws' house (or his books) for more than four hours a week. In March 1786, Adams was admitted to Harvard as a junior. His father crowed a bit at JQA's admission to "our dear Alma Mater": "You are now among Magistrates and Ministers, Legislators and Heroes, Ambassadors and Generals, I mean among Persons who will live to Act in all these Characters" — exactly as his parents wished him to do.

Adams arrived at Harvard sporting European manners, which made him a bit of a fop. Although he resembled his mother, he enjoyed striking poses like his father: head cocked, one eye half-closed, his right hand in his pocket. He had his hair fashionably groomed and carried a sword like a European gentleman. JQA soon shed all this, however. He did little but study. When two of his nieces, the Cranch girls, visited his room in Hollis Hall, they found it littered and filthy, and Adams disheveled, wearing a soiled gown, his fingernails dirty and his uncombed hair greasy about his shoulders. His room smelled of stale tobacco — JQA had taken to smoking as he read — and he was pale and drawn. He complained of headaches. Aunt Cranch urgently sent Dr. Tufts to the young man's room, and the doctor prescribed more exercise and a better diet. His mother, when she learned of her son's health, advised: "Our bodies are framed of such materials as to require constant exercise to keep them in repair, to brace the nerves, and give vigor to the animal functions."

Adams put whatever spare vigor he summoned into playing his flute. He had started lessons at The Hague, and continued at Harvard, playing a German flute purchased in Cambridge. He reassured Nabby that playing did not affect his health, and he sometimes joined, during holidays, the Cranch family's musicals, when cousin Eliza played the pianoforte and Billy scraped the violin.

John Quincy Adams was graduated from Harvard on July 16, 1787. Aunt Mary Cranch prepared the graduation feast, and all available Adams relatives were invited to a roistering afternoon devouring two shoulders of beef, four boiled hams, six tongues, and a plum cake that took 24 pounds of sugar, plus an ample supply of porter, hard cider, punch, and wine. They had much to celebrate. John Quincy ranked second in his class of fifty-one, and joined the newly founded Phi Beta Kappa society. Throughout the family there was excitement and pride over the young scion of this American dynasty.

The excitement was not shared by the *Columbian Centinel*. Newspapers seldom admired the Adamses as much as the Adamses admired themselves. The *Centinel* noted that JQA made one of the two English orations at graduation: "The publick expectations from this gentleman . . . were greatly inflated." John Quincy, however, was pleased both with his speech and Harvard. Attending the college, he said, "was my own choice, and the most judicious choice I ever made. My short discipline of fifteen months at Harvard University was the introduction to all the prosperity that has ever befallen me, and perhaps saved me from ruin."

Abigail, in London, was equally pleased. She wrote her sister, Mary Cranch, that the graduation gave her "great satisfaction." Now, she continued, if JQA's life be spared let him not "be an idle or useless spectator." She took paper and pen, and immediately wrote to her son: "We may be a great and powerful nation," she said. But it will require "industry and frugality, wisdom and virtue" to make it so. "I hope you will never lose sight of her interests; but make her welfare your study, and spend those hours, which others devote to cards and folly, in investigating the great principles by which nations have risen to glory and eminence; for your country will one day call for your services, either in the cabinet or field. Qualify yourself to do honor to her. Your affectionate mother, AA."

6

LOUISA GREW UP schooled in the style that society and her parents decreed proper for a young woman. Men like Louisa's brother and her future husband went to Harvard; women remained at home in the parlor. Any subjects taught them outside the correct and requisite female education were viewed suspiciously as having "a tendency to render [women] masculine." Louisa, however, loved to read, and her interests under Miss Young's brief but profound guidance had encouraged her to seek a more classical, "masculine" education. After leaving boarding school, however, Louisa was gently but forcefully redirected by her parents and governess to the traditional role, her proper place: Louisa and her sister Nancy became belles of her parents' evening parlors.

At sixteen, about two years older than Louisa, Nancy already "gave promise of great beauty." Louisa was herself growing into a lovely young woman, and she was envious of her older sister, in a revealing way. Although Louisa was a good student, she never considered herself as spectacular as Nancy, who had, Louisa thought, "a sort of intuitive genius." Study came easily to Nancy, and she could master any subject. But it wasn't only her sister's brains that Louisa coveted. It was also Nancy's social ease, her parlor skills so valuable to a young woman's prospects. Louisa was painfully shy, she admitted, "reserved and cold" before an audience. She entered into the woman's world ill-equipped, emotionally, for her social role. Her knees trembled when she was called upon to entertain.

The Johnsons entertained a great deal, especially after Joshua was appointed by George Washington in 1790 to fill the post of U.S. Consul in London. Their home and family gained a reputation for hospitality and amusement, and diplomats and travelers from America made it a point to stop by Cooper's Row on Tower Hill. There they savored "little unceremonious dinners," the very essence of social festivity, when Louisa's mother conversed brilliantly and her father, she thought, looked at his wife with admiration, his "sparkling eye" conveying rich approval. In the evening, the oldest daughters, as expected, joined the family and guests in the parlor, and each played a musical instrument or sang to entertain the company. Sometimes the Johnsons rolled up the carpet as a reward for an especially flattering performance, and everyone would dance, including Joshua and Catherine. Louisa, Nancy, and Carolina were always pushed forward, in the manner of exhibiting marriageable daughters, for music and dancing. Carolina, however, presented a danger, for her true talent was not music, but "the most admirable" mimicry. Carolina brought her sisters to tears of laughter and rolling about the floor with her imitations of well-known guests — including, later, a stuffy young diplomat named Adams. Her father, wisely checking this unusual talent, did not push Carolina too hard to perform before the guests, lest she allow her real talent to emerge in public. So it fell to Louisa and Nancy to carry the burden of the evening's entertainment. And while Louisa was "timid to shyness," she enjoyed dancing, singing with her sisters, and could read music with speed and skill. She sang with a pleasing and flexible voice. Joshua loved showing his daughters off, and "required" Louisa to sing upon demand. He listened critically to every performance, and he refused to go to bed without having his girls sing to him every night; the habit became, Louisa said, "almost as regular as our meals." Despite her father's demand for performance, all her life Louisa agreed that "Musick is a passion with me, and the love of it often makes me silly."

So the Johnson girls passed their winters in London, performing at their parents' bidding, and enlivening evenings in the parlor while emerging into society in the full blossom of readiness. The London social season lasted from New Year's until June, and sometimes continued over into a major watering place, perhaps Bath, Brighton, or Lymington, or Highberry, where the Johnsons took their summer holidays and Joshua would visit from London on weekends. In the country, Louisa, Nancy, and Carolina were free — unburdened from the continual encounters

of the parlor, the restrictions of society, and best of all, the re-
straints of fashion that, like the social rules themselves, laced
and bound women to a certain requisite form. Fashionable dress
around London those days included grotesquely enlarged breasts
and buttocks, the former created by wire work and the latter by
cork attachments. The wire stays and cork rumps, one man complained in 1801, were like putting "your arm around an oaken
tree with the bark on." In the country, Louisa and her sisters
were relieved of wire and cork and inhibitions, and they swam
and fished — a favorite sport of Louisa's — and exercised muscles
in most unladylike fashion. Here, each was free to be her own
person, not an object.

There were, of course, young men now paying attention to
the Johnson girls, and one summer when Louisa was seventeen,
her father's nephew, Walter Hellen, lived with them in the
country house at Highberry. Walter, a very handsome but also
very sickly young man, was destined to become Louisa's brother-
in-law. She thought him "possessing no shining qualities and
very indolent," an opinion she never retracted. Obviously not
the object of Walter's interests, and both attracted and repelled
by him, Louisa took to luring Walter out of his bedchamber for
rigorous exercise. She got him to row her and Nancy about a
pond, but Louisa enjoyed best of all thrashing Walter at battle-
dore, a badmintonlike game, which she played as often as she
could with him until she "turned" her neck and injured herself,
thus ending the summer of Walter's defeat. Beating Walter,
Louisa felt, was almost as satisfying as beating Nancy at the skill
of attracting a suitor.

Louisa and Nancy were almost interchangeable. So close in
age, they were introduced together to society. Both were educated, talented, highly desirable young women; and, as visiting
bachelors noted, daughters of obvious wealth. Louisa, by age
eighteen, stood barely over five feet tall, small busted, with fair
complexion, hazel eyes flecked with green, curly auburn hair,*

---

* Shortly after Johnson's appointment as American Consul, the family
had their portraits painted "in small," each about six by four-and-a-half
inches. One guess is that they were painted in 1792, when Louisa was
seventeen. Any portraits are always suspect as a source of a person's ap-

graceful hands, sloping shoulders. Nancy, also short and fair, employed a "brilliant" dimpled mouth which contained, Louisa observed with envy, "a beautiful set of teeth." If Louisa had a flaw in her beauty, it was her mouth, which appeared straight in her portraits, and not voluptuous or enticing, but narrow. She may have been concealing her teeth, however, for Louisa always had trouble with them, perhaps the result of an early and uncontrolled love of sweets. She started having her teeth pulled early in her adolescence; the extractions, fortunately for her appearance, were made from back to front. The loss of her teeth might explain Louisa's "bewitching smile": not wishing to show too much decay, she developed a mysterious, quick smile that gave both the impression of sparkle and enigma.

Despite the two dazzling sisters, and Carolina (no less a lure), only twenty months younger than Louisa, the Johnson house was not swarming with suitors. One major problem was their father. Joshua, when his oldest daughters entered society, received a letter from his older brother, Gov. Thomas Johnson, whom he admired to excess. Thomas wrote Joshua that he had heard, all the way back in Maryland, of the beauty of the Johnson girls, and worried about their marital prospects. Why one brother was meddling in the social affairs of another 3,000 miles distant remains unclear, but Thomas implored Joshua to have his daughters "form connections with none but men of note and distinction in his own Country." In no hurry to lose his parlor full of song and dance, Joshua concluded that Thomas, as always, was right. Calling his family together, he announced that henceforth his daughters would be prohibited from meeting with eligible young Englishmen. As a result of Thomas's "silly letter," Louisa said, "although we lived in the midst of the city of London we were kept almost entirely out of English society and visited only one family in the street where we lived."

Thus restricted, Louisa and her sisters had to fall back upon

---

pearance, but Louisa said of these that "most of them were thought good likenesses," though hers did not please John Quincy Adams. Elsewhere Louisa said that, at age seventeen, her head was shaved "in consequence of a severe illness," and her hair may have been a wig, or the artist's recollection and liberty.

whatever young men visited London from the United States. Further complicating the process, suitors asking for the attentions of the Johnson daughters had to meet the approval of a Colonel Trumbull, then living with the Johnsons, and his word was law; when a beau failed to impress the old colonel, the young man was dismissed. Other eligible men arrived from America to work in Joshua Johnson's office, and formed a pool of bachelors. One, a small but handsome man, courted Nancy and asked her hand. But Joshua declined permission until the young man had finished his studies, and returned to America and established himself. On these terms, Nancy and her beau considered themselves engaged, but the separation proved the match too weak, and the young man, Louisa noted, was "lured to his destruction" in the United States by the wiles of a married woman. Eventually, Nancy would have to settle for the sickly and defeated Walter Hellen.

Louisa was allowed "a number of ardent admirers," including one John Taylor from Massachusetts, "whom I disliked more than I can express." She received verses from another, a charming young fellow from North Carolina "and a dashing Beau," but Colonel Trumbull took a dislike to him. Vance Murray, a student and banker under her father's tutorship, "almost lived at our house," and became Louisa's admirer for a while. But the love of her life was David Sterrett. He was twenty, and also worked in her father's office, and Louisa still remembered many years later his voice and good looks, and manners that captured her heart. "He was equally fond of me," she said. He wrote verses to her, and she to him, which "naturally produced a great deal of intimacy." David called Louisa his "little Wife" and "everybody delighted to tease me about him until a sentiment was forming in my heart, which no one doubted, least of all myself." But when David returned to the United States, the romance, at one time so bright, faded; the memory, however, did not.

7

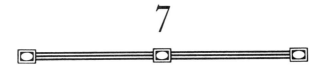

SOON AFTER GRADUATION, John Quincy Adams rode by horseback forty miles north from Boston to Newburyport, a seaport village on the mouth of the Merrimack River. There, Theophilus Parsons charged a hundred dollars each for law students who wanted to study under him, and he had several in his office. This was the standard way of studying law, and Adams became an "articled clerk" in Parsons' office. But the study of law never excited JQA; he felt pushed toward it by his father and mother. Parsons, moreover, was a strict disciplinarian who enjoyed sitting in a rocking chair in his office, cutting a quid of tobacco with a penknife, sliding the brown chew between his teeth and right cheek, and grilling his students between spats into the fire. Bacon's *Essays* was a favorite text, and Adams remembered Parsons' praising the book to his law students with a warning: "Lord Bacon observes that reading makes a full man, conversation a ready man, and writing a correct man. Now, Gentlemen, I would have you all full, ready and correct."

Adams thought Parsons tough and demanding, and the study of law boring. The adjectives "quiet" and "tedious" are sprinkled through his diary during this early period, and soon the conflict made Adams a troubled man. He suffered headaches, dizzy spells, colds, a sour stomach, sore eyes, insomnia, and, when he could sleep, troubled dreams and nightmares. The conflict with his parents over his future, evident in Europe and postponed at Harvard, emerged. Their dreams for him were his nightmares. If he disliked law, how could he meet his parents' wishes? He wrote in his diary: "The question, what am I to do in this world recurs to me very frequently and never without causing great anxiety, and a depression of spirits. My prospects appear darker to me every day, and I am obliged sometimes to drive the subject from my mind to assume some more agreeable train of thought." Adams soon discovered temptations in Newburyport of a more pleasing, yet troublesome nature.

Newburyport was isolated, separated by Old Town Bridge from Newbury, and by the dark and wild Lynn marshes from Boston. Beyond the seaport, America was shaking into life. Shays' Rebellion had erupted in western Massachusetts only a few months earlier, and the convention framing the new Constitution was then sitting in Philadelphia; George Washington was still two years from being the nation's first President. But the distant stirrings underscored the town's solitude, and the young law clerks and doctor's apprentices, including John Quincy Adams, added a sense of restlessness. These young men, alone and bulling their way through difficult studies, clustered for enlivening company and relief at the local taverns, where Adams soon discovered a previously unknown passion for drink, ladies, and serenading. He and his friends frequented Wolfe Tavern at the corner of Threadneedle Alley and Fish Street, Samuel Richardson's under the sign of the eagle, or the Blue Anchor on High Street, where the locals gathered about the ten-foot-long, walk-in fireplace in the taproom to sing "Why Should Our Lot Repine?" or "The Parson and the Barrel of Beer," an old favorite. Adams and his friends soon discovered a short route to intoxication called a Stonewall, named after the New England boundary line, which by combining cider and rum rendered its participant as horizontal and silent as its name. Another, first concocted down in Salem, was the infamous Whistle-Belly-Vengeance, irresistible to a young law student, in which sour beer was simmered in a kettle, sweetened with molasses, filled with brown-bread crumbs, and consumed piping hot. With his parents an ocean away, and his stern relatives and their New England morals on the other side of the Lynn marshes, Adams also discovered the hangover, tardiness, and late-sleeping. When he found he could not pay attention to his studies, he and his friends met at the taverns at seven ". . . and from that time till between three and four in the morning we were continually dancing. I was acquainted with almost all the company; but I never saw a collection of ladies where there was comparatively so much beauty. Two or three gentlemen got rather over the bay; but upon the whole the proceedings were as regular and agreeable as might be expected. . . . The clock struck four just before we went to bed."

Some days his drinking and roistering left him so shaky that he could neither read nor write, nor attend church on Sundays. On Monday, October 1, 1787, he wrote in his diary: "I have not yet got over the consequences of our frolick on Saturday evening. Three whole evenings I have by this means entirely lost; for I cannot yet write with any comfort. How inseparably in all cases of intemperance is the punishment allied to the fault!"

During the autumn, Adams suffered from depressions. His future seemed to him dark and confusing, and "the bubble reputation," so important to his parents, false. He noted in his diary that "not even dissipation has been able to help me." He visited a local doctor and got a prescription for "the bark" for his "nervous system." He also wrote Dr. Tufts, who suggested (again) exercise. But what troubled John Quincy lay at the very soul of his being, unreachable by medicinal brews or physical vigor. He was rebelling against his parents, their authority over him, their control of his life. They had allowed him little self-examination or doubt, and expected him to follow the straight path they selected to their dreams. Much could be made here in modern psychological terms of John Quincy Adams's behavior, but what was clearly observable was that he was unhappy, ill, depressed, and engaging in behavior that he knew would upset his parents if they discovered it. Study of the law was making him sick; his drinking and late hours were making study difficult; his parents' dreams for him were depressing.

Adams had always observed women — not always favorably — but denied himself much time for visiting or courting them. He joked that he had loved but one woman of all he saw in Europe, and she had been a fourteen-year-old actress glimpsed once in Paris, and never seen again. Otherwise, his closest female acquaintances were his sister, Nabby, whom he had regularly taken for walks in the Bois de Boulogne or to the theater in Paris, and his mother.

In America, Adams soon discovered that he was a young man among young women. Socially immature, when he first returned to the United States he made the rounds of teas and parlors, as a prominent young man was expected to do, and evaluated American women. He entered into his diary that he found these young women "very fine," "amiable in character," or "perfect beauties."

But to his disappointment, many of them were also "great talkers," or "too affected" for his European conditioning. They could, however, make Adams lose his cool and detached manner. A graceful and fetching young lady on Long Island momentarily turned JQA into a dithering blubberer when she sang, with clear, strong voice accompanied by harpsichord, a song with the words "One fond kiss before we part."

Awakening, Adams found himself confronting two problems: He disliked the law and his chosen profession; he loved the "frolicks" and the ladies. Unfortunately, in those days of precarious birth control, one had to work before one could love. So as Adams grew from observer to participant, he discovered that young women were another obstacle in the path to his parents' dream.

In winter there were sleighing parties, which prompted JQA to recall with fondness when in his late sixties: "The art of making love, muffled up in furs, in the open air, with the thermometer at Zero, is a Yankee invention, which requires a Yankee poet to describe." He and his friends "paraded round town till about four in the morning" serenading the ladies, or spent snug evenings warm and dry before the great fire at Sawyer's Tavern on the Bradford Road about three miles outside town, where Adams drank and danced and, on January 21, 1788, fell in love.

In his diary he noted that he "danced with the oldest Miss Frazier, with Miss Fletcher and with Miss Coates." His observations dwelled upon Miss Fletcher's "very genteel shape," animated eyes, and fair complexion, and upon Miss Coates' "agreeable" manners and easy conversation — noting with approval that she was an only daughter "and her father has money." But of Miss Frazier he wrote not a word; what could be said about losing your heart? John Quincy had met Mary Frazier before, and only a few weeks earlier, with his law-clerk friends, spent an evening at her home playing "pawns," a kissing game. "Ah!" Adams wrote, "what kissing! 'tis a profanation of one of the most endearing demonstrations of love."

But in Adams's ecstacy there was pain. Mary Frazier, then only fourteen, offered a temptation he could not satisfy. He disliked his studies, he loved the girl; he knew he was headed down a path without hope: In these days a young man married only when he could afford a family, or married into wealth. Adams could not afford love. He had always been dependent upon his father for funds, and his complaints to his parents that his advancement in a career had been delayed by service in Europe met little sympathy. Four days after dancing with Mary at Sawyer's, JQA confided in his diary, "I feel dull and low spirited. I have neither that insatiable ambition, nor that ardor for pursuing the means to gratify it." In February his "low spirits" continued for ten days, and "not even dissipation has been able to support me. My nerves have got into a disagreeable trim." When he stayed up late, Adams again found he could not sleep; and when he slept, he was disturbed by "extravagant dreams."

By May 1788, Adams's dissipations and love were causing depression that was giving way to "terror" as he contemplated two more years of study for a profession unpromising of personal fortune. The arrival of his parents did not ease his burden; nothing did. On July 11, 1788, he woefully noted his twenty-first birthday, his coming into manhood. The occasion, he said, hiding the truth, "emancipates me from the yoke of parental authority, which I never felt, and places me upon my own feet, which have not strength enough to support me. I continue therefore still in a state of dependence." As long as his parents had to support him, he knew, he would never be free to live and love as he wished. At the end of his first year of law studies, Adams became so ill that he took several months to recuperate. When he tried to return to Newburyport in the autumn of 1788, after a summer in Braintree, he broke down completely. He returned to his parents' home. In Braintree, JQA tramped the fields, rode horseback, went duck hunting along the sea marshes, worked outdoors on the farm with his father, and helped build bookshelves for the library the older Adams had brought back with him from Europe. His mother and father worried about him, and Aunt Cranch brewed her special teas. In early December, he again left for Newburyport, but after three weeks returned home.

In his diary, Adams made clear what was troubling him. On his first day back in Newburyport in December, he had gone dancing, but did not reveal with whom. Safely back home, he wrote several quotations on the last pages of his almanac diary for 1788, one of which said:

> Perfect he seems & undefiled with sin,
> But is this Saint without, a Saint within.

Adams knew he was no "saint within." His appearance to his parents did not coincide with his inner feelings for Mary Frazier. He lusted after the young woman. He had dreams of his own. On the fly leaf for the new almanac for 1789, he wrote: "There is small choice in rotten apples." Below the gloomy reflection JQA wrote Prince Hal's bright line from "Henry IV:" "A fair hot wench in flame-colour'd taffeta." The two connected in his mind: pursuit of the "fair hot wench," a phrase later used by one of Adams's closest friends to describe an outing, would make the young man, who must appear a saint, much the rotten apple.

At home that winter, out of temptation's reach, John Quincy followed Dr. Tuft's prescription of riding, skating, shooting, walking. His friend James Bridge, a fellow law student, wrote JQA a kind "get well" letter, and playfully teased him that no thoughts "are more concerned with the Flesh than those excited by the Ladies," as though Adams needed reminding. In March 1789, when his father left to take the oath of office as the nation's first Vice President, John Quincy Adams returned to Newburyport, and opened another year in which law was second to love.

Adams and his friends continued sporting "the Ladies" at Judge Bradbury's, Colonel Wigglesworth's, or Moses Frazier's, father of Mary, where they danced, played cards, or dined. In warm weather, they sometimes ate picnics in "the grove," and JQA enjoyed his walks with other young men and women, including Mary. At this time, Adams also started writing poetry, discovering a romantic interior hidden or suppressed, which pleased him. Some of his poetry appeared in the *Massachusetts*

Magazine and other publications in Boston. One of the favorite poetic forms of the day was a literary puzzle, called a "rebus," in which the poet furnishes clues to a hidden message. JQA spent much of his time and creativity composing these poetic forms, and in one of his best efforts made an acrostic of the name Mary Frazier.

The year 1790 was a fateful one for John Quincy Adams. His health regained, his love for Mary increased — although a formal declaration and courtship had not been reached — and his law studies finally ended. He was beginning to feel like his own man. Without question, Mary Frazier had given him reason to study and complete his law work. She was, according to a friend of JQA's, "so exquisitely beautiful, so faultless in feature, complexion, expression. . . ." Mary's plump cheeks and full lips, her gentle blue eyes, captivated Adams. Together they went to melon parties, picnics, snow parties, dances, and sometimes walked home side-by-side from church. Without question, but with some reserve, Adams was in love. Newburyport during these last few months of law study contained iridescent days of joy. Adams visited the Fraziers so often that rumors circulated of his engagement to Mary.

In July 1790, John Quincy Adams was admitted as an attorney in the Court of Common Pleas for the County of Essex. The time had come for him to leave Newburyport and start practicing his profession. JQA was in a race with his heart. Could he get his law practice underway fast enough to allow himself to marry? A week after his admission to the bar, Adams opened his law office in Boston in the front parlor of one of his father's houses, at 10 Court Street. He settled in Boston only because business for a young lawyer was poor elsewhere. The day after engaging his office, Adams rode back across the Lynn marshes forty miles to Newburyport, where he spent the evening at the Fraziers'. When he returned to Boston and opened his office, he was in low spirits.

Now began an exchange of letters with his mother and father, lasting from August to November 1790, in which the parents reasserted their control over their son. In April, JQA had unwisely confided to Nabby his attachment to Mary, and word quietly spread through the family. But this was a period when a man's "declaration" must soon be followed by marriage; long engagements risked the woman's reputation. Adams could not afford marriage. Nor would his parents allow a diversion now that their son was launched. He had always been dependent upon them for financial support, and never more than now as he started his practice.

In August 1790, Adams detailed to his father the circumstances that delayed his career — and denied his own dream. Unfortunately, this was not the time to speak to John Adams of finances. He was complaining of his miserly salary as Vice President (five thousand), the meager returns on his houses, and his investments in government securities. The older Adamses were also helping Nabby, who had married a man who appeared unwilling to work; she had just given birth to their third child. "Heaven grant that she may add no more to the stock until her prospects brighten," Abigail wrote to John Quincy. She used the event to warn him about falling in love before he could support a family, and she playfully — but pointedly — hinted that he search for a wealthy woman. In September, John Adams told his son that he could not assist him financially any more than he was doing: "I only ask you to recollect that my Circumstances are not affluent; that you have Brothers and a Sister who are equally entitled." Abigail also wrote, when JQA was depressed over lack of work and income: "You must expect to advance slowly at first . . . but it must be some dire misfortune or calamity, if I judge not amiss, that will ever place you in the shallows." His mother tried to cheer him up: "I will prophecy for you," she wrote, "that you will be able by the close of one year to pay your own board and if you do that it's as much as you ought to expect, and if you do not, why don't worry your face into wrinkles about it, we will help you all we can, and when you are better off than those who assist you, you shall help them again if they want it, so" — and here she gave hint of a warning — "make yourself easy and keep free from entanglements of all kinds. Thomas says you are in love." For the moment, Abigail played down the fact, and even made it trivial. "So far as it will serve to make you more attentive to your person — for you are a little inclined to be negligent — so far it may be of service to you."

His parents had their doubtful son where they wanted him. Both underscored his dependence upon them, and his mother's warning to "keep free from entanglements of all kinds" made clear to JQA that he must support his lady or not have her. Later, she wrote again, making apologies for "moralizing," but warning him to control his impulses, and never allow a woman to become indebted to his poverty; that is, don't marry until you can afford it. That this needed saying indicated JQA's seriousness about Mary Frazier. Abigail opened a careful trap for her son, and he entered it. John Quincy replied that he would never marry a woman for wealth, nor join a woman to poverty. "You shall never be requested for your consent to a connection of mine, until I am able to support that connection with honor and independence."

During this correspondence, however, John Quincy continued seeing Mary. He visited her in Newburyport in August, and in September returned again for evenings at the Fraziers'. On October 29, he wrote in his diary: "M.F. came to town." Mary, in fact, made several visits to friends in nearby Medford and JQA met her there. Four days later, his diary showed another entry: "Conversations with M.F." The conflict between his love for Mary, and the exchange of letters with his parents made JQA "perplexed" and "in anxious expectation." He would either have to announce his intentions soon, and thereby run the risk of a quick marriage and family, or break off his love. He strung out the romance as long as he could, measuring the summer and early autumn with Mary, and perhaps savoring the mildly scandalous meetings in Boston and Medford.

But on November 13, Adams wrote and underlined in his diary: "*Letter from my mother, N.B.*" The letter he had anticipated and dreaded, had arrived. His mother's insistence that he end his Newburyport romance and love for New England's prettiest woman had come. Abigail wrote from her sickbed — and she made the most of that fact — that she was very ill, but had heard of his love for the young lady, and felt she had to act, however sick she might be. Since her son had no financial means to enter into a formal engagement, and since he had promised never to make a connection joining a woman to his poverty, he was now in danger of breaking his word to her and hurting the young lady. "Do you not know," his mother asked him, "that the most cruel of situations to a young lady is to feel herself attach'd to a Gentleman when he can testify it in no other way than by his actions, I mean when his situation will not permit him to speak?" JQA's situation would not allow him to ask for Mary's hand. Why continue misleading her?

John Quincy replied to his mother within a week, first expressing anxiety for her health, and then telling her that his love affair had ended. "I wish to give you full satisfaction by assuring you that there shall never more be any cause on my part for the continuance of it," he wrote. "The Lady will henceforth be at the distance of 40 miles from me and I shall have no further opportunities to indulge a weakness, which you may perhaps censure," but which, he added in a defiant tone, "if you knew the object, I am sure you would excuse." Three weeks later, after a final visit with Mary Frazier, Adams again wrote his mother. "I believe I may add I was never in less danger of any entanglement, which can give you pain, than at the present." John Quincy Adams had done as his mother instructed; he had quickly, almost surgically, broken off with Mary. He had, in the words of Edward Gibbon, sighed as a lover, but obeyed as a son.

John Quincy wrote his brother Thomas a letter that, in part, revealed his deep pain. "I must," he said, "bid a long and lasting farewell to the juvenile Misses." He was also saying farewell to much within himself. He was putting aside the things of youth; he was stifling his love; he was placing duty before the woman of his life. He was, as well, suppressing his sexuality, his youthful desire to love without calculation, his spontaneity. John Quincy told Thomas that he was also ending his poetry writing; the magazines, he said, would have to publish without his rebuses and acrostics. The statement carried a symbolic meaning as well: poetry was his love, his dalliance, his fun. These he suppressed also. He must turn instead, he told Thomas, "to the severer toils" of the law; to his country and his duty. Some members of the family disagreed with Abigail's decision for her son, and watched sympathetically as JQA suffered. Four years later, Aunt Eliza would write him of how she shed "tear for tear" as he struggled to make his sacrifice for *"Situation & filial Duty."*

But John Quincy Adams did not simply toss Mary Frazier aside. The letters to his mother, conveying the breakup as being accomplished with ease, concealed the hurt and anger Adams felt for the rest of his life. Mary Frazier was his heart; he surrendered to her his youthful love without reason or condition. In September, Adams had confided to his friend Bridge that "all my hopes of future happiness in this life, center in the possession of that girl." When the break came, John Quincy said that he and Mary had parted with "a mutual dissolution of affection." But they also made a promise to one another that neither would marry someone unworthy of their lost love. Mary waited until after John Quincy married Louisa Johnson in 1797 before taking one of his friends, Daniel Sargent, Jr., as her husband, in 1802; Mary died in 1804 of consumption. Adams did not visit Newburyport again until 1837, and then with feelings of "chaos." On June 30, 1864, the Newburyport *Herald* carried an account of the love affair, and claimed that Adams, when seventy years old, had stated "that in all which constitutes genuine beauty, loveliness, personal accomplishments, intellectual endowments and perfect purity of life and heart, Miss Mary Frazier excelled" anything he had known of "the most attractive and recognized beautiful among the female sex in Europe and America." He had declared that he "loved her then" and loved "her memory" still.*

Further evidence of the depth of this wound comes from Samuel Breck, who first met John Quincy Adams in 1788 during a visit to Newburyport, and who became his close friend and fellow club member. Breck, too, long remembered the "exquisitely beautiful" Mary Frazier, and said that Adams "was exceedingly in love with her, but she did not respond to his passion." Thirty-six years later, Breck and Adams met at a din-

---

* Charles Francis Adams, John Quincy's son, later labeled the *Herald*'s account an "over-colored and extremely apocryphal narrative."

ner for General Lafayette, who had returned to the United States for a triumphant tour. In conversation at table, Breck happened to mention Mary Frazier, and Adams, somewhat surprised, replied that their love "was a consuming flame kindled by her. Love such as I felt for that Lady is a distressing malady; it made me restless, sick, unhappy; indeed, I may say wretched. It was a long time before I was cured; or able to transfer my love to another object, which I did very sincerely when I married my present wife, who has fulfilled by her kindness and affection all my expectations and wishes in reference to connubial happiness." In 1790, Adams struggled to part with this unpossessed love; as the new decade began, he symbolically lost his cloak at a New Year's party.

John Quincy Adams was so serious about this young woman that he went to Braintree, and made a difficult overland trip from Boston to Philadelphia, the new seat of the Federal government, at great cost to himself, to argue with his parents for his financial independence, and his love — in vain. His parents dismissed him casually. His mother wrote to her sister that John Quincy seemed to have lost "his sprightlyness and vivacity" and was depressed because of "the want of Business in his profession and the dismal prospect for the practitioners of the Law in Massachusetts . . . & that He should still be obliged at his age, to be dependent upon his parents for a support. . . . He wishes sometimes that he had been Bred a Farmer, a Merchant, or an anything by which he could earn his Bread, but we all preach Patience to him." The letter was touching and sad. Farming would have allowed John Quincy freedom to marry. One imagines the young man making his case about income, and arguing that a farmer earned more than a Boston lawyer.

John and Abigail had won. John Quincy would later complain of his "blunted sensations," and of the painful lesson, coming when it did in his life, that certainly contributed to his later icy and stern character. But in 1791, Adams was still young, and his eye for form and beauty soon roamed again. On the trip home by packet from Philadelphia, Adams spent several hours admiring among the passengers "the prettiest Quaker girl" he had ever seen. While Adams might honor his father and mother by putting aside love for law, there were, he soon learned, other ways to deal with passion.

John Quincy Adams spent the next four years trying to earn a living as a lawyer in Boston. But attorney's fees were low: seventy-five cents to two dollars for drawing up indictments for courts and sessions (one dollar for Superior Court), and twenty-five cents for every action entered in the Court of Common Pleas. Not until his last year did he earn a profit as a lawyer.

Central to his life at this time was the "Crackbrain Club," a cluster of eight to ten young men who met irregularly for wine and conversation. Among them were Nathan Frazier, Jr. (a cousin of Mary's), John Gardner, Jr., Tom Crafts, and the Sargent brothers. They were tight friends, confidants, and roisterers who called each other by descriptive nicknames such as "Starveling," "The Fat Knight," "Sir John," "The Squire," "Longwharf." They drank and danced with the Boston ladies at Julien's opposite the Quaker Meeting house ("excellent cooking and good cheer"), or gathered for bowling and drinking at Bird's. Adams's life took on regularity: work at his office and matters of court during most days; drinking and dining with his friends most evenings, and a bath twice a month.

But Adams found that his depressions returned. He spent much of his time (and income) at Bird's or Julien's, and grew reckless. Some evenings he danced until two, wandered home around three, and then spent the next morning "much fatigued" in his office. His conversations became sloppy, and he developed an affection for "macaroni" expressions that fit his rakish pose. At a dance, Adams "made an intentionally offensive reply" to a young woman. Two days later he said that he was "Heavy and dissipated," "Staid late" at the club "and was injudicious."

For exercise, and to overcome his depression and drinking, Adams took walks almost daily, either after meetings of his club, after work, or late at night, when he was alone. He preferred Boston Commons, which was close to his office on Court Street and contained several malls designed for strolling. The Commons offered opportunities for exercise, and other pleasures. In 1784, its low areas had been filled in, the holes covered, fences repaired, and a large number of trees planted. Adams walked along the Great Mall, next to Tremont Street, from the old Burying Ground to the Public Granary, and along the New Mall, now called Beacon Street, or under the English elms lining the little mall of Paddock's Walk. Sometimes he followed the path behind the Granary and crossed obliquely to Beacon Street and the walk that curved westward ending in the region of Boston called "Mount Whoredom."

In 1792, Adam's walks along the mall took on tones of danger, or adventure. On August 27, he wrote in his diary that following an afternoon at Bird's with Crafts and Frazier, he went "Walking in the Mall all the Evening. Fortunately unsuccessful." The next night he again spent an hour on the mall, and three days later while there with Daniel Sargent they "parted accidently, and I got fortunately home." His walks in the mall became nightly adventures, and continued despite a smallpox epidemic ravaging Boston: "Small pox not my only evil," Adams confided. On October third, he recorded another encounter: "Disconcerted madame [in] walk in the Mall." He returned to the mall the next two nights, but noted only once that he went "for exercise."

What was John Quincy up to? His diary reveals little but implies much. Adams was being both allured and repelled by someone. Even in December, following a party at Nathan Frazier's, he walked the mall, although it was after midnight and cold. In April, with the warming of spring, his walks became more frequent; following one, he wrote: "Foolish adventure afterwards. Discretion prevailed." May 16, after church, he walked until ten in the evening; "Was rather fortunate than otherwise." His diary that month also speaks of his being "prudent" during a walk with Gardner, but after a party at Bird's, "guilty of extragavance," and the next day "silly again" during a walk in the mall. June 20: "Day at office and evening in the Mall as usual. Not so wise as sometimes. Home this evening almost despairing." What had upset him? Eight days later he met Gardner "& two Ladies but made a lamentable mistake again. There is a fatality in it I think." On July 5, he parted in the mall from his friend Gardner "very foolishly," and a week later, after an evening at Julien's with Gardner and Frazier, Adams wrote, "Adventure in the Mall. No harm." In September, Adams made "a foolish but fortunate walk" in the mall, and in November, after dinner with Daniel Sargent, he walked in the mall and "went beyond old former hazards" — an act that upset Adams so much that two days later he was still "Trembling for the wages of my own sins."

This series of strange and highly personal experiences continued from December 1793 through June 1794. On the first, second, and third of December, JQA made appointments with someone to meet him at the front of the porch of the Brattle Street Church. The church, newly built in 1772, occupied a curve of Brattle Street; it was conveniently near Adams's law office on Court Street, and one block from the Commons where Adams walked. Each night, however, John Quincy went to the church and waited at eight, but the other person did not appear. Adams claimed he was "fortunate" at this lack of "correspondent punctuality." He was, he wrote, "luckily . . . unsuccessful" and "escaped unhurt."

Adams put on weight. He fretted over his legal work. Troubled, he went through "severe smoking" fits, broke out with boils on his face, and tossed at night in bed with "not a wink of sleep." He used "exercise by way of punishment — walked a great deal." But his efforts at reform — and reform from what? — were half-hearted. He continued his escapades. In February, 1794, Adams walked the mall and "escaped one bad adventure." He pledged "repentence yet." On March 1, during his evening walk he "Met with several adventures. One really affecting. . . ." Three days later he made another appointment for eight on the porch of the Brattle Street Church, but again "failed," which he said was "Very well" with him. Adams now began sleeping during church services, and at the end of March cried out, "When will the vulture leave my bosom?" He committed a "double folly" in April that left him "unwell and spiritless," and asked himself miserably, "Anticipations for futurity — what?" He again promised reform: "commencing a new regime."

The mysterious entries ended in 1794, probably because

Adams's life changed suddenly. What had occurred? These oblique diary statements may be combined with some speculation. First, Adams planned at least four rendezvous with someone during late 1793 and early 1794. He did not want to meet this person at his office, club, or room. This person was interesting enough to him to make Adams wait four times on the church steps in the cold of December and March. Second, it is highly unlikely that this person was male. Adams would have met any man in his office or club; in later years, he even received potential assassins in his home and office. This person was a woman, and someone Adams did not want his friends to see. That leaves two choices. Either Adams was meeting Mary Frazier on the sly — and not even entering her initials in his diary as he had previously — or he was engaging a prostitute, met during his walks on the mall in 1793. Mary Frazier was a young and beautiful woman. She was able to have her choice of young men. Her romance with Adams had been broken off publicly by his wish. Most convincingly, Breck's recollection instructs us that JQA's love for Mary exceeded her love for him. Once denied, she was unlikely to have pursued alone and in the night a man who could not marry her, and who had broken with her.

The argument that John Quincy Adams engaged a prostitute is strong. Nothing else would have upset him as much, nor caused him to plead with himself for reform. Prostitution, moreover, was not uncommon in Boston or any American city; New York, for example, had seven thousand prostitutes in 1795, and Philadelphia's streets, said Benjamin Franklin (an experienced source on the topic), were teeming with women "who by throwing their heads to the right or to the left of everyone who passed by them, I concluded came out with no other Design than to revive the spirit of love in Disappointed Batchelors and expose themselves to sale at the highest bidder."

Adams was certainly one of those "Disappointed Batchelors," and his walks in the Boston Commons brought him close to "Mount Whoredom," an appropriately named community that formed one of the hills near the Commons. On its slopes lived Boston's poor, and its north side was indeed a disreputable place of vice and crime. It was, in fact, of such notoriety that when

Charles Bullfinch sought to make Beacon Hill a respectable residential area, the name of nearby Mount Whoredom was dropped from Boston's maps, and the more wholesome Mount Vernon substituted. Women living along Mount Whoredom's slopes did walk the mall throwing their heads in suggestive ways, and it is likely that JQA encountered many of them, and found one attractive.

Adams had several good reasons to engage a prostitute. He was young and his friend Bridge described him as passionate, while another friend, Putnam, said Adams was as "capable of strong attachts as any person I know." He couldn't afford a mistress, and the liaison, although morally repugnant to him, would have been as emotionally invigorating as it was sexually satisfying. Adams was also, of course, rebounding from a lost love, and was vulnerable. But most of all, loving a prostitute would have made a satisfying personal rebuttal to the preaching of his parents, especially his mother. It was his way of getting even. For if they wouldn't let him possess the immaculate Mary Frazier, he would have instead the common street girl of Boston. And so much for his Puritan heritage.

Unknown to John Quincy Adams, however, a *deus ex machina* was about to sweep across the stage of this young Boston lawyer and burgeoning roué. On June 3, 1794, Adams received letters from Philadelphia stating that President Washington had appointed him as Minister Resident to the Netherlands. He was to sail for The Hague as soon as possible. The appointment, ending his idleness and tiny law business, and plucking him from the perils of pleasure, made John Quincy sick. Conversations in Braintree with his father, who was "more gratified than myself at my appointment," didn't help. Abigail and John considered the appointment the splendid start "in the cabinet or the field" that they had raised John Quincy to accept. The young man took sick on June 6, and remained "extremely unwell" through the eighteenth, when he spent a very bad night, and was bled. His spirits remained "at lowest ebb," and even by the twenty-eighth, as he packed to leave Boston for Philadelphia, and as his friends collected to drink a final toast to him (and he to them), Adams was still "unwell. . . . Cannot prepare myself sufficiently." He found "the idea of leaving all my friends very painful," yet on June 30, once more the dutiful son, John Quincy departed from the private life of Boston for the public arena.*

Alone, John Quincy Adams slowly rode the stage out of Boston to Providence, where he caught the packet *Clemantine* for Newport (he dined on board, and noted "fare wretched") and then the packet *Romero* to New York. He went by stage over the jarring clay roads of New Jersey — the whole like a plowed field in furrows two feet deep — and arrived in Philadelphia at sunset, July 9, after a trip of ten days. From that hour, with only two brief intervals until the hour he died, John Quincy Adams devoted himself to public service.

In Philadelphia, his family could scarcely contain their excitement. His father was ecstatic. His mother showed him a letter from Martha Washington, consoling her on losing a son to diplomatic service, but extolling that son's prospects. Aunt Eliza of Haverhill wrote that she knew John Quincy had obtained "the Palm" by following the path of virtue. But while the "Palm" was his, JQA was never asked whether or not he wished to accept it. No one ever suspected that young Adams might choose what he wished to do with his own life. The parental dream was overwhelming. "I have indeed long known that my father is far more ambitious for my advancement, far more solicitous [sic] for the extension of my fame, than I ever have been," said JQA, "or ever shall be."

On September 15, John Quincy sailed, with his brother Thomas as his secretary, from Boston for London and the Netherlands. Two close friends boarded and went as far as the

---

* Why had President Washington selected John Quincy Adams? Some historians argue that the appointment came as a reward for JQA's spirited articles in the *Columbian Centinel* on matters of foreign policy — much of it supporting Washington's position. Also, the Vice President was the young man's father, and not above championing his son in his career. President Washington, both flattered and coaxed, also knew that this new nation needed young diplomats, that the post was peripheral (London, Paris, Madrid, and Lisbon being more important), yet a good training ground. With one appointment, therefore, Washington filled a diplomatic post, pleased a friend, rewarded an admirer, and assured his nation of an experienced diplomat for the next century.

Boston lighthouse: Nathan Frazier, Jr., cousin of the woman Adams loved; and Daniel Sargent, Jr., Mary's future husband. The irony of their presence was underscored by a gift Adams received from his father before departing: an order on Dutch bankers for five thousand guilders, a large sum of money. This was the father's reward for the son's painful choice. The money, which would have meant so much to John Quincy four years earlier, now meant little. He arranged to have some of it paid to his Aunt Eliza — who had shed "tear for tear" with him then — for the education of her son. Adams turned the rest over to his brother Charles to invest, for a handsome commission. Both were acts of generosity and kindness, the one to Charles particularly troublesome, for the younger brother would squander the investment, lose the entire fortune, and thus cause JQA to spend the rest of his life without financial security. So John Quincy Adams sailed toward his new arena, and a life where he was more sure of himself, where the control of emotion, the suppression of passion, were rewarded with the only thing men value more than sex or money — power.

8

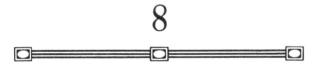

A⸺T THIS MOMENT in John Quincy Adams's life, the appointment to the Netherlands proved fortunate. The Hague was the least significant of the five United States diplomatic posts overseas. France, England, Spain, and Portugal ranked above it. Adams's salary of forty-five hundred dollars a year allowed little extravagance, but made him independent. He was single, and his instructions from Secretary of State Edmund Randolph created much free time: Adams had only to tend to the Treasury loans borrowed during the war from the Dutch by his father, and keep a watchful eye on European affairs, especially the French Revolution now sweeping the Continent. These benefits of free time and income combined with others. Adams was an ocean distant from his parents, and letters, the only communication, took two or three months, door to door. John Quincy was also older, more mature, and experienced in both pain and pleasure. Best of all, as he wrote to his friend John Gardner in Boston, Adams found himself "once more my own man again." Given the diplomatic position, the leisure, the income and freedom, John Quincy was ready to whirl the ladies, and he wasted no time. On his way through England delivering dispatches to John Jay and Thomas Pinckney, JQA and brother Thomas spent two weeks sporting "around in the fling of London." Adams confided to his diary: "There is something so fascinating in the women I meet in this Country that it is not well for me. I am obliged immediately to leave it."

John Quincy stayed at The Hague only two months before being sent back temporarily to London in the autumn of 1795, on a small diplomatic errand. With Jay sailing to the United States and Pinckney in Spain, Adams had to complete the exchange of ratifications and other diplomatic sweepings necessary to the conclusion of Jay's Treaty. Such diplomacy, then as now, dragged. Adams found himself at the Adelphi Hotel with little to do but receive invitations to balls and dinners; among these was a request to visit and dine with the Joshua Johnsons of Tower Hill.

This came at a time when the Johnson home was well known among American young men as a place of fine wines and dinners, and excellent parlor entertainments performed by three daughters of marriageable age, heirs to Joshua's fortune. In November of 1795, therefore, John Quincy Adams passed through the immense front doors of the Johnson home for the first time, a willing bachelor shopping in London's richest bazaar. Adams had dressed for the occasion in his new, heavy Dutch clothing, which featured a thick white overcoat, and he spent the evening in "high spirits" visiting with Joshua and Catherine, dining, and sitting still for a sampling of the daughters' talents. Immediately after he left, the family collected, as they did on such occasions, to evaluate the young man. All agreed that Adams was a solid prospect, but a shoddy dresser. John Quincy returned frequently, and soon became a favorite of Louisa's mother. Her father, however, found him a nuisance. "He always had a prejudice towards the *Yankees*," Louisa said of Joshua, "and insisted that they never made good husbands."

When Adams visited, Louisa and Nancy were put forward by their parents to play the piano and sing, which they did for two or three hours after dinner. Adams liked some kinds of music, but female singing was not one of them. JQA preferred the songs he and his fellow clerks sang in the taverns of Newburyport. At the Johnsons', if Louisa or Nancy began singing a song Adams found "disagreeable" — usually one Colonel Trumbull requested — John Quincy immediately put on his hat and bid them all goodbye.

But he always returned. This was the marketplace, and JQA needed a wife. He was lonely, and almost twenty-nine, and thought this might be his last chance. Everything came together at once: profession, income, leisure, age, his freedom to choose. Marriage was the business at hand, and John Quincy Adams was prepared to complete one period of his life, and start a new one.

Adams had a further reason for seeking a wife. In November 1795, his mother wrote that brother Charles was marrying Sarah Smith. Charles had no profession, no income, and was younger than John Quincy had been during his romance with Mary Frazier. When he received this letter, JQA exploded. He had surrendered his heart to his parents' demands for duty and career; Charles would gain his wishes where John Quincy had been forced to suppress his own. The unfairness, the bitterness burst out. Adams wrote his mother a stinging letter. He resented, he told her, his parents' having forced him to make his "prudential sacrifices," and having done so he now suffered frigidity and his natural warmth of character had been replaced by a coldness; he had suppressed all love, all passion. Seven months later, his mother replied coldly that she recognized "the sacrifice you had made" but told him not to despair, that "a kindred soul" waited "in reserve for you." If he needed one, this gave Adams an additional reason to marry, and get on with his life.

Adams dallied at the Johnsons' frequently. He knew what he wanted. He was determined to marry a short woman; he worried that a tall woman might appear superior to him. He wanted an intelligent woman, a good conversationalist. Adams had disabused "the state of female education" in the United States, where he said he found "very few young ladies who talk and yet preserve our admiration." He found conversation with them difficult; he was more comfortable with serious, European women. The Johnson ladies, therefore, were doubly attractive: all of them were small; they openly, and with a rare intelligence, conversed like European women in a manner Adams thought proper for a lady, and found enticing.

At first, the Johnsons believed John Quincy fancied Nancy, their oldest; this made Louisa feel more relaxed around him. They gently teased one another about her music and his poetry (and musical dislikes), and Louisa asked John Quincy to prove he was indeed a poet by writing a poem to her. He did, and one evening at dinner he passed it to her across the table in full view. Louisa was surprised and pleased. She opened the paper and started reading aloud, embarrassing Adams and Nancy, and stopped only when her governess sitting next to her whispered that it was impolite to read at the table. Briefly saved, John Quincy made known his intentions to Louisa almost impetuously. On February 12, 1796, Louisa celebrated her twenty-first birthday with a ball, and John Quincy spent the evening dancing with her and escorting her about on his arm. His "decidedly publick" attentions "brought much trouble on my head," Louisa later wrote, especially from Nancy. But her sister's sulks and pouts amounted to little compared with John Quincy Adams's demands for Louisa's improvement, and his uncertainties.

Louisa, too, was uncertain. For one thing, she was not impressed with Adams's career: "An American Minister was to me a very small personage," she later wrote, "and in my eyes is so still, in as far as place goes." Wasn't love supposed to laugh, to sing, to make her heart run fast? Instead, Louisa found herself having to be "coaxed into an affection." She too, was immature, and although twenty-one in age, "in knowledge of the world I was not fifteen." She had properly kept herself always in the company of chaperones, and had never been alone with a man, anywhere, anytime. Louisa could recall only one occasion when she had left her home without her father or mother, and that was when she went to a ball at Chiswick under the "protection" of the elderly Colonel Trumbull. John Quincy Adams, she said, was the first and only man with whom she had ever been left alone; he was the first man she had ever kissed, and the first man who ever touched her with passionate embraces. "I can swear before the living God," Louisa wrote, "that I came pure and virtuous to his arms."

Instead of passion, however, JQA's courtship of Louisa Johnson created fear and doubt. "Love seem'd to chill all the natural hilarity of my disposition," she said, "and those hours which had been spent in cheerful mirth were passed in gloom and anxiety." Louisa sensed, she later wrote, "something wrong without knowing to find the error." They walked in the parks and took rides together, but Louisa and John Quincy squabbled almost from the start. Adams was dull-quiet, slovenly in dress, and clumsy at dancing. Louisa was none of these. Any efforts at reform by her met with harshness from him. When Louisa invited him to a family picnic, she jokingly suggested "that if he went with us he must dress himself handsomely and look as dashing as possible." Louisa, as she admitted later, was unaware that "on this subject he was very sore," and her demand made Adams angry. When they called for JQA in their carriage at the Adelphi, however, "he was very handsomely dressed" in an elegant blue suit and large Napoleon hat. Louisa was extremely pleased, and when they entered the party, Adams offered Louisa his arm, which she took, and they strolled about, but when she complimented him on his appearance, "he immediately took fire," and told her that *his wife* must "never take the liberty" of interfering in his dress. John Quincy spoke in a tone "so high and lofty and made so serious a grievance of the affair" that Louisa felt offended, and told him that she rejected his marriage offer, and left him "free as air to choose a Lady who would be more discreet." She joined her mother and stayed close to her for the rest of the evening. Both made apologies to the other on the way home, but lessons had been learned. John Quincy now understood Louisa's strong "fixedness of opinion," and her temper. Louisa, for her part, felt the "sting" of his. They had discovered a trivial issue — his dress — that would be one tender sore among many repeatedly touched, indicating the deeper weakness of their marriage. As Louisa said, the incident gave her "a secret and unknown dread of something hidden beneath the rosy wreath of love."

After asking Joshua for his daughter's hand, and getting a quick approval, John Quincy suddenly departed in May for The Hague. He thought he had frittered away too much time in London, and should return to his public duties and private reading. He told Louisa to ready herself for marriage. He laid out a course of study for her with the hope of improving her mind. They exchanged miniatures, and he promised to return for her — perhaps in a year, or in seven.

Abigail learned of her son's betrothal through hinting letters from Thomas, and her deductions led her, she said, to suspect the Johnson family. She wrote John Quincy, approving of his decision to return to The Hague without marrying "to accumulate some solid property before you take upon you the charge of a Family." This was what she expected of him, but not of Charles, and JQA, back at The Hague, replied defiantly that he was "old enough to get married." His mother, recognizing the distance and her son's age, replied: "You are certainly old enough. Your father was married nine days younger than you are now." But Abigail continued to raise doubts. Did her son have any lingering thoughts of Mary Frazier? "As you tell me the enthusiasm of youth has subsided," she probed, "I presume that reason and judgment have taken its place." Abigail worried that Louisa was too English — anti-British feeling still ran high in the United States — and said: "I would hope for the love I bear my country that the Siren is at least *half-blooded.*" John Adams, too, voiced his concern: "I wished in my heart it might have been in America. But I have not a word to say. You are now of age to judge for yourself."

But John and Abigail remained unwilling to let John Quincy make that judgment alone and simply give him their blessing. They expected much for him, and Louisa appeared unlikely to fit those expectations. Would Louisa survive "at so early an Age, without any knowledge or experience of the World . . . the manners, luxuries, dissipations and amusements of a foreign Court?" Abigail asked. Would she find the continental style of living incompatible with their later prospects in America? Louisa, she wrote, had been raised by "kind and indulgent parents," who gave her "a virtuous Education, taught her to have domestick virtues, and at the same time accomplished her in musick, dancing, French, etc." But wouldn't a European court with its glitter and pomp "unfit her for the discharge of those domestic duties which cement the union of Hearth, and give it the sweetest pleasures?" Abigail suggested that JQA place country before "contentment and delight."

But John Quincy had made this sacrifice once; never again. He replied sharply to his mother, ending the discussion, that "if upon the whole I have done wrong, I shall be the principle sufferer." But if he waited until everyone — father, mother, brothers, sister — approved of his choice, and all doubts were overcome, "I should have been certainly doomed to perpetual celibacy." "Prudence," he told his mother, "is a sorry matchmaker." In fact, Abigail worried about something that John Quincy remained blind to: that Louisa's upbringing made her unfit to adapt to the conventional expectations society, especially American society, had for women her age. How would she accept Quincy and New England after she'd tasted London and the Continent?

During the summer of 1796, Louisa lived at Clapham Common in a small house that her father rented for her. Here she had the privacy needed to devote full-time "to such studies," she wrote, "as I hoped would lesson [sic] the immense distance which existed in point of mind and talents between myself and my future husband." She was so isolated that her jealous sisters called her "the Nun," and Louisa agreed that she became "miserably dull, stupid and cross." John Quincy soon inquired, however, whether she was employing her time "to advantage," and asked that she send him "a detail of everything interesting to yourself in your situation. . . . Your progress upon the Harp, I am persuaded is great," and he hoped that her reading equaled it. He wanted her attentive to her studies and her music, for they would make her valuable in a marriage to a public man.

9

LOUISA, AND JOHN QUINCY were separated longer than they had been together before their marriage. They conducted a strange, formal, and dispassionate courtship almost entirely by mail. At first, Louisa dreaded receiving his letters, and held to the etiquette of responding only when he wrote to her. But Adams wrote only between diplomatic correspondence, letters to his family, and diary entries, and Louisa sometimes didn't receive a word for more than a month. Thirty-six years earlier, John Quincy Adams's parents had enjoyed a passionate courtship, and the contrasts between father and son, and between Louisa and Abigail, reveal not only their different personalities, but also the different social periods. These contrasts mirrored the sharply changing roles of men and women at this time. Here was a period of social transition, and Louisa was a victim, if not a symbol, of it. Here, too, was a time from which we can measure the oppression of women in America, and of a person, Louisa Johnson, whose life spanned that time.

Nowhere are the disparities of this period sharper than between the lives of Louisa and Abigail. This New Englander was the quintessential Puritan woman: purposeful, frugal, independent, diligent, courageous, passionate, and self-righteous. She was also well educated, for a woman. When Abigail was raising her family, colonial women were considered the equals of colonial men. Few activities were thought unsuitable for women, and they moved freely into occupations where they were needed, rather than what was thought proper. They ran businesses, worked as shopkeepers, teachers, blacksmiths, innkeepers, silversmiths and tinworkers, shipwrights, gunsmiths, barbers. Eleven women ran printing presses, and ten published newspapers in America before 1776. Of Boston's fifty-four taverns, twenty-four were run by women in the mid-1700s. A few women taxpayers even appeared on the records of New Jersey and other colonies, and cast ballots at voting places. During the colonial period, 1620 to 1760, American women were people of unquestioned value and importance. They were needed; they were essential to the process of nation-building that was under way.

John and Abigail had courted and married in 1764. They had lived about thirty miles apart, and during their courtship could hardly keep their hands off each other. After one meeting, John wrote Abigail that his ardor was aboil, and that "Itches, Aches, Agues, and Repentence might be the Consequence of a Contact in present Circumstances." When a summer storm kept them apart one day, he wrote (with relief) that their passion had fortunately been held at a distance. He showed up on Abigail's doorstep with a letter for her, which demanded that she "give [the bearer] as many kisses, and as many Hours of your Company after 9 O'Clock as he shall please to Demand and charge them to my Account." Abigail coyly protested that John owed her for purloined kisses, and John, playing the lawyer, advised that she could not sue for payment "unless I refuse Marriage; which I never did, and never will, but on the Contrary am ready to *have you* at any Time." The italics were his.

No such demands for Louisa slipped from John Quincy's pen. At his most passionate he called her "My amiable friend," and told her "You are the delight and pride of my life." He saw himself, he told her, as "a faithful and anxious though not a romantic lover." Louisa, in turn, called him "my beloved and most esteemed friend," and often signed her letters during their courtship, "your still tenderly attached and truly faithful Louisa C. Johnson."

During his years in Philadelphia, John had written Abigail: "I intreat you to rouse your whole attention to the family, the stock, the farm, the dairy. Let every article of expense which can be spared be retrenched; keep the hands attentive to there [sic] business and the most prudent measures of every kind be adopted." He placed his entire family and farm totally in his wife's control. She hired and fired farm workers, bartered for animals and food and farm products, hired tutors for her children or educated them herself, clothed them all, and still melted bullets for the revolution and read aloud to JQA every evening from Rollin's *History*. Abigail replied that, in time, she hoped "to have the reputation of being as good a *farmeress* as my partner has of being a good statesman." The essential word was "partner."

The American Revolution, however, freed men and gradually imprisoned women. Louisa Johnson, born on the eve of the Declaration of Independence, grew up at a time when women were becoming less outspoken and equal partners with men, and more ornaments for the home and marriage. Her life connected the pre-Revolutionary War American woman with those of the Victorian era; the brief period of comparative equality with the confinement and suppression of the nineteenth century. After the Revolution, as men left the farms to work, women remained at home with little purpose. A woman's life narrowed and her importance beyond the home diminished. Society confected a new role for her: Guardian of the home. Even the home itself physically changed: Special rooms were needed for the new society. Calling cards were invented, and the social institution of receiving visitors or making visits, which required a room, brought about the parlor. Family conversation, letter writing, indoor games, reading aloud, entertaining with music, also came into vogue. Women who had shared the American frontier and farm now had to preside gracefully over drawing rooms and levees. By 1800, Abigail Adams, the "farmeress," had become a fussy hostess burdened with a cultivated social life.

While John Quincy Adams enjoyed a classical education, including Harvard, Louisa Johnson learned music, needlework, and dancing for a gloss of elite manners. Only by an unusual encounter was she made aware of something more. Louisa and other women her age were educated not to become individuals, or arbiters of their own destinies, but to be absorbed into a family unit as homemaker, guardian of Virtue, Morality, and Piety. Female education had never been equal. Few women could write or read; colonial records show them signing their names with an X. As early as the mid-1600s, men like John Winthrop asserted that intellectual development would rot the female mind, and cause madness. By 1775, one Boston squire thought that "girls knew quite enough if they could make a skirt and a pudding." Not Abigail Adams. She would see the ladies educated. "If you complain of the neglect of Education in sons," she wrote John, "what shall I say with regard to daughters who every day experience the want of it." Abigail pushed John to urge a new constitution in Massachusetts Bay Colony that would provide "Learning and Virtue" for all children. "If we mean to have Heroes, Statesmen and Philosophers" for this new nation, she wrote him, "we should have learned women."

But after the war, by law and by economic and social design, women took less of a part in American society. Men diminished them to fragile, delicate creatures; they repressed feminine sexuality. How women should behave was interwoven into the fabric of society by magazines and literature, tutors and governesses. The passive woman was much admired; the active male her master. Women became preoccupied with good manners and social graces that emphasized proper conduct; how to enter a room, greet a hostess, sit, talk, place one's hands. Specialists even determined how women should raise their skirts: for passing through muck, one allowed the use of a single hand — never two — to bunch and lift the skirt to the right. There were lists of topics of conversation. Unlike their frontier grandmothers, these young women conformed to elaborate rituals of behavior that included increased modesty about their bodies, their fluids and odors; dexterity with rows of forks and knives, and separate plates and dishes for every course; the use of perfumed handkerchiefs instead of fingers or cloths for noseblowing; the control of spitting (but not its demise); the wearing of nightclothes; the introduction of washbasins, portable bathtubs, "showerbaths," and soap. The upkeep of appearances was essential, and exhausting. Aqua Vitae, a nighttime potion, required the lady's skill at mixing thirty ingredients, two months' cultivation, and the impossible final order to "shake the bottle incessantly for ten to twelve hours." Diaries became popular, and the common theme of leisure ran through them: "At home with company," "Dined out," "Attended ball."

Women had one purpose: to become "stewards and guardians of their husbands' property." Louisa learned to play the harp and pianoforte, as other women did, so she could "soothe the cares of domestic life" with song. She learned geography, religion, penmanship so she could provide domestic comfort and educate her sons. She prepared for private life; her education directed at controlling servants, raising children, creating intelligent conversation. Louisa, like other women, had been instructed to dispel gloom, maintain ease and comfort, make her home a refuge set apart from society where she would dispense, like some private psychological service, domestic comfort to her husband, whose major concerns would take place away from her, outside the boundary of her life. "Sweetness is to woman what sugar is to fruit," said one authority. "It is her first business to be happy — a sunbeam in the house, making others happy."

Here, then, were the seeds of conflict for Louisa's adult life. Educated to be subordinate, she had witnessed the worst example of subordination — enslavement of a person — and dared to test her intellect on masculine ideas and education. But she was also taught the lesson contained in *A Father's Legacy to His Daughter*, printed the year Louisa Johnson was born: "If you happen to have any learning, keep it a profound secret, especially from the men, who generally look with a jealous and malignant eye on a woman of great parts and cultivated understanding." All her adult life, however, Louisa would rebel against this instruction; she would refuse to be a mere bright ornament, a decorative sunbeam in a man's house.

Preparation for marriage and learning proper behavior, she knew, were essential to a woman's life. Benjamin Rush wrote to a young woman on the eve of her marriage in 1792 that "you will be well received in all companies only in proportion as you are inoffensive, polite, and agreeable to everybody. . . . From the day you marry you must have no will of your own." The perfect wife was "kind, obsequious, uncontradicting." Was this how Louisa Johnson perceived herself? Brought up in a care-free home, educated more than the average woman, Louisa had been exposed to ideas unusual for her time. Her home served as a crossroads for American and European visitors, newspapers, books, ideas, rules, and standards. More French than English, and more English than American, Louisa was alert to events around her. It was an impoverished Englishwoman, Mary Wollstonecraft, who wrote in 1792 against female oppression. Her *Vindication of the Rights of Women* argued for equality, and stated that marriage, which once had offered dignity and value to women, had become in the 1790s a degrading relationship. Men were at fault. To praise a woman for her "elegancy of mind, exquisite sensibility, and sweet docility of manners," Wollstonecraft warned, was a masculine trick to keep women in "slavish dependence." Louisa was surrounded by these ideas, these women advocates who planted seeds of questioning and doubt that, nurtured in the acid soil of Louisa's marriage, sprouted late in her life. Make no mistake: Louisa Johnson was an upper-class woman who had been spoiled and sheltered. She was no impoverished weaver's daughter like Mary Wollstonecraft, shocked by the oppression of women after the French Revolution. Louisa started her adult life preparing herself for marriage to John Quincy Adams, asking not How shall I be free? but, How shall I behave?

10

LOUISA AWAITED John Quincy's first letter from The Hague with "anxiety." When it finally arrived in the late spring of 1796, "the terror which assailed me at the idea of answering it" was great; the formidable Adams frightened her. Louisa had never before carried on a correspondence with any male, and she was "too much afraid" to write anything to her suitor without the approval of her governess. For the first few months of their correspondence, Louisa wrote a draft reply, and her governess corrected Louisa's draft by giving it the proper tone, as she knew it, of elegance and romance. In this system, the level of passion between Louisa and John Quincy could not have ignited any but the most inflammable love.

John Quincy proved a cautious, even reluctant, fiancé. He told Louisa that their separation would teach them control, fortitude, endurance, duty. He wanted Louisa to be happy and contented, but told her that this was achieved only by controlling "our own wishes and passions." Her desire to be with him matched his to be with her, he said, but she must learn, as he had, "to acquire the faculty not merely for acquiescence, in unavoidable circumstances, but even of cheerful conformity to things which must be endured. . . . As long as we cannot command Events, we must necessarily learn to acquiesce in them, and the more carefully we prepare for them, the more easily we content ourselves under them."

But Louisa was not interested in learning how to endure. To her dismay, she discovered that John Quincy actually welcomed their separation. Deprivation, even misfortune, were ways he tested himself and improved. He told her to "reconcile" herself to a long separation, and "derive satisfaction from the reflection that it cannot be avoided." He advised her to "consider untoward Events as a test of character, and that a large portion of all human merit consists in *suffering* with dignity and composure, without weakness or unavailing regret."

Louisa found this "boasted philosophy" a "*dreadful* thing," she told him. "I see too plainly that it dictates every action, and guides your pen I hope in contradiction to your feelings." Now her shock and anger let her write without her governess's assistance. In another feisty letter, Louisa accused John Quincy of having "very little knowledge of my disposition . . . and I hope in time to convince you that I possess both fortitude and dignity, sufficient at least to conceal any unbecoming emotion, if not entirely to conquer them." True, she agreed, we are unfit for life's path if we think "our way strewn with flowers or its borders lined with down. . . . No . . . I have never dreamt of *cloudless skies*, yet did I not expect that *you* would have been the person to have strewn my path with needless thorns."

Testing his character or not, Adams was in no hurry to be married. In May 1796, President Washington with Senate approval had appointed John Quincy as Minister Plenipotentiary to the Court of Lisbon. His salary would double from forty-five hundred to nine thousand dollars a year. Adams could afford a wife, and he wrote Louisa that he planned, at a time unspecified, to sail to Portugal by way of London, "taking you as the companion for the remainder of the Journey or Voyage, and of my Life."

Hearing of Adams's appointment to Portugal, Joshua Johnson, with his daughter's gentle urging, wrote JQA that he might outfit a ship to sail to the Netherlands, perhaps carrying the Johnson family to America, and Louisa might visit Adams there. John Quincy recoiled at the suggestion. He quickly wrote Louisa that the plan contained too many "obstacles" and that he saw behind it a scheme for her to disembark in Holland, and remain with him. Louisa denied this, and said her father's suggestion was an impulsive act "of the most honourable feelings" and the wish to promote "the happiness of a child so dear to him." She found John Quincy's letter "so severe, so cold and so peremptory" that it made her furious. "I adored my father," she later wrote, "and I was proud." She regretted "most sincerely ever having expressed a wish to *meet* you in Holland," she told John Quincy, "since it appears to have given you so much uneasiness." She was not, she said putting herself in the position where he, or anyone, could ever say that she forced herself "upon any man or into any family." Louisa's feelings and pride were hurt. Obviously, John Quincy was not rushing to her side. She felt "a sense of unnecessary harshness and severity of character . . . which often led me to fear something . . . and put a damp upon my natural spirits which I never overcame."

John Quincy thought so little of this match that he closed 1796 by writing in his diary his concerns for that year: "The situation of two objects the nearest to my heart, my country and my father, press continually upon my reflections. They engross every thought and almost every power, every faculty." He didn't mention a young woman and her heart.

It is essential in understanding this relationship to know one other important fact. That autumn, when Joshua Johnson so casually offered the use of one of his ships, when Louisa and her mother had prepared a wardrobe and trunks and Adams's harsh letter had sent the marriage trousseau back into storage, Johnson had learned some bad news. He had recently received a letter informing him that his partnership was being dissolved "by mutual consent," and terms entered into. Lawyers in Maryland urged him to sail for the United States, leaving his family in England, to settle the matter. But Catherine Johnson had never been separated from her husband, and refused to let him go; care of the family, she said, would be "too great for her nerves." Although Johnson had also received word of a possible embezzlement of the profits of the business, he remained with his family in London. Nevertheless, he kept a ship standing by, just in case. Therefore when, in the spring of 1797, Johnson again offered Adams a ship to carry him from Holland to England, and then to Portugal, or to place his daughter in the Netherlands, it is unclear whether he wished to get his family out of England and back to Maryland, or whether he was making the kind gesture of a loving father. In retrospect, the facts appear suspicious. With his daughter married, Johnson could sail to the United States with his family; but as long as Adams remained stubborn, Johnson and his family had to remain in London.

In April, John Quincy received a packet of letters from the Secretary of State and President directing him to proceed to Portugal. Still he delayed. There were problems, he told Louisa. He should await his replacement. He saw no prospect of peace between France and Portugal, nor any means of passage from England through the French privateers. Perhaps she should not accompany him "into so dangerous a situation." Perhaps he should wait a month or two. Perhaps he would depart on a Danish vessel, for safety. But even his mother thought the time had come: "I advise you to marry the lady before you go to Portugal," she wrote; "give my love to her and tell her I consider her already as my daughter."

When Joshua's second offer of a ship reached Adams that spring, he could feel the trap closing. He tried to hold it off. He wrote that he hoped "for a time of more tranquility." But Johnson, in a letter dated April 25, 1797, offered Adams the use of several of his ships. The schooner *Mary*, fifty tons, outfitted in Virginia for passengers "and remarkably handsome," could be outfitted to carry only Louisa, John Quincy, Thomas, Louisa's servants, their baggage and ballast. It could be sent to Rotterdam, bring John Quincy to London, convey the blissful couple on to Lisbon. Or, wrote Johnson, another vessel, the *Holland*, was expected in port in May in preparation to take Johnson and his family home to the United States; it could stop at Rotterdam or Amsterdam for John Quincy.

Adams had no single, strong reply to Johnson's kind and encompassing offer, and so he made several small and weak rebuttals. He wrote that, unfortunately, he was "obliged to go directly from Amsterdam to Lisbon" (obliged by whom?) and although this was "a great disappointment," he must, he said, "bear it, like so many others." Further, the *Mary* "would suit *me* very well," but at this time of year for a lady unused to the sea, "I feel it would be too unpleasant." This, of course, was nonsense: the next month marked the opening of the best sailing season of the year; Louisa had also been at sea enough to know what to expect. She had written in 1796 that she sometimes thought of the severity of their life together, the "dark side," and concluded that "with you at the hand [I] find every idea of danger vanished." She was ready to be courageous; he was not. Yet, Adams said in closing his letter to Joshua, if Louisa felt strong enough and had "all the papers and necessary documents," he might reconsider.

That same day, John Quincy also wrote Louisa. He played his final card, and offered her a chance to say no. He told her that, in his manners toward her and his letters, he had disguised none of his true character. She knew the man she was to marry. Speaking of himself in the third person, Adams told her:

> You know the chances for hardship, inconvenience and danger, which you may be called to share with him. You know his inviolable attachment to his Country, and his resolute determination not to continue long his absence from it. — You know that upon his retirement, the state of his fortune will require privations, which will be painful to him only as they may affect you. Choose, Louisa, choose for yourself, and be assured that his Heart will ratify your choice.

John Quincy said he would remain in The Hague long enough to receive her reply. If she said yes, he would then "immediately come to you"; but if she said no, he would submit to "the will of Providence." Louisa, however, hesitated not a moment:

> Why my beloved friend did you tell me to choose, what I have always declared, required not a moments hesitation to determine. No my Adams, I have long ardently wished you might be enabled to return . . . your return would make me happy and . . . I anticipate it with the utmost pleasure — I only fear my friend that you will find *me* a troublesome companion.

Before leaving bachelorhood, Adams made a final scold. He did not like the term "my Adams." "It is a stile of address that looks too much like that of novels. A bare proper Name does not sound or look well for a Man in real life." Adams worried that Louisa might not be dignified enough for a public man. Perhaps she had been indulging in novels, instead of the more serious matter detailed by him for her studying. John Quincy left The Hague on July 9, arranging his own passage, and sailed for London, where he would learn that the Senate on May 30 had confirmed his appointment, made by the new President, his father John Adams, as Minister Plenipotentiary not to Lisbon, but to Berlin.

11

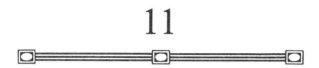

JOHN QUINCY ADAMS arrived at the Adelphi Hotel in London on July 12, at five in the afternoon, with time to stroll over to the Johnsons'. But Adams delayed one more day. He had told Louisa that the nuptials could take place "immediately after" his arrival, as he could spare only a few days before speeding on to his next post. He had planned to marry enroute between The Hague and (he thought) Lisbon, scooping up Louisa Johnson in London as though she were an incoming diplomatic pouch. When he saw her on the thirteenth, Adams asked Louisa to set a date. She named July 26 — two weeks hence — and John Quincy was shocked. Even Louisa's mother was surprised at so early a date, and scolded her. But the bride held firm; that's when they would marry. John Quincy Adams agreed.

In the midst of wedding preparations, as Louisa's trunk was once more brought out and filled, Adams learned about Berlin. His father wrote that he hoped his son's plans were not upset "by the Alteration I have made in your destination." The mission to Portugal, he told JQA, was "less important" than that to Prussia; the north of Europe was "more interesting" to the United States. John Quincy was to conclude a treaty with Prussia, and perhaps go on to Sweden or Denmark.

The President asked his son to be both diplomat and spy. "I

thought your Talents, Sagacity and Industry might be more profitably exerted in collecting and transmitting Intelligence of the Views and designs of those Courts and Nations than they could be in Lisbon where there will be little to do, that I can foresee, besides Sleeping Sastas." The father thought the son, not one for siestas, would soon be bored in Lisbon. It was equally important, he told JQA, to transmit information about the Emperor of Russia and the Emperor of Germany, both "important Luminaries for the political Telescope to observe." President Adams wanted to know "the Part which the King of Prussia means to take either during the War, or at and after the Peace, and what his Relations are to be in future towards France and England." What might be the future systems of Europe, he wished to know, and how might the United States best preserve friendship with them all? "Send us all the Information you can collect. I wish you to continue your practice of writing freely to me, and cautiously to the Office of State."

John Quincy Adams was hurt and furious. Here, again, his parents had not considered his plans or feelings. More immediately painful, he had already bought passage and shipped personal effects to Lisbon, and rented a house there; he had committed twenty-five hundred dollars in expenses that he never recovered. He told his father that the appointment to Berlin was "so totally contrary to every expectation and every wish I had formed" that he considered not accepting it. He had resolved, he said, never to hold any public office under his father's administration, and "had explicitly declared that resolution to my Mother." The appointment, he told his mother, tainted the "satisfaction" he had enjoyed so far in being a public servant. Yet after the bluster, Adams agreed; Berlin was the more challenging post. He would go.

And so John Quincy and Thomas Adams gathered with Louisa and Catherine and the Johnsons at the parish Church of All Hallows Barking on Tower Hill, on Wednesday the twenty-sixth to join together two of America's leading families: the Johnsons of Maryland and the Adamses of Massachusetts; the daughter of a prominent merchant and the son of the President of the United States. After the brief ceremony, the wedding register was brought out. Under number 202, marked "John Quincy Adams of Boston in the United States of America and Louisa Catherine Johnson of this Parish," below the signature of the kind and guiding Rev. John Hewlett, B.D., John Quincy signed his name, and Louisa, her handwriting strikingly like his, signed hers. Then James Brooks, Thomas B. Adams, Joshua Johnson, Catherine Johnson, and one smudged signature, probably Joseph Harris, followed.

But the marriage started off sourly. Louisa was now the wife of a man whose ambition was to gain the highest political office in America; but she was a private, shy woman who had never been away from home before. Heights of any kind – political or personal – troubled her; Louisa had acrophobia and would not climb any open staircase. John Quincy was grumbling about his lost trunks and money, sent to Lisbon instead of Berlin. Thomas would accompany the bridal couple on their honeymoon, and on to Berlin, but his rheumatism was so painful that he dreaded a winter journey across northern Europe. He had already written to his mother imploring her to send out someone else.

The idea of a honeymoon as a time of leisurely travel – but not a time of privacy or mutual exploration of mind and body – was now popular. Chaperones accompanied every bride and groom, and it was not unusual, therefore, that Louisa and John Quincy set out in the Johnson carriage to explore parts of England accompanied by Louisa's maidservant and John Quincy's brother. Other couples traveled with their parents, bridesmaids and grooms, brothers and sisters, maiden aunts, and even family clergymen – all of them joining together for rounds of sightseeing and elaborate dinners. They were not mere hangers-on, but performed functions of supervision, counsel, service. After some weddings, the guests carried the bride and groom from the reception to the bedroom, accompanied by horseplay and ribald jokes, and left them alone for only a short time before rising for more sightseeing. One ritual called for the curtains of the four-poster wedding bed to be drawn open so the bride might scramble into it stark naked except for long white gloves (it was not genteel to come to bed without them on her wedding night), which the groom symbolically removed. During the day, the groom might disappear with the men to shoot, course hares, or play billiards, while the bride gossiped in the drawing room with the ladies.

The Adams honeymoon, like the wedding, was more somber and quiet. The only reference to anything that occurred during the entire honeymoon came from John Quincy Adams, who noted carefully in his diary, after their visits to Tilney House, that it was "one of the splendid country seats for which this country is distinguished." Nothing else.

Two days later, John Quincy wrote his "dear and honoured Parents" that he had "the happiness of presenting to you another daughter. . . . The day before yesterday united us for life." Louisa attached a note at the bottom "to solicit your parental affection" and promised to fulfill her "duties as wife and daughter." But John and Abigail Adams, in East Chester, New York, where they had fled to avoid a yellow fever epidemic, first learned of their son's marriage from newspaper accounts, in October. The *Independent Chronicle* of Boston, not an Adams paper, had gleefully noted that "Young John Adams's negotiations have terminated in a marriage treaty with an English lady, the daughter of one Mr. Johnson on Tower-Hill. It is a happy circumstance that he made no other Treaty." Abigail sent the newspaper clipping, "which, as usual, made an ill-natured reflection," rebutted by the *Centinel*, and added: "For myself I sincerely congratulate you upon the Event." But even Louisa complained, after reading the newspaper account, that the "scorpion tongue of political slander assailed me." It would continue to do so. There was some muttering through the New England Adamses as to whether the lady was tough enough to stand up to the rigors of marriage and the public political life. Only Thomas was unreservedly taken by his new sister-in-law. He wrote home that she was beautiful and intelligent, and "has much sweetness of Temper and seems to Love *as she ought.*" Soon after the wedding, Thomas wrote his mother that Louisa was "indeed a most lovely woman, and in my opinion worthy in every respect of the Man for whom she has with so much apparent Cheerfulness renounced father and Mother kindred and Country to unite her destinies with his." Abigail sent his letter to Mary Cranch, with the footnote: "This is a great deal for Thomas to say."

Thomas could only sense Louisa's sacrifice. In October, her parents had sailed from England for the United States, and Louisa was undergoing a painful ordeal. When Louisa married John Quincy, her father was a prosperous commissioned merchant. Joshua was expected "to give each of his children a small fortune"; he had promised Louisa five thousand pounds sterling. John Quincy, of course, was not unaware of Joshua's wealth, or the promise of a large dowry. But after two "happy weeks" of marriage, Louisa learned that her father had suffered a major financial collapse. The details are not precisely known, but from her accounts written several decades later, Louisa indicated that her father lost a large, valuable East India ship at sea, and that he was in addition swindled by a treacherous partner in Maryland. Had he left earlier, had his wife not demanded that he stay, or his daughter not wished to be married, or his future son-in-law not hesitated more than a year, Joshua Johnson might have returned to Maryland in time to save himself. Louisa said that her "poor mother" was "severely reproached" for her selfish act; the burden of the family's misfortune was placed upon her, but belonged to others.

Johnson's actions did not help appearances. He quickly outfitted a vessel, and with his family left London just forty-six days after Louisa's marriage. His departure gave the impression of his fleeing creditors, and indeed creditors knocked on the newlyweds' door and appealed to Louisa for payment of her father's delinquent accounts. One wrote a letter "of the most barbarously insulting character" to John Quincy Adams, demanding that he pay his father-in-law's debts. Worse, events suggested that, with her compliance, the Johnsons had lured a very eligible bachelor into marrying a daughter who would have been left penniless, just as her parents fled to America. In Louisa's troubled words, it appeared that her father was "palming his daughter" off upon the Adamses, and that JQA had "connected himself with a ruined house." Louisa felt a shame and guilt that never left her; it would always surface in her letters and diaries even into her old age, a "phantom" that would shadow her life.

Not surprisingly, John Quincy Adams was unsympathetic. He, too, found himself exposed to an embarrassing situation just at the moment when his career seemed so promising. One can imagine his temper when, only two months after leaving the tranquility of The Hague, JQA was plunged into marriage and scandal. He worried about "disgrace" — and was not oblivious to the loss of a handsome dowry. Louisa soon discovered that she had forfeited all of "my husband's esteem."

Joshua Johnson wrote his new son-in-law immediately after boarding ship at Gravesend. Contrary winds, gales, rough seas caused sickness and alarm, but they were nothing, he said, compared to his humiliation, and "my sufferings on this occasion of leaving England." Adams, however, would not accept so oblique an apology. He was angry. He wrote Johnson a tough and direct letter. His sudden departure, said Adams, had cast suspicion on the Johnsons in England and on the Continent. "Appearances and allegations are advanced which bring in question something more than your credit," JQA wrote. He urged Johnson to "consider Justice to your creditors as the most imperious of your obligations. — To render it speedily and amply, however unkind you may think their treatment of you has been. I urge it, because I cannot suspect you of an unnecessary misrepresentation of your affairs to me."

But Joshua Johnson was beaten and doomed, reduced, Louisa said, "to a state of the utmost distress." Within three years, Johnson would be bankrupt, and would turn desperately to President Adams for help. The older Adams, a family friend, would appoint Johnson as Superintendent of Stamps in Washington, which enabled him to survive with his family in a modest house on K Street near the Alexandria Bridge. But two weeks before Joshua Johnson died in 1802, his post would be stripped from him by President Thomas Jefferson, and Johnson would leave this world, Louisa said, "destitute, with the horrible conviction that he left his widow and family penniless, and dependent upon the charity of their relations, and the exertion of an only [son]."

Louisa Johnson Adams was alone in Europe, shamed by her father's financial collapse and flight. This was the first time that she had ever been apart from her family, and she found the separation the most painful kind of wound. When Adams arrived in London for their marriage, Louisa had met him with a feeling of "dread at the idea of my immediate parting with my parents that almost broke my heart." Even after her marriage, she asked that she might spend a few days with her mother, from whom she had never been separated more than a few hours. When the Johnsons sailed, therefore, Louisa was doubly shattered: by her father's financial embarrassment, and by her sudden separation. "When I arose and found them gone," she wrote, "I was the most forlorn miserable wretch that the Sun ever smiled upon." Louisa withdrew into a depression and illness, and suffered "anguish of mind and deep feeling of wounded sensibility," which, in turn, created "a total loss of sleep." The thought of traveling in winter to Berlin over churning seas and rock-hard roads was no less painful than the remembrance of a family that had sheltered and nurtured her. Nor did her discomfort diminish with the realization that she had married a man who would spoil no one, not even himself.

"Such," Louisa said, "was my honeymoon."

II
Berlin;
Washington

1797–1809

1

IN NOVEMBER 1797, the three Adamses left London for Hamburg on their journey to Berlin. When they reached Gravesend, their vessel had already sailed, and although it was dark, they scrambled into a small boat and were rowed several miles downriver to overtake her. Once aboard the Danish ship, Louisa immediately vomited, and remained seasick for eight days, while John Quincy enjoyed the excellent food and noted that every morning and evening the crew was rung to prayers, heavy sea or not. He approved even more of the sailors' economy in the use of sugar: a piece of white sugar tied to a string was passed among them, and each then dipped it into his tea. Adams admired frugality.

The Adamses rested ten days in Hamburg. Louisa remembered the air as smelling dank, filled with the fumes of peat, the winter fuel, which hung in stinging, thick clouds over narrow, dreary streets lined with "dirty and gloomy" buildings. It rained most of the time and waterfalls cascaded from rooftop spouts onto the middle of the cobblestone streets with a sound that was thunderous. Louisa felt desolate, alone. She had broken from her sheltered past, from parents, sisters, freedom, innocence; even her old servant Celia had stayed behind. Raised in a protective manner, Louisa had no preparation for — or even sound information about — what marriage held. The separation, and the sex, surprised her. She had been taught that the "normal" woman had no sexual drive, only the generosity to submit to sexual intercourse with her husband. Louisa entered the marriage bed in the spirit of self-sacrifice, and she was not encouraged to be a willing, or eager, sexual partner.

Most women of this period, and Louisa was no exception, were treated as objects of reverence, too pure and refined for the harsh world, for sexual pleasure. The virtuous woman was fragile, and given to believe that a wide range of "feminine illnesses" so weakened her that she had to be treated gently, to be confined. Menstruation, surrounded by superstition and prudery, was used as a sign of a woman's inferior health and vitality. Men declared it a hereditary disease that was part of "the curse" that a woman must bear for the sins of Eve. Thus, every month a woman's menstrual period was surrounded by social myths that themselves made a woman ill: She was confined; given rest, bland food, medicines often accompanied by medical bleedings. Told she was sickly, a woman became ill in a self-fulfilling prophecy. Women suffered from fainting spells (or vapors), weakness, headaches, bad backs, "fevers," and a variety of nervous disorders, all of which reminded them that they were delicate creatures, diseased in some strange, recurring way, who needed masculine care and protection. The woman who rose above this cycle of fact and myth to become a strong individual was rare indeed.

Society considered it unfeminine for women to be active sexual partners. This was soon after the time when Addison frowned upon the naked arms of English women, when proper ladies blushed at the mention of a leg or chemise. Women were bashful about their body functions, or ignorant of them, and too modest to allow doctors to touch their bodies or see them entirely nude. "American women divide their whole body into two parts," said Moreau de St.-Méry, a French observer of American life in the 1790s. "From the top to the waist is stomach; from there to the foot is ankles." Louisa Adams, like many women of her class, rarely removed all her clothing at once, even when bathing. Sex and pregnancy were surprising, shocking, threatening. Her obligation to John Quincy Adams was to produce a certain number of children, after which sex might be avoided. For many women marriage was not a joyful experience, but part of their subordinate relationship with a man, based upon fear, subservience, and obligation. Louisa's journey to Berlin, therefore, was not only a voyage from her treasured past, but also a venture into a threatening future, and womanhood. One thing now was certain: She was no longer the indulged young daughter of a rich man.

From Hamburg, the "dreadful" journey to Berlin continued in a heavy wooden English carriage, which swayed and jolted across two hundred miles of what Milton called "a windy sea of land," washed into bogs by the rains. When the Adamses reached Berlin, Louisa was "seized with a violent and dangerous illness," which was in fact the first of seven miscarriages that she would suffer.* She spent eleven days of anguish huddled in her room at a public tavern, surrounded by two well-meaning but inept men, and the sounds and smells of a foreign country.

Ailing, homesick, Louisa became a recluse. For three months she remained in her chambers, alone. Not one woman visited her. Rumors spread among the wives of the diplomatic corps that the new American minister's lady was ugly, horsefaced, ashamed to be seen at court, perhaps not even married to Mr. Adams at all. Louisa herself thought that John Quincy did not wish to appear in public with her "owing to his mortification at his marriage." And in effect, John Quincy Adams abandoned his wife in Berlin; he paid far more attention to his diplomatic duties than to her.

Louisa met and was befriended by Countess Pauline Neale, a member of the royal court, who was astonished to find the wife of an ambassador at home alone. Countess Neale took Louisa to the theater, so she would be noticed, and the rumors about Louisa's appearance quickly dissipated; "they found me pretty." More than six weeks after her arrival, Louisa was fi-

---

* Thomas sent a letter home describing "the delicate constitution of Mrs. Adams. . . . [S]ince our arrival she had undergone severe illness, illness of such a nature as an experienced Matron would easily divine upon calculation and comparison of dates, but which a young Bachelor knows not how to describe."

nally presented to the Prussian King and Queen, and as required, she visited each princess of the court and the seconds in command, and later left her card at the residence of every member of the diplomatic corps as well. For the next four years, Louisa Adams was "launch'd in the giddy round of fashionable life" in Berlin, "a world altogether new to me, and little to my taste."

But it was not John Quincy Adams who escorted his wife and made her popular in Berlin society. It was his brother, Thomas. The younger brother loved to joke and dance, unlike the somber JQA, and one evening soon after Louisa's presentation at court, at a private ball for five hundred, she boldly asked Thomas to dance "and he danced so well and with so much spirit, I was quite delighted." Louisa attracted a succession of partners that evening, and danced until two in the morning, "when I returned home perfectly exhausted." From that time on, Louisa declared, Thomas's dancing with her "made me the fashion and I became a Belle." His kindness and humor gave Louisa confidence and made her feel appreciated. He brought her into Berlin society, and escorted her to balls and dinners, and occasionally to parties at country estates. As an escort, Thomas became Louisa's surrogate husband. But far more important, before he resigned as Secretary of Legation and left Berlin for Philadelphia in September 1798, Thomas protected Louisa, temporarily, from the coldness of John Quincy and the harsh realities of her marriage. He was, she said, a "kind brother" who "provided a solace in my moments of mental anguish . . . [and] soothed me in my afflictions." Thomas also made John Quincy's flaws clearer. "I have always believed," Louisa later wrote of Thomas, "that he both respected and loved me and did me justice in times when I needed a powerful friend."

Once launched, Louisa went everywhere. With other capitals engaged in war, the Prussian court was one of the most splendid in all Europe. St. Petersburg, Russia, displayed more wealth and ceremony, while a court ball in London or — between revolutions — in Paris brought out silks and jewels, military clankings and sashes to bedazzle the most jaded. What made Berlin unique at this hour was not the splendor, the brilliance or carat of its diamonds, the glitter of its uniforms or medals or ribbons — but its sheer madness. When a handsome young officer dropped dead during a lively quadrille at a ball, for example, his wife donned his uniform and paraded about the city for days. Another time a young woman became so drunk at a court ball that, being spun about during a vigorous waltz, she threw a cascade of vomit over the Queen — who kept dancing. Nothing stopped the fun. When the Prince of Orange died just before the annual Carnival, the suppers and balls continued; mourning was postponed. One young prince received all his officers while in bed at five in the morning, smoking his meerschaum pipe. Even young King Frederick Wilhelm III was a bit daffy, and insisted that the royal family and any foreign prince who might be in Berlin take time to play one of his favorite diversions — blindman's buff.

John Quincy Adams's observations of this court contrasted sharply with Louisa's. She, of course, enjoyed the advantage of "my good little friend" Countess Neale, a maid of honor to the Queen, who gave her "a peep behind the scenes" in Berlin. Adams thought Prussia "little more than a nation of soldiery." He reported to his father that King Frederick III was "a very military man" with qualities "very uncommon among kings." He was distinguished, in John Quincy's mind, by his "private and domestic virtues, and makes not his high station a shield to protect a dissolute life, or to indulge himself in luxurious indolence and dissipation." Louisa's "peep", however, offered a different view. She wrote about the King's dalliances with beautiful young women, including one Princess Lucia, who as soon as she became pregnant by the King was shipped off to a frontier town with her husband. Another, "a very beautiful cousin" with whom the King was "smitten, . . . had twins supposed to be his majesty's and this winter [was] married off to an officer in the army who was promoted suddenly for the occasion." The Queen herself was young and beautiful, and often pregnant. She was so nearsighted that she couldn't see down the length of a dinner table without squinting; she bumped into things. But few obstacles discouraged her: In 1798, only twenty-one and bulging with her fourth child, she went, true to the spirit of the Berlin court, "into company" and danced "from 6 in the Evening until 6 in the morning."

Berlin dazzled. "Every night of the week," Louisa wrote, "was engaged for Courts, Parties, or Dancing Teas. Operas twice a week in full dress. . . . A masked ball on Thursday. . . . Dance and supper at one of the Ministers and Sunday ball at Court." The royal family also held courts twice a week, and every Monday the great-aunt of the King, who wore an iron collar to support her head, entertained a card party, where Louisa was required to sit for three hours at whist. There were parties and balls at the homes of the diplomats, or lesser royalty, and fortnightly visits to the King's great-uncle and his sister, the Langrave de Hesse, "a very fine looking woman" with coarse manners and a stentorian voice that vibrated the crystal two floors above her.

John Quincy Adams pronounced himself offended by this "sea of dissipation." He viewed jewels and ornate clothing as ostentatious. Formal court dress annoyed him. He complained that life in Berlin was boring and unprofitable for an ambitious man. But he kept busy. He rewrote and negotiated a new treaty with Prussia, bringing it into agreement with Jay's Treaty with England, which had become the new standaru of American neutrality; this took a year, and he signed the treaty on his thirty-second birthday, July 11, 1799. He sent observations to his father, and his Berlin dispatches and private letters detailed the diplomatic history of Europe at the time. These were convulsive years, with the French Revolution taking place, and John Quincy's intelligence, sent freely to the President but cautiously to the Secretary of State, helped President Adams pursue peace instead of war against France between 1798 and 1800. But peace was unpopular in the United States, and one reason John Adams was not re-elected President in 1800 was his determination not to lead the nation into war, especially a war only to keep the Federalists in power.

But the slow pace of diplomacy, however helpful to his father, was not enough for the younger Adams, and he undertook a severe habit of work. He studied German several hours a day; completed, after some struggle, a poetic translation of

Wieland's romantic *Oberon* from German into English; and compiled a seventy-three-page pamphlet translation of Gentz's work on the American Revolution. In truth, John Quincy considered that his major accomplishment in Berlin was learning German. But where he struggled to learn the language, Louisa picked up idiomatic fluency at the balls and dinners; languages, like laughter, came easily to her.

At social and diplomatic gatherings, John Quincy often left Louisa to wander by herself while he played cards. It never occurred to him that she might feel lonely, even in this glittering crowd. Sometimes, when John Quincy left early, Louisa stayed late for supper and dancing. If he refused to attend at all, she would give her dance card to the hostess, who always made sure it was full. Louisa loved the attention and flattery, and as the daughter-in-law of the American President and the wife of America's minister to Berlin, she was addressed as "your Excellency" and "Princess Royal." She soon found herself "the fashion" in Berlin. She danced frequently with the King, and sang at court parties. It was not unusual for her to stay out until two, return home to bed, rise, eat, and go once more to a gathering of the "Elegant Mob." Although she sent a disclaimer to her mother — "I do not think I am calculated for a Court" — Louisa was, indeed, the Belle of Berlin.

2

For louisa, Berlin was both a last childhood fling and a shocking awakening. She constantly tested her relationship with John Quincy, always searching for a way of asserting her rights, or at least defining their limitations. Louisa's desire to be her own person conflicted with John Quincy's belief that his wife was subordinate to him. He was having difficulty dominating this woman. Their contrasting attitudes toward each other's role in the marriage, and rights, are best exemplified by three problems that now emerged: pregnancy, money, and, of all things, the use of rouge.

For more than a year in Berlin, Louisa and John Quincy Adams fought over her assertion that she should wear rouge to the balls. Louisa had been offered a box of rouge by the Queen, who thought she looked pale. But John Quincy ordered Louisa to refuse the gift. A month later, the Queen again "threatened me with the box" of rouge, and Louisa again refused it. During the Carnival ball in the winter of 1800, however, Louisa had second thoughts. She admired, even envied, the effect of rouge on the women in their black costume dresses, and wrote with some petulance that "those who were pale look cadaverous particularly when not relieved by the brilliancy of diamonds." It was a double complaint, for Louisa had neither diamonds nor rouge; she thought she "looked a fright in the midst of Splendour." When the Queen offered her rouge for the third time, therefore, she accepted it.

Now Louisa undertook her first open defiance of her husband. While the issue — wearing rouge — appears petty, the confrontation was not. Adams expected his wife to be like other women: docile, obedient, subservient to his will and person. One evening in February 1800, as Louisa dressed to attend *The Marriage of Figaro*, she stealthily applied some rouge to her cheeks, which she thought relieved the dullness of her homemade dress "and made me look quite beautiful." When John Quincy saw her red cheeks, however, he was furious, and took a wet towel and washed her face clean. Louisa noted that "a kiss made the peace, and we drove to the [opera] where I showed my pale face as usual." That, however, did not end this strange confrontation. In December 1800, almost eighteen months after the Queen first offered her the rouge, Louisa made her final defiant stand. This time, unlike before, Louisa applied the banned rouge as she dressed for court, and walked boldly up to John Quincy. He was shocked, as she expected him to be, and ordered her to remove the offending cosmetic. "With some temper," Louisa refused. Here was a major effrontery: Few women of this time stood up to their husbands on any issue, and fewer still defied a man's direct order. Louisa did both, and by her act underscored her refusal to be a compliant, docile wife. This seemingly insignificant issue challenged John Quincy's male right to dominate Louisa, and represented her wish to be independent from that control. Without a word, John Quincy turned and ran down the stairs, out the door, and into his waiting carriage. He attended the royal court alone. Louisa felt a rush of triumph. She had asserted a small right, and won a temporary victory. Each had learned a valuable lesson: Louisa could stand up to her fierce husband; John Quincy had to contend with more than a docile wife.

Louisa and John Quincy fought repeatedly during their marriage about the circumstances of her father's financial collapse, and money. To understand John Quincy's feelings about Louisa, one needs to understand his feelings about money. Adams always felt poor, from Newburyport until his death. When he had loved and wished to marry, he couldn't because he had no income. When he married Louisa, the wealth of her father and the promise of a large dowry evaporated as swiftly as a dream. How could he love her passionately, without reserve, when there lurked the feeling that he had been cheated?

John Quincy Adams supported himself and his wife largely from his salary for public service, which in Berlin came to nine thousand dollars a year. But an American foreign minister's life contained pinching expenses: housing, carriages, entertainments, clothing, servants. Louisa sewed almost all of her court dresses, both in Berlin and, later, in St. Petersburg, and they "made out in a very economical manner," she said. With some bitterness, she noted that "The Salaries [of an American minister] are too mean to place you on a level with your Colleagues." The Adamses furnished their small Berlin apartments with the "very plainest and cheapest" furniture. They could afford no carriage during their first social season, and only later bought a secondhand one with a pair of old horses. They kept the minimum number of servants: John Quincy's manservant, Louisa's maid, a footman, a coachman, a housemaid, and a cook. The cook proved no bargain: she drank so much she often couldn't stand upright in the kitchen to prepare the meals.

Beyond this, or perhaps running beneath it, was a major problem with money that John Quincy only discussed with his mother. This concerned the large sum that JQA had received from his father in 1794 as he sailed for his first diplomatic post, and which he had turned over, in part, to his brother Charles for investment.

In so many ways, Charles represented the side of the Adams family that it wished to hide. There were flaws in this dynasty, embarrassing deep weaknesses that ran beneath the family like fissures through New England granite, and tore and cracked each generation. Money was one weakness, serious mental depression another, and alcoholism a third.* In the case of Charles Adams, the three connected. Charles was a liability, a cracking fault that jarred the entire family.

Charles was the unchosen, the middle of three sons, frail and shaky. He had sailed with John Quincy and their father in 1779 to Europe, when the ship had hit heavy gales and had blown to a landing in Spain, and the three had made their harrowing overland journey of a hundred days to Paris. But Charles had been homesick from the start, and his father sent him back, alone, at age eight. The little boy did not reach Braintree and the comfort of his mother for six months. At Harvard, Charles had enjoyed what his parents and older brother deemed "bad company." His mother had directed John Quincy to look after Charles, and John Quincy remembered, when selecting a brother to accompany him to The Hague and choosing Thomas, that Charles had been too difficult, and played too much and drank too hard.

By 1798, Charles was sliding into alcoholism. He had married his brother-in-law's sister, Sarah Smith, in 1795, and they had two daughters, Susanna (born in 1796) and Abigail Louisa

* Serious depression troubled John Adams; his sons Thomas, Charles, and John Quincy; JQA's son Charles Francis; his sons Brooks and Henry; and Henry's wife, Marian Hooper Adams, who committed suicide. Alcoholics included William Smith, Abigail's brother; Charles and Thomas; John Adams 2d.

(1798). Charles was broke and in debt. His mother's theory that marriage might stabilize him had proved a grievous error. Through a series of missteps, which involved Dr. Thomas Welsh, the Adamses' family friend in Boston with whom they had invested some money, Charles slipped into complicated financial trouble. Dr. Welsh and Charles had been placed in charge of some of the family's investments, which included John Quincy's gift and whatever else he might squeeze from his salary. Charles had been allowed to withdraw sums and invest them in real estate.

But Charles was vulnerable to charm and fast talk, and his brother-in-law, Colonel William Stephens Smith, was expert at both. Colonel Smith was handsome, and gallant to obnoxiousness. He was the spoiled son of a wealthy New York merchant, and he lived long and caused much trouble for the Adamses and their children. Colonel Smith had been appointed Secretary to the first American Legation in London, headed by John Adams, and there had married Nabby, Charles's and JQA's sister. Colonel Smith liked punch, conviviality, and money, and he soon began staying away from home for long periods, during which he seldom bothered to write or contact Nabby and their four children. He also ran up a debt, and in December 1798, John Adams wrote his scoundrel son-in-law an unusually candid letter scorning his "pride and ostentation," his "dishonorable conduct," and vowed that such behavior would not be forgotten nor forgiven. But the colonel continued his expensive habits, and planned to make a fortune speculating on land. His scheme was to buy land low, on credit, and sell it high, for cash. He bought large tracts in central New York State, and became bankrupt in the crash of 1797. Alexander Hamilton had to intercede on Smith's behalf and fend off a swarm of creditors.

William Smith's whirlwind took in poor Charles Adams like a tornado sucking up a dropped leaf. When Smith's land speculations went bankrupt, Charles, to save his brother-in-law from immediate imprisonment for debt, exchanged JQA's money for a note drawn by Smith's younger brother, who had the ironic name of Justice. But the collapse of land prices prevented Smith from paying the note, and when Dr. Welsh also went bankrupt in 1798, Charles was done. He could not handle financial trouble, and with the dishonor of losing his older brother's funds, Charles stopped functioning. Perhaps he could win the amount back at cards, or find it in a bottle. For two years, Charles slowly sank into a personal nightmare. As the Adamses discovered what had happened to their investments, their disapproval buried Charles. At first, he remained silent to his mother's inquiries; she spoke of his difficulties in oblique terms. But as the full extent of the loss became known, and as Charles continued drinking heavily, Abigail became frantic. With foreboding, she wrote John Quincy: "Indeed my dear son, I am not without fears that you will lose all you have been so prudently and carefully saving." Where had she gone wrong? Charles's "habits are so rooted, the temper so soured, the whole man so changed that ruin and destruction have swallowed him up and his affairs are become desperate." For a year in New York, Charles tried to quit drinking, and go to work, but it was no use. Sarah and their younger daughter went home to her mother; Abigail took in Susanna. "Your brother Charles is . . . ," Abigail wrote John Quincy. "What shall I say that will not pain us both?"

In November, 1800, Abigail stopped by Charles's small chambers in New York City. She found her son alone, in squalor, drunk and in the last stages of his sickness. "All is lost," she wrote, "poor, poor unhappy wretched man." But though her heart went out to Charles, she could not stay long. Dutifully Abigail continued her journey southward to the new Federal city, Washington, under construction in the swampland and wilderness along the Potomac River. The White House, or President's House as it was then called, was a cold, uncompleted mansion — the Adamses kept thirteen fires going against the damp November weather — which contained a sense of tragedy. Only a few weeks earlier, John Adams had become the first President to fail to win re-election. He had remained in the President's House and never visited his son. Humiliated, he had renounced Charles, and refused to acknowledge his illness. On Sunday, November 30, 1800, Charles Adams died alone in New York, an alcoholic.

On March 4, 1801, President Adams rode out of Washington

at sunrise rather than attend Thomas Jefferson's inauguration. The reason often cited by historians was the father's mourning over the tragic death of his son. But in truth Charles had been dead more than three months when the second President climbed into his carriage that winter morning. Adams had refused to see his son, had renounced him, and in the end, Charles's death merely provided a convenient excuse for John Adams to flee an awkward confrontation with a political enemy.

During his last two months in office, President Adams had made several last-minute appointments: John Marshall as Chief Justice of the U.S. Supreme Court; Joshua Johnson to the stamp office. He even gave his son-in-law Colonel Smith, the catalyst of Charles's tragedy, employment as Surveyor-General of the Port of New York. Charles, the embarrassing family drunkard, was forgotten. The Adamses viewed Charles's frailties as a weakening fissure deep within the family; they would unsuccessfully try to overcome or ignore alcoholism and depression in future generations. Thomas spoke for them all when he wrote of Charles: "Let silence reign forever over his tomb." For John Quincy, however, the loss of that money went noisily onward.

3

PREGNANCY, as for so many women, defined Louisa's role. More than money or rouge, it made clear who she was, and what she could do. Louisa Adams was pregnant during each of her four years in Berlin. In her first thirteen years of marriage, she was pregnant eleven times, and her twelfth and final pregnancy occurred in 1817, when she was forty-two. Louisa's twelve pregnancies created tension between her and John Quincy, and explain her chronic disabilities and pain. Yet they also underscore the deep inner strength of this woman. Nineteenth-century women, largely ignorant about their bodies, were doomed to poor obstetrical care and prenatal diet. Louisa was terrified of childbirth every time she got pregnant, but she endured pregnancies as God-given, the "normal" trials of being female. John Quincy, as one might expect, regarded pregnancy and childbirth as " 'the pleasing punishment that women bear.' "

Louisa's pregnancies and miscarriages drained her health. The first miscarriage occurred, as we've seen, in December 1797; the next came in April 1798, and the third that December. When the fourth miscarriage occurred in early 1799, Louisa's doctor recommended a health-restoring journey, and the Adamses decided to travel to the hot mineral baths at the fashionable spa Töplitz. This was the first of two such journeys that the Adamses made during their Berlin years to help Louisa recover from miscarriages.

The village of Töplitz nestles deep in a valley through which courses a stream that swirls into rock-lined pools, some of which form basins where both hot mineral water and cold mountain snow-runoff collects. Here, the villagers constructed baths of rough wood, forming circular tubs, at intervals along the stream, taking advantage of the various temperatures. Physicians of the village assigned patients and guests to the baths according to their illnesses and the bath's curative powers. At first, Louisa was so weak that her physician would not let her attend the public baths, but directed that the soothing waters be brought to her room, where she had a special wooden tub. Three times a week, Louisa bathed in the hot tub in her room, and every day she drank a bottle of Pyrmont Water, a mineral water, although she found it "disgusting to the smell and taste." She considered both the bathing and the drinking purely medicinal. For a while, the baths tired her, and she could not go out. Within two weeks, however, the Adamses settled into an idyllic routine. Music from the nearby cathedral filled their chambers, and their windows overlooked a park where deer gamboled across meadows of mountain wildflowers. Louisa and John Quincy took mineral baths along the village's stream, drank the mineral water, and went for walks. Louisa started hiking 4½ miles each day, and learned in conversations with other women the hidden truth about spas: They were also places women went to escape oppression. At Töplitz, Louisa met the Grand Duchess Constantine, who arrived so severely beaten by her husband that she remained in her room for two weeks, taking the mineral baths, until the bruises disappeared from her eyes, neck, and shoulders.

The Adamses' regime of walks, baths, mineral water was restorative. Louisa felt a new and surprising strength and vitality: The contrast of Louisa Adams, free and exercising, with the same woman confined and restricted in her home was the stuff of tragedy. One day, Louisa "Walked with Mr. Adams to the Schlosberg, and ascended the mountain, having derived much benefit from the Pyrmont Waters." Another day, Louisa returned to climb the mountain again, where she "took new milk" at the top, and she and John Quincy amused themselves by reading the names of the visitors carved in the walls of the hut, some of them almost a century old. Louisa and JQA "wrote our own to pass down like the rest."

After almost eight weeks at the spa, the Adamses departed for a leisurely journey back to Berlin. In all, Louisa stayed out of Berlin society for five months in 1799 before re-entering the "same treadmill" of ceremonies and festivities. Despite her holiday and regained strength, however, Louisa Adams was trapped, as so many women were, in an almost inescapable cycle of pregnancies. Only five birth control methods existed: the tentlike condom which, despite its flourishing ribbon, men usually wore only with prostitutes to avoid venereal disease; exotic recipes for douche solutions; male withdrawal; and a poorly thought-out rhythm method that assured women that if they abstained from sex in the first ten days of their menstrual cycle, pregnancy would never occur. Abortion was possible, but dangerous, and newspapers carried advertisements from its practitioners as late as the 1830s. The most reliable birth control method of all was abstinence, and it appeared that American women of the early nineteenth century abstained from sex for months or years. Society indirectly backed this form of birth control. Manuals and counselors let it be known that sexual relations were regarded as weakening, and sexual ejaculation was thought to expel the vital energies concentrated in the male. Excessive intercourse was wasteful, destructive to a man's health, offensive to frugality. Marriage manuals were stingy in their recommendations for the frequency of sexual intercourse: once a month, once every twenty-one months, ninety times a lifetime – all were recommended formulas. Nineteenth-century physicians considered abstinence a healthy regimen, and at least one doctor thought two years of celibacy a prudent method.*

But John Quincy Adams had married to assure his family of male heirs, and Louisa understood above all else that her first role was to produce children, and be a dutiful mother. After her fifth miscarriage, by 1800, with the treaties with Prussia completed and signed, the Adamses again rode out of Brandenberg Gate, to Silesia, a region not frequented by holiday travelers. They spent another two months free from the diplomatic ceremony and Berlin court ritual, and explored the mountains dividing Silesia from Bohemia. In October, Louisa discovered "I was once more as 'Ladies wish to be who love their Lord,' and in a very bad way." Her sixth pregnancy created such alarm that the Adamses hurried back to Berlin. Louisa had miscarried each previous time, and the Adamses were so worried, that they kept her pregnancy a secret from their families in America. Louisa enjoyed better health than at any other time since her marriage, and while "very feeble and delicate" she still considered these months of waiting "the most splendid Winter since we have re-

---

* Another form of birth control was personal cleanliness of men and women. There were few private bathrooms, and even the upper classes were careless about personal hygiene. The Earl of Rochester complained in 1670:

> *Fair nasty nymph, be clean and kind*
> *And all my joys restore*
> *By using paper still behind*
> *And sponges for before.*

One hundred years later, Englishmen still complained that among England's fair ladies "the parts concealed are more neglected than among the regions of Italy." Mary Wollstonecraft asserted that among English women "that regard to cleanliness . . . is violated in a beastly manner." As late as 1897, in France most women died without ever taking a bath, and the same would have been true for men, if not for their military service.

sided here." Best of all, for the first time in her life, Louisa carried successfully to term. On April 12, 1801, she was "blessed" with a son.

But childbirth was then dangerous, and ignorant and poorly trained midwives often botched the job. Unsanitary conditions also carried the danger of puerperal fever. A drunken midwife handled Louisa so roughly that she almost died, and for five weeks her left leg was paralyzed. She could only move about with help. The King and Queen, almost as excited as the parents, inquired daily about Louisa, and, to keep her home quiet from marching troops or noisy carriages, ordered the streets around the Adamses' house barred and closed. For all the pain and fuss, Louisa was joyful: "I was a *Mother*. God had heard my prayer."

John Quincy wrote with equal fervor in his diary of the "Long expected, ardently desired, painfully born and only child." He was cooler about the birth to his parents and brother Thomas. After writing four pages of European news, quotes from Cicero, speculations upon his term at Berlin, inquiries about the health of mother and father, JQA finally noted in the last paragraph that Louisa "gave me a Son" two days earlier at 3:30 in the afternoon.

John Quincy's reserve might have been caused by the controversy about his son's name. Louisa preferred something from both families. Abigail wanted the baby boy named after his paternal grandfather Adams — an unimaginative family predilection that led to such biographer's nightmares as Abigail Adams 2d, John Quincy Adams 2d (twice in the same generation), Louisa Catherine Adams 2d (twice) and so on. John Quincy, however, had been saddened a year earlier by the death of George Washington, his benefactor. When JQA's son was born a little more than a year after the first President's death, the choice was clear. Adams named his first-born son George Washington Adams. He told Thomas:

> I was not induced merely by the public character of that great and good man to show his memory this token of respect. President Washington was, next to my own father, the man upon earth to whom I was indebted for the greatest personal obligations. I knew not whether upon rigorous philo-

sophical principles it be wise to give a great and venerable name to such a lottery-ticket as a new-born infant — but my logical scruples have in this case been over-powered by my instinctive sentiments.

Recalled by President Adams, in June 1801, Louisa and John Quincy prepared to leave Berlin. Louisa could neither stand nor walk, and the Adamses delayed their departure as late as they could, for her health. She was lifted by servants into an armchair and carried to the coach, but the "change of air" during the long stage ride, the spring flowers brightening Europe's fields, and the prospect of seeing her family made Louisa progressively stronger. By the time she reached Hamburg, Louisa could walk leaning on John Quincy's arm. On July 8, she climbed the gangplank of the *America* without help, and embarked upon the first of several journeys by sea that she would make with small children. The crossing took fifty-eight days, and little George Washington Adams, just ten weeks old, fell so severely ill from dysentery that his parents feared he might die. The *America* landed in Philadelphia on September 4, an intensely hot day. Thomas Adams met the ship, happily embracing brother, nephew and sister-in-law, whose pregnancies had made her so thin and weak, Louisa said, that Thomas was "shocked and distressed when he saw me."

4

LOUISA WAS in no hurry to confront her formidable parents-in-law. Instead of traveling north with John Quincy, she instead went south to Washington and her own parents' home. Louisa knew the Adamses' attitude toward her: They called her "an *English* bride," and openly asked whether she was bright enough or tough enough to be the lifetime partner of New England's favored son. Could she measure up? America was a rough frontier country, and Louisa was European, more comfortable among the Continent's courtly ritual and manners. Her education was broader, finer than most American women's, and certainly more formal than Abigail's had been, although less practical. Europeans, on their part, saw Americans as unsophisticated citizens of a small nation of the third class, unworthy of comparison with France or England, or even Portugal. While the Adamses imagined Louisa too delicate and elegant, Louisa considered the Adamses, members of America's small aristocracy, coarse replicas of the real thing. Status and family in New England did not impress Louisa Johnson Adams. But by the same reasoning, Louisa Adams and her comfortable European upbringing did not reassure the doubtful Adamses. Rather than ride to Massachusetts, Louisa took George and, escorted by servants, separated from her husband for the first time and rode the stages to Washington, "a forlorn stranger in the land of my Fathers."

Joshua did not recognize his favorite daughter when she climbed down from the carriage. Louisa, too, thought her troubled father had "fearfully changed" during their four years of separation. Joshua complained of an undefined illness, and throughout Louisa's two-month stay with her mother and father in Washington, she could not get over how much altered he appeared. He held his grandson on his lap all the time, as though trying to assure himself of a future. In September and October, Louisa wrote frequently to John Quincy, who was enjoying "the inexpressible delight" of seeing his parents after seven years of absence. Adams was in no hurry to travel more than six hundred miles to fetch his wife, and the couple exchanged a series of unintentionally humorous letters, as she tried to coax him to Washington, and he found a list of excuses not to make the trip.

The journey, in truth, was dangerous. The early roadways were nothing more than cleared paths angling down from Boston to Providence and Newport, where one caught the packet for New York, then crossed the waist of New Jersey to Philadelphia, the neck of Delaware-Maryland, and on to Baltimore. Only in the last three years had the route south to Washington been cleared through the wilderness. These roadways were terrifying, dark, rutted corduroy* log roadbeds; the ride was perilous. Stagecoaches were built of oak and metal, and suspended on strong leather straps for springs. But the vehicles underwent terrible strain on the road, plunging into deep mud holes, or jarring over rocks, stumps, and logs. No lights illuminated the way. There were few bridges, and swollen streams sometimes swept away the stagecoach; or, with nine people riding inside and four more holding on outside, and trunks and boxes piled on top, the stage's center of gravity shifted, and the coach rolled over. Toppled by overloading or swollen currents, stagecoaches sometimes crushed or drowned their passengers. Every journey was hazardous: In 1835, Chief Justice John Marshall suffered "severe contusions" on his head riding the stagecoach across flat tidewater lands from Washington to Richmond, Virginia. Even as late as 1842, Charles Dickens wrote of his travels upon America's stage roads: "The very slightest of the jolts with which the ponderous carriage fell from log to log was enough, it seemed, to have dislocated all the bones in the human body."

John Quincy, however, gave in to Louisa's demands for an escort — like all upper-class women, she was not allowed to travel alone — and on October 13 boarded a stage in Boston for his journey to Washington. Adams traveled from stagecoach to packet to stagecoach as fast as he could. When alone, he always recorded the details of each trip, its costs, and the time between major cities. He tried to cut this time by sitting up all night — also saving hotel costs — and throughout his life, even as an old man in his seventies, JQA gleefully noted when he had safely journeyed between Quincy and Washington in record time. By so doing, Adams also measured the growth of his nation's transportation system. During this trip, in 1801, he arrived in Washington on October 24, his first visit to the city, having covered the distance from Philadelphia in thirty-four hours.

* The name originated in France, where a Cordon du Roi was a lace ribbon from which royal orders hung; the Corde du Roi crossed the Channel to emerge as a democratic fabric of cheap ribboned cotton and durable linen. The corduroy road consisted of straight trees six to eight inches in diameter, with their branches trimmed, laid across a cleared roadbed. The surface, after a few rains, was like corduroy.

The return trip, however, was a nightmare. After a week in Washington, Louisa — ill with a "dreadful Cough" — and John Quincy set out on the two-thirty A.M. stage for Frederick, Maryland, with Joshua and Catherine Johnson, little George, and Louisa's maidservant, Epps. But Joshua Johnson took sick during the first stage, and they reached Frederick only with "utmost difficulty." Adams, fidgety to move along, planned to stay two days; they paused for eight, and when Joshua remained seriously ill they left him at his brother's home with Mrs. Johnson. George, too, was very sick with dysentery, but John Quincy, behind schedule, loaded his family on the northbound stage at two A.M., and hurried toward home. Louisa never saw her father again: he died in Frederick on April 17, 1802. The Adamses traveled all day, stopping but once, with George "constantly shrieking." They rode stagecoaches, then the ferry in the dark, then the stage again at two in the morning in such penetrating cold that Louisa, without warm clothing, could not stop shivering. She protested that the pace was "too violent," and took sick, but John Quincy said that her "spirits were more depressed than herself ill." They slept jammed together in the stage, or in crowded hotel rooms, and banged along the log roads, crossed the Hudson in an open boat in pouring rain, and sailed in subfreezing weather to Newport, Rhode Island. They arrived in Boston tired, ill, and fortunately too late for the stage on to Quincy. For Louisa, the trip from Washington meant sickness, cold, wet, exhaustion. "These," she said, "were my first impressions of America."

The older Adamses received Louisa "very kindly," and were "much pleased" with baby George. Dozens of Adams relatives, arriving in carriages or on horseback, filled Abigail and John's rooms. But Louisa was in a foreign country; she could not believe her eyes or ears. The clothes, the food, the nasal Yankee accents all seemed strange and unfriendly. "Had I step[p]ed into Noah's Ark I do not think I could have been more utterly astonished. Dr. Tufts, Deacon Cranch! Mrs. Cranch! Old Uncle Peter! and Capt. Beale!!! . . ." On Thanksgiving Day, Louisa accompanied the Adamses to services. "Even the Church," she said, "its form, the snuffling through the nose, the Singers, the dressing and the dinner hour, were all novelties to me, and the ceremonious parties, the manners, and the hours of meeting, ½ past four, were equally astonishing to me."

The Adamses treated Louisa with care. They placed a special dish for her at dinner. They prepared special foods, and opened special preserves for her. Yet every dish, every delicate specialty made Louisa feel separated from the Adams family, "and though I felt very grateful, it appeared so strongly to stamp me with unfitness, that I often would not eat my delicacy and thus gave offence." She grew reserved, and seldom spoke, "which was deemed pride," and soon discovered that the qualities sought in a Quincy lady were directly opposite to those she had learned. "Do what I would," Louisa said, "there was a conviction on the parts of others that I could not suit. . . . I was literally and without knowing it a *fine* lady."

Louisa felt especially unsuited to the standards of her mother-in-law. Abigail Adams, she said, "was in every point of view a superior Woman," and someone spoken of as being "much above the common standard of her Sex." Louisa found Abigail "the equal of every occasion in life." But Abigail found Louisa wanting. Her first impressions confirmed her judgment that John Quincy had married a weakling not up to the Adams standards. Abigail remarked on her daughter-in-law's physical frailty and her inability to please her paragon son. Louisa's persistent cough, aggravated by the trip northward, brought scoffs of displeasure from Abigail, who reported to Thomas that Louisa was "in a most distressing state," and worried that John Quincy "could get no rest." Abigail thought Louisa's "frame . . . so slender and her constitution so delicate that I have many fears that she will be of short duration." Rather than try to comfort Louisa, however, Abigail was far more concerned about the effect of such a burdensome wife upon John Quincy; Louisa, she said, "has added a weight of years to his brow."

But John Adams immediately liked Louisa, and she him. "The old gentleman took a fancy to me," she said, "and he was the only one." Louisa found her father-in-law a warm, approachable and protective man. When her own father, who never recovered from his illness during her trip north, died in Frederick, a broken and sad shadow of himself, Louisa had no warning, and the death of her favorite man "overwhelmed" her. Slowly, over the years, John Adams would become a willing and loving replacement. Their fondness for one another found expression in their letters, and thirteen years after the old gentleman's own death Louisa still wrote lovingly of him. On his part, John Adams told a friend in 1824 that John Quincy's marriage to Louisa Johnson had been "the most important event" of his son's life. Abigail did not agree. The two women, while alive, remained antagonists and rivals for John Quincy's indifferent attentions to them. Louisa's awe, however, would turn in the 1830s to profound admiration of Abigail Adams, and regret that they had not been closer.

For now, Louisa's continuing lessons came not in her meeting of the Adamses, nor even in her father's sudden and unexpected death, but in her mother's life. Catherine Nuth Johnson was left destitute; Joshua died in poverty. In her old age, Catherine Johnson did the cooking and drudgery of the family herself; she lived without servants or children at home. Louisa was made sharply aware of the "conflicting duties" a "poor feeble powerless Woman" must bear: In her widowed mother, she first saw the injustice of being a sacrificial woman. Catherine Johnson had given birth to a large family, done her duty to husband and children. Yet she had lived a life robbed of its essence and meaning, "without a possibility of acquiring the means of entering on any useful career" for herself. She had given her life to a man now dead, and would spend her last years impoverished, and robbed of self-worth.

In these interlinking episodes we see continuing evidence of Louisa's increasing sensitivity to the traditional, narrow role that society, and her husband, were directing her to assume. These were pivotal years for Louisa as she emerged from the comparative freedoms of her childhood to the narrowing perimeters of womanhood and marriage. She was now recognizing, and would later struggle to reconcile, the traditional role of women — nonpolitical, reserved, ornamental — with her own feelings and views and interests. In Boston, where Louisa and her husband and child lived, she spent time discussing Rousseau with Hannah Adams, a prominent historian and distant relative of JQA. "I really felt proud to have had the power to draw out a mind of such strength and such purity," Louisa reported. Hannah and Louisa could not reconcile their observations of themselves as women with Rousseau's view:

> The education of women should be always relative to the men. To please, to be useful to us, to make us love and esteem them, to educate us when young and to take care of us when grown up, to advise, to console us, to render our lives easy and agreeable; these are the duties of women at all times.

These were not the themes of Louisa's life; these were not her duties or role. She admired strong-willed, well-educated women "of masculine mind," women like Miss Young, and now Mrs. Martha Sullivan, wife of the Massachusetts Attorney General, whom Louisa also befriended. "They always appear to me to be what God intended woman to be, before she was cowed by her Master *man*." The destitution of her mother, the exploration of her own mind, her continuing admiration for educated and strong-minded women alerted Louisa to the unfairness of her own life. She began asking: Did not God create man and woman equal? And she also began examining her fear of living a life without meaning or purpose, overshadowed by her husband.

At this same time, John Quincy Adams was also worried about his future. He had, of course, greater choice and assurances. Restless, concerned about expenses, uninterested in practicing law in Boston, he wrote in his diary in 1802: "I feel strong temptation and have great provocation to plunge into political controversy." He also understood that if he entered politics it would be on his own terms. "A politician," he continued, "in this country must be the man of a party. I would fain be the man of my whole country." Adams would adhere to his family's creed: Duty to God, Country. Politicians and parties who might later try to hold him to lesser allegiances would find Adams a maverick. On February 8, 1803, the Federalists asked John Quincy to fill the vacant U.S. Senate seat for Massachusetts, selecting him over Timothy Pickering, the fifty-eight-year-old former Secretary of State, who had been dismissed from office by President John Adams three years earlier. Only thirty-five, John Quincy Adams became a U.S. Senator.

As John Quincy prepared for the Senate, Louisa, pregnant

for the seventh time, prepared for birth. In Boston, on July 3, 1803, she went into labor just after midnight, as John Quincy lay sleeping soundly on a visit to his parents' home in Quincy. This birth was the first without her husband nearby, and as Louisa's contractions came more frequently, her groans awakened Carolina, her young sister, who jumped out of bed almost naked, and ran into the room to assist. Two older women staying at the house to help, however, ran off, frightened, which made Louisa angry. She later cited it "as an example of the false delicacy which is too often practiced [by women] even at the expense of life." At three, just as the first cannons fired celebrations for the Fourth of July, Louisa gave birth with only Carolina's shaking assistance to another baby boy. The baby was placed on the carpet of Louisa's chamber until the other women could be collected and brought back. As soon as Louisa was well enough, she and the baby rode out to Quincy, where the little boy was named – with everyone's approval – after his grandfather: John Adams 2d.

So Louisa entered her next phase: raising children. She often disagreed with John Quincy about childrearing, but he was, if nothing else, a proud and determined father. Since George's birth, John Quincy had studied all the works on education from Locke to Lady Edgesworth. He understood the heavy responsibility placed upon the Protestant father as head of the household to oversee, guide, and control the conduct of his children (and wife). Louisa and John Quincy both accepted Locke's idea of the child as a plain sheet of paper, who needed guidance and nurturing. How that would be done, however, was a matter of fundamental disagreement between them during their entire parenthood. The child might be a plain sheet of paper, but JQA would have it filled in correctly, neatly, and promptly. John Quincy applied intense pressure and expectations to his sons to shape them in the way he thought best. There were no beatings in the Adams house, but the repetition of stern demands, the withholding of love and approval, struck as hard upon the Adams children as hickory rods.

Childrearing, therefore, was another lesson in Louisa's induction into womanhood. "He ruled his children," she wrote of her husband years later, "and I quietly acquiesced to his right of controul." Louisa could produce the babies. John Quincy would educate them.

5

FOR THE NEXT six years, until 1809, Louisa's life snagged upon the whirls and gnarls of reality. She moved downward from lover to mother to caretaker to servant to ornament to, she felt, burden. She found her life filled with contradictions. She told John Quincy that she was raised for domesticity, her "whole Soul devoted to you and the children." But, she admitted, she was also "ambitious to excess, my heart and head are constantly at war." She knew there would be sacrifices so he might gain his "future hope" of attaining "the highest honours your Country admits to." But Louisa, alert to "these seeming contradictions" in herself, was completely unprepared for the price she would pay.

John Quincy Adams, having sired two heirs, now turned his full attention to his real passion: politics. The Louisiana Purchase revealed again the persistent conflicts between party and region in Congress, and as the Federalists struggled for power, and President Jefferson confronted the French and British, Senator Adams shifted his allegiance so he might remain a man of his country, not his party. His health was sometimes poor, his clothes frazzled, his appetite erratic, but Adams loved this politics business, and applied incessant application to it. William Plumer of New Hampshire, a colleague in the Senate and lifelong friend, described John Quincy in 1806:

> He is a man of much information, a bookworm, very industrious. A man of handsome natural and acquired abilities far

exceeding his age. He is a very correct and animated speaker. A man of strong passions and of course subject to strong prejudices, but a man of strict undeviating integrity. He is free and independent. On some subjects he appears eccentric.

For Louisa and John Quincy Adams, these years in the unfinished wilderness of Washington contained promise, and warning. Washington was an incongruous arena. The whole of it contained no more than six hundred buildings, most made of wood, and two magnificent stone and marble structures, the Capitol and the President's House. One Representative called it "both melancholy and ludicrous . . . a city in ruins." Streets were ungraded, pitted pathways, and bridges a mere layering of loose planks. Because of the expense, few Congressmen brought their wives with them, and most members roomed together in boardinghouses. The Adamses, short on money and with little choice of housing, moved in with Louisa's sister Nancy Hellen and her husband, Walter, who lived in a "lonely and dreary" house in the country. John Quincy walked five miles every day to and from the Capitol, sometimes in driving rain or snow.

Washington was a meager, tattered, backwater third-world capital with few diversions. Attention to dress, soap and water (which had to be hauled by buckets from wells in the public squares) had not yet achieved popularity. The snowy neckcloths and brass-buttoned coats of Gilbert Stuart's portraits were uncommon in this town, where chewing tobacco replaced snuff, and waistcoats, walls, and fireplaces were streaked with the juices. Ladies overcame infrequent bathing with heavy powdering, and the British ambassador, for one, ordered his embassy stocked with white, pink, and lavender powders. There were occasional dinners and balls, and social functions at the President's House. But President Jefferson was cheap with firewood and coal, and more than once the Adamses huddled with other guests around the President's parsimonious coal grate, shaking with cold, their breath visible.

Louisa Adams disliked Thomas Jefferson intensely. He had removed — or been the cause of removal of — three of her closest relatives from public office: her father, her husband, and her beloved father-in-law. Louisa called Jefferson "the ruling Demagogue of the hour — Everything about him was aristocratic except his person which was ungainly, ugly and common." She abhorred his "awkward" manners, his "peering restlessness." She compiled a list of Jefferson's weaknesses: "the hypocrisy of his nature"; his "tricky cunning"; his manners that "were neither elegant nor refined." He had obtained his office, she said, by a "sneaking greatness of mere good fortune attained in a lucky hour." Louisa even criticized the Presidential housekeeping: "The aspect of the House *below* Stairs was very handsome — Up Stairs there were strong indications of the want of female inspection."

Louisa complained when President Jefferson, the champion of democracy, declared that European court rules of precedence had no place in his republic, and that henceforth all official functions would be "*pêle-mêle*." Guests scrummed for the best seats at table, jostled the President, and spoke to anyone they wished. For the first time — but not the last — an Adams aristocracy, defeated in a Presidential election, was swept aside in the name of democracy and the common American people. The traditional New Year's Day at the President's House became a horror to Louisa Adams. On January 1, 1804, for example, she was shocked by the "unruly crowd of indiscriminate persons from every class" who bumped and ruffled the *corps diplomatique*, and stared at the carriages and fine clothing. "Tom Jefferson as the founder of democracy," Louisa wrote, "was obliged patiently to submit and to *permit* these indignities, and to have his wardrobe ransacked that the People might admire his *red breeches* &c &c and amuse themselves at his expense and *not a little* annoyance." An aide to the British ambassador agreed, and, miffed, sent off an official dispatch observing that "the excess of the democratic ferment in this people is conspicuously evinced by the dregs having got to the top." It was a sentiment the Adamses could not have faulted.

Nevertheless, the Adamses were frequent guests at dinner in the President's House, and despite a long-term falling-out between his father and Thomas Jefferson, John Quincy retained his friendship and admiration of this older statesman begun in Paris more than twenty years before. And despite the impoverished fires, and by contrast with *pêle-mêle*, Jefferson's private dinners, which started promptly at four, pleased both JQA and Louisa. The President spent fifty dollars a day to feed and wine these guests, and even Louisa thought the French servants in livery, French butler, French cuisine, "and a buffet full of choice wine and plate" very handsome.

During John Quincy's six-year Senate term, he frequently rode home in the summer to be with his mother and father, often without Louisa. Life in Quincy, alone with his parents, was comfortable, and cheap. Abigail complained to Louisa that her son arrived home looking shabby, pale, and thin. She sent her daughter-in-law instructions for caring for John Quincy when he was in Washington, and she set about fattening him up. Abigail told Louisa to make John Quincy pay attention to his personal appearance. She fussed over the cut of his coat, his wig, the color of his neckcloth. " 'A good coat is tantamount to a good character,' " she believed, and scolded him:

> Now I hope you never appear in [the] Senate with a beard two days old or otherwise make what is called a shabby appearance. Seriously I think a mans usefulness in society depends much upon his personal appearance. I do not wish a Senator to dress like a beau, but I want him to conform so far to the fashion as not to incur the Character of Singularity nor give occasion to the world to ask what kind of mother he had, or to charge upon a wife negligence and inattention when she is guiltless. The neatest man, observed a Lady the other day, wants his wife to pull up his collar and mind that his coat is brushed.

Abigail nagged John Quincy about his eating and instructed Louisa to feed him more regularly. "I wish you would not let him go to Congress without a cracker in his pocket. The space between breakfast and dinner is so long that his Stomach [grows sour] . . . and his food when he takes it neither digests nor nourishes him." John Quincy, however, remained indifferent to everyone, and everything, except his career. He was, clearly, a man used to having his own way, and as Louisa discovered, this meant his will, his choices, his life over hers.

John Quincy now made a series of unilateral decisions that

shocked and damaged Louisa, and made finally clear her subordinate place in his life. In the spring of 1804, he went home alone to his mother's care, and left Louisa and her two boys at the Hellens'. "My health and spirits were sadly depressed," she said. Louisa was lonely and ill with "spasms" and "a considerable degree of Fever." "Oh this separation life," she wrote, "is not worth having on such terms." George, she told her husband, talked of his father "incessantly, though he has never forgiven you for your desertion. John calls every body papa . . . poor little fellow he was too young when you left us to remember you."

Louisa's "separation life" grew harsher. In November 1805, after the family had spent the summer together in Quincy, John Quincy ordered that the boys be left behind and that Louisa accompany him back to Washington, alone. George stayed with his Aunt Mary Cranch, and John with Grandmama and Grandpapa Adams. John Quincy, Louisa said, was finding the boys "troublesome," and "I thought that I had no right to refuse what Mr. Adams thought just." His decision bore "very hard" on her, and their journey southward that November was "dreadful." Her reaction, however, was revealing of Louisa's inner strength. Other women might simply have acquiesced, or remained silent. Louisa exploded in anger: She wrote Abigail that she had been "compelled" to leave her sons, coerced without any discussion. John Quincy had treated her as though her opinions and feelings did not matter, like one of Rousseau's women. Abigail, however, was unsympatnetic, even nasty. She replied that the children were much better off in Massachusetts than "at any boarding House in Washington." She told Louisa to toughen up: "A cheerful heart doeth good like medicine."

The pattern of John Quincy's dominance over Louisa was established. In the spring of 1806, he again left her in Washington at the Hellens' and went on alone to Quincy. Louisa was pregnant for the eighth time. She gained too much weight, her feet swelled, she could not leave the house to walk. During her last month, Louisa could not even leave her chamber. She had small abscesses on the back of her throat and in her ears that broke repeatedly and caused "excruciating pain." On June 21, Louisa's sister Harriet, who a year earlier had married George

Boyd, sent word that her new baby was dying. Louisa, like many women, was sought for her nursing skills and medical knowledge, and without a carriage and in pain from her pregnancy, she walked "a long Mile" to Harriet's, in vain. She arrived after the baby had died. Louisa rested, and then walked home at nine in the evening. Six hours later, she went into "a very bad" labor, and after twelve hours, with her mother and a nurse midwife with her, Louisa gave birth to a stillborn baby boy. This was the second birth without her husband nearby, and years later Louisa remained resentful of his absences. She was unwilling to suffer childbirth alone so he might comfortably visit his parents in Quincy. And however strongly she might urge him to political success, she was unwilling to suffer actual pain for it. "I was not patriotic enough," she said, "to endure such heavy personal trials for the political welfare of the Nation whose honor was dearly bought at the expense of all domestic happiness."

Adams knew that his political future in the Senate was dubious; he was only nominally a member of the party that had placed him in the office. In 1804, he was selected for the first Boylston professorship of rhetoric and oratory at Harvard, and he started his lectures in the summer of 1806. Seeing an end to his public life, and wishing to settle his family, John Quincy purchased in July, 1806, a house at the corner of Nassau Street (now Tremont) and Frog Lane (now Boylston Street) in Boston, for $15,000, which put him into debt.

That autumn, when John Quincy returned to the Senate, Louisa found herself alone in Boston in the house with her two young boys, "and there we were to remain while he passed the Winter in the Sunshine of Washington." Louisa felt trapped with her sons, her sister Carolina, and a maidservant far from the southern city she loved. Worse, just before John Quincy departed in November, he had impregnated her again. Abandoned, swelling with her ninth pregnancy, Louisa thought Boston "gloomy beyond description," and the house the coldest she ever lived in; it leaked from every part, and three times during the winter fires erupted inside or on the roof.

In fairness, John Quincy Adams was correct on one point: He cut expenses by traveling alone. In 1805, the trip to Washington with Louisa had cost, not including meals, $118.58. In 1806, making the same trip alone, riding the stage through the night to avoid hotel bills, treating himself only to a handful of cigars, Adams spent just $33.55, for a savings of $85.03.

Louisa's suffering, however, had no price. On August 18, 1807, she gave birth in the Boston house to her third son, as John Quincy listened from the next room. The baby was born at eight-thirty in the morning, after six hours of "extremely severe" labor, and was apparently dead; the midwife left Louisa's room in tears. But Louisa was determined to save him, and she struggled with the baby; within five minutes he took several deep breaths and appeared to breathe on his own. For two days, Louisa watched every move while this newborn tentatively grasped life, and by the third day as he started nursing and thriving, she wrote, "Thanks be to God!" This baby was going to live. The Adamses baptised him Charles Francis — there was no consideration of a Johnson name — after John Quincy's unfortunate younger brother and Francis Dana, with whom Adams had traveled to St. Petersburg, Russia. Louisa proudly wrote her mother that she was doing well, and "the little Gentleman is likely to do so too. . . . He is born to be lucky."

On October 10, 1807, the Adamses set out on the six o'clock stage for Providence, and Washington. John Quincy once more arranged to have George and John boarded with relatives, and "thus again was the family scattered to the winds," said Louisa. But while she had been persuaded to surrender George and John to the wishes of her husband, Louisa held tight to Charles. As the three traveled toward Washington, Fate reached out once more and almost snatched this new baby from her. After landing in New York, Louisa and her maid walked from the ship to a carriage John Quincy was fetching. The maid was carrying Charles when a man suddenly snatched the baby from her arms and ran off. Louisa and the maid screamed and started chasing the man along the street, but he turned quickly and entered a doorway. When the two women followed, they saw no one. Louisa was about to pound on the house doors, when the man suddenly reappeared and placed Charles in her arms. He excused himself, and said that the "Child was such a perfect beauty, he thought he would show him to his Wife." Momentarily flattered, Louisa turned away, and the kidnapper disappeared. From that moment, however, she would always hold her youngest son close to her, and he alone among her children would survive his perilous birth, and brief kidnapping, into adulthood, and the next generation of Adamses.

In 1808, Louisa and John Quincy again left George with Aunt Cranch and John with his grandparents. Taking Charles, they returned to Washington. This was the third winter of separation from their older sons. Politics, Louisa said, "were growing very hot, and Mr. Adams was very busy and very anxious." The Whigs were "jealous" and the Federalists "hated him; so that we were fast getting into hot water," she added, placing herself alongside her husband. In 1807, John Quincy Adams, the man of his whole country, had split with his party and had courageously risen above sectional loyalty to support Jefferson's embargo. He was repudiated by the New England Federalists, and without warning, but with ample reason, they dumped Adams for disloyalty. Stung, he resigned before the end of his term, and moved with Charles and Louisa back to Massachusetts, where once again Louisa noted with pleasure "we were a family." But not for long.

In January 1809, while alone in Washington to argue a case before the U.S. Supreme Court, John Quincy was called suddenly to the President's House, where he found the newly elected James Madison flustered and in a hurry. Would Adams accept the post of first U.S. Minister Plenipotentiary to Russia? President Madison already had his name on a list to be submitted to Congress in half an hour. As John Quincy later wrote in his diary: "I could see no significant reason for refusing the nomination."

He would have had reason enough had he bothered to ask his wife. In Boston, Louisa had heard rumors of a foreign post, "a thing perfectly abhorrent to me and which I hope was done with forever." When the confirmation reached her, Louisa was "stunned." "I had been so grossly deceived," she said, "every apprehension lulled. — And now to come on me with such a shock!" When she complained to John Quincy, he laughed and called her suffering "affectation." He would discuss no decision with her. He alone had decided the separation of Louisa from her sons, and the acceptance of the ambassadorship. He made another, fateful decision. John Quincy wanted this post, and to be certain of a smooth exit, he sent his brother Thomas, who had been so kind to Louisa in Berlin, to be kind once more. It was Thomas, not John Quincy, who told Louisa that she must leave her two older sons behind, and travel to Russia with only Charles and her sister Catherine. George and John would remain with relatives in Massachusetts. "Every preparation was made without the slightest consultation with me," Louisa later wrote, "and even the disposal of my Children and my Sister was fixed without my knowledge until it was too late to Change." It was also Thomas, not John Quincy, who took Louisa out to the Adamses' to visit her sons for the last time before leaving for Russia. They would be young men before Louisa saw them again. Worse, while John Quincy Adams refused to face his own wife, he plotted to keep her from confronting his father. JQA mistrusted his own father's will and his love for his daughter-in-law; he refused to allow them to meet alone to say goodbye. Louisa said that Abigail and Thomas were instructed to keep her away from the old gentleman "lest I should excite his pity and he allow me to take my boys with me."

Moving toward the Continent and war, toward Napoleon's Europe and Alexander's Russia, the Adamses took only a month to prepare for sailing. "In this agony of agonies," Louisa wrote, "can ambition repay such sacrifices? Never!!!

"Adieu to America."

III

St. Petersburg;
London

1809–1817

1

O N SATURDAY, August 5, 1809, just as the Boston church
bells tolled noon, Louisa, John Quincy, and Charles
climbed into the carriage waiting outside their house at the corner of Frog Lane and Nassau Street. They made room for
Catherine Maria Frances Johnson, Louisa's sister, and William
Steuben Smith, John Quincy's young nephew and private secretary. Behind them, on the dickey outside the carriage, rode
Martha Godfrey, Louisa's chambermaid, and the family's free-
man black servant, known only as Nelson. The hired carriage,
drawn by two horses and piled high with trunks and baggage,
lurched through the narrow Boston streets, rumbling across the
wooden planks of the Charlestown bridge before pulling into
William Gray's wharf on the Charlestown waterfront. There
the Adamses and their entourage boarded the *Horace*, under
Capt. Beckford, a simple merchant ship outfitted for this voyage
directly to St. Petersburg, Russia.

Few Americans traveled anywhere during this period, and a
voyage overseas was a major expedition with its own ritual. The
Adamses had purchased special sea trunks, and put together a
large medicine chest to meet their needs. Although the *Horace*
had been outfitted for their personal use, without other passengers, the Adamses had to purchase their own bedding, food,
clothing, and wine – all in addition to the six-hundred-dollar
fare. Because so few Americans went overseas, those who did

took on special obligations, such as delivering mail or packages, watching small children en route, or taking along older sons for the exposure and education of travel. As the Adamses boarded the *Horace*, therefore, they were greeted by two young men placed in JQA's care: Alexander H. Everett and Francis C. Gray, both sons of family friends with the title of Secretaries to the Legation, but who were being sent for seasoning under Adams's careful scrutiny. John Quincy himself had first seen St. Petersburg in this manner as the secretary to Francis Dana.* Thus Everett and Gray entered Adamses' enlarged family. John Quincy, a fussy record-keeper, carefully noted that the young men were paying their own way, and not living off the United States government. He also recorded that the carriage to Charlestown cost two dollars. He gave no tip.

In another ritual of travelers, Louisa and John Quincy the evening before sailing had walked over to Henry Williams' studio, and asked the artist to cut their silhouettes in black paper, which he placed against white — much as people later took photographs to record moments of passage. John Quincy was forty-two, with a large nose, double chin, and rounded forehead; he wore a high hat for his silhouette, and under it he was bald except for a fringe of hair. Adams conveyed an air of self-contained strength, even pugnacity. He often lost his temper, and was animated and brusque, yet this harsh landscape was softened by a paradoxical inner kindness. In middle age, Adams was softening, even mellowing; he sometimes laughed, when the occasion demanded it, preceded with a warning sibilant uptake of breath. Louisa's silhouette showed a pretty woman, at age thirty-four, with a slightly upturned nose, recessive chin, and straight forehead. Outwardly, she had changed little, nor would she change much. But inside, Louisa continued struggling with the contradictions of anger and ambition. She was really two women: the outwardly docile, lovely wife of a hard-edged public man, and the seething inner captive searching for a way to break free. The coming trials of Russia would more strongly delineate this

---

* Dana headed the first American Legation to the Russian capital, but was not received because the Revolutionary War taking place in America at the time made Russia's relations with Great Britain delicate.

dichotomy. The Adamses left their silhouettes with Abigail and John, to be looked at during the long years ahead as part of a precious, fleeting moment of time.

The *Horace* cast off precisely as the Charlestown and Boston church bells were ringing one o'clock. Leaving their likenesses and their hearts behind, Louisa and John Quincy watched their homeland slip by. How clear and large Boston appeared that summer noon. The town was almost a city, and church spires and new homes, factories and warehouses closely followed the curves of its coves and arching hills. Landfill already extended Boston's size and narrowed its harbors, and would soon embrace and disguise forever the long, sea-swept neck across which John Quincy Adams, as a nine-year-old post rider, had galloped during the war. Now Boston and America were sending this son half-way around the world on a mission that, in part, would finally settle hostilities with Great Britain. As it hoisted sail and pulled away from Boston harbor toward the open sea, the *Horace*, carrying America's first Minister to Russia, was bid farewell salutes from the Navy Yard; then from Fort Independence on Castle Island, where the garrison paraded as the ship eased by; and from the revenue cutter *Massachusetts* and the frigate *Chesapeake*, anchored two miles outside the light. The boom of small signal cannon echoed along Boston's hills. As evening descended, and "a tolerably fresh Breeze" came up, the crew of the *Horace* started cranking and hauling sail to catch it. Thomas and the family friend Dr. Thomas Welsh, who had boarded to sail with the Adamses to the port's lighthouse, now slowly embraced each person, leaving Louisa and John Quincy for last, and both men cried without trying to hide the tears. The two Thomases climbed down the ship's ladder and were rowed to the revenue cutter, which came about for the slow tack back into the harbor. The *Horace* then "stood out, with a light breeze and fair weather," and ran briskly toward the open Atlantic while its passengers lingered on deck until they lost sight of the domed hills of Boston, as darkness intercepted the shore from their view.

Beyond the smell of land, in the night with the sea cool and foggy, and light winds south by southwest pushing them along,

Louisa and John Quincy sat apart, in private thought. Adams tallied the number of Atlantic crossings he had made to Europe: His first in 1778 and second in 1779, accompanying his father; and his third in 1794, as U.S. Minister to The Hague. This crossing, however, was the most painful and most significant, both to JQA and Louisa. The separation from parents and children carried with it a sense of foreboding. Louisa knew that she would never share the childhoods of her two older boys. She had been badly scarred by the compelled separation from them, by not being included in the decision, by being ignored, unneeded. She was, she wrote, "broken hearted miserable, alone in every feeling." It had not been her choice to leave America, to part from her sons, her sisters, her aged mother. Louisa found no attraction in the courts of Europe. "I had passed the age when Courts were alluring," she said. "Experience had taught me years before the meanness of an American Ministers position at a European Court." Had the choice been hers, she said, she would have sent JQA on alone; "nothing on Earth could induce me to make such a sacrifice, and my conviction is that if domestic separation is absolutely necessary cling as a Mother to those innocent and helpless creatures whom God himself has given to your charge. A man can take care of himself. And if he abandons one part of his family he soon learns that he might as well leave them all. . . . I alone suffered the penalty."

John Quincy worried not about his sons, but his parents; their old age meant that he might never see them again. He had parted from them reluctantly with sadness. Before boarding, Thomas had given John Quincy a letter from their mother "which would have melted the heart of a Stoic." Abigail had written, she said, because she could not come into town and say goodbye. "I know I should only add to your and my own agony. My Heart is with you, my prayers and blessings attend you." The separation, Abigail told her sister, was too much "like taking our last leave of him." When five hundred miles at sea, John Quincy replied to his mother: No other parting in his life had been "so painful." His mother's few lines, he said, written on the morning of his sailing, he would keep always, "as a treasure." And he did.

Throughout the Atlantic crossing, during heavy seas and "frightful" roaring gales, Louisa and Catherine remained very sick below decks. Louisa's recollection of the crossing was of spending one dreadful night after another with the seas running "mountains high"; or, when the ship edged through fog, of dampness penetrating the mattresses and blankets. John Quincy, however, could "scarcely perceive that we are at sea." He involved himself with the ship's routine, as he had during his first crossings. He rose at six, often earlier, and after reading ten to fifteen chapters of the Bible and breakfasting at nine, he walked the deck for exercise and made observations of the ship's position by quadrant, which he had learned to use during the 1779 crossing. Adams and members of the crew cast lines over the side, and one morning caught sixty cod. He also measured the sea temperature with a thermometer. JQA spent most afternoons reading and writing, followed by another walk upon the deck until seven, and dinner, after which he read or played cards until eleven or twelve. He concluded that there was "much time for study and education at sea," and read over again Plutarch's life of Lycurgus, taking notes, and Massillon's sermons, first one on forgiveness, another on the word of God, and a third on reverence.

John Quincy considered the assignment to Russia "the most important of any that I have ever in the course of my life engaged in." He prayed that the result would prove "beneficial to my country, prosperous to my family and myself, and advantageous to all who are concerned in the voyage." Adams entered the world stage at a dramatic moment. Since 1801, when the Adamses left Berlin, Napoleon and his armies had conquered Europe, from the Danish Sound to Gibraltar, from the Baltic Sea to the Strait of Messina. New puppet states, ruled by the Bonaparte family, took their places in a ruined Europe. After his plans for a land-sea invasion of England were halted by Lord Nelson at Trafalgar in 1805, Napoleon had pivoted his Grand Army around to the east, and swiftly advanced to the Danube. Austria fell in 1805, Prussia in 1806, and eastern Russia in 1807. After the Battle of Friedland, Napoleon ruled mainland Europe west of the Russian and Ottoman Empires, except for Portugal, which his troops soon swallowed, and Sweden, protected by the British Navy. The French Emperor paused only at the Russian Czar's Baltic border. Peace with Russia allowed consolidation of Napoleon's Continental System; his objectives were not Russia, but England and the Ottoman Empire leading to the Near East and India. Napoleon and Czar Alexander I met on a raft in the middle of the Niemen River in the summer of 1807, and, with the Treaties of Tilsit, pressed their imperial seals on a new map of Europe, and pledges of alliance.

By 1809, war between France and England made the ports of Europe dangerous for United States ships. America's trade was thriving: Tonnage tripled between 1790 and 1810; its value for the twelve years from 1800 to 1812 would not be equaled again during the century. New England and New York put to sea almost half the tonnage of all of England. Neutral trade was lucrative. But British ships halted American ships, and British officers impressed American seamen. Even the peaceful Danes seized several hundred American ships between 1807 and 1812, and this issue would be quickly placed upon John Quincy Adams's agenda even before he reached St. Petersburg.

The Adamses' Atlantic crossing progressed without event. The *Horace*'s officers hailed four schooners, and spoke with one by megaphone, which carried homeward the news of their progress toward Europe; they later came upon a fishing vessel, the *Dove*, at anchor on the Banks of Newfoundland, and rowed a packet of letters over to her to be conveyed back to Massachusetts. But as the American ship entered the North Sea and then the Baltic, it was repeatedly hailed and stopped, first by an armed brig that refused to identify itself, then by a British brig of eighteen guns, the *Rover*, which sent over an officer and four men, who boarded the *Horace* and inspected her papers. Within two hours after the British sailed off, a Danish brig passed close under stern, hailed them, and asked where they came from and where bound. Later that afternoon, a small Danish two-master with swivel gun came up and fired to bring the *Horace* about, and showed fifteen armed men. A Danish lieutenant told them to board the American ship, but Capt. Beckford ordered his sailors to hold them off, "and," said John Quincy Adams, watching the confrontation, "pikes and swords and axes were on immediate opposition to each other." With a wave of his hand, the lieutenant signaled his men to stand down, and the Danes rowed back and hoisted sail.

Continually halted, sometimes putting into port, the *Horace* made slow progress across the Baltic Sea. Gales delayed them further, and by mid-October Capt. Beckford asked Adams if they might put in for the winter. But Adams was firm: In the pursuit of a public trust, he would not abandon any means of reaching his destination. They pushed on through rain and fog on flat seas, reaching the Gulf of Finland in late October, as ice threatened to seal it for the winter. On October 22, before a light and favorable breeze, they were in sight of land on both sides, and soon slipped by the Tölbacken lighthouse about six miles below Kronstadt. The next day, the *Horace* warped "out of the Mole," and in three hours, passing Russian men-of-war at anchor, reached St. Petersburg. At four in the afternoon, October 23, 1809, the ship docked at a quay just across from the Winter Palace and the enormous statue of Peter the Great. A carriage took Louisa, Charles, and the women to temporary lodgings, while John Quincy and the young men walked, safe at last after eighty days "of tedious and dangerous navigation."

2

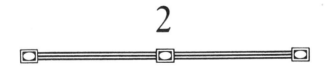

No OTHER EUROPEAN capital rivaled the splendor and luxury of St. Petersburg, except Paris, and no other European ruler equaled the power of Czar Alexander I, except Napoleon. No other court — none — cost as much, exhibited diamonds in such profusion, luxuriated in such ceremony and raw power and ostentation as the Czar's in St. Petersburg.

For Louisa and John Quincy, St. Petersburg marked a time of contrasts, when he ascended in power and stature, and she, temporarily, receded into the first of two long periods of reclusion. Louisa's years in St. Petersburg were lonely and sad. They began and ended with the death of a child: in July 1810, pregnant for the tenth time, Louisa suffered her seventh miscarriage. She thought of her older sons daily, and wrote them frequently, but her letters were often intercepted or lost at sea; it took six months for replies to reach her. Louisa's only companions were Catherine and Charles. She complained of vague, undefined illnesses, continuing pain in her hands, a temporary blurring of her vision, headaches. But while Louisa was eclipsed, her husband entered almost five years of increasingly important diplomacy, and found himself among the rising constellations of American statesmen. She temporarily faded, as he shone brighter. Yet Adams continued to expect Louisa's presence at every ball, dinner, and court. She should, he insisted, add to his brilliance in this socially demanding capital, and not indulge hypochondria, melancholia, or even personal tragedy.

St. Petersburg was, with Paris, the jewel of Europe. Its wide boulevards, open squares, palaces, and cathedrals went beyond the dream of Peter the Great, who started building the city in 1703 after driving the Swedes from the Neva delta. Peter built a fortress on one of the islands, and planned a city that would be Russia's western seaport, its "window on Europe." By 1809, with its active sea trade, St. Petersburg filled the left bank of the Neva, and its palaces, fortresses, and ornate gardens spilled across the surrounding rivers to a scattering of large islands and the countryside beyond. The old city itself, where the Adamses lived, was a large, almond-shaped island on the left bank, with the Neva forming one curve and the grand Fontanka, a 150-foot-wide waterway, the other. Narrow canals and streets looped through it, and the Nevsky Prospekt, then as now its major thoroughfare, its Champs Elysées, stretched in a straight line 130 feet wide from the countryside four miles into the very heart of the city, to Palace Square.

Opposite the quay where the Adamses disembarked, and where the *Horace* now spent the winter as ice shut the Bay of

Kronstadt and the rivers, two large public squares formed the focal point of St. Petersburg, and the Russian Empire. Here, along the Neva embankment, stood the Admiralty, under construction since 1806, its exquisite 230-foot needle spire not yet in place, and before it a spacious and magnificent square, called Senate Square, or St. Isaac's Square, after the marble Church of St. Isaac in its center. The whole was dominated by Catherine's incomparable bronze memorial to Peter the Great, seated upon a rearing horse with trampling hooves that struck the sky, rising above its columnal plinth of Finnish granite. To the north along the Neva, connected by public walks in front of the Admiralty, was another, equally large and magnificent expanse, called Palace Square. Along it, and the object of its spaciousness, sprawled the Winter Palace, the largest royal palace in the world, dwarfing Versailles, with three hundred rooms decorated with paintings and sculpture, and a maze of apartments and halls and chambers that could accommodate sixty-five hundred overnight guests in luxury. The Winter Palace connected with the Imperial Palace of the Hermitage, which contained, in John Quincy Adams's words, "one of the most magnificent collections of masterpieces in many of the arts that the world can furnish."

From Palace and St. Isaac's squares, which formed the center of St. Petersburg, streets and boulevards radiated out reaching toward the rest of the Russian empire. St. Petersburg was a city of palaces, such as the opulent Marble Palace, which Grigori Potemkin designed, on the banks of the Neva, with its large rooms and salons and enclosed garden with an aviary and "trees of full growth," all for his mistress, Catherine II. The Anichkov Palace on the Fontanka contained bronzes and ornamentals, gilded sofas and chairs, Siberian vases of agate, and steam and water baths for the royal family. These included a tin bathing tub fitted into the floor in the middle of a room, and above it a vessel "with holes like a cullender," Adams said, "from which the shower bath is poured when they choose it." Clocks ticked in every room, marking the Czar's time, and one with a bronze figure of Venus chimed the hours with a little Cupid bursting from an eggshell she held in her hands. The

Czar lacked nothing: His greenhouses produced fresh large pears* through the Russian winter, so he might present them to his mother on her birthday.

St. Petersburg was also a city of cathedrals, and John Quincy Adams would worship during the next five years in almost every one of them. He would return so often to the Roman Catholic church, where he found the music "exquisite," that the Father General of the Jesuits in 1812 would make a strong effort to convert the New England Protestant. Adams would stand packed into the immense crowd of the common people for five hours at the consecration of the new Church of the Mother of God of Kazan, and attend orthodox services at the Church of St. Isaac, and Good Friday services at St. Nicholas the Assumption with its twenty lighted shrines. He would admire the "very magnificent" paintings in the cathedrals, especially the portrait of the Virgin of Kazan with its dazzling headdress of diamonds and precious stones, in the Cathedral of Our Lady of Kazan along Nevsky Prospekt, and he would run his eyes, but never his fingers, over the massive silver sarcophagus in the Cathedral Church of St. Alexander Nevsky. Adams would watch the annual procession of the Imperial family into the church for a solemn Mass on St. Alexander's Day, after which the Czar and his wife and mother prostrated themselves before the shrine. This was no mere genuflection, Adams would note, not a simple falling to the knees, but a bowing of the head and a slow lowering of the entire body until the forehead was pressed against the stone pavement of the church floor. Adams would worship in these great cathedrals with the lowest classes of Russian society, the muzhiks and foot soldiers, whose religion and superstition gave the Czar power and served his needs. The only thing that distracted from the richness of these cathedrals was the poverty of the parishioners, and the beggar boys and girls, some not older than four or five, who wanderd through

---

* The Czar gloried in these pears, and at least once allowed fresh ones to be used as a centerpiece for a dinner dance at the French ambassador's in mid-winter. When the Emperor returned to collect them the next day, however, they were gone. The French ambassador had paid 100 rubles apiece for them.

the standing congregation asking for alms and rattling cannisters with narrow slits in the lids for kopecks.

The Adamses would walk everywhere, and discover the common little wood hut in which Peter lived while planning and dreaming of his window on Europe. Little did he know that it would be a window on Russia as well. The center of St. Petersburg, and the heart of Russia, were the two large squares, and the Czar. Here, emanating from the Winter Palace, were its richness, court, and ceremony; its fears, hatreds, and oppression. At ten o'clock every Sunday morning, the Czar reviewed his empire's soldiers, and as many as forty thousand men filled Palace and St. Isaac's squares from the Winter Palace to the bridge over the Neva River. Here, too, in the squares, the Czar and nobility celebrated, promenaded, rode their opulent carriages to luxurious dinners and balls. And here, as well, the common Russian people gathered, first in veneration of their Czar, and then in revolution.

One of John Quincy Adams's first expenses in St. Petersburg was 35 rubles for a wig, and 170 rubles to the wigmaker for his styling. Only twenty-four hours after his arrival, told that the Russian foreign minister wished to see him immediately, Adams "was dressed from top to toe much to his discomfiture in a superb style," said Louisa, "Wig and all, to be presented to the Chancellor of the empire."

Adams had been caught by surprise. He was, after all, only the minister from a third-rate nation, radical in its politics and the antithesis of a Czardom. Adams entered a nation ruled by one of the two most powerful men in the world, while he headed a tiny legation whose principal underling was a corrupt little ferret named Levett Harris, who had been sent to St. Petersburg in 1803 by President Jefferson, and had used his time getting rich.* When Harris dutifully communicated notice of

* Harris made a fortune by accepting money from American merchants to clear their ships through the Russian neutrality commission. In 1819, William D. Lewis, one of these merchants, accused Harris of using his office for personal gain, and Harris sued for libel. Adams's papers contain summaries of arguments on the two sides, and his own deposition. Despite his guilt, Harris won $100 in the case.

Adams's arrival to Count Nikolai Petrovich Rumyantsev, the Russian High Chancellor of the Empire asked to see the American minister that same day. This was an unusual honor, and a curiosity. Harris scurried back, instructed Adams on how to be received and how many bows to make. Promptly at seven, John Quincy departed, attired in his best court clothing, "looking very handsome," Louisa said, "all but the Wig," which she thought changed his appearance "not to his advantage."

The elderly and distinguished Count Rumyantsev greeted John Quincy "in full dress," and apologized that Czar Alexander could not give the American minister an immediate audience. The Czar had overturned in his droshky during one of the ceremonial processions so popular during his reign, and injured both his legs, which kept him confined to a sofa. Rumyantsev was "courtly," and his character and strong pro-French views fit precisely Czar Alexander's strategy in his alliance with Napoleon. Alexander had confidence in Rumyantsev, for a while, as the man whose talents best served as the skids for launching the Imperial will. Adams found Rumyantsev pleasant and useful. He appreciated the Russian's classical scholarship, and his huge library attracted the American, who himself knew the value, both intellectual and monetary, of a wealth of books.* Adams and Rumyantsev also shared another common characteristic: both men were exceedingly ambitious. In 1810, the French ambassador wrote home in code (intercepted by the Czar) that Rumyantsev was "always politically ambitious in outlook," and in 1811 the ambassador again encoded the message that Rumyantsev was "personally interested" in maintaining the pro-French policy; "if things change, he is ruined." Unhappily for the ambitious Rumyantsev, in Czar Alexander's Russia two rules obtained: The Czar knew everything; and things always changed. Rumyantsev's French sympathies proved his downfall.

The Czar was already feeling Napoleon's wrath. The French

---

* Rumyantsev owned one of the most important collections of books and manuscripts concerning the history and culture of Russia and the Slavic world. This collection was later established as the Rumyantsev Museum, and later still as the Lenin Library in Moscow.

Emperor wanted Russia to halt all trade with the United States. But Russia, the farthest European nation from Napoleon's power, was becoming one of the United States' most important trading partners. Between 1808 and 1812, the Stars and Stripes appeared more frequently than any other flag in Russia's ports. Within two summers of John Quincy's arrival, and largely because of his friendship with Count Rumyantsev and Czar Alexander, one hundred vessels flying American flags would lie in the Bay of Kronstadt at one time; one-tenth of all American exports would go to Russia.* Alexander needed American trade, and the United States needed Russian commerce. The Czar would soon refuse to enforce Napoleon's decree, essential to his Continental System, against ships carrying goods under the American flag. This refusal would be a major factor in Napoleon's invading Russia, and his invasion would bring the powerful French empire to defeat upon "the white reefs of the Russian winter." John Quincy Adams had arrived in St. Petersburg with far more political muscle than he, or his Secretary of State, had estimated. Adams's instructions were vague: continue good relations, attend to the rights and interests of the United States, be attentive to favorable treatment for American commerce. Those instructions had been in force for ten years. The day-to-day conduct of affairs, therefore, fell to Adams's discretion, and he quickly learned that he was in a special position with Rumyantsev and Alexander, and that personal friendship and the social festivities of the Russian court would smooth his diplomacy. Ships and trade, Russia's necessities and Europe's exigencies, placed the little American minister between two large powers, and in a position of importance.

Adams went to work at once. Only four days after donning his new wig, he and Harris rode back to Count Rumyantsev's for a special diplomatic dinner. The Chancellor's guests, forty-

---

* Not all these ships were American. The British disguised their own merchantmen with American flags and papers. At one point, Rumyantsev uncovered thirteen forgeries of British ships as American. John Quincy spent three years gently lecturing Rumyantsev about American exports — especially cotton and sugar — which the Russian was certain did not grow in the United States, and explaining the difference, with imitations, between a British seaman's accent and an American's.

five male diplomats—the Count was an "old bachelor"—sparkled and flashed with stars and medals, ribbons and bright sashes beyond anything John Quincy had seen in any capital. They spent the evening at a table and dinner "magnificent in every detail."

In 1809, the diplomatic corps consisted of a French ambassador; ministers of the second order from the kings of Denmark, Prussia, Sardinia, Saxony, Bavaria, Würtemberg, Holland, Spain, Naples, and Westphalia; and a chargé d'affaires from Portugal and a minister from Sweden who enjoyed the formal powers of an ambassador but not, said Adams, "the formal character." The British ambassador had been sent home in 1807. Seven of these gentlemen represented kings created within the last nine years and descended from the French Revolution. The King of Naples, for example, was Napoleon's brother-in-law. This diplomatic corps changed rapidly with the shifting politics of the Continent. When the Hanseatic Cities incorporated with the French Empire, their ambassador in St. Petersburg "vanished," said Adams. "I have not seen him since. . . . His name was Wiggers." Three months after the Adamses arrived, the Duke de Mondragone, minister from the King of Naples, was recalled and took his leave. This enabled the Adamses to purchase some of the Duke's used furniture. When the minister from the King of Saxony was recalled, Louisa and John Quincy rented his house. And when the Bavarian minister, the only diplomat other than Adams with his family in St. Petersburg, took leave in 1809–10 to thaw out in Naples, that left Louisa Adams as the only wife of any foreign diplomat in the Russian capital. The craziest diplomat in St. Petersburg was Count St. Julien, an aged envoy from the Emperor of Austria, who dressed wildly, and raced about the winter streets on a noisy, six-foot-high sleigh. Adams always enjoyed his company. St. Julien was a sociable old soldier who could bow himself into a hoop. He claimed title as one of the noble rakes of the last century, but his desire, JQA reported, "has long outlived his performance." Count St. Julien confided to Adams that what he wanted most in life now was a chair on rollers so he could glide about any ballroom "from lady to lady and coquette them all."

The center of attraction at Rumyantsev's, however, was none of the satellite diplomats or the shiny-eyed eccentrics, nor even the host. It was John Quincy Adams's principal adversary: Armand Augustin Louis de Caulaincourt, Duke de Vicence, Grand Ecuyer of France, Napoleon's dashing emissary to St. Petersburg. Caulaincourt was, Adams thought, "one of the most accomplished as well as one of the greatest noblemen of the Napoleon creation," and the only representative of true ambassadorial rank at the Czar's court. Caulaincourt enjoyed unequaled prestige in addition to rank, and he lived "in a style of magnificence," Adams wrote, "scarcely surpassed by the Emperor himself." The diplomatic corps always called Caulaincourt, and his successor, *the* ambassador, and because of this, and the critical nature of French–Russian and Russian–American relations, Adams cultivated him shamelessly. To Adams's surprise, he found Caulaincourt an easy, unassuming man, unusual among such grandees.*

From 1809 to 1812, Napoleon's ambassador to St. Petersburg, first Caulaincourt and then the much-inferior Lauriston, battled John Quincy Adams for the Czar's attention. Their struggles, always mannerly and genteel, made every *Te Deum*, court, ball, dinner, and ceremony take on significance. The staggering complexity of the Russian court ritual, with its intricate political nuances, required constant attendance. Diplomatic success depended upon it. At St. Petersburg, unlike any other capital, one attended every social occasion, and played every card.

* Caulaincourt was indeed unusual. In 1811, opposing Napoleon's plans to invade Russia, he asked to be recalled, and was. During Napoleon's retreat, however, the French minister bravely escorted the Emperor he opposed to Paris. In 1815, in yet another twist of fate, Caulaincourt was saved from exile by the conquering Russian Czar, Alexander I.

3

C̲ZAR ALEXANDER received John Quincy Adams at the
Winter Palace a week after the new minister arrived
in St. Petersburg. This formal ceremony was necessary not only
for presenting credentials, but also for entering the Russian court and diplomatic society. Without being presented,
one did not socially exist. The court employed a Monsieur le
Commandeur de Maisonneuve and staff to insure the proper
repetition of its rituals; one never forgot, for example, to make
three bows on advancing toward a member of the Imperial family, and three when withdrawing. Le Commandeur himself
arrived at the Adamses' and instructed John Quincy on the
ceremonial procedures for his presentation. The American was
not a good pupil. Adams considered court formalities "so trifling and so insignificant" and "much more embarrassing . . .
than business of real importance," but he went through them.
He especially abhorred the ritual of diplomatic visits, when
one made the rounds to diplomats and royalty in person, in
full court dress, yet never got out of one's carriage nor inquired
whether or not the person was at home, but simply left one's
card.

Louisa, too, had to be presented, and one Countess Litta, "very
handsome and very fat," the royal Dame d'Honneur and a niece
of Potemkin, visited her to rehearse the ceremony. Louisa's
presentation was very formal. She wore a silver hoop skirt,
heavy crimson robe, and long train lined with white; she climbed
from her carriage at the Winter Palace only with great difficulty. Inside Louisa was made to stand in the center of a vast
empty room, facing tall double doors. Two large black men—
the Czar being fond of them—dressed like Turks "with Splendid
Uniforms" took position by the doors, and drew sabers with
gold handles. When the double doors opened, Louisa could
glimpse a corridor lined with identically dressed black men,

their swords drawn, and down the long corridor the Grand Marshall, resplendent in uniform with medals and sword flashing, preceded the Czar and Czarina, who marched together toward Louisa followed by a long train of ladies and gentlemen. As this procession passed the doors, the Grand Marshall fell back, allowing the Czar and Czarina to enter the room, and closing the doors almost shut behind them. The Emperor wore his uniform, and the Empress "a rich court dress." Louisa's eyes followed every move, but her body, trembling with nervousness, remained stationary. Like a porcelain figurine decorating an ornate Russian music box, Louisa slowly curtsied.

This Empress, the German Princess Louisa Maria Augusta of Baden, had been married in a political union to Alexander when she was fourteen and he sixteen. She disliked being touched; now thirty, the Empress had no children, and her marriage was not a happy one. Alexander turned his attentions to other women, and his favorite mistress was Madame Marie Antoinette Narishkin, the wife of a high court official who preferred silence to duty elsewhere. Alexander and Madame Narishkin had five children, but he made it a point of honor to give no political power to this woman just because she was beautiful and he was young and full of passion.

When Louisa finished her curtsy, Czar Alexander, always eager to break formality, walked up to her and made small conversation, in French, while the Czarina said nothing; then their Imperial majesties withdrew as they had entered and left Louisa in the same position, unmoved.

By contrast, John Quincy's audience with the Czar was informal, without ceremony at all. Czar Alexander,* the heart of the Russian Empire, the jewel of the Russian crown, the absolute ruler, "the Blessed Czar," was a friendly man of inner conflicts. When Adams stepped into the Czar's private cabinet, in which the Emperor waited alone, Alexander walked forward to greet him and said in French: "I am so glad to see you here." The Czar was young, only thirty-one, yet his appearance projected power. He was tall, fair-haired, strong. In Palace Square,

* Born December 23, 1777.

reviewing his troops, Alexander cut a dashing figure upon a horse. He radiated an imposing sense of grandeur and nobility, benefitted by his persuasive and captivating eloquence. Yet he preferred, in his private cabinet, an informal, almost familiar manner that relaxed Adams. After presenting his credential letters, John Quincy told Alexander that he should consider the American mission as proof of President Madison's respect for His Majesty, and his desire to strengthen relations between the two countries. Alexander replied that he, too, sought friendly relations with the United States. The Czar spoke about the political alignments of Europe, of United States neutrality, which he thought "wise and just," and his support for a fair and lawful system of commerce for all nations. Adams, also, emphasized his nation's wish to remain free from political ties to Europe, and its interest in open commerce among all nations. John Quincy also got a glimpse of the flawed Alexander: At one point in their conversation, the Czar took Adams by the arm and walked him from near the door to an open window overlooking the Neva, "a movement," Adams thought, "seemingly intended to avoid being overheard." Spies, of course, flourished in any court, and informers in Alexander's Russia received handsome rewards. But the gesture had about it a sense of foreboding, for the Czar trusted no one. When John Quincy left his first meeting with Alexander, he felt both puzzled and elated. His mission to Russia was off to an excellent start, but depended entirely on a man troubled by doubts and suspicions.

Alexander at this moment was nearing the apogee of his power. He would govern Russia for almost twenty-five years, and under his rule that nation would reach a pinnacle of influence in Europe unequaled in the century. Alexander would match Napoleon, and their decisions shape the destiny of Europe. In a wonderful irony of history, each would march at the head of an invading army into the other's oldest city: Napoleon into Moscow in 1812, and Alexander into Paris in 1814. Russia's ruling class already considered itself part of aristocratic Europe. The Russian peasants, too, loved Alexander, and called him their "Angel." Even John Quincy, not one to lavish adjectives on others, would call Czar Alexander "the darling of the human race."

Alexander's great magnetism, however, also contained the mechanisms of his destruction. He was a man divided against himself; a man who personified the contradictions of his own empire. Beneath his brilliant display and handsome appearance lay disease and emotional imbalance, marked by explosions of rage and frenzy later soothed only by daily seances with the religious mystic Baroness de Krüdener. His weakness for sex —sex of all kinds—was happily exploited by St. Petersburg's voluptuous society, and may have contributed to his instability by slowly driving him mad from syphilis. The seeds of true madness, however, had been implanted in Alexander in boyhood. As a child, he found himself caught between his grandmother, Catherine the Great, and his father, Czar Paul III. His libertine grandmother spoiled him, and engaged a Swiss tutor — a shocking idea for an heir to the Russian throne—who imbued Alexander with dreams of a Russian utopia, but neglected to acquaint him with a history of Russian realities. Catherine hated Paul, her only child, and with reason. Alexander's father ruled his empire and his family with cruelty and violence; he excluded foreigners, censured free thought, burned books, substituted military discipline for government. Czar Paul even confined his son for years to the grounds of his estate at Gatchina. While Alexander gained a sense of freedom and an education from his grandmother, from his father came the conflict of confinement and burned books—and a passion for military parade. When Alexander was twenty-three, he learned of a coup against his father, and did nothing to prevent it. In March 1801, Paul was strangled in his bedroom in the fortress-like Michael Palace he had built as a safe refuge against his many enemies, and Alexander became Czar.

The Russians loved symbols, and Alexander's Hamlet-like ascension to the throne on March 24, 1801, in the second year of a new century, contained, they thought, good omens. This Czar was young, open-faced, considered the man who would restore the glories and privileges of Catherine's Russia, who would free the serfs, reorganize the bureaucracy, and keep Russia at peace. But Alexander did none of these. The Russian Army marched, and met defeat. The serfs remained oppressed, the bureaucracy huge and unresponsive. Bribes and cash gifts formed a way of life in Russia by 1809. Russian officials lived above their salaries, and many of them went into debt with no intention of repayment, viewing frugality as a far more serious crime than corruption. The corruption was so extensive that the French ambassador complained to Paris that "there was perhaps no government employee who did not have his price."

Czar Alexander controlled everything. Adams soon found an impenetrable Russian foreign ministry, the largest in all Europe with some three hundred employees. The British Foreign Office, by comparison, oversaw an expanding empire on three continents with a staff of just twenty-eight, including the librarian. Napoleon's French foreign ministry numbered just fifty-five. The bloated Russian staff was also inefficient, and the dearth of qualified ministry workers caused one foreign diplomat to report that "perhaps no court is as poor in able men as that of Russia." More than once the Russian foreign minister himself had to go as a supplicant to the home of an official he had dismissed and order him back to work at the ministry because no one else could (or would) complete some urgent work.

For John Quincy Adams to accomplish anything in St. Petersburg, he had to read, spy, socialize, and cultivate the Czar. The Adamses subscribed to *The English Magazine*, and read Everett's and Gray's newspapers when they arrived six months late from the United States. John Quincy and Louisa both read the *St. Petersburgischer Zeitung*, a German-language edition of the local Russian paper, for news, but its political section was controlled by the Russian foreign ministry. In 1806, the ministry also started publishing the *Journal du Nord*, which after 1813 became the *Conservateur Impartial*, a misnomer, for this controlled-news source was designated specifically for diplomatic consumption in St. Petersburg. The Adamses subscribed for twenty-four rubles a month.

The Czar not only controlled the press, he also intercepted the mails, including all the private letters and diplomatic dispatches sent by Louisa and John Quincy Adams, and employed an extensive network of officials in this business. Every letter was opened and read. There was little foreign diplomats could do. Some tried writing in invisible ink. Adams sent dispatches to the State Department written in a code that, by modern-day standards of espionage, appears childlike. A typical diplomatic letter from the American Legation in St. Petersburg to the State Department in Washington in 1809 started: "From the enclosed 1045 1576 1501 879 999 134 1024 601 1102 377 569. . . ." Rewards flowed to those who could decipher such documents, and the bribery of messengers, couriers, and mistresses kept the flow steady. The Czar's staff read all correspondence, and compiled a register containing the interesting parts of letters, which was shown to Alexander daily.

The social festivities of St. Petersburg, as we shall see, offered the best source of gossip and rumor, with a light dusting of news. The idea was to meet other members of the diplomatic corps, the nobility, the Emperor himself, and gather what one could. A slip, a casual remark, an oversight took on special nuance. If one made a bow too shallow, it became a matter of international observation and discussion. Are the nations at difference? Social skills, therefore, had such high value in the Russian capital that one diplomat wrote anxiously home in 1810 for a new secretary, and directed that the young man must have all the usual qualities of that job, and be as well a good dancer and a musician with a sense of humor. "I should have—in a milieu of the most futile and the most immoral society in the world," the diplomat requested, "a man who would serve me as an informer with the women to learn the secrets of their husbands." Louisa Adams watched, amused, another aspect of this game: Russian officers employed at the court balls to dance with any woman, however ugly or lacking, for political purposes. Louisa called them "Waltzing Machines," these windup soldiers who charmed women for information delivered to other men.

The corruption, the inefficiency, the gossip and rumors, all took on an almost charming aspect in this most unreal world capital. In Russia, the really essential things remained secret, for the Czar alone decided them. Like a magnet, power emanated from this man, and events gravitated to him. As Count St. Julien acknowledged: "How absolute the will of the sovereign is in this empire." Alexander allowed few diplomats close access to him; such men he saw informally. Adams knew that the Czar made foreign policy, and that Alexander, encountered at a formal dinner or ball, walking along the quay, dancing with Louisa Adams or flirting with Catherine Johnson, was a friend and political asset. The best way, the only way to know Russia's intentions, therefore, was to know Alexander—and even then, one couldn't be sure. Friendly but suspicious; brilliant yet erratic; handsome and flawed, Czar Alexander at his most powerful moment contained his most destructive weaknesses. He was also called, for good reason, The Enigmatic Czar.

4

WITHIN A WEEK of their court presentations, Louisa and John Quincy Adams were socializing until four every morning, rising at eleven, dining at five in the afternoon, taking tea at ten, and going out once more. Adams scarcely had time to write the Secretary of State. By January, 1810, he and Louisa found themselves in a constant round of balls, suppers, masquerades, court circles, and a continual round of visits. Court parties and diplomatic balls were held to fend off the winter darkness, and the Russian nobility kept perpetual open house where the Adamses found card parties and gaming tables of every kind piled with large amounts of international currencies. Gambling was "the only genteel and *interesting amusement*," said Louisa, and at one party learned a new definition of envy when she watched the Dutch minister win four thousand rubles in ten minutes. In this free-wheeling milieu, John Quincy prayed that he and all the members of his family, male and female, would "preserve steadiness of brain in this sudden and violent whirl, to come out of it still in possession of our Senses and our reason. But we all, to begin with myself, need the care of the guardian Angel, more than we did in the Baltic or the Gulph [sic] of Finland."

Nothing protected the Adamses from seas of champagne, shoals of caviar, reefs of meats, and desserts that left them drowning, deliciously, in dissipation. No capital anywhere maintained such an exhausting round of ceremony and banquet. Czar and nobility, ministers and diplomats, intertwined in embroidered circles of power that defied even the seasons: they danced when their rivers froze, and drank when they thawed. They elevated dancing the polonaise and the politics of digestion to a new diplomatic art form. Where such power gathered for pleasure, lessons of history were taught, and Louisa and John Quincy Adams found themselves as students, unprepared for the rituals, the weather, or the expense.

St. Petersburg turned raw and dark in October, when the first snows fell and the Russian winter swept in after summer had barely warmed the earth. By September, the Adamses were dining by candlelight at four in the afternoon. The November ball for the Empress Mother not only signaled, Louisa said, "the approaching dissipation of winter," but also the approaching time of cold and darkness. As though to hold back that hour, the Russians illuminated this ball with fifteen thousand wax candles, which cost eighteen thousand rubles,* and concluded a full day of court circles, French opera, and dancing with a magnificent supper for 250 guests wearing a profusion of diamonds and precious stones and sashes and ribbons greater than Louisa or John Quincy had ever seen. This was followed by thunderous fireworks high above the Winter Palace and the frozen Neva River. By the Czar's birthday fête in December, winter embraced St. Petersburg, and the capital was dark by three. During the shortest day, John Quincy measured sunrise at 9:14 and sunset at 2:26. He noted that the sun rose so little above the horizon that there was not a street in the city where it reached the ground; the capital huddled in "gloomy semi-dark-

---

* About forty-five hundred dollars.

ness." By January, JQA was also recording nightly readings of minus thirty and minus forty degrees Fahrenheit. Louisa wrote Abigail that during the winter her body "was almost congealed by the intense cold of these frozen regions." To keep warm, the Russians constructed houses with walls three feet thick, and installed double windows, hanging the second, external window in September. They put airtight wood stoves in every room, which held the heat like ovens and needed stoking only twice on very cold days. At these temperatures, the Emperor dispensed with his Sunday morning review of the troops across Palace Square. Horses' steel hooves made musical notes striking the hard snow, leather boots cracked, metal adhered to finger or tongue of those foolish enough to touch it outside. The winter air in this festive capital appeared as though filled with frozen confetti: Tiny motes of ice crystals blew and skittered through it, invisible everywhere except when they coruscated across the rays of sunlight, which, shining through the suspended vapor, formed dancing rainbows.

In winter, a psychological darkness embraced the inhabitants. With the canals and rivers and bays sealed by an impenetrable layering of ice five to six feet thick, which moaned and boomed with the temperature changes, food had to be hauled in on sleds. The last vessel sailed in early November, and the Adamses received no letters from America until May or June; the only communication was by diplomatic courier overland in carriages on runners. To ward off the terrors of such darkness, the Russians confected entertainments, superstitions, festivals of light and pageantry. In January, the Czar and Czarina and Imperial family wrapped in luxurious furs and, followed by shivering diplomats, joined the Archbishop in blessing the waters of the Neva—a blessing that penetrated six feet of ice. The Russian New Year celebration, started with a Mass at noon, swirled into a Diplomatic Circle, followed by an enormous masquerade ball—at which no one wore masks or danced—with as many as sixteen hundred guests swarming the Winter Palace "like an ant hill" dressed in ornate Russian costumes.

No one in the Adams family escaped these rituals. Every year, Louisa took baby Charles to the Children's Ball, where elegantly attired mothers sparkling with diamonds watched their youngsters dance the polonaise, the English country dances, the Polish promenades, and the Russian *Golobalist*, or Dove Dance. Bowing to the customs of St. Petersburg, Louisa said, "we have been obliged to initiate [Charles] very early in the school of dissipation." He appeared in a variety of costumes: as Bacchus, or as the Page from Beaumarchais' *Marriage of Figaro*. For his first ball, Louisa dressed him as an Indian chief "to gratify the taste for Savages," and prolonged applause greeted little Charles as he entered the dance floor, where he "led out Miss Vlodek . . . and they, with the assistance of their Mamas, opened the Ball." Charles was three years old. Following the dance, the children ate an elegant supper with "oceans of Champagne" while their mothers stood in full dress behind their chairs. Afterward, there was a lottery for expensive toys, but John Quincy Adams would not allow any member of his family to accept gifts; every year he pulled Charles away, and they went home empty-handed at two in the morning.

Winter ended, with great rejoicing, as the ice blocking the Neva River broke open. Five cannon salutes from the Peter and Paul Fortress brought the Czar and the people of the city to the embankment. Church bells rang, and as the first boats crossed, dodging chunks of ice, the Governor of St. Petersburg brought the Czar a glass of water from the river to drink. Summer now began. The Adamses could write again directly to Boston, and within a month Louisa happily noted: "Letters from America now come more frequently God be thanked," and then added, "but the dreadful long Winter must come again." Louisa and Catherine strolled along the quay until dark—that is, almost midnight. In June, John Quincy climbed the round tower on the corner of the house they rented, and watched the sunset and sunrise occur at the same time; on the summer solstice, he noted, the sun rose at 2:46 A.M. and never really set at all.

With the ice cleared in the rivers, the people of St. Petersburg floated a chain bridge of boats, connected with thick planks and secured by heavy ropes, across the Neva and Little Neva, which once more opened the countryside beyond the city. Now the rich could ride in a procession of summer dresses, uniforms, and opulent carriages to their country palaces. The highlight of the summer was the annual carriage procession into the countryside to the Palace at Peterhof on the Bay of Kronstadt, where Czar Alexander gave a ball, a dinner, and guests rode about the gardens in carriages and watched the illumination of three thousand lamps ignited at once by sixteen hundred servants, followed by a fifteen-minute fireworks display. John Quincy never stayed overnight, but rode back to the city in the semi-darkness, and passed perhaps fifty thousand of the common Russian people, who had walked out in their own procession on foot to share this midsummer night with the rich and their carriages.

This contrast troubled Louisa and John Quincy. On the banks of the Neva, it was the law of nations that the Czar and each minister be ostentatious. Most members of the diplomatic corps received high salaries, and spent well. At the grand ball for the Empress Mother, held at Rumyantsev's home, those at the Czar's table dined from solid gold dishes; diplomats ate upon silver, and the rest made do upon ornate porcelain. They were all waited upon by three hundred servants wearing magnificent liveries. The French ambassador spent more than a million rubles ($350,000) a year on entertainment, maintained a household of sixty-five people, and kept fifty-six horses. Napoleon liked to have his ambassadors spend well, which gave them little cause for independence and kept most of them loyal.

John Quincy Adams's salary in St. Petersburg was just nine thousand dollars a year, plus an equal amount as "outfit" for traveling to a post and establishing a residence. Only the President earned more (twenty-five thousand dollars a year); the Vice President and Cabinet officers received five thousand dollars, and the Chief Justice of the Supreme Court, four thousand dollars. To the American people, Adams's salary appeared extravagant, but in St. Petersburg, no matter what economies he took, JQA felt pinched and embarrassed. He found himself faced with the choice of spending beyond his means, which would put him into debt and reduce his meager property in America, or incurring a reputation for parsimony. He accomplished both. Only once in St. Petersburg by luck, did his salary ever equal or exceed his expenses; Adams was always overdrawn.

Old arguments, like bad luggage, have a way of tagging along and breaking open in public. Once more, Louisa and John Quincy struggled over money. "What mortifications attend an American Mission!!!" Louisa said. She tried cutting back. She and Catherine sewed their dresses for every social occasion. Louisa refused to attend the Czar's birthday ball because she had only one dress in which she had already appeared several times. Her absence brought the Adamses' comparative poverty to public attention, and the Empress Mother openly warned her that if she refused again, she would not be admitted into any future court functions—a disastrous exclusion that might have dashed John Quincy's growing friendship with Czar Alexander. In disgust, Louisa wrote Abigail that "the manners, customs and expenses of the Country are insurmountable." John Quincy was used to pinching, she said, but every bill "makes ruin stare him in the face. *He* has borne it very patiently but *I* cannot. It has ever been a maxim with me knowing I brought him no fortune, to make my expenses as light as possible." In January 1810, therefore, seeing expenses mounting beyond her husband's income, Louisa asked to return home with Charles in the spring. But John Quincy refused; he could not maintain a household in Boston and one in St. Petersburg. "I cannot conceive what plan we can adopt here," said Louisa, "to avoid the difficulties into which we are plunged."

Money problems shadowed them. When the Adamses first reached St. Petersburg, they moved into small chambers where Louisa's room, she said, "was a stone hole entered by Stone passages and so full of rats that they would drag the braid from the table by my bedside." For a year, the Adamses huddled together in a "horrid hotel" on Nevsky Prospekt, where the walls were so thin that whenever Louisa and Catherine sang and played the piano, the neighbors applauded and shouted "*Brava, brava.*" Louisa and John Quincy moved almost every year, as landlords raised their rents or sold houses out from under them. They never found a comfortable residence they could afford.

In addition to the costs of a household, the number of servants who "must" be retained, John Quincy said with dismay, was three times more than elsewhere. The Adamses, who lived frugally, kept fourteen. "The expense is intolerable and the trouble ten times worse," said John Quincy, who made a list of the hangers-on and hungry mouths:

> Since we entered this house my monthly expense books amount to double what they were the first month. We have a maitre-d'hotel, or steward; a cook, who has under him two scullions — mujiks; a Swiss, or porter; two footmen; a mujik to make the fires; a coachman and postilion; and Nelson, the black man, to be my valet-de-chambre; Martha Godfrey, the maid we brought with us from America; a femme-de-chambre of Mrs. Adams, who is the wife of the steward; a house-maid, and a laundry-maid. The Swiss, the cook, and one of the footmen are married, and their wives all live in the house. The steward has two children, and the washer-woman a daughter, all of whom are kept in the house. I have baker's, milkman's, butcher's, greenman's, poulterer's, fish-monger's, grocer's bills to pay monthly, besides purchases of tea, coffee, sugar, wax and tallow candles. The firewood is, luckily, included as part of my rent.

The cook and the steward made a profit on every purchase, and then stole some of the purchases anyway. The steward also drank, or stole, the Adamses' wines. John Quincy complained that he had to pay "the most constant and minute attention to keep this pilfering within tolerable bounds," and for him perhaps the most costly loss of all was "the loss of time swallowed up in the business of such drudgery." To cut some of the deficits and pilfering, Adams fired the cook; he also dismissed the steward and chambermaid within two days of each other, perhaps for reasons of other liberties. In place of the cook, Adams hired a caterer to furnish the family dinners at twenty rubles a day. "You will readily conceive the embarrassment in which I find myself," John Quincy wrote his parents, "and of the desire which I feel to get out of a situation, irksome beyond expression."

Abigail, shocked by Louisa and John Quincy's letters, interceded, and wrote President Madison asking him to order her son home from Russia. The President and Secretary of State promptly obliged, and sent letters of recall to Adams to present when, and if, he wished to return; President Madison—with Senate approval—also sent John Quincy a commission as Associate Justice of the Supreme Court. But Adams refused both offers: Louisa was pregnant for the eleventh time, and his diplomacy was going well.

Not one member of the diplomatic corps ever questioned the Adamses' poverty, or snubbed them for it. Perhaps they found parsimony charming, as though the Adamses were the poor that the rich always had with them. Czar Alexander, wealthy as he was, seemed to understand this unusual economic situation. One cold May morning, Alexander and John Quincy met while walking on the Fontanka, near the bridge where the canal joined the Neva. As the Czar approached, he greeted Adams warmly, and despite the threat of snow in the air asked John Quincy if he intended to take a house in the country for the summer. Adams replied no; "I had for some time had such an intention, but had given it up."

"And why so?" Alexander asked, and seeing Adams hesitate, relieved him from embarrassment by saying, with humor and a smile, "Financial considerations, perhaps?"

"Well yes, Sire, in large part," Adams replied, trying to make the phrase sound lighter than it felt.

"Well enough," the Czar continued. "You are quite right. One must always balance income and outgo."

A maxim worthy of an Emperor, Adams thought to himself, but one few Emperors practice.

5

JOHN QUINCY ADAMS and Czar Alexander both walked for exercise.* They often met along the Neva or the Fontanka, and discovered a mutual bond. Both men disliked what Adams called the "dissipation" of St. Petersburg, and Alexander frequently avoided "gala days" whenever he could. Unfortunately, the mechanism was in place, and thousands of court employees, diplomats, and the powerful Russian Orthodox Church encouraged and depended on these rituals.

The minister and the Czar took their first walk together along the quay of the Neva on February 2, 1810. They spoke about the weather, and Adams discovered that the Czar walked for the benefit of his foot, which had not recovered from the injury in the droshky accident. John Quincy and Alexander met frequently after that. They walked the quay, by the Admiralty, to the Summer Gardens, or along Adams's favorite path to the foundry and back. Rarely did anything of substance pass between them: They debated when the Neva would break up, or discussed the merits of flannel to ward off the cold. But their walks and conversation brought a closeness and admiration for one another that helped John Quincy conduct foreign policy of benefit to the United States.

Louisa and Catherine, too, met Alexander out walking, or at court balls and dinners, which provided the men of the

---

* Adams walked not only for exercise, but also to measure distances in St. Petersburg. With repeated experiments, he precisely calibrated that, as a man 5'7" tall, he had a pace he said of "two feet, six inches and eighty-eight one-hundredths." At an ordinary walk he took 120 steps to the minute. Adams walked at what today would be called an aerobic pace, and covered a mile with 2,040 steps in seventeen minutes. He measured everything: He paced the distance from the Winter Palace to the Marble Palace (1,360 paces; eleven minutes and twenty seconds); from the St. Isaac Church to the Fontanka (thirty-four minutes); across the long bridge spanning the Neva (2,213 feet). By the time he left St. Petersburg, he had paced off almost all its buildings and distances.

Adams household—Gray, Everett, and Smith—occasion to tease and question the women. As John Quincy well understood, Louisa and her sister Catherine were both assets to his diplomacy. Russian women were large, heavy, with handsome features that faded early. Never in any of the Adamses' records did any diplomat mention seeing a beautiful Russian woman. Quite the contrary; all of them despaired of the dearth every time they went into society. Count St. Julien, for example, spent an evening at the French ambassador's in February 1811, looking "through his glass at the dancers and lamenting that the sex in Russia was not handsome." At Vienna, said the Count, a babble of chambermaids would be more attractive. John Quincy Adams agreed with St. Julien's observation. When Adams met Princess Woldemar Galitzin at a dinner party, he was unpleasantly shocked "by the length and thickness of her beard." This was not uncommon among Russian women: Adams had also observed at the Academy of Sciences a painting of a Russian noblewoman with a beard "equal to that of Plato." By contrast, Louisa and Catherine looked spectacular. Both were small, pretty, trim, and alluring women. Catherine bubbled with easy laughter, and Louisa practiced her fanged wit, both unusual characteristics for women appearing in public.

Alexander found each enticing, especially the unmarried Catherine, and acted foolish over them almost immediately. At a ball at the French ambassador's in May 1810, Czar Alexander, in a very unusual and public scene, danced the opening polonaise with Louisa, and when the music ended asked where her sister might be. "I don't know," Louisa replied, "but I will go immediately and seek her."

"No," said the Czar, "I will go and do that myself."

Alexander found Catherine in another hall, and led her out to dance. Catherine, not understanding that etiquette called for her to be silent and stiff, laughed and talked with the Czar as they danced, as she might have done with an American partner. Alexander was so charmed by this impudent woman that he delayed Caulaincourt's delicately prepared supper for twenty-five minutes by prolonging the polonaise, insisting that the orchestra continue playing so he could hold this lovely and vivacious lady in his arms a little longer. Catherine had never been presented at Court—that is, she had never been formally introduced to Alexander or the Czarina—and the extraordinary distinction the Czar paid her, said the watchful Louisa, "produced a Buzz of astonishment." Within a week, as part of a Court invitation, Alexander ordered that since Louisa Adams was (at the time) the only lady of the diplomatic corps in St. Petersburg, Catherine should also be invited to the Hermitage and all royal functions. This startled St. Petersburg society, and Louisa herself called the invitation "one of the greatest honors ever conferred upon a foreign young Lady"—as well as, of course, upon a minister of the second rank.

As a single woman, however, Catherine needed protecting, and Louisa found herself acting both as a sister and a chaperone. The two women had started a regular walking regime along the broad boulevard of Nevsky Prospekt, and Alexander soon discovered them there, and often stopped and spoke politely in French to Louisa and in English to Catherine, charming them equally. After several months of walks and brief meetings with Alexander, Louisa, usually an excellent diplomat, made a small and almost costly error—the kind diplomats at St. Petersburg dreaded. It was possible, of course, considering her role and concern, that Louisa made it deliberately.

Walking with Catherine along the Neva one December day, Louisa suddenly felt fatigued. Although she saw Alexander gaining on them with long, eager strides, and believing that the Czar would not notice the gesture, Louisa beckoned to her servants to drive up with her carriage. She and Catherine immediately climbed in and rode off, but as they turned toward Nevsky Prospekt they passed the embarrassed Alexander, who averted his head and looked out across the river, and took no notice of them. Louisa's act was not entirely innocent: "The great distinction shown to my sister at the Invitation to the Hermitage," she admitted, "had occasioned so much talk I thought it was injudicious to encourage it." Unwisely, Louisa also stopped their promenades for the winter.

Czar Alexander behaved like a chastised adolescent. Three weeks later, when Louisa and Catherine, riding in a carriage, passed the Emperor walking along Nevsky, he turned his head again and would not look at them. "I could not help laughing," said Louisa, "but was sorry when I found that he had taken offence." Louisa heard gossip at the Court balls about Alexander's hurt pride. She worried that it might reflect upon John Quincy and his carefully prepared diplomatic work. During the warm days of spring, therefore, Louisa and Catherine resumed walking along Nevsky Prospekt, this time carefully looking for the Czar, and sometimes venturing down to Palace Square and the Neva embankment. One day, Alexander spotted them along the Fontanka, and immediately stopped and spoke, a little coldly at first, to Catherine, and asked why they had discontinued their walking. Without waiting for an answer, he turned to Louisa and lectured her. Walking, he said, was good for her health, and he expected them – here looking at Catherine – to meet him every day when the weather was fine. "This was a real Imperial command, in its tone and manner," said Louisa. As they parted, Alexander turned again to her, repeated his instructions, bowed, and touching his hand to his hat, walked on.

At dinner that evening, "the usual question and sour looks greeted us from the young gentlemen," said Louisa, and Catherine burst out, "Yes! we met him and we've been ordered to walk every day to meet the Emperor." The young men now "were all in a blaze. . . . The Minister looked very grave but said nothing." The others, however, disapproved of Catherine's walking outside and meeting and speaking to the Czar in the streets, and ordered that she not do it. Louisa was of another mind and overruled them, continuing her walking regime with Catherine. Sometimes they brought Charles, "who always had a kind greeting from his Majesty and a shake of the hand, but the Emperor complained that he could not make him sociable."

With her smile and laughter, Catherine Johnson had broken into the most regulated and etiquette-conscious court in all Europe. Indeed, the Czar gave the Adamses informal privileges and recognition accorded only to the higher-ranking French ambassador; not only did he show special favor to Catherine, but he also allowed them all to use the private entrance at the Hermitage, and attend all court functions. Catherine, for her part, played the role coolly; she gave her hand and smile to Alexander, but her heart to William Steuben Smith, John Quincy's private secretary. Catherine and William would marry in 1813, in St. Petersburg, with the Czar's blessing. Louisa, who had wished to leave Catherine home, now concluded: "I thank my lucky stars that my Sister is with me as things have turned out." And, she added with amusing understatement, "A young lady in the family is quite an acquisition."

The political results of these social encounters is difficult to measure. In October 1809, John Quincy Adams had counted fifty-two American ships seized by the Danes and held in their ports; the ships had a total value of more than five million dollars. Adams pressed Rumyantsev from their first meeting to ask Czar Alexander to use his influence with Denmark for the release of the captured ships. John Quincy could have avoided this issue; Danish-American affairs lay outside his mission. He could not, without permission of his government, make formal application to the Count and the Czar. Instead, he used his friendship with them, and approached them informally. He also met with Baron de Blonde, the Danish minister, at balls and dinners and even on the French ambassador's ice hills at a sledding party, to press the issue. Alexander moved with surprising speed, and in part due to his perceived value of good relations with the United States, and his friendship with the Adamses, pressed the American case. In 1810, the ships were released, occasioning a formal letter of thanks from President Madison to the Czar, and John Quincy Adams had the satisfaction of knowing that hours of socializing had been worth millions of dollars to his maritime countrymen.

Adams also pressed the issue of American ships detained in Russian ports; during the winter of 1810–11, twenty-three ships were held at Archangel, Kronstadt, Riga, and other seaports. His direct contact with Alexander, and the Czar's interest in freeing himself from Napoleon's Continental System, won the release of these ships, too. By the end of 1811, American merchant ships were sailing freely into and out of Russian ports, much to Napoleon's growing anger.

In the eyes of the French, there was no doubt about the

value of the friendship between the Adamses and Alexander and Rumyantsev. Defeated, Caulaincourt himself confided to John Quincy Adams: "It seems you are great favorites here. You have found powerful protection." Not a little of his importance Adams owed to his wife and sister-in-law.

6

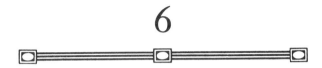

WITHIN TWO WINTERS, even as the Adamses' lives assumed a mosaic of ceremonies, walks, visits, and festivals, the shadow of war drew near. Napoleon was sending arms and men to Danzig and Warsaw, and Alexander was countering with two hundred thousand Russian soldiers on the frontier from Riga to Kiev. The movement of troops, the rumors of war, cast a new anxiety over St. Petersburg. These were bittersweet days, filled with the awesome prospect of death and the promise of birth. Louisa started 1811 burdened with her eleventh pregnancy.

On June 26, she and John Quincy spent an unusually quiet and relaxed afternoon. About four, they boarded a small boat on the quay opposite the Winter Palace, and were rowed up the Neva by muscular boatmen in plumed hats, to the island of Crestoffsky, where they landed and took tea in a shady spot in the open air. The day was filled with the hues of summer, the blues and greens and yellows and shades of white that reminded them of those few precious days of their honeymoon, when their lives together were briefly without care. Louisa, in her seventh month, stretched on the grass and admired her belly. Only four weeks earlier, she had been filled with fear over the impending birth. On May 23, Louisa had received a letter telling her that her "love," her closest sister, Nancy, had died in childbirth, and the infant with her. Nancy's death terrified Louisa: was it a sign, a warning? For two days, the fear of death during childbirth tormented Louisa, and only heavy doses of opium "freely resorted to by my physician" let her sleep. Now lying in the grass, she felt the day was too beautiful, the moment too keen, to allow such thoughts to constrict her senses. Before ten, she and John Quincy walked to the small boat, climbing aboard and floating down the river with the current. The boatmen lifted their oars as they drifted, and turning to face one another across the width of the boat, softly sang Russian songs while two of them played a pipe and a tambourine. Drifting with the music, the Adamses momentarily let the cares and dangers entering their lives ripple by them, and they landed tired and peacefully at the quay near the Admiralty at midnight, just as the sun was setting.

The Adamses were spending the summer at a rented house on Apothecaries' Island in the Nevka River, one of the small tributaries flowing into the Bay of Kronstadt. The location was idyllic, near the Botanic Garden with its large public walks, and they looked out upon the river and, on the other side, the Imperial Summer Palace. Louisa walked in the garden, listened to the Czar's military bands give dinner concerts across the water, or watched the boats from the Adamses' pier. She had a chair placed on the river bank where she sat with Charles and caught fish. She and Charles loved fishing: "It is an indolent sort of amusement that just suits me for I do not think" of the approaching childbirth. "When I look forward," she said, "I tremble."

On August 11, 1811, Louisa gave birth at seven in the evening to a baby girl, "the first I was ever blessed with. . . . God was very merciful to me for I had been in great danger ever since morning." John Quincy, too, was joyful, and wrote his mother: "I think this will convince you that 'the Climate of St. Petersburg is *not* too cold to produce an American.'" A daughter made the perfect blessing for their summer, one of the most serene and quiet of their lives; as John Quincy wished, they christened her Louisa Catherine Adams 2d.

But as one life began, others ended. The Adamses received

letters telling them of the death of Louisa's mother, of her brother-in-law Andrew Buchanan (Carolina's husband), and of Uncle and Aunt Cranch within twenty-four hours of each other. They learned also of the hopeless illness of Nabby Adams, John Quincy's beloved sister.* "God help us," Louisa cried. "My Poor Mother! After ten years of poverty dependence and severe suffering which at this great distance it was so utterly out of my power to mitigate or assuage. How different will home appear should we live to return. God's will be done!" John Quincy tried to place these deaths in his religious beliefs. The primary good, he wrote, other than knowing that the deceased were all in a better world, was to learn by meditating upon death "to be better prepared for our own."

So, as the leaves turned and the river grew stormy, and with the days of cold and darkness again at hand, the Adamses sought the comforts of St. Petersburg. They had been married fourteen years. John Quincy thought their union had been not "without its trials, nor invariably without dissensions between us," and noted that he and Louisa differed in tastes, opinions of economy, and matters of education of their children. But while they both had "quick and irascible" tempers, their marriage was comfortable, settled. Louisa was proving, he said, "a faithful and affectionate wife, and a careful, tender, indulgent and watchful mother to our children, all of whom she nursed herself." Adams considered his lot in marriage "highly favored."

And Louisa seemed equally contented as she tended her baby daughter. "O she grows lovely," Louisa rejoiced in a letter. "Such a pair of Eyes!! I fear I love her too well." When Louisa walked her daughter along Nevsky Prospekt or the wide

---

* In the spring of 1813, Nabby Adams Smith, living in Lebanon Valley, New York, set out for Quincy. Emaciated, her breasts ulcerating from cancer, she ordered a bed constructed in her carriage and rode in deep and fatal pain over three hundred miles of dirt roads to her parents' home, to die. They gave her opium whenever she wanted it, which was often, and three weeks after she arrived, on the last Sunday of August, Nabby passed to a better world. Neither her husband nor her children were with her. Abigail wrote John Quincy of the death of his favorite sibling: "My only source of satisfaction, and it is a never-failing one, is my firm persuasion that everything — and our oversights and mistakes among the rest — are part of the great plan."

Neva embankment, the Russian *babushkas* stopped them and told Louisa how beautiful, too beautiful, the baby girl with the huge black Adams eyes was. "Born for Heaven" — an angel —they told her.

7

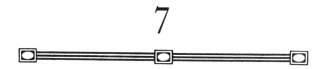

THE THREAT OF WAR made the splendor of St. Petersburg fade quickly. By the end of February 1812, eight regiments of Russian soldiers had paraded across Palace Square to the front, and by mid-March three regiments were leaving every week. Alexander reviewed each of them, and the sight caused him anguish. On a walk along the Neva on March 19, Alexander poured out his heart to John Quincy Adams. Another regiment had marched from the capital that morning, and yet another would go on Saturday.

"And so it is after all," said Alexander with sadness in his voice, "that war is coming which I have done so much to avoid — everything. I have done everything to prevent this struggle but thus it ends."

John Quincy tried to console him. "But are all hopes vanished of still preserving the peace?"

"At all events," Alexander said, "we shall not begin the war; my will is yet to prevent it; but we expect to be attacked."

Adams replied that if the Czar was determined not to commence, perhaps the issue would pass without war.

"I wish it may," Alexander said. "Everything points to war, however. *He* keeps on advancing. *He* began by taking Swedish Pomerania — now he has just occupied Prussia. He can't advance much further without attacking us."

As Spring unfolded, as the sun again warmed the land and

the people of Russia, there arrived with this eternal gift of life the promise of death. To be sure, Butter Week, that prelude to Lent when the Russian Orthodox Church allowed its faithful to eat anything except meat, still thrived with festivity, with processions of nobility in carriages and the common people upon the ice hills. Only a few dances continued, but the masquerades — one at eleven, another at two, and a third at nine the same evening — still ended precisely at midnight when the full rigor of Russian Lent commenced. But this year when Lent ended, on a brilliant Easter morning, at the moment of celebration of the greatest holiday on the Russian calendar, Adams watched "a very splendid parade" of 40,000 fresh, young Russian soldiers, who marched "immediately" to the frontier of Poland. For them in their season, the Lenten sacrifice would have a new meaning.

At no time was the contrast between the Russian Czar and nobility, and the people of Russia, clearer than at Lent, and no Lent underscored this contrast better than that in the Spring of 1812, as the Russian people sent their sons off to die for their Czar and homeland. The nobility and the common people began Easter Week at midnight in their churches celebrating the Resurrection, and ended it massed together in the two major squares of their empire. For this week, on one side of the square at St. Isaac's Church, the commoners erected booths in which they put rope-dancers, Chinese Shadows, puppet shows, a small zoo, tumblers. On the other side of the church, and filling the square, the people erected swings and whirligig chairs, and men, women and children screamed and yelled as they swirled and spun. Beyond Peter the Great's statue, other Russians skidded down new sliding hills. In place of ice and snow, they erected planks, and instead of sleds on runners they rode sleds with little wheels or rollers held in place by channels or tracks that guided them down the plank slopes. With twenty or thirty swings and whirligigs in St. Isaac's Square, and the sliding hills in Palace Square, these magnificent spaces filled with whirling, bouncing, spinning, sliding, screaming mobs of Russian people.

"Of these Sports," Adams said, "only the lowest classes of the People partake." Every afternoon, those of "better condition" rode for two or three hours in a procession of carriages, which they owned or hired. Three rows of these carriages rolled sedately around the periphery of St. Isaac's and Palace Squares. They formed, outside the whirligigs and swings and sliding hills and booths of puppets and captive animals, a slow-moving boundary of the elegant and the privileged, perhaps 1,000 carriages in all, most of them pulled by four horses. The privileged exhibited themselves, their dresses and uniforms, their carriages and liveries and horses in spectacle to one another, and the muzhiks.

8

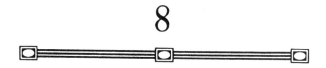

BY THE END of Easter Week, 1812, the music and laughter of St. Petersburg fell silent. Fifteen of the best Russian regiments had left the capital for the frontier. Alexander, John Quincy estimated, now had more than six hundred thousand of his young men under arms, from the Baltic to the Black Sea, matched man for man by an equal number of French, Prussians, Poles, and Germans facing them. These were, John Quincy wrote his father, "the Millions destined to fatten the Corn fields [of Europe] with their blood."

In St. Petersburg, everyone awaited the French attack, and the ensuing shock of two immense powers colliding. The diplomats hurriedly packed and left; only the ministers from Sardinia and Denmark remained. Count St. Julien, mistakenly believing that Russia was still courting Austria, lingered, and the French ambassador had to confide in him that it was over, finished, and give him "a touch of the spur" to depart. On June 28, when the secretary of the French embassy called upon the Adamses to take his leave, he told them that a courier had arrived last night after riding hard from Wilna in forty-seven hours with the news that the French troops had crossed the Niemen River at Kovno, and that the Russian troops were retreating. Russia and France were at war.

While French and Russian men died on the corn fields of Europe, the Adamses' young daughter, not yet a year old, became sick. What caused the illness is uncertain; the little girl had grown six teeth, and was fat and dimpled, but when five more teeth suddenly appeared after weaning, the physicians advised Louisa to take her back to her breast. Her daughter suffered "a violent Dysentery." For eight weeks, with a strange physician and a nurse who did not speak French or English, Louisa watched her beloved daughter slowly waste and die. She was helpless, frantic. Following the doctor's orders, Louisa and Catherine took the child into the country for a change of air, but they returned speedily in six days, with the baby "in Convulsions." John Quincy said that his daughter's sufferings were "so severe that the sight of them would have wrung with compassion a heart of marble." Louisa attended her daughter day and night, and tried everything to save her. Catherine remained at the baby's cradle with Louisa. But on September 15, 1812, Louisa Adams ended her Russian diary — there were no further entries — with one sad sentence: "My Child gone to Heaven." Part of her had died as well.

For more than a year, Louisa mourned her lost daughter, the little angel born for heaven who was, said John Quincy, "the darling of her Heart." Louisa turned to her religion. She taught Charles his prayers and commandments, and John Quincy read prayers to her. But no matter what she did, the pain did not diminish. "I read. I work, I endeavor to occupy myself usefully but it is all in vain. My heart is almost broken and my temper which was never good suffers in proportion to my grief." Louisa blamed herself for weaning the child too soon, which might have caused her illness. "My babies [sic] image flits forever before my eyes and seems to reproach me with her Death. . . . My heart is buried in my Louisa's grave and my greatest longing is to be laid beside her."

John Quincy Adams allowed no time for mourning. He

forced Louisa to attend the dinners and court circles that continued despite the war, and when she sought "affection and gentleness," she said, she was rejected with "harshness or contempt." Louisa buried her own sorrow in reading; she listed fifty-three books during the winter of 1812–13, many on religion and the promise of a better life to come. She had strong and recurring dreams of trying to please a demanding father, of being in "a deep vault," of stumbling over a murdered body, of thunder and lightning flashes and streams of fire stretched across the sky. Louisa read for the first time Dr. Benjamin Rush's book *Treatise on Diseases of the Mind*, which John Quincy gave her, and it became her reference book. She read it through at least twice in her lifetime, seeking answers for her own troubled psyche. "I confess it produced a very powerful effect upon my feelings and occasioned sensations of a very painful kind," she said. Louisa sensed "a great change in my character" since her daughter's death, "and I often involuntarily question myself as to the perfect sanity of my mind." She struggled "in vain" against these feelings.

John Quincy had no time for his burdensome wife. Paralleling his diplomatic duties were his duties, as he saw them, to the upbringing of his sons. As a father, Adams felt obligated to guide the education and morals of his children. In August 1809, Adams had begun a system of instruction by letter for his sons, especially George, whom he invested with his belief and the burden of being the leading Adams of the next generation. This correspondence continued into the 1820s, and formed a major thread through the Adams family — a thread that documents what kinds of parents Louisa and John Quincy Adams were, and what tragedy resulted.

John Quincy sought to manage his sons' lives with harsh, scolding letters that demanded far more than boys of eight or ten could fulfill. His "Letters to My Children," started on board the *Horace*, revealed not only his advice to his sons, but also what Adams regarded as his own lifetime obligations: "You should each of you," he wrote them, "consider yourself as placed here *to act a part* — That is to have some single great end or object to accomplish, towards which all the views and the labours of your existence should steadily be directed." He pursued this theme in his letter to George telling him of the death of baby Louisa, and his directions for George's "steady and continual improvement in piety and virtue." He went on for four pages, discussing George's deficiencies in his education, his need to be more rigorous. He wanted George, then eleven, to study Greek and Latin "until you can write them correctly and read Homer, Demosthenes, and Thucydides, Lucretius, Horace, Livy, Tacitus and *all* Cicero with *almost* as much ease and readiness as if they were written in English." And he hoped that George would read them not for the "vain glory" of saying he had done so, but for their wisdom. "Learning is but the *food* of the mind. Reading, says Lord Bacon, makes a *full* man." John Quincy directed his son to prepare himself to be "most beneficial to your country and most *useful to mankind.*"

John Quincy also undertook, in a series of letters addressed to George (but intended as well for John), to direct his son's study of the Bible. Reading this book, Adams said, made men "good, wise, and happy," and the earlier his children started, to continue throughout their lives, the greater their chances of proving themselves "useful citizens to their country, respectable members of society, and a real blessing to their parents." John Quincy methodically read the Bible through every year, usually during the first hours before sunrise. He wished his sons to follow this rigorous example.

These demands tumbled in upon the young and fragile George. The list seemed without end. When George wrote in September 1810, in a letter obviously dictated to cousin Susanna Adams, John Quincy in disgust responded with a prototypical, staccato series of directions. The next time you write to me, he told George, do so in your own hand. Tell me what books you are reading, and what you have learned from them. Tell me that you have been a good Latin scholar, "and that you will before long be a good Greek one." Improve your handwriting, your English and French grammar; treat classmates kindly and be respectful and obedient to your elders; make only good boys your friends, and learn faster than they do; and remember above all to worship God, piety, and virtue. The strange, demanding voice of the letter, coming from such a distance and from a father so long absent, may have seemed like the voice of God to a nine-year-old boy. Who could ever fulfill the demands of such a deity?

Even at this age, George's retreat from this omnipotent parent was evident. He studied quietly with the Cranches until 1811, when they both died suddenly, and was then shuffled to school in Quincy taught by a Mr. Whitney. George found studying difficult, and was not cast in his father's image: Unlike JQA at nine, George much preferred chasing after birds' nests and trifles to reading and ciphering. He eased the inner pains of separation from his family, and the realities of his father's unmeetable standards, by drowning himself in fiction – what his father considered the trash novels of the day. When Whitney closed his school, George was sent to Atkinson, New Hampshire, to live with Aunt Elizabeth Smith Peabody, Abigail's sister and the wife of the Rev. Stephen Peabody. George thought Elizabeth Peabody a kind and gentle woman, more patient with those in her care than Aunt Cranch. "They were both examples of a race of women," George said in 1826, "formed by the Revolution and taught by its trials to acquire and exert great qualities." George, now twelve, began searching and reaching, but not always in directions his father approved. He loved poetry, and he wrote five plays. He read Virgil and Cicero, his father's favorite, and when Grandmama Adams gave him four broken little volumes of Shakespeare's plays, he read then "with utter astonishment" at their strength and beauty. In Hingham, his fourth school since 1809, George kept a journal, and continued to "scribble verses." He also fell in love for the first time, but the feeling of passion stirring within him conflicted with his father's instructions to subdue his feelings. The Bible, John Quincy told George, gave every human being "the *power* of controlling his passions," a power that, if neglected or misused, he would "be answerable for."

At first George had reacted to his father's demands by fleeing. Before his tenth birthday, he had often run away from school. After that, until his death, with the flood of instruction and demands not ceasing, George escaped into the distant archipelagoes of his mind. Poetry, writing, the theater, music, art all attracted him, as they did his mother. He soon called Grand-father Adams's library his "home," and he grew into the personi-fication of his grandfather's dream. John Adams had written Abigail from Paris in 1780, during the Revolution: "I must study Politicks and War that my sons may have liberty to study Mathematicks and Philosophy. My sons ought to study Mathe-maticks and Philosophy, Geography and natural History, Naval Architecture, navigation, Commerce and Agriculture, in order to give their Children a right to study Painting, Poetry, Musick, Architecture, Statuary, Tapestry and Porcelaine." George might have become a writer, poet, or actor. But his father demanded much more of his son than fulfilling the gentle wish of his grand-father. Trapped between a dream and a nightmare, separated while at Atkinson from every member of his family, George had isolated himself in reading and writing, and discovered his rich fantasies. One day he found in the township a large meadow, in the middle of which was an "island" of seven or eight acres. George played there often. When the meadow flooded, the island remained above the water, and there George retreated, pretend-ing that he was afloat, free, unburdened. And so he was, and so he would always be, unanchored, a floating island himself drifting in the flood of his father's relentless expectations.

While John Quincy was strict and unrelenting with George, he was easier with Charles. During his first four years in Russia, John Quincy was Charles's only instructor; he was persistent and cajoling, Charles stubborn and crafty. Adams had difficulty controlling his temper, especially when Charles appeared de-liberately "perverse" by "reading or pronouncing words wrong when he knows perfectly well the right." But Charles read the Bible in French and English every day, sometimes for several hours. He also learned Russian and German, and, at five, started arithmetic. If he was deficient, it was in English, which he was embarrassed to speak. Charles was the beloved son. When her daughter died, Louisa said that Charles "seemed to read my heart," and showed his mother a tenderness and affection beyond his age. While his brothers hardly knew their father or mother at all, Charles grew up under their care and attention. His only absence from them came during the French invasion, when

Charles attended Mr. Fishwick's school in St. Petersburg, to gain regularity and order, and find playmates.

Freed from the private instruction of his son, Adams turned to a major, public diplomatic task. French troops had entered Moscow, one of the most magnificent and populous cities of Europe, and were burning it to the ground. In September 1812, the war itself blazed in the Russian countryside only three days' horseback ride from St. Petersburg. With the French invasion of Russia, the War of 1812 between Great Britain and the United States had begun in America. The causes were complex: the impressment of seamen, neutral shipping rights, American agrarian expansion eager for Canadian and Floridan lands. The irony of this war was the fact that the first two reasons for fighting it – impressment and neutrality – had already been resolved, but a week before the final British concessions arrived, Congress had voted to take up arms. Slow communications aided the start and delayed the conclusion of this war. Equally bizarre, negotiations for peace in North America began almost as soon as the war started.

Here, once again, Adams's friendship with Alexander aided United States foreign policy: The Czar, seeking to balance France against England, sounded out Adams on the Russian's mediating an end to war in America. The United States was eager for peace. Its armies had been beaten in Canada and in Florida, and the British Army would soon march through Baltimore and Washington, burning the Capitol and the President's House and sending the United States government fleeing. When word of the Czar's offer reached President Madison, he quickly sent out two special envoys to serve with Adams as a negotiating team: Albert Gallatin, Secretary of the Treasury, and Sen. James A. Bayard of Delaware. But the British, so successful on land (yet, strangely, so inept at sea), rejected the Czar's offer, and Bayard and Gallatin lingered six frustrating months in St. Petersburg before heading for home by way of London, where, with a stroke of luck, they found the British agreeable to direct negotiations. Alexander's overture of mediation had opened the dialogue. After some haggling, everyone agreed on a compromise location: Ghent, in Dutch Flanders (Belgium).

In Russia, meanwhile, by the end of 1812, Alexander was reversing his defeat. Adams joyfully read newspaper accounts reporting that Napoleon, two thousand miles from his supplies, had lost half his men to a tenacious Russian army, and was retreating back into Europe toward Paris "in disguise." Of his immense Grand Army, John Quincy wrote, "nine tenths at least are prisoners of war, or food for worms. They have been surrendering by the tens of thousands at a time," and Alexander, now at the front, had taken 150,000 prisoners. The Russian people spoke thankfully of the two Russian generals who had defeated Napoleon: General Frost and General Famine.

"From Moscow to Prussia," Adams wrote his mother, "eight hundred miles of road have been strewed with his Artillery, Baggage, Waggons, Ammunition, Chests, dead and dying men, whom he has been forced to abandon to their fate." They were "pursued all the time by three large armies of a most embittered and exasperated Enemy and by an almost numberless militia of peasants stung by the destruction of their harvests and Cottages which he had carried before him, and spurr'd to Revenge at once their selves, their Country and their Religion."

Louisa and John Quincy attended celebrations at the Kazan Church for the delivery of Moscow and then for the defeat of the French troops retreating across eastern Europe. The church filled with the spoils of war: field marshals' truncheons, ten French Imperial Eagles, forty standards, the keys to Warsaw, Lübeck, Dresden, Hamburg, suspended by ribbons. A dinner for sixty at Count Rumyantsev's was twice interrupted with messages of victories from the front and champagne toasts to the Czar; the Count became so overwrought that he embraced the muzhik footman who brought the second note, and made him drink a glass of wine, and kissed him on both cheeks. With the celebrations and champagne came tales of heroism in death, and funerals. The Adamses attended the "elegant, but plain" funeral of a Russian general, whose legs had been crushed by a cannon ball, and who asked only for his flint and steel and some cigars, which he calmly smoked one by one as he lay dying on the battlefield. The solemnities for Field Marshal Prince Koutouzof Smolensky surpassed anything Louisa or John Quincy had ever seen. Peasants pulled the carriage with his coffin through St. Petersburg, followed by five thousand infantry and one thousand cavalry in slow step, to the Kazan Church, where the coffin was placed on a twelve-foot-high catafalque covered by a crimson canopy under the cathedral's dome.

Count Rumyantsev also suffered a burial of sorts. In 1812, after the French had crossed the Niemen, Rumyantsev still counseled Alexander to favor accommodation. But the Czar refused to make peace with the Grand Army on Russian soil, and he excluded Rumyantsev from his entourage. When Alexander left for the front in December 1812, he took Count Karl Robert Nesselrode with him for any diplomatic negotiations. Rumyantsev remained in St. Petersburg, the guardian of archives, humiliated. In February 1813, he confided to John Quincy Adams: "I have nothing to do." A year later, Alexander advised the diplomatic corps that "due to the ill health of the Chancellor," they should refer all their work to the chief clerk. Rumyantsev was as good as dead.

Adams himself would see Alexander again only once. The ruler John Quincy had befriended for five years, who created the first signal leading to negotiations in Ghent, would pass from Adams's life almost without notice. In Ghent, on a hot June day in 1814, Adams would stand amid a cheering, excited crowd as the victorious Alexander rode by on horseback with fifteen officers "distinguished from them only by the greater simplicity of his dress — a plain green uniform, without any decoration, and even with facings. Very few in the crowd knew him as he passed." Alexander stopped for ten minutes in one of the town squares and reviewed a Prussian regiment, and then proceeded toward Antwerp. He never saw Adams, and John Quincy never saw him again.

Alexander was at the pinnacle of his life, "the Titus of his Age," Adams called him, "the Delight of Human Kind." That year, as Europe's monarch, Alexander would play the dominant role at the Congress of Vienna. But his flaws, his contradictions would betray him. With a growing mystical piety, he would become the driving force behind the Holy Alliance, a political confection to restore peace in Europe, but more the product of

Alexander's religious exaltations than a union of nations. Later, darkened by melancholy and speaking only to his own deity, Alexander would become almost a monk. The most powerful emperor in Russia's history, and in Europe of that day, Alexander had always dreamed of escape, of his desire to flee to America or to the banks of the Rhine or to a farm in Switzerland. Instead, he would isolate himself from contact with all men in mystical communication with a god of his imagining. In November 1825, Alexander would die suddenly in Taganrog, the Crimea, and in his death the Russian people would create another enigma, the legend that the unhappy Alexander had cast off his crown and continued to live as a monk, Feodor Kuzmich, who wandered shrouded in mystery until he died in Siberia in 1864.

Alexander's life cannot be concluded without one further detail. On coronation day, December 14, 1825, when Nicholas I prepared to ascend to the throne to replace Alexander, officers of the Imperial Guards led out three thousand troops opposed to taking the oath of allegiance to this new Czar. These dissidents planned to seize control of the Russian state, and were soon joined by the ragtag muzhiks of St. Petersburg, who filled St. Isaac's Square. Nicholas and troops loyal to him lined up in Palace Square, facing the dissidents, who shouted epithets in defiance of this Czar. Three times Nicholas patiently sent emissaries across the vast squares, to ask the protesters to leave. Three times his emissaries were shot, their frightened horses galloping riderless back to the Czar. Exasperated, worried that the coming darkness would shield marauding soldiers and peasants, Nicholas finally ordered a charge. His Cossacks drew their swords and, slowly at first, gaining speed across Palace Square, their steel flashing in the fading daylight, they crashed their horses into the screaming mob, and sliced and skewered and pursued them even onto the ice of the Neva, which turned red with blood.

Other skirmishes in the south of the empire and five hangings ended the first public demonstration against a Russian Czar, but not the last. For the Decembrists' protest and the repressions that followed inspired dissenters for several decades, and again and again, in these massive squares at the heart of Russia, where the common people had spun on swings and whirligigs, where soldiers had marched before their Czar to war, where the nobility had paraded in unspeakable opulence, the people of Russia gathered in protest, until 1917, when they entered the Winter Palace for good.

9

I N THE WINTER OF 1813–14, John Quincy Adams searched the heavens, checking his knowledge of the stars and planets, and one clear morning saw a cluster that he couldn't recognize. It was Orion. "That I should have lived fifty years without knowing him," Adams castigated himself, "shows too clearly what sort of an observer I have been." He now scanned the heavens every morning, reviewing each star and watching his newly discovered constellation rise above the roof of the house across the street. In 1814, appointed to join Gallatin and Bayard in the negotiations with the British at Ghent, Adams sensed that his moment was approaching. His sign was in the heavens. Napoleon had abdicated his throne, and the war in Europe had ended with the victorious Allies, led by Alexander, entering Paris on March 31. "With this prospect of a general peace in Europe," Adams said, "I commenced my journey to contribute, if possible, to the restoration of peace to my own country."

The news from home, however, was bad. The American army had fewer than twenty-four regiments, and the British regulars pushed them around at will. By the second year of war, the Americans had been beaten and cleared from Canada. At sea, the United States had put out its three "superfrigates," the *Constitution*, the *United States*, and the *President*, which were larger and more heavily armed than their British counterparts, and battles raged along the Atlantic coast and as far away as

West Africa, with the British Navy taking serious losses. But with the end of war in Europe, Britain was able to carry the war to the United States, concentrate her navy off the American coast, and force peace on her own terms. The British planned to invade the United States at Niagara, Lake Champlain, Chesapeake Bay, and New Orleans. And as John Quincy said goodbye to Louisa and Charles on April 28, 1814, at the posthouse at Strelna where they dined together before his departure, the land and sea forces of this plan were moving toward final confrontation.

Adams spent fifty-four days on the road in a carriage he specially outfitted himself. He had installed a new reclining couch for sleeping, a small lamp (with extra wicks) for reading, and purchased provisions that included a tin kettle, a knife, forks, a corkscrew, and five bottles of wine. John Quincy had also taken a bath for good health, and purchased two traveling pistols, for protection. Thinking he would return in a year, he left Louisa only about eight hundred dollars for her expenses, and carried a thousand dollars himself, most of it in Dutch ducats. Leaving his wife and son, Adams set out on a mission he regarded as one of major import: "On the providence of God alone is my reliance. . . . The welfare of my family and country, with the interests of humanity, are staked upon the event. To Heaven alone it must be committed."

John Quincy arrived in Ghent on June 24. He and Jonathan Russell, the youngest delegate and first American ambassador to Sweden, joined Bayard, Gallatin, and the irreverent Henry Clay, Speaker of the House of Representatives, who preferred being in Kentucky smoking cigars, drinking bourbon and branch water, and playing poker. The five waited, in bachelor quarters at a hotel on the Rue des Champs, almost six weeks through the heat of summer for the British to arrive. The Americans found themselves killing time. Adams, whose constitution drove him to rise early and write by candlelight, kept himself busy. His colleagues, meanwhile, hung about the coffeehouses, played billiards, smoked, and drank.

When the British Commissioners finally did appear for their first meeting on August 8, they were a cut below the Americans in diplomatic ability. The British first string remained in London, preparing for the opening of the peace conference in Vienna that would settle the European situation. With Napoleon defeated on the Continent, and regiments of crack troops sailing for the United States, the British had time on their side; negotiations at Vienna were the focus, those at Ghent the periphery. From the beginning, the British at Ghent took a hard line: They insisted on an Indian buffer territory north of the Ohio River, abandonment of U.S. rights to fisheries off Newfoundland and Labrador, and revision of the boundary line between Canada and the United States that would give British Canada access to the upper Mississippi. They completely ignored the reasons for the war: impressment of seamen, blockades, freedom of the sea for neutral ships. For four months, however, the Americans cautiously but firmly held their ground, and the British slowly shifted theirs. Negotiations took the form of memorandums exchanged between the two sides, which caused long delays while the British sent everything back to London for consideration.

With little to do between afternoon meetings and the slow exchange of communiqués, the Americans turned to what Adams considered a frivolous social life. Clay welcomed poker players to his room, which was unfortunately near Adams's, and more than one morning as John Quincy was rising to read his Bible he heard Clay's company ending its card party. Adams, however, did bend a little, and attended the receptions, dinners, concerts, and plays with the other commissioners. He even took up smoking his favorite "Corbisier Segars" despite an effort to stop in 1812, at age forty-five, after reading a paper by his old friend Dr. Benjamin Waterhouse of Harvard on the injurious effects of tobacco.

The British negotiations at Ghent seemed to follow the fortunes of their expeditionary forces in America. In July and August, British navy and army units were defeated at Niagara and Plattsburg, New York; negotiations started at Ghent. But in September, word reached London that the British Army had taken Washington, D.C., after meeting only feeble resistance, had sent President Madison and his administration scurrying into the Virginia countryside, and had burned the President's

House and the Capitol building.* Negotiations at Ghent dragged through the fall, while the fourth British expeditionary force sailed from Jamaica to New Orleans, where it would be engaged in December. With the capture and burning of the American capital, the war looked good to the British. To make matters worse, the legislature of Massachusetts summoned a New England Convention at Hartford, Connecticut, to draft a new Constitution and discuss the possibility of secession. Only events at New Orleans and Ghent dramatically altered its impact.

Despite the bad news from home, the American commissioners at Ghent stood firm during the autumn negotiations. And despite their different priorities — Adams for American fishing rights, Clay equally stubborn over the right of navigation on the Mississippi — and the slow response of the British, a Treaty of Peace was reached in December 1814, just as the final battle of the War of 1812 was taking shape. The British withdrew their claims to territory, and the Americans dropped their demands for seamen's rights. The Treaty of Ghent stated simply that the two nations, at war, wished to be at peace. It did keep open access to the American West, making expansion to the Pacific Ocean possible. On Christmas Eve, the envoys met at Chartreux, where the British had been residing, and signed the treaty of peace and friendship. Louisa, when she read a report in St. Petersburg, was not pleased: "I think it is indeed pointed at the Eastern States and that our good Friends the Yankees have some ground for discontent, but I must learn not to say all I think."

At seven that Christmas Eve, after the signing, the secretary of the British Commission ran with copies of the treaty to a carriage, and started for Ostend where a ship awaited him to sail to London. The treaty was, therefore, officially given to the King of England on Christmas Day, "the day of all the year," John Quincy wrote Louisa, "most congenial to the proclamation of Peace on Earth." But getting the news to America, where the war continued, proved more difficult. The Americans had the treaty written and copied in triplicate to guard against any loss

---

* Marylanders, however, stood firm at Baltimore, August 25 and 26, and the naval bombardment at Fort McHenry inspired Americans, including a young Georgetown lawyer and lyricist named Francis Scott Key.

in passage. On December 26, at ten in the evening, Henry Carroll, Clay's secretary, left Ghent for New York and Washington with one copy of the treaty. He sailed first to England, where the British sloop-of-war *Favorite* departed Plymouth for New York on January 2, 1815. The envoys also dispatched another secretary with a second copy, by way of Bordeaux, where he was delayed until the fifth. The third copy went with a secretary to Amsterdam, but his ship was locked in by ice.

The war, meanwhile, continued. On January 8, with word of the peace at Ghent still at sea with Carroll, Gen. Andrew Jackson, fortified on the left bank of the Mississippi between the levee and the swamps at New Orleans, took on a frontal assault by British troops under Sir Edward Pakenham. In the assault, against earthworks protected by artillery and riflemen, the British general was killed along with his second and third officers in command, and their troops suffered two thousand casualties. Only thirteen Americans fell. The Battle of New Orleans, and the Treaty of Ghent, which had little military or diplomatic value beyond ending the war, would help popularize and nominate two men for the U.S. Presidency: Andrew Jackson and John Quincy Adams, general and negotiator.

The *Favorite*, blown by strong winds, took just thirty-eight days to reach Sandy Hook, on Friday evening, February 10, and as news of Carroll's arrival swept before him in New York City, lower Broadway filled with men and women, lighted candles in their hands, shouting: "Peace!" During Carroll's swift journey southward the word flowed before him like a large quenching wave upon dry ground, and as he rode without stopping, sleeping in his post-chaise, eating when he could, his presence brought Americans into the streets of their towns and villages, cheering. By Tuesday evening, when Carroll's chaise lumbered past the charred Capitol and plunged and splashed along Pennsylvania Avenue, rutted and deep with mud after a week's rain, a crowd of men and boys followed it wildly shouting "Peace! Peace!" After stopping for James Monroe, the Secretary of State, Carroll continued down Pennsylvania, passing the burned and shell-pocked President's House, to President James Madison's temporary residence, where he and his family lived while the President's House was being repaired. Madison sat conversing with his wife, surrounded by members of his household staff, when Secretary Monroe and Henry Carroll were announced.

Madison was not a demonstrative man, but Dolley, when told of the treaty, shouted to the rest of the house: "Peace!" Someone started ringing the dinner bell and echoed the cry — "Peace!" — and a cousin ran to the foot of the huge spiral staircase, where the black servants now crowded over the railing, and bellowed *"Peace!"* and they took up the cry. Soon guests began arriving, the house filled with friends celebrating the end of the war, bells rang in the capital city, and the streets filled with people shouting that one glorious word: *"Peace!"*

In Ghent, the American delegation had slowly broken up after more than a week of celebrations and dinners. The parties and banquets and too little exercise caused John Quincy to write Louisa: "I am grown so fat you will hardly know me. My health is good, but I cannot wear my clothes." And Louisa kindly replied: "I think at our time of life fat is very becoming." The Americans drank, ate, and sang; they gave their landlord permission to auction off their hotel furniture, and the enterprising man sold at top prices all the beds, dressers, desks, and bureaus he could find anywhere in Ghent. "Even the furniture from the British hotel was sold at our house," said John Quincy, "for the sake of putting it in favor. The worst part of the joke was that they put off quantities of bad wine, as if it had been ours. We did not leave a bottle for sale." Adams, the last American negotiator to depart, showed Ghent to Catherine Johnson and her husband, who had sailed to Holland by the Baltic that autumn on their way to the United States. Before leaving for Paris, John Quincy sent Louisa instructions: "I therefore now invite you to break up altogether our establishment at St. Petersburg, to dispose of all the furniture which you do not incline to keep, to have all the rest packed up carefully and left in the charge of Mr. Harris . . . and come with Charles to me at Paris, where I shall be impatiently waiting for you."

Louisa had spent the months from April 1814 to February 1815 hiring and firing servants, and following events at Ghent as best she could by newspaper. She went to the court balls and dinners, and considered so essential the task of keeping her husband's name before the elite of St. Petersburg and American merchants in the capital that she invited guests to dinner every few weeks. But she expected her husband to return to Russia, and when his letter of instructions arrived, Louisa was shocked. John Quincy's charge to her was extraordinary. Most women of Louisa's class were hauled about in style from place to place, with the luggage and the servants. But he instructed his wife to sell or ship all of his European possessions, including his valued law books and state papers; to dismiss and hire servants, to outfit herself and Charles and a carriage, and ride more than eighteen hundred miles from St. Petersburg, across the cold heart of winter, in the wake of Napoleon's retreat, to Paris. Louisa herself was uncertain that she could do what he asked. "Conceive the astonishment your letter caused me if you can," she wrote. "I know not what to do about the selling of the goods and I fear I shall be much imposed upon." A less trusting man might have directed Levett Harris to the task. Adams's charge, therefore, contained a marvelous contradiction: He often treated Louisa as a frail underling, a woman; now he asked that she act with the skill and toughness of a man. Selling furniture and closing a house, crossing the frozen Russian Steppes in an unheated carriage, required a person of courage, skill, resilience, stamina. Adams instructed Harris to draw up letters of credit on an Amsterdam bank for five thousand florins, and told Louisa: "I have only to ask you to keep a particular account of all your expenditures and of all the monies you receive."

Louisa spent all of January and early February packing, crating, selling — and keeping records. "I am turned into a woman of business," she wrote, "but I much fear you will find your affairs in bad hands." Louisa discovered that it was difficult to sell the furniture to advantage; few people had cash, and sought to barter with diamonds and pearls, but she could not determine their value. By February 4, not half the Adamses' furniture had been sold. Harris obtained a *padorojna** from the Military Gov-

---

* The *padorojna*, as Louisa called it, was attached to a letter from the Military Governor stating her purpose and arrival times at various stages in Russia, and directing the postmaster at each stage to give her horses and not delay her "on pain of punishment." It served, in effect, as a letter of introduction, passport, and credit card.

ernor for post-horses, and Louisa hired "good servants" and purchased "an excellent Carriage." She had a special bed made in her carriage for Charles, and outfitted the vehicle (for $378.61) with a tea kettle, tin cups, bread, and provisions that included rum, butter, cheese, chocolate, and the family medicine chest. With John Quincy already in Paris, and George and John, unknown to Louisa, soon embarking to cross the Atlantic, her family was slowly moving from cities halfway around the earth to be together one more time.

On February 12, 1815, the day she turned forty years old, Louisa Adams hastily scribbled a note to John Quincy: "I am this instant setting off and have only time to say that nothing can equal my impatience to see you." She had left some business to be completed,

> . . . but I hope you will forgive all that is not exactly correspondent to your wishes and receive me with as much affection as fills my heart at this moment for you. I could not celebrate my birthday in a manner more delightful than in making the first step towards that meeting for which my Soul pants and for which I have hitherto hardly dared to express my desire but in the full conviction, that the sentiment is mutual. . . . be prepared to expect your most affectionate Wife & Child. L C & C Adams.

At five that evening, Louisa and Charles set out across the winter wastelands of Russia and eastern Europe for Paris. Almost three decades later, Louisa wrote an account of this adventure, which she titled "Narrative of a Journey from Russia to France, 1815." She wrote it, she said then, to fill an idle hour, "to recall the memory of one, *who was*," and to demonstrate "that many undertakings which appear very difficult and arduous to my Sex, are by no means so trying as imagination forever depicts them." The journey, therefore, symbolized to Louisa an event in her life that gave her definition; a journey during which she relied only upon herself; an ordeal demonstrating that under such circumstances women were the equal of men. Louisa hoped her account would overcome "the fancied weakness of feminine imbecility."

At first, Louisa and Charles and Mme. Babet, her French maid, traveled in a carriage on runners, for the snow; behind them, in a *kibitka*, followed two menservants, who were armed. The weather was so cold that, by the time they reached Riga, all their provisions including the Madeira wine had frozen solid. The carriage sank so deeply into the snow that on occasion they had to stop and awaken peasants, who came out with shovels and pickaxes and dug them out. Louisa, Charles, and Mme. Babet kept warm only with fur blankets, and their carriage rolled, pitched, and lurched in a nauseating motion that forced them to brace themselves continuously. The road was, at best, a cleared way through a vast wilderness, rutted, torn by gullies, falling off in precipitous slopes, cut by frozen streams and rivers that, with sudden spring thaws, could sweep them away without a trace. The two carriages got lost at night beyond Mitau, and "jolted over hills, through swamps and holes, and into valleys into which no carriage had surely ever passed before." To cross the frozen Vistula into Poland, Louisa hired men to walk ahead of her horses with poles to test the ice. The men went forward, pounding the ice with the heavy prods, to find the firmest path. With a resounding boom the ice would crack in parabolic curves, and they would all halt, holding the horses steady, watching the break for signs of water, poised motionless above sudden death. They just reached the other side when the ice gave way, and only the driver's violent whipping of the horses pulled Louisa's carriage out of the water and prevented it from over-turning on the bank.

In Poland, Louisa and her servants traveled in wheeled car-riages, through "the most filthy and beggarly Villages," and when late at night the front wheel of her carriage tore off, the nearest farmhouse was "little more than a hovel consisting of two rooms and a blacksmith's shop," occupied by a "dirty, ugly and ill-natured" woman and two or three "surly ill-looking men." They would fix the wheel, they said, but — as at all repair shops — it would take time. Louisa reluctantly spent the night; she brought in Charles's bed, ordered one servant to sleep in the carriage to guard it, and posted the other outside the door to one of the two rooms in the shack, where she and Mme. Babet sat awake all night, "neither of us feeling very secure." The next morning, a clumsy and unpainted wheel was fitted onto her carriage, and it worked well enough for them to proceed to Berlin along "the most beautiful road in the world," constructed by Napoleon's troops. Louisa now heard, for the first time, praise for the French Emperor, and fear of the Russian Cossacks.

Louisa spent a week in Berlin while her carriage was repaired and re-outfitted. She felt nostalgic for that time fourteen years before, and recalled George's birth and visited "some of my old friends," including Countess Pauline de Neale and remnants of the royal family. But while the Lindenstrasse, the Bradenburg Gate, the bridges and palaces remained grand, Berlin felt "cold and flat," and Louisa's friends had all suffered greatly from the invasion. She left Berlin for the last time with feelings of gratitude and regret. Departing, Louisa recalled a warning she had received in St. Petersburg, when she had called upon Countess Colombe to take tea and bid her farewell. Louisa had met there a Russian lady, the Countess Apraxin, "a fat, coarse woman," who, because Louisa was leaving on her journey, insisted upon reading her fortune. Louisa had agreed, and drew "a Queen" from a deck of cards, and was told, first, that she was glad to be leaving St. Petersburg (embarrassingly true), and that she would soon see her loved ones. But, Countess Apraxin had warned, when Louisa had covered about half her journey — after Berlin — she would be "much alarmed by a great change in the political world" caused by "a great man" who would produce "consternation and set all Europe into a frenzied commotion." Louisa, she continued, would encounter this on the road and be forced to change her plans and find her journey "very difficult, but that after all I should find my husband well, and that we should have a joyous meeting after so long an absence." Louisa had laughed, and thanked Countess Apraxin, but had assured her that the journey was well arranged and "simple." Still, Louisa and Countess Colombe "were very merry at the skill with which she had strung together so many improbabilities." The fortune-teller told her to "*remember*," and Louisa had replied, "I was certain I could never forget."

The roads from Berlin were sandy through pine barrens, and Louisa proceeded "quietly," occasionally meeting small straggling parties of disbanded soldiers. In the evenings, riding after dark,

Louisa wore Charles's military cap with a tall feather, and placed his toy sword across the carriage window, which made her feel more protected. Her two servants rode with their pistols displayed. In a small fortified village, an innkeeper told Louisa that Napoleon was rumored to have returned to France from Elba, and she "started with astonishment" and thought of Countess Apraxin's fortune for her. Wherever she stopped to change horses, Louisa now heard of Napoleon's return, and after riding across a broad plain outside Hanover, where the Bavarians had intercepted the retreating French and Louisa saw the remnants of uniforms, boots, "and an immense quantity of bones, laying in this ploughed field," she entered the city and found troops being called up. In Frankfort, Louisa's two manservants, fearful of having to join the French army, refused to continue to Paris, and she had to engage a "Prussian lad of fourteen" as a servant and escort, who fortunately "proved very smart and active." They hurried on toward Paris — from Strasbourg, where she was warned against going on and engaged a manservant named Dupin; to Nancy, where "the square was full of [French] troops, who were mustering to make preparations for joining the Emperor"; to Château-Thierry and Epernay.

In Paris, meanwhile, John Quincy Adams followed the news of Napoleon's approach with the calmness of a journalist. On the first of March, Napoleon had landed at Cannes with 1,140 men and four pieces of cannon, and five hundred miles to Paris. In ten days he had marched into Lyons at the head of an army of 12,000, and by the end of March had reached the outskirts of Paris, with the king fleeing northward. On March 21, Adams watched a detachment of Napoleon's advance guard enter the capital to great acclamation of the people, who only a fortnight earlier had been screaming "*Vive le Roi!*" Proclamations acclaiming Napoleon were hastily pasted over proclamations declaring him a traitor and commanding every civil and military authority to seize him for courts-martial. Adams also noted, with wry humor, that when Allied troops had entered Paris a year earlier the *Journal de l'Empire* had metamorphosed in a single evening to the *Journal des Debats*, but with Napoleon's troops at the city gates, the newspaper had a counter-metamorphosis and appeared the next morning as the *Journal de l'Empire* again, retaining the Timbre Royale on its masthead, just in case. With the House of Bourbon headed north, and Paris in tumult as Napoleon approached, masses of foreigners and loyalists were fleeing, heading directly toward Louisa Adams.

On the road, wagons filled with soldiers rushed past Louisa's carriage toward the frontier, with the men "Roaring national Songs, and apparently in great glee at the idea of a renewal of hostilities." Louisa was stopped and questioned at every stage and village, her baggage removed and inspected, and her passports closely examined. At a roadhouse, she sat up all night guarding her son and possessions. But only a mile outside Epernay — after "a capital dinner" that included Louisa's first taste of the "superior" champagne of the region — she suddenly found herself in the middle of boisterous, drunken Imperial Guards on their way to meet Napoleon. The soldiers, seeing her Russian carriage, cursed her — Louisa was more shocked by the language of the women camp followers — and threatened her manservants. "Madame Babet was pale as death, and trembled excessively." The soldiers shouted, "Tear them out of the Carriage, they are Russians, take them out, kill them." They seized her horses and halted the carriage, and pointed their guns at her drivers. Louisa tried to show them her passports, but the soldiers, determined to kill them, refused to look at her papers. An officer rode up to her carriage, and after formally addressing her, read Louisa's passports, and then called out to the angry troops: "This is an American lady going to meet her husband in Paris." Now the soldiers shouted, *"Vive les Américains!"* and Louisa called out *"Vive Napoléon!"* and waved her handkerchief, and the cheers and shouts carried along the line of soldiers, adding *"ils sont nos amis"* ("they are our friends"). The officer ordered several of his men to march before the horses, and he and his aides rode on either side. He warned Louisa that her situation was precarious: "The army is totally undisciplined." The soldiers obeyed only orders they approved of, and she must appear unconcerned and whenever they shouted *"Vive les Américains"* she must reply *"Vive Napoléon."* Louisa behaved coolly — Charles "seemed to be absolutely petrified and sat by my side like a marble Statue" —

and she cheered and waved her handkerchief continuously. Along a road lined with intoxicated men, the soldiers threatened the people they passed with bayonets and "loud and brutal" shouts. Louisa reached a posthouse at midnight, and only after lengthy argument did the landlady allow her in, on the condition that she stay in a darkened room, conceal her servants and Charles, and hide her coach where it could not be seen. Louisa "gladly" consented, and was put into "a comfortable room" with a good fire and the shutters closed and barred. The officer continued on with his troops, but all night other soldiers crowded into the roadside house drinking and shouting. Charles slept, but Mme. Babet clasped her hands and wept that the revolution had begun again and this was the start of "its horrors." During the night, three soldiers discovered the boy Louisa had hired, and threatened him with a bayonet. They forced him to burn his Prussian hat, and only the landlady's chance intercession prevented them from killing the lad. At five in the morning, the inn's doors were barred, and from that time stragglers pounded and shouted outside. Louisa, however, went to sleep, and did not awake until nine. After an "excellent breakfast," she took her carriage out of hiding and continued on the long route to the Marne River, the Seine, and Paris.

Now Louisa's only delays occurred when her carriage again lost a wheel, in the wilds of the *Forêt de Bondy*, or when edging through raucous troops. The rumor that she was Napoleon's sister on her way to Paris swept before her, which Louisa encouraged with smiles and waves of her handkerchief, and on March 23 she safely passed through the gates to the French capital, descending from her carriage at eleven that evening at the Hotel du Nord on Rue de Richelieu. John Quincy was at the theater, but when he returned, Louisa said, "I was once more happy to find myself under the protection of a husband, who was perfectly astonished at my adventures, as everything in Paris was quiet." It never occurred to John Quincy that it might have been otherwise elsewhere. The journey was so harrowing that Mme. Babet was "seized with a brain fever," caused by the frightening trip, and had not recovered when Louisa left Paris two months later for London.

Louisa kept careful accounts of her expenses, as John Quincy had instructed. She recorded them first in Russian rubles, then Prussian thalers, German florins, and French francs. Including the cost of her carriage and provisions, Louisa spent $1,606.38. She worried that the expense of the trip would shock her husband. It was not her fault, she said, and "I wish it was possible for me to prevent it but the government will perhaps be in good humour with the Peace and make it up to you."

10

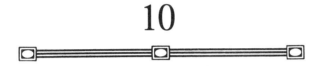

O N MAY 7, 1815, John Quincy Adams received word from President Monroe appointing him Minister Plenipotentiary to Great Britain, a post first held by his father. In eleven days, after a parting visit with Lafayette at his ancestral home at La Grange, the Adamses sailed for London. News of the appointment had long before reached Quincy, and George and John had set sail on April 18 for Liverpool.

The next two years in England passed quietly and swiftly; they were the best the Adamses ever had. Louisa gathered her family about her, savoring this treasured moment she knew would not last. She found them a little country house at Ealing, eight miles from Hyde Park Corner in London — far enough to avoid the constant round of diplomatic parties, but close enough to allow Louisa and John Quincy to ride the carriage to the theater and opera; sometimes the Adamses remained overnight in the ambassador's chambers at the American Legation's chancery on Craven Street. But the house at Ealing, with its laurel-bordered garden and bucolic English countryside, bound the family together, and held them momentarily. They fondly nicknamed it their Little Boston home. Louisa and John Quincy played the pianoforte and flute. They walked the fields with their sons. Adams hired a fencing master to teach them that skill, and bought a pair of pistols for target practice – but promptly injured his right hand with a kickback. The boys performed scenes from plays, with their parents as an appreciative audience, and they all spent long hours at cards, walking, or on rides to Kew, Richmond, Harrow, Cambridge. John Quincy also bought a telescope; at night he gathered his sons and young friends around him in the backyard, and taught them the names of the major constellations, especially his newly discovered Orion.

The family also started what became a major form of communication among them. They wrote poems to one another, and during the next two decades not only used this device to say obliquely what they couldn't say directly, but also as a form of psychotherapy. John started a round of poems with his effort titled "What is Youth!" A sampling of each person's entry suffices. John:

> What is youth! tis but a rose
> That now is in its prime.
> But soon it buds it blooms and goes
> All in an hours time.

Louisa caught the spirit, and replied with eight verses of her own. Verse five:

> What is youth! that blushing morn
> Whose orient beams announce the day
> Ah, may no lurking treacherous thorn
> Envenom'd round its guileless prey.

She signed the work "your Mother." George, too, picked up the idea – adding a question mark, perhaps reflecting his own uncertainties:

> What is youth? A fading flower
> Some little while loved
> Tis but the offspring of an hour
> By every passion moved.

He went on to ask what is beauty, pleasure, and:

> What is life? A fleeing dream
> Which fades away and dies
> Affords a cheerful pleasant gleam
> A spark it upward flies.

John Quincy, too, wrote poetry — but disdained the chance to add to this family inquiry — and put to use his rides in and out of London composing an "Ode" in six stanzas, "To Fortitude, Written in the Manner of Gray." The verses he wrote all his life were like him: metrical exercises without warmth or inner feeling:

> Nor crown, nor sceptre would I ask
> But from my country's will,
> By day, by night, to ply the task
> Her cups of bliss to fill.

Ambassador Adams had little else to do. The British Foreign Office's attention was diverted to the Continent, where the One Hundred Days of Napoleon's return ended at Waterloo, on July 3, 1815. Adams, with his Ghent collaborators Gallatin and Clay, negotiated and signed a commercial convention with Great Britain that month, but he largely occupied himself during these two restful years in England by preaching peace and improving relations between the two nations after the War of 1812. He had plenty of time for visitors to his office, one of whom was a young American painter, Charles Robert Leslie. John Quincy and Louisa both sat fourteen times for Leslie, and Louisa thought her husband "never looked so well or so handsome as he does now." The "handsome" Adams was forty-nine, plump, with double chin and soft dark eyes, bald with his hair swept forward in the manner of men his age who wish to cover a spreading bare crown. Louisa's portrait showed a woman with long, delicate hands, a small double chin to match her husband's, tight brown curls and a slightly disgusted expression, which one might expect from a woman of her experience.

The Adamses' house in Ealing was a mile from an excellent boys' school run by Dr. George Nicholas, an Oxford graduate. George, John, and Charles attended the school, and George thought Dr. Nicholas "the best master I ever knew for he gave an interest to the studies which made them agreeable as well as useful." Charles, on the other hand, found the school difficult. He made slow academic progress, unsatisfactory to either his master or his father. He had, John Quincy complained, an "intractable" memory, "particularly with regard to everything relating to numbers," and he thought his son "a dull boy," who nonetheless (when he wished to) had "a great aptitude to learn whatever spontaneously strikes his own fancy."

George was tutored, as well, by his father in preparation for Harvard. He lived at home, and enjoyed having his own room. On Tuesdays, Thursdays, and Saturdays, when extra study was omitted at Nicholas's school, George returned home around three and spent his time writing until six, when the family dined. He wrote elaborate letters to his grandparents in America, poems, plays, and papers "circulated at school." He found it difficult, however, to keep up with his class, and he was often deficient. His father urged him to read French, and George struggled to obey. He preferred collecting English plays, which he had bound together into a book, and often rode to London to the theater, his "very favorite amusement." "The wonders of London," he exclaimed, "the delights of her Theatre, Paintings galleries Museums, Tower and Parks. . . ." It was a new world to George, and he absorbed all of it.

But for the first time, in close proximity to his sons, John Quincy Adams got a hint that his children might not reach his expectations, that his letters of instruction from Russia had been in vain. He expected his sons to play major roles upon the world stage — and not in the theater. Adams wished to inspire his sons with "the sublime Platonic idea, of aiming at ideal excellence." But they disappointed him early, and he took it hard. He found that they preferred "the great and constant effort . . . to escape from study." He might have to content himself, he wrote his mother, with seeing his sons grow up to be "like other men." He wished for "something more flattering than all this."

George was discovering his own interests, separate from his father's direction. He traveled away from the family, both literally and figuratively, and visited friends, went riding, took moonlight sails on the Thames. With Charles Storer, who had been John Adams's private secretary in Europe, 1781–85, George traveled to the Continent, and on his sixteenth birthday arrived in Paris. Less than two years after Waterloo, British troops still garrisoned the city, but that didn't diminish George's "highest pleasure" of attending the Parisian theater, where he saw works of Molière, Racine, Voltaire. He also traveled alone and without passport to Ghent, Antwerp, Brussels, and Calais. George was growing independent, educating himself, and discovering his deepest interests: writing and the theater.

When he returned to Ealing, however, George learned that his father had been appointed Secretary of State by President Monroe. The position meant a cut in pay, but it was also known as the stepping-stone to the Presidency. Abigail wrote John Quincy that people back home already spoke of him as "worthy to preside over the Counsels of a great Nation." The Adamses bought two sea trunks, wood to pack their furniture, mattresses, and the provisions for their voyage. They bid farewell to their Little Boston home at Ealing, and to a time of togetherness and relaxation. In London, Louisa and John Quincy attended a cordial farewell dinner given them by Lord Castlereagh, and Adams went through the ritual of leavetaking, which included the traditional ceremony with "the obtuse, frivolous and dissolute" Prince Regent (George IV), "A Falstaff without the wit, and a Prince Henry without the compunctions." On June 14, 1817, the Adamses embarked from Cowes on the *Washington* for New York.

Louisa and John Quincy, Charles, and John looked forward to being home again. On the other side of the Atlantic, old John Adams missed his grandsons and their noise about the house. "Oh, how I want John to divert me and George to assist me!" he wrote wistfully. "I can scarcely get a book from my Office without him. Charles is a little Jewell too! How delighted I should be to have them all about me. Yet they would devour all my Strawberries, Raspberries, Cherries, Currents, Plumbs, Peaches, Pears and Apples. And what is worse, they would get into my Bedchamber and disarrange all the Papers on my Writing Table." He could not wait. But George could. He left Europe reluctantly to return to the United States and prepare for college, for growing up.

As the Adamses sailed from Europe for the United States, the old order was passing to the new. With the Treaty of Ghent, the nation started upon its separate and independent path from Europe. The United States was small and rural, but its population would increase to almost ten million by 1820, and it was filled with expansion fever and sectional rivalry. The gathering clouds were forming over what would become the central issue of John Quincy's and Louisa's lives, and America's history: slavery. That issue was already tied to the admission of the new states of Missouri and Maine, and Americans who disputed large tracts of land in East and West Florida and beyond the Mississippi River found slavery interconnected with expansion. In politics, the days of the Founding Fathers were ending. Only six signers of the Declaration of Independence lived on (including Jefferson and Adams), and only eleven framers of the Constitution. Power was passing to young men in Congress, such as Henry Clay, just thirty-nine, and John C. Calhoun, thirty-two. John Quincy Adams, the new Secretary of State, turned fifty during this sea voyage. His struggle against the younger order was just beginning.

On board the *Washington*, John Quincy found time to fish, try out "one of Burt's patent sounding machines" (without success), converse with the crew, read passages from Bacon's *Novum Organum*, play chess, write in his diary, and read his Bible. He still complained that "Our life on shipboard is as usual dull; and I fear my time will be much wasted on idleness." The voyage would have been uneventful for Louisa as well, except while at sea she suffered "a bad miscarriage," she said, and was extremely ill. It marked her twelfth and last pregnancy.

Above: The Old House in Braintree (later Quincy), Massachusetts, painted by E. Malcolm in 1798 before large extensions were added on.

Right: John Quincy Adams at fifteen. Engraving by Sidney L. Smith, 1887, after the pastel by Isaac Schmidt, 1783.

John Quincy Adams. Oil by John Singleton Copley, painted in 1796, while Adams, then almost thirty, was on diplomatic business in London.

Louisa Catherine Adams. Detail of an oil ascribed to Edward Savage, about 1801, within four years after her marriage to John Quincy Adams.

The Signing of the Treaty of Ghent, oil by Sir Amedee Forestier, 1814.

Ball given by Mrs. John Quincy Adams in Washington, January 8, 1824, in honor of Andrew Jackson. Photoengraving from *Harper's Bazaar*, March 18, 1871.

Louisa Catherine Adams in an oil by Charles Bird King, about 1824.
Louisa sits with a volume of music open to Thomas Moore's song,
"Oh Say Not That Woman's Heart Can Be Bought."

Abigail Brooks Adams, painted by William E. West, about 1840,
was the wife of Charles Francis Adams, right, painted by
Charles Bird King in 1827.

George Washington Adams, left, at twenty-two, six years before
his suicide, and John Adams 2d, at about the same age. Both oils
ascribed to Charles Bird King.

The Old House in Qunicy as it looks today.
Below: John Quincy Adams in a daguerreotype by Southworth and Hawes, 1843.

IV
Washington

1817–1825

1

A FTER FIFTY-THREE DAYS at sea, the *Washington* dropped anchor off the Sandy Hook lighthouse. John Quincy Adams impatiently paced the deck at sunrise, and noted that "The morning was fine, the sun rose clear, and Venus was visible more than a quarter of an hour after she had risen; air and water both at 67." Capt. Jacob Forman waited for the tide to turn in his favor, and then brought the ship slowly through the narrows and across the wide bay to dock safely at the southern tip of New York City. John Quincy directed the offloading of his family's trunks and possessions; he hired a carriage (for $2) to carry them to Mrs. Bradish's lodgings, and they slowly jostled through the narrow cobblestone streets swarming with people. The Adamses crossed Broadway, thirty feet wide and reaching four miles northward to the very edge of the city, and Wall Street, already the location of "the banking houses, exchange, brokers, insurance, auctioneers, and custom house offices." The crowds of people surprised the Adamses: New York was America's largest city, and when a ship arrived it was difficult to pass along Wall Street where "throngs of gentlemen" surged out of their offices to get the commercial papers and the latest news from Europe.

For nine days, the Adamses plunged into the teem and jostle of New York. They covered the city like tourists, and the *New York Evening Post* covered them, announcing their arrival and following their activities. John Quincy dined at Tammany Hall, where one hundred prominent New Yorkers, including Gov. DeWitt Clinton and John Jacob Astor, turned out to greet their new Secretary of State. Adams visited such public exhibits as the New-York Historical Society and the Academy of Fine Arts. He also sat for his portrait, to William Shiels, a Scotsman he met during the crossing. Louisa and the boys shopped, and she went through the music at William DuBois' store at 127 Broadway, which carried Thomas Moore's "Sacred Melodies" and sheet music for his recently published song, "There's Nothing True but Heaven." Louisa admired Moore; she had met him during the summer of 1804, while she was alone in Washington, when the wife of the British ambassador brought the popular musician to the Hellen home. Moore had stayed several hours, and had played the piano and sung "in the Italian style & with exquisite taste." Louisa invited Moore back frequently, and she and the composer had filled the Hellens' home with piano and tenor melodies. "He said that I sang beautifully," Louisa wrote John Quincy, "but I wanted *Soul*."

Word reached John and Abigail in Quincy that the Adamses had landed safely. "Yesterday," old John Adams wrote with the trembling hand of age, "was one of the most uniformly happy days of my long life." He added, in wobbling capital letters, "*ALL WELL*. . . . A thousand occasions exalted the delight . . . a succession of warm showers all day: my threshers, my gardeners, and my farmers all behaved better than usual, and altogether kept me in a kind of trance of delight the whole day. Kiss all the dear creatures for me, Wife, George, John and Charles. I hope to embrace them all here in a few days. God Almighty bless you all. So prays John Adams."

In Quincy on August 18, Louisa Smith, one of Abigail's nieces, watched impatiently outside the Old House in the rising heat of a summer morning. About ten o'clock she let out a whoop of excitement, and raced inside shouting that a carriage and four was coming down Penn's Hill on the turnpike from Milton. Abigail ran to the door, her heart thumping. In a few minutes, the stagecoach rolled to a stop before the house, and Adamses filled the yard expectantly. First from the stage was young John, who rushed up to his Grandmother Adams and threw his arms around her neck. Then came George, half crazy with joy, calling out all the way: "O Grandmother! O Grandmother!" Only Charles hesitated, having been away from Quincy eight years and unable to remember his grandparents; he walked up to the old folks and shook hands. Louisa and John Quincy climbed out of the stagecoach, and began kissing and embracing the relatives. Abigail sized everyone up: The boys had grown much taller, and their mother, Louisa, appeared "better than I ever saw her, and younger I think." All of them looked sunburned, brown, in good health. John Quincy, too, was pleased by his parents' appearance. "I had the inexpressible happiness," he wrote rather stiffly in his diary, "of finding my venerable father and mother in perfect health."

Aunts and uncles, nieces and nephews soon filled the Old House, John Adams's clapboard farmhouse in Quincy. Brother Thomas and his large family walked over to share dinner. He and his wife had five children: Elizabeth, Abigail 2d, Thomas Jr., Isaac Hull Adams, and John Quincy Adams 2d. The neighbors, led by Peter Adams, JQA's uncle, rode up on horseback and in carriages. Hard cider and wine and Abigail's fine food started a slam-bang good time; everyone ate and celebrated. They grabbed the boys and took their height, marking each of them off against a doorjamb: Charles, measured first because it was also his tenth birthday, stood 4'4"; John, 4'9½"; and George, 5'7½" — already half an inch taller than his father.

For the next twenty-two days, the Adamses luxuriated in the welcome and love at the Old House. They put the place in turmoil, Abigail wrote goodnaturedly, and her rooms were "covered with trunkes Bookes and papers . . . [in] every chamber in the house." She got up from her letter to count the trunks: ". . . No less than Eighteen large packages, addrest to all the Governours in the United States." Each package contained inquiries about weights and measures, a complicated project that John Quincy had started in St. Petersburg and now, with the official urging of Congress, was preparing. For the next four years he would continue to work on this subject in his spare time, rising at three or four in the morning to write, and in 1821

Adams would publish his *Report on Weights and Measures,* a lengthy, heavy, and neglected classic. Even John Adams, awed by the prodigious output of his son, could not read it all, although he felt by its volume and heft that it was a "mass of historical, philosophical, chemical, metaphysical and political knowledge."

For John Quincy, coming home meant touching once more the verities of his life: his parents, the farm, and the Old House. He swam again at Black's Wharf in Quincy, where he had gone swimming as a youth, and walked the fields and hills of his boyhood. He and Louisa rode into Boston; the town had grown to 32,250 people, with new shops and houses, some five stories high that darkened the narrow city streets. But Boston people didn't forget: two hundred of them gave a party for John Quincy, to wish him well.

Louisa spent her days fishing with her sons, and getting to know Abigail and John better. Her mother-in-law was seventy-two, content at last with home, family, and Louisa Adams. The two women shared a friendly, respectful, but wary time together. "We did not understand one another," Louisa wrote two decades later, and she thought that half the enjoyment of knowing Abigail had been lost by their rivalry and petty jealousies. Louisa spent hours in Abigail's chambers in the Old House, in the west bedroom, overlooking "the yellow and green brilliancy of the garden" below. Around Abigail's fireplace were the picture tiles John Quincy had brought her in 1801, from Berlin; next to it was her favorite armchair, where she sat when her rheumatism troubled her; then in a circle were her long sofa, her four-poster bed, and John Adams's highbacked armchair where he liked to sit to be near her, and where Louisa now ensconced herself. Here, Abigail in one chair with her dog, Satan, and Louisa in the other, they talked in their animated way, sorting out their differences. "She herself told me she was worried she had not better understood my character," Louisa said, "and proved herself on every occasion a kind and affectionate Mother." Abigail had seen in her daughter-in-law a stronger woman than she first suspected — a durable, resilient person who had proven unafraid of adventure and uncomplaining of her life, but not her role. The pregnancies, the fatiguing Courts, the sea voyages, and the journey with Charles across western Russia impressed Abigail. Louisa at this point only sensed Abigail's depth; full recognition would come after Louisa had asked herself some troubling questions as a woman, and discovered that Abigail had asked the same things, and demanded answers. The two women found they shared much in common: their mutual ambitions for John Quincy, and admiration for each other's inner strengths. Their reconciliation, which had been developing slowly for several years, came just in time. Abigail Adams would die in fourteen months from typhoid fever.

The Old Gentleman, as Louisa fondly called John Adams, was almost eighty-two, and blissfully happy planting, pruning, farming. Old political scars, especially those with Jefferson, had healed, and both ex-Presidents understood that the curtain was falling. Louisa loved John Adams, and thought him as kind and gentle as a New England Indian Summer, and as delicate. He proved a warm surprise among the cold Adams men, and unlike them always knew how to show her tenderness and sympathy. He never spoke a cruel or harsh word to her, but "treated me with the utmost tenderness and distinction." She was, she said, eternally thankful to him for this respect and love, and the kindness shown her father. For Louisa, John Adams made the Old House, the fields, Quincy itself welcoming and pleasant; when he was no longer there, they would seem colder and forbidding.

On September 9, Louisa and John Quincy said goodbye to his aged parents and left for Washington. Once again they parted from their sons. On the surface, their separations revealed no severe difficulties. John and Charles were enrolled in Mr. Gould's Boston Latin School, and moved into the city where they boarded with Dr. and Mrs. Thomas Welsh. Charles briefly rebelled at this first separation from his parents; for ten years he had enjoyed their attentions and undivided love. He tried to remain at Quincy with his grandparents by feigning dysentery, but when Grandmother Abigail brought forth the home remedy of medicine and emetics, Charles's symptoms suddenly disappeared and he went on to Boston with John. George soon wrote his mother that his brothers were "very well contented and now have no wish but to remain at Mr. Gould's school." But Uncle Thomas, with difficulties of his own, kept a careless eye on the two lads, and John drifted into sports, shooting, and fishing, while Charles struggled to remain faithful to his books.

George, too, was studious, although sometimes nervous and awkward, and his grandfather thought the young man had about him the air of erratic genius. Louisa and John Quincy placed George with Samuel Gilman, a mathematics tutor at Harvard, and George moved into the Gilmans' home in Cambridge. He was, at age seventeen, "generally speaking happily situated," he said, "but it was the first year of entire separation from my whole family and the first time when I had been left wholly to my own guidance." George's preparation for Harvard's entrance examination made his life "regular even to monotony." He worked hard on his Latin grammar, but he felt deficient, and pushed himself to master arithmetic and geography, subjects in which, he confessed, "I was and still am shamefully ignorant." On February 13, 1818, prepared as much as he could be and full of his father's admonitions, eager to please his parents and do honor to the family name, George took the Harvard examination — and vomited. He was, despite everything, accepted; he entered the college one term in advance that spring, and graduated in 1821.

So the family split apart. The closeness and gaiety of Ealing finally ended. For several years, the young Adams men visited their parents in Washington during school holidays. But they relied, once again, on their grandparents to be their loving, sheltering family and protectors. The old folks tried, but after Abigail's death in 1818, John, delighting in every visit and marveling at each lad's progress, became a feeble substitute for parents. The feelings of abandonment persisted.

In the service of his country, John Quincy Adams thought no sacrifice too great, for himself and for others. This time, the separations and arguments would exact their price. Now began a twelve-year stretch perhaps without equal among public families. John Quincy Adams would become one of the most outstanding Secretaries of State the nation ever produced. He would expand with treaties the territory of his country to its present continental boundaries — almost doubling its size; resolve old conflicts between the United States and Europe; and create with President

Monroe an American policy still central to the nation's foreign affairs into the last quarter of the twentieth century, almost 200 years later. But unresolved problems have a way of demanding solution: the separations, the harsh letters, the unmeetable standards, the trinity of honor to Duty, Country, Family also came to bitter fruition. As John Quincy Adams's political career approached the goal his parents and he so ardently sought, beneath the strong foundation of service and duty and sacrifice, this dynasty began to show cracks.

2

LOUISA AND JOHN QUINCY entered Washington by stage at about four in the afternoon of September 20, 1817, precisely when Adams had promised President Monroe he would arrive. The Adamses' trip took eleven days to cover the 460 miles from Boston, and cost $237.44, which included porters, hackneys, carriages, six steamboats, and six stages. The journey was long, arduous, dangerous. Steamboats shortened the trip, but sometimes exploded, killing hundreds of passengers; stagecoaches could overturn.

Life in America was simple, but not easy. Adams often had steamboats leave without him — waiting for wind and tide but not the Secretary of State — and thought it not at all unusual when, as President of the United States, he would ask for a room at the City Hotel in New York and be told that it was full, and have to walk over to Bunker's to find a place to sleep for the night. The seasons regulated and disturbed lives, and darkness shut down villages and towns; only New York and Philadelphia were illuminated by the new gas lamps and stayed open for business after sunset. This was a time of nationalism, unity, growth. The continent was opening to the plow. With the peace at Ghent, there was a feeling in 1817 that the nation's dangers had passed, and that its expansion was beginning. Americans voiced their optimism, and when President Monroe, a Virginian, toured New England, the *Columbian Centinel* in Boston, capital of Federalism, cheered his visit as the start of an "Era of Good Feelings."

Nothing symbolized better the nation's growth and energy than the changes taking place in transportation, and nothing revealed as well the hardships encountered by its people. The Adamses left Boston by stagecoach at five A.M., making themselves as comfortable as possible on the horsehair-cushioned seats. They rolled out through a sea fog, with the driver running the horses across the dangerous Neck connecting Boston with the mainland; the road was so low in places that spring tides washed over it, and unwary travelers who lost their way in the fogs or night or high tides drowned in the marshes. As the coach crossed the Neck, it encountered clusters of marketwomen, who had slept the night at Roxbury, just on the mainland, and with dawn started walking toward Boston, their horses burdened with butter, cheese, eggs in tow sacks, and poultry tied in twos by their legs and tossed over the animals' backs. They formed a human tide flowing through the dawn fog to Boston and the markets around Fanueil Hall, before returning again in the afternoon to gather the farmers' harvest in an eternal nurturing rhythm, back and forth, like the sea just beyond this tiny neck of land and its peninsula town.

The Adamses' stage reached Indian Point, below Providence, in time for the New York steamboat departing precisely at noon. Immense quantities of wood filled the dock, for each steamer consumed between thirty and forty cords a trip. At each change the Adamses and other passengers scurried from stage to steamboat, elbowing each other for berths, or from steamboat to stage, scrambling for the best seats in the front coaches, which set the pace and were therefore more comfortable to ride. As competition between the lines increased, older or weaker passengers were actually carried by porters to waiting stages or steamboats to speed them to their next destination ahead of rival lines. This competition, these steamboats, were opening up America. In the next three years, some seventy-five steamers would push from New Orleans against the flow of the Mississippi and Ohio Rivers to Cincinnati and Pittsburgh. The steamboat went against the current; this flatbottomed floating mansion and its hoarse whistle broke the silence of America's wilderness, and brought its people closer together. This was speed and luxury: ladies' salons, berths, ballrooms lined with mahogany paneling, dining rooms where the Captain occupied the head table and distinguished passengers sat with him. The eastern steamboats that the Adamses sailed were smaller than the western; one traveler on both thought that the eastern steamboat would fit into the grand ballroom of a western steamer. The little easterners also lacked satin spreads and gold fringe on the berths. By 1816, all the steamboats came equipped with a new high-pressure engine connected directly to the crankshaft of the paddlewheels. They were cheaper to operate and more powerful, but they were also unsafe. The whole ornate, glorious, puffing, paddling thing could explode, and when it did the vessel, adrift with its dead and dying, burned with great display to the waterline.

And so the Adamses sailed and scrambled and rode until their stage was bumping along the broad expanse of mud of Pennsylvania Avenue. The evening he arrived, John Quincy reported to President Monroe, and two days later took the oath of office as Secretary of State.

The State Department was located in a large brick building just beyond the President's House at Seventeenth Street and G, N.W.* Nearby were the War Office, Treasury Department, City Hall, the poorhouse, and the prison. Adams' entire staff consisted of Daniel Brent, his chief clerk (and his landlord), and seven assistant clerks. The State Department expenditures at home and abroad totaled just $123,062.04, which was less than the British Foreign Office spent for secret service alone.** And while Adams earned $3,500, his counterpart Lord Castlereagh received about $72,000 a year.

* In 1820, State moved to the corner of Fifteenth and Pennsylvania.
** The British government's expenses in 1822 for its diplomats reached $1,200,000, excluding expenses for the Foreign Office on Downing Street.

Adams found the State Department in disarray. Monroe, his predecessor, had been a bit of a scatterbrain, disliking the details of being Secretary, and Richard Rush, the Acting Secretary before John Quincy's arrival, merely held things together as best he could. Accounts were in arrears and inconsistently kept. Back correspondence and diplomatic dispatches lay about the Secretary's office; some of them were dated more than a year earlier. Important letters had been misplaced. The translation of the Swedish Treaty of 1816 couldn't be found anywhere, nor could documents relating to claims against Sweden. Adams ordered an index prepared of all diplomatic correspondence, and directed that each dispatch from every American minister abroad be entered, numbered, and summarized as to its contents and enclosures — much as he directed his family to do with their own private letters. He organized another register for consular correspondence and one for notes from foreign ministers. This allowed him to rank matters according to their importance, and freed the Secretary to undertake urgent business as it came into the department. Adams was everywhere; he established the State Department library, put together the Secretary's instructions for newly appointed ministers to foreign nations, organized a register of letters within the department, redesigned the agency's financial accounting, supervised office routine. He scrutinized every detail, and alone performed the work that, in later years, would be delegated to a sprawling bureaucracy. He read all dispatches to and from U.S. ministers and consuls abroad, and the notes from foreign representatives in Washington. He drafted and redrafted replies in his own hand; at home, Louisa Adams copied all of John Quincy's private letters into his letter books "to save his hand and Eyes," his mother said, "his Eyes being very weak, and his right hand . . . much upon the tremble like his Fathers." This was no small task. Scattered throughout the Adams papers are voluminous, handwritten letters and petitions from private citizens, with sloppy writing or blotches of ink or scratched-out words. Some correspondents employed a style of writing horizontally across the page, and then — perhaps to save paper — turning the page sideways and writing perpendicular over the previous message, thus forming a lattice work that at first glance is indecipherable but upon closer examination created a readable artistic pattern unlike anything written since. It took excellent handwriting to pull it off, and patience to read.* Secretary Adams read and replied to each one. John Quincy also superintended the census and managed the custody, printing, and distribution of all congressional acts and resolutions. He collected the laws of the different states, handled extradition warrants and pardons of criminals, countersigned and recorded commissions signed by the President.

During his seven-and-a-half-years as Secretary of State, Adams negotiated several major treaties with the Spanish and British settling the Floridan, Canadian, and western boundaries. He also stood firm against Spain and Great Britain at a time when, as Lord Castlereagh later said, "war might have been produced by holding up a finger." Adams was a nationalist at a time when nationalism in the United States was a driving force; he was a continentalist when the opportunity came to expand his nation from the Atlantic to the Pacific. On February 22, 1819, Adams signed the Transcontinental Treaty under which Spain, for five million dollars, ceded all her lands east of the Mississippi, surrendered her rights to the Oregon Territory, and settled the boundary between the United States and Mexico — excluding all of present-day Texas, and leaving an issue John Quincy would face in the 1840s. So essential were these gains to Adams, and his nation, that he called February 22 "the most important day of my life." John Quincy also formulated the foreign policy of nonintervention and noncolonization in the Americas, which became the backbone of the Monroe Doctrine that remains today a basic part of American foreign policy.

To perform all these functions, Adams regulated his life. He rose before sunrise, read his Bible, and exercised regularly, either by walking or swimming. On warm days from April through October, Adams dressed in pea-jacket and pantaloons and, towel in hand, strode briskly the mile to his favorite old sycamore and

---

* The papers also contain the quaint handwritten accounting of the United States Treasury, which appeared like a small business or household account. One report showed that as of June 30, 1827, the United States of America had a treasury balance of $4,272,523.74.

a large rock where Tiber Creek flowed into the Potomac. Adams would start peeling off his clothes as he approached the tree at the river's edge, and fling them on the riverbank before plunging headfirst into the water. He came up noisily, stroked out about fifteen yards, turning occasionally on his back, spouting water as the sun's first rays played through the wooded shoreline to the river. For almost three decades, John Quincy Adams would swim at this spot by the sycamore and rock. Occasionally, he was surprised by a few early-rising residents, such as Stratford Canning, the dignified British ambassador, who reported seeing the American Secretary of State out for a swim wearing a black cap on his head and a pair of green goggles covering his eyes — and nothing else. Washington wags enjoyed spreading the tale that Anne Royall, a daring young journalist from Alabama, sat upon John Quincy's clothes early one summer morning until he promised to grant her an interview. Whether true or not, Miss Royall did indeed visit the unsmiling Secretary of State in his office not long after such a swim, and marveled in her report at, among other things, his "vigorous constitution." After returning home and breakfasting, Adams walked the mile (in twenty-two minutes) from the house he and Louisa rented for $650 a year from Chief Clerk Brent, to the State Department.

Adams walked along Pennsylvania Avenue. He joined the Avenue near the Capitol building, which stood alone on its hill, with its towering dome eighty feet above the tidewater of the Potomac held safely above the flood, Louisa liked to joke, by the hot air of its inhabitants. As John Quincy walked up Pennsylvania, he often stopped among the shops lining its sides. He was not above a timid wager, a practice started in Ghent, and sometimes played the horses at the Washington Race Track or paused at Allen's Lottery and Exchange, three doors west of Davis's Hotel, or at Davis & Force, one door west, to play the national and state lotteries. Adams, however, was cheap, and always bought the lowest lottery ticket possible, one that covered only a twentieth of a whole ticket, and cost $5. The lottery probably attracted him because he was always broke; he had taken a cut in salary as Secretary of State. (Congress raised the salary to $6,000 in 1819.) Family expenses for 1818, the Adamses' first full year in Washington reached $10,980.14, and exceeded income by at least $4,000 every year as Secretary. Fortunately, Thomas Adams had wisely invested his brother's money during the Adamses' years abroad, and by 1817 John Quincy showed a personal estate worth $100,000 on paper, much of it in land and buildings. A little of this was in bank and other stock paying 6 percent a year, and John Quincy and his family lived off this and his meager salary during the rest of his public service. So a stop at Allen's or Davis & Force — or the "Truly Fortunate Lottery Office" near Dr. Ott's on Pennsylvania — carried the elusive promise of winning up to $30,000 with just $5. Adams never did, but he bought his shares and hoped. To indulge another, more permanent habit, the Secretary of State also stopped at the Snuff, Tobacco and Fancy Store at Twelfth and Pennsylvania, which offered tempting "Woodville Segars and James River sweet smell and best Cavendish chewing tobacco."

Adams, then, arrived at the State Department fresh from his walk and ready for work. Officially, the office opened at nine and closed at three, when the clerks promptly shut their desks and departed. John Quincy found these hours scarcely long enough for the duties of his official papers. To reorganize the department, handle American ministers, write in longhand the dispatches and orders, meet and negotiate for treaties, and write his *Weights and Measures* tome, John Quincy had to rise early and work late. He cut back his reading, and squeezed in only the daily Bible chapters before breakfast. Cicero and Tacitus he put aside, and he declared that the sacrifice was equal to losing a leg to stand on. With his office open to a succession of visitors, and with interviews, Cabinet meetings, and diplomatic conferences, Adams was often delayed late into the evening. More than once the janitor locked the Secretary of State into the building after everyone else had gone home.

3

THE CAMPAIGN TO SUCCEED James Monroe as President started early in Monroe's first administration, and went on for almost six years. From 1818 until 1824, Louisa Adams was John Quincy Adams's best asset, and filled the place that today would be called campaign manager. She took on a social role for which she felt ill-suited, and which she basically detested. Yet she stepped into the arena, and we find in her a bewildering mixture of repulsion and enthusiasm. Washington demanded an elaborate system of social activities, but this time the objective was not diplomatic information, or a favorable treaty, or even peace, but the goal of John Quincy's life, and his parents' dream: the Presidency.

Before Monroe's first term ended in 1820, members of his cabinet were jostling for position in the Presidential campaign of 1824. Three of the leading contenders were Adams; John C. Calhoun of South Carolina, the Secretary of War; and William H. Crawford of Georgia, Secretary of the Treasury. A fourth candidate, Henry Clay, had opposed Adams's appointment as Secretary of State, seeking that stepping-stone for himself, but lost, and he now used his position as Speaker of the House to raise his voice in opposition to Adams and Monroe. A fifth aspirant, depicted in political cartoons of the time as a dark horse coming up fast on the outside, was Gen. Andrew Jackson, the hero of New Orleans, who would win a seat as U.S. Senator from Tennessee in 1823 that gave him a forum. Almost from the start, Adams found the Cabinet a display platform for the Presidential campaign, and its meetings a "play of passions, opinions and characters" unlike anything he had experienced. In public, John Quincy restrained his temper and his slicing tongue, a prerequisite for a successful candidate, but privately he opened to his diary his feelings about the men around him. Of Monroe, he wrote: "There is slowness, want of decision, and a spirit of procrastination in the President." Of Crawford: He was "a worm preying upon the vitals of the Administration within its own body." Of Clay, with echoes from the card parties of Ghent: "He has more than once won and lost an affluent fortune at the gaming-table [at one time more than eight thousand dollars]. Clay is essentially a gamester, and, with a vigorous intellect, an ardent spirit, a handsome elocution, though with a mind very defective in elementary knowledge, and a very undigested system of ethics, he has all the qualities which belong to that class of human characters." As early as 1818, Adams concluded: "This Government is indeed assuming daily more and more a character of cabal, and preparation, not for the next Presidential election, but for the one after — that is, working and counter-working, with many of the worst features of elective monarchies."

Neither gaming nor ambition remained outside John Quincy Adams's character. But he would not campaign himself for this office; he wanted it in a special way. The Presidency, he believed, must come to him, seemingly unsolicited, as a reward for service to his country. There was only one other person who could gain for John Quincy his coveted place: Louisa. And so the groundwork was laid for an elaborate six-year ritual, a campaign without election speeches, a seeking of the nation's highest office by a man whose candidacy was put forth by his wife. Appropriately, Louisa started her diary in 1818 with the Shakespearean quote: "All the world's a stage, and all the men and women in it players. . . ."

On this political stage, Louisa Adams became a major player. She paid strategic visits to the wives of Congressmen, spent whole days at home receiving them and filled her spare time dispatching cards of invitation. At night she and John Quincy maneuvered through dinners, drawing rooms, and balls, always "Smilin' for the Presidency." There was not a single day from 1818 until early 1825 when Louisa Adams did not campaign for her husband. She often got up from her sickbed, or went out on Christmas Eve or during a driving February snowstorm to visit the wives of Congressmen scattered throughout Washington and the back reaches of Georgetown, sometimes arriving to find no one at home, and then returning the next day. So serious was this business of visits that Louisa and other wives got embroiled in an "etiquette war" over who should make the initial social call at the opening of Congress, Cabinet wives or the wives of Senators and Representatives. The U.S. Senate passed a resolution decreeing that Senators' wives would not make first calls on anyone except the President's wife. Feelings ran high, and in December 1819 the question came before the President's Cabinet, and official state papers were written about it. Louisa resolved the issue by declaring that she would return all visits from the wives of Congressmen, but not visit first; she still didn't miss a single member. John Quincy Adams clearly understood the value of Louisa's social calls. Every morning before going to the State Department, he took time to prepare a set of visiting cards, Louisa said, "with as much formality as if he was drawing up some very important article to negotiate in a Commercial Treaty. But thus it is, and he has been brought to it by absolute necessity."

What necessitated Adams's minute interest was the complex process of nominating Presidential candidates. No country-wide system prevailed, and anyone — party members of a state legislature; a group of judges, lawyers, spectators at a court session; a public mass meeting; even a newspaper or a crowded barroom in the West — could recommend a man for the Presidency, and did. The Congressional caucus was the earliest method of nominating a President, and still prevailed. Since 1800, members of Congress had met in election years as a nominating convention, which in the past had virtually selected the President. The practice was increasingly unpopular — and, in fact, would end with the election of 1824, to be replaced in the next decade by the national convention system — but it could not be overlooked.* While friends of Andrew Jackson, for example, denounced the Congressional caucus system, Jackson himself rightly called it "King Caucus." John Quincy saw the system clearly:

> The only possible chance for a head of Department to attain
> the Presidency is by ingratiating himself personally with the

---

* The Nashville *Gazette* put forward Jackson's name in 1822, and the Tennessee state legislature nominated him that year. The Kentucky legislature nominated Clay in 1822, and the Massachusetts legislature placed Adams before the people in February 1824. The Congressional Caucus nominated William Crawford.

members of Congress; and, as many of them have objects of their own to obtain, the temptation is immense to corrupt coalitions. . . . [This is] one of the numerous evils consequent upon the practice which has grown up under this Constitution, but contrary to its spirit, by which the members of Congress meet in caucus and determine . . . upon the candidate for the Presidency . . . — a practice which . . . leads to a thousand corrupt cabals between the members of Congress and the heads of the Departments, who are thus almost necessarily made rival pretenders to the succession.

This courting of Congressmen brought its members and their wives into the social life of Washington, and made their presence at any event essential to a Presidential candidate's aspirations. Congressmen were prized. By 1820, when their role as President-makers was clear, and as Congressional committees began overseeing the executive departments and their budgets, no visit nor any drawing room or ball or dinner by any member of the President's Cabinet could omit its cluster of gentlemen (and their ladies) from the Hill. In 1824, in fact, Louisa and John Quincy would boast of having sixty-eight Congressmen as steady guests.

Rival social formations created salons loyal to one or another Secretary, and special evenings were set aside when members of Congress and other guests might visit the Secretary's home or the homes of his supporters. The rivalry created elaborate formats for attracting and holding followers: games, sideboards heaped with food, an enticing variety of drinks, entertainment. Wives and daughters read poetry and sang, or played a variety of instruments that included one pyrosistic combination of mother on piano and daughters on trumpet and trombone. Louisa's drawing rooms mixed American hospitality and European sophistication: She played the harp and pianoforte, and sometimes recited her plays or poems; in a city without choral groups or much entertainment, this was high-class fare. Other Secretaries competed for ensembles from the Marine Band, or a Philadelphia lady who kept the guests alert with her tambourine. Notables passing through Washington were grabbed by eager hostesses, and such men as Fenimore Cooper, Washington Irving, and Baron Humboldt became major salon attractions — as did a reformed opium eater who wandered into town and cashed in on both the salon society and its enchantment with all things classical by giving recitations in a Roman toga. Rival coteries were recruited early every autumn and expected to remain with the candidate of their choice throughout the season. If one attended Secretary Adams's dinners or entertainments, he became known as an "Adams man," or by frequenting Secretary Calhoun's let it be known that he backed "Mr. C's politics."

In addition to her visits, therefore, Louisa Adams also developed a regular drawing room with entertainment, and accompanied the sour Presidential non-candidate to every social engagement. Louisa opened their home every Tuesday evening during the social season, and to her husband's astonishment the wine and entertainment attracted prominent members of Congress and cabinet, and from December to May between fifty and a hundred ladies and gentlemen crowded into their home. Moustaches, muttonchop whiskers, epaulettes, stars and ribbons, and high starched collars were in abundance.* "Greek fever" was sweeping America, and women wore adaptations of Greek costumes with turbans of spangled muslin or drooping ostrich plumes in their hair, long chains entwined about their necks, bracelets and armlets, and low-cut gowns with skirts that trailed along the ground and in a few years would evolve into trains. To entertain them with food and music, the Adamses spared little expense. Musicians cost $20 a party, and the members of the Marine Corps band, which Louisa engaged in 1823 and '24, received $5 apiece plus wine and dinner. The Adamses had the piano tuned regularly ($1.50), replaced the carpeting every year ($120), paid grocer's, baker's, miller's, and butcher's bills, and maintained horses, coachmen, and carriages for hauling themselves about Washington on visits and to parties. The cost of tailoring of the coachman's uniform ($34.17) almost equaled his yearly salary ($36). The Adamses hired extra waiters and an extra cook, bought hogsheads of wine ($29) and coal twice a winter ($56 each time to warm their guests). There were other,

---

* Starch, long popular in Europe, had reached the United States, and men's shirt collars stood stiffly against their chins, sometimes reaching their ears.

less obvious costs. They bought calling cards ($8) and a new door knocker ($2.50) to announce the guests' arrival. Before the social season started, they subscribed to the Washington Baths, for $10. Finally, at the end of the social season, the Adamses notified the city's scavengers, and had their outhouse drained and scoured ($6).

Just how valuable were these Tuesday entertainments and Louisa's visits? It is safe to say that John Quincy Adams would not have been elected President without them. Louisa carefully planned each visit and evening, selected the food and wine, and provided entertainment. She hired the musicians and extra servants, decorated, plotted the nuances of guest lists and seating, and ultimately — with her charm, wit, and beauty — compensated for her socially backward husband. Without Louisa, John Quincy would have offended in one way or another the very men who later awarded him the Presidency. One Tuesday evening, for example, Senator Elijah H. Mills, who seemed to attend almost every dinner during his fifteen years in Washington, arrived late for his first social evening at the Adamses', and left early. After a bow to Louisa, a brief chat with the Secretary, a cup of tea and some ice cream, he concluded: "A more unsocial and dissonant party I have seldom been in, even in this wilderness of a city." Two nights later, however, Sen. Mills returned for dinner and "passed the time very pleasantly." He thought Louisa "on the whole, a very pleasant and agreeable woman; but the Secretary has no talent to entertain a mixed company, either by conversation or manners." Indeed, while other Secretaries spent just six hours in their offices, and then at least as much time in the important social rounds, John Quincy Adams had to be dragged from his desk. He was the only Presidential candidate publicly reprimanded in a newspaper advertisement for neglecting his social obligations.

Adams was, socially, as dull as granite, with only small flashes of color or seams of interest. He greeted everyone solemnly with his old pump-handle shake of the hand. He disliked changing his manners or clothes, but he was fastidious and arrogant intellectually, and alienated guests he did not admire. He was self-righteous, dogmatic, filled with wrath, forgetful of small courtesies in society, "cankered with prejudice." An Englishman had written of him in 1812:

> Of all the men whom it was ever my lot to accost and to
> waste civilities upon [he] was the most doggedly and sys-
> tematically repulsive. With a vinegar aspect, cotton in his
> leathern ears, and hatred to England in his heart, he sat in
> the frivolous assemblies of Petersburg like a bull-dog among
> spaniels; and many were the times that I drew monosyllables
> and grim smiles from him and tried in vain to mitigate his
> venom.

Adams confessed to a friend that he was growing frigid in manner, and as he gained experience in politics he was developing a cold heart. While he performed service to his country "with a passion as powerful as it was crabbed," he also lost everything he had treasured from his youthful days in Boston: his good looks, his hair, his sparkling eye, his carefree poetry, his sense of pleasure. Now he enjoyed good jokes, but couldn't tell one; at least one visitor wondered whether he ever laughed in his life. He described himself as a man "of a reserved, gloomy, unsocial temper." He thought drawing rooms boring, and was acutely aware of his weaknesses. "I was not formed to shine in company," he wrote in his diary, "nor to be delighted with it." Yet he worried that guests would laugh at him, or not come to his parties. Adams's political prospects, therefore, were diminished by his personality and social ineptitudes. He recognized his difficulty: "I am a man of reserved, cold, austere, and forbidding manners," he wrote, "My political adversaries say, a gloomy misanthropist, and my personal enemies, an unsocial savage. With a knowledge of the actual defect in my character, I have not the pliability to reform it."

Understanding so well his own weaknesses, John Quincy relied upon Louisa's strengths. In Washington, Louisa's charm, beauty, fluent French, European manners, and ambition enhanced her husband's political aspirations. One guest called her "the most accomplished American lady I have seen," and others praised her as a stylish hostess with gracious manners and a fondness for romantic poetry and music that compensated for her husband's stumbling social skills and stony silences. Charles later described his mother as understanding "the *ways* of kindness"; she quickly made guests feel at ease. Louisa could create ripples of laughter with her wit, and, as a natural mimic facile with languages, she was soon charming the wax out of Congressmen's ears with her new, beguiling Southern accent.

But Louisa Adams was uncomfortable in this public setting and role. She did not like large gatherings or crowds of people, and she struggled even now to overcome her lifelong shyness. Louisa hated the visits; they made her ill. She hated the attention, the loss of privacy, the gossip, the press attacks. Why, then, did she do it? She could have withdrawn, and let John Quincy suffer his own consequences. But Louisa understood that she was central to her husband's success, to his dream. Left to him, the social evenings cultivating Congressmen would have been disastrous. She was, first of all, a victim of her husband's ambition.

Louisa's reasons for putting herself — and John Quincy's candidacy — forward are open to speculation. There is one, clear statement. She was, of course, motivated by a sense of obligation as wife to her husband's wishes. As a man, his life came before hers, and Louisa's place in the family was third, behind her husband and her children. It is not unlikely that John Quincy requested, or even directed Louisa to enter society for him. Second, Louisa was also, as we have seen, ambitious for John Quincy; she shared Abigail's wish that JQA achieve his goal, perhaps because that was what he wanted above all else. Third, and most interesting, by achieving his goal, John Quincy also gave Louisa a new identity. That is, if he became President, she became First Lady. More to the point, Louisa's role in her husband's campaign gave her definition, a purpose. She was no longer merely wife, mother, household supervisor. Her role made Louisa feel special, important, not a mere ornament as she had been in Berlin and St. Petersburg where she had to smile and chat with people vital to her husband's career, but unimportant to her own life. In Washington, so essential was Louisa's role in this campaign, so completely did John Quincy Adams depend upon her — need her — that she gained, for the moment, status beyond being a mere woman. For these years, in the center of her own crowded rooms and the high-stakes politics that would always fascinate her, Louisa Adams became an important *person*.

Remember that women in this time were entrapped by men and society in their homes, made dependent for every need, denied the right to their own lives. The only money women had was given them by men. Women could not travel without male chaperones. They obeyed society's command that they be delicate, submissive, suppressed, unable to engage in intellectual conversations or express their own opinions. Louisa Adams was no "feminist." She clearly understood her own subordination and dependency. She never lost sight of the boundary lines of her life, but she also constantly sought to push them out a little farther. Campaigning for her husband, she could go far beyond these confected limitations: She traveled about Washington freely, and her opinions and reactions were observed and sought. Several times, for example, at drawing rooms in the President's House or elsewhere, she engaged Andrew Jackson and Henry Clay, separately, in gentle debate and humor.

Louisa also knew people observed her closely. "I find that the most trifling occurrences are turned into political machinery," she said. "Even my countenance was watched at the Senate hearing Mr. Pinckney's speech. . . . If my husband's sentiments are to be tried and judged by such variations the gentlemen will have hard work." In a time when women's opinions were kept to themselves, when their spheres of influence extended only to the walls of their homes, Louisa's special role contained enormous significance for her. Valued for her opinions, watched for her reactions, listened to and sought after, Louisa found herself outside the traditional woman's role. Committed, she soon spoke of her visits and invitations and Tuesday drawing rooms as part of "my campaign."

One other point must be mentioned. Louisa was sacrificing none of her own standards, none of her self. She was reaching, exploring new identity; this was a fair exchange of duty for growth, insight. During the height of this campaign, Louisa sat for her portrait by Charles Bird King. He had painted John Quincy Adams in 1819, and eventually would do other members of their family as well. Louisa's finished portrait is large — more than four feet by three feet — and brilliantly colored. She sits in a billowing gossamer white gown, her hair piled upon her head, her graceful hands resting upon a harp and holding a book of music open to one of Thomas Moore's songs. Here, Louisa clearly left her message: The title of her song, painted into her portrait in the middle of this important Presidential campaign, is "Oh Say Not That Woman's Heart Can Be Bought."

4

FROM 1818 THROUGH 1824, while Louisa Adams conducted her "campaign" furthering her husband's career, she also supervised a roaring houseful of children. The Adamses not only raised their three sons, but also took in orphaned children from Louisa's side of the family, and abused and abandoned nieces and nephews from John Quincy's. By 1820, the Adamses had living with them between eight and ten teenagers. It was not an easy parenthood, and much of the burden fell upon Louisa.

John Quincy had little time for his own sons. His father, in 1818, had to remind him that "children must not be wholly forgotten in the midst of public duties." John Quincy translated attention to mean instruction, and continued writing letters to his sons detailing their studies, habits, duties. He fumed over defects, real or imaginary, in their characters that might prevent them from fulfilling his wishes. He preached at his sons, and demanded that they rise early, be punctual, and temperate, attend church regularly, keep diaries. He sought to regulate their lives hour to hour. But his sons almost always failed him. On Christmas Day, 1820, for example, Adams gathered his boys and read Pope's *Messiah* to them, and was keenly disappointed in their reactions. "Not one of them, excepting George," he lamented, "appeared to take the slightest interest in it; nor is there one of them who has any relish for literature." Adams was convinced that his sons' "indolent minds" were contented with "the blast of mediocrity." He confided in his diary that they would never answer his hopes; he prayed that none would realize his fears.

Each son went on to Harvard, but only George did well. He won the Boylston prize in his junior year,* and, significantly, it was his grandfather who praised him, not his father. "Our George," John Adams wrote proudly to JQA, "has gained the first prize, and bears his honour meekly. He is a dutiful son." At least once, Louisa had to intercede between her husband and George, and stop John Quincy from sending him a cruel letter about joining a student romp during his junior year instead of studying. George graduated and studied law in Boston under Daniel Webster. John entered Harvard in 1819, and underwent a four-year struggle with his father's expectations. He complained of having to study hard, and of not receiving a large enough allowance, and John Quincy accused John of taking "dissipation and extravagance" as his twin companions. "Are you so much of a baby," John Quincy wrote him, "that you must be taxed to spell your letters by sugar plums? Or are you such an independent gentleman that you can brook no control and must have everything you ask for? If so, I desire you not to write for anything to me."

When Adams learned that John, in his junior year, stood only forty-fifth in a class of eighty-five students, he refused to allow his son to come home to Washington during the Christmas holidays. He must stay in Cambridge and study. "I could take no satisfaction in seeing you," he wrote. "I could feel nothing but sorrow and shame in your presence" until he redeemed "that disgraceful standing." Even when John rose to sixteenth in his class, his father was unsatisfied, and said that if he stood lower than fifth, JQA would not attend his son's commencement. John Quincy never got to carry out his threat. John was

---

* George defeated Ralph Waldo Emerson.

expelled from Harvard for participating in "The Great Rebellion," a student riot, in 1823,* and returned to Washington and moved in with his mother and father.

Charles entered Harvard at age fourteen, but his father had to intercede to get him accepted into the freshman class. By the end of his term, Charles rested near the bottom: fifty-first out of fifty-nine students. He wrote his parents, pleading to quit college, and confessing that he was "addicted . . . to depraved habits" that he could not resist, such as smoking cigars, playing billiards, and drinking wine with his friends. John Quincy thought the culprit was idleness and living off campus, while Louisa was certain that vice was indigenous to Harvard. Had John or — worse — George confessed to drinking and billiards, and languished at the bottom of his class, John Quincy's wrath would have seared them. Instead, once more underscoring Charles's favored position within the family, John Quincy told his youngest son that if he would employ his time upon his studies, the father would be satisfied "be his standing what it may." Charles agreed that there was a "higher end" to college than a steady round of billiards, oysters, champagne, and whist, and undertook serious reading (but resolutely avoided mathematics). He graduated in 1825, within hailing distance of the upper ranks of his class, but returned to Washington without attending commencement to avoid embarrassment to the family. He started studying law under his father.

Throughout these years, Louisa and John Quincy also raised nieces and nephews, and endured daily turmoil and disruption in their home. In 1818, the three children of Louisa's sister Nancy, who had died in 1810, and her husband Walter, who had died in 1815, moved permanently into the Adamses' household. Their two sons, Johnson and Thomas, gave the Adamses five rebellious young men to raise; their daughter, Mary, romantically entangled each Adams son, and finally married one of them.

* Letters of protest from the Secretary of State to the president of Harvard to have John reinstated failed, and not until 1873 did the Harvard Corporation consent to posthumous degrees for John Adams 2d and his classmates.

Johnson Hellen, one year older than George, was quiet and studious; he attended Princeton and later became a lawyer. Charles loved arguing politics with Johnson, who turned out to be a secret Jackson supporter under the Adamses' roof; Johnson and Charles both placed bets *against* John Quincy in 1824. Like many of their guests, Johnson had difficulty leaving the Adamses. He moved out in 1822, moved back in a few days later, moved out again to Rockville, Maryland, to start his law practice, moved back in with President and Mrs. Adams at the White House, moved out for the last time in 1828, but visited "very often" while building his own home. One time, John Quincy wrote Louisa that Johnson had moved out that morning "with a tear in his eye. God bless him! I told him he must let us often hear from him, and often come and see us.—And that he would always find his chamber ready to receive him." Thomas Hellen, born in 1809, caused Louisa and John Quincy much trouble. Thomas would enter Harvard in 1825, after John Quincy had paid his way through Exeter, but in 1827 would be dismissed for "licentiousness." He received $125 a quarter from Uncle JQA, a handsome sum (compare that to their coachman's salary), and still ran up large bills at college; licentiousness then as now was not cheap. Louisa, sounding like John Quincy, told Thomas to overcome his bad habits with fortitude, temperance, "No chaises, no nonsense of any kind. The only cause of your unhappiness is the unbounded indolence of your character." But her scolding did no good.

Opposite these young men there fluttered a small, brilliant array of butterflies: a twirling of young female cousins, the first generation of Victorian America, already adept at the coquettish sigh, the feathered fan, the swoon and the faint. They raised confinement to chambers to a social art, and when they emerged, their sole and glorious purpose was to enhance, bedazzle, allure, captivate. They kept the Adamses' house in a perpetual season of tremulous excitement. The best of this species was Mary Catherine Hellen, born in 1807, who burst forth as a lovely young woman, flirtatious, irresistible, short and plump with shiny brown hair, a radiant complexion, bright hazel eyes that together made a gaudy, frivolous, and elusive lure that each young

Adams would, in turn, pursue. Other young women joined Mary. Abigail Adams Smith, Nabby's oldest, stayed with Aunt Louisa and Uncle John Quincy for long periods. When Thomas Adams started drinking heavily and becoming violent, his daughters, Elizabeth and Abigail 2d, and his sons, Isaac Hull and John Quincy 2d, took shelter from the alcoholic storms with the Adamses in Washington.

Louisa and John Quincy never complained — not for long, anyway — about the arrival of these children, and they fed, clothed, educated, and cared for them all. The Adamses treated each child like their own, perhaps better. The doors of their homes, and the White House, were always open, and each guest remained as long as he or she wished. Mary Hellen stayed a lifetime, and became Louisa Adams's closest female friend; after 1834, Mary lived with Louisa for the rest of her life.

It is difficult to imagine Louisa conducting the Presidential campaign, or John Quincy conceiving some of the most important foreign policy of the nineteenth century, given the uproar of the Adamses' home. One Tuesday, for example, Louisa had a severe headache and recorded the day's irritations. Mary took music lessons at ten, scraping on the violin, accompanied by her music master. Charles then started his lessons, which lasted an hour and a half, after which the dancing master arrived and all the young people in the house rolled up the parlor carpet and danced for three hours. George and Charles then played the flute and violin for an hour. When they finished, the first guests for Louisa's weekly drawing room began arriving.

The presence of a young female guest, coinciding with college holidays, sometimes spilled the turbulence of the Adamses' house into Washington politics and society. When Miss Fanny Johnson, a teenage cousin from Frederick, Maryland, stayed fifty-one days with the Adamses, in December and January 1820, her flirtations embroiled George, John, Johnson, and a U.S. Senator in an issue of manners and the threat of a duel over what the lady did or did not say. The turbulence even sucked into its vortex the Secretary of State, who tried to negotiate between Fanny and a misled suitor by drawing up a document — a domestic treaty of peace — to be signed by the aggrieved parties. Louisa found it all "so irritable, what with the coquettish airs of the young lady who was alternately playing upon them all and I believe very willing to foment the discord. My home was pretty much like a bedlam broke loose." When Fanny finally departed, she left the young men "in the depths of belle passion," and the Adamses wondering about the thin line between sanity and insanity.

5

THERE WERE OTHER distractions from the politics and campaigning in Washington. By the winter of 1821–22, Louisa Adams had turned forty-seven and the rounds of society, the roaring household, the psychological burden of being watched and examined and criticized were making her physically and emotionally ill, "and I really sometimes think they will make me crazy." Louisa suffered from several ailments, not all of them real, but all painful. Hemorrhoids troubled her greatly, and she complained, as she had in St. Petersburg, of erysipelas, a disease not uncommon among frequently delivered women, which sometimes resulted in acute endocarditis. Louisa's symptoms included rapid rising fever, tension of the skin, a "nervous irritability," and severe swelling of a hard, well-defined ridge across her forehead. Her face puffed until her eyelids closed; her lips, ears, and scalp swelled until she was unrecognizable, and the disease so inflamed her hands and feet that she couldn't write or walk comfortably for several days after an attack. She suffered this disease the rest of her life. One of the most beautiful hostesses in Washington, Louisa turned ugly when erysipelas visited; at least once in 1821 she was so severely disfigured temporarily that John Quincy would not let her go to a ball. Louisa, in fact, complained that year of being "under the most gloomy auspices in respect to health and totally unable to meet the exigencies of the bustling season." Her illnesses carried political importance. Because of them, during the 1821–22 season, Louisa worried that many new members of Congress coming to Washington did not know her, or her husband.

In the spring of 1822, after the Washington social season had ended, Louisa's brother Thomas Baker Johnson arrived in Washington for an urgent health consultation with her. He had left New Orleans, where he had been postmaster since 1808, because he was suffering from bleeding hemorrhoids and in extreme pain. Thomas Johnson's problem was serious: Hemorrhoids can reach egg size and cause painful spasmodic contractions. Diagnosing Johnson's condition and treating it, however, were two very different issues. Louisa discovered that in dealing with her brother's poor health, she found help for her own.

Diseases of every description scoured the United States, and the sick often depended upon unlicensed, sometimes uneducated doctors; only one physician in ten had a medical degree or its equivalent in training, and the medicines they dispensed were of dubious help and often harmful. Doctors had few diagnostic aids — no stethoscope or oral thermometer — and understood little about diseases. Pulmonary consumption was regarded as incurable, and dyspepsia thought to be caused by "ardent spirits" in salt meat and spoiled cooking. Doctors said that gout followed gluttony, drunkenness, and debauchery; patients considered it proof of living well, enjoying fine wines and rich foods, and a man sick with gout never concealed it. The disease carried the mark of class. Physicians and clergy together assured people that cholera was divine punishment for sin, and attacked only those who had been corrupted by drink, immorality, gluttony. Yellow fever swept America's cities in 1817 and 1819, and when the disease broke out people shuttered their homes. Some thought smoke prevented it, and even women and children puffed cigars. Others chewed garlic, or put it in their shoes, or burned gunpowder, tobacco, or nitre, or sprinkled the walls and floors with vinegar. Those who ventured out covered their faces with handkerchiefs soaked in camphor, or carried pieces of tarred rope or smelling bottles filled with "thieves vinegar." None of it did any good.

The great medicine of the day was mercury, often administered as calomel, or mercurous chloride. Louisa sometimes worried that during her illnesses she might "be killed by Calomel as my poor mother was." (Exactly how Louisa's mother died, and whether the overdose was deliberate or not, remains speculative.) Doctors also gave opium freely, and patient-addicts were common. The most widely used treatment for any illness was bleeding. Disease was still thought to be caused by bad humors and bile — hence "bilious fever" — and doctors thought that bloodletting lessened "the morbid and excessive action in the bloodvessels," eased pain, induced sleep, prevented hemorrhages, and safeguarded against relapses. Before being bled, a patient was usually given an emetic purge and mercury to produce excitement and inflammation of the glands of the mouth and throat. The patient might also be blistered.

Louisa was often the best doctor in the Adamses' house. She learned her skills through practice — one hesitates to say trial and error — and by sharing remedies with other women. The Adamses, like many families, kept a well-stocked medicine chest, which opened like an accordion, and contained six rows of shelves that displayed labeled bottles ranging in size from six one-pint containers to sixteen one-ounce vials. The contents give a good idea of the opportunities available to the imaginative healer. Included were castor oil, a variety of medicinal wines, tincture of rhubarb, paragoric; calcined magnesia, Peruvian bark, epsom salts, nitre; sweet oil, spirits of hartshorn, syrup of squills, spirits of turpentine, tincture of bark; camphor, laudanum (opium in alcohol), "elixir vitriol"; ether, tincture of foxglove, tincture of steel, arsenic, sugar of lead; borax, tartar emetic, "corrosive sublimate," "lunar caustic," oil of wormseed, essence of peppermint. The chest also contained drawers with scales and weights, mortar and pestle, lancets, syringes, injection pipes and bags.

Thomas sought Louisa's advice about his hemorrhoids both because of her affliction (hemorrhoids were prevalent among the Adams family, too), and because Louisa was a smart and good physician. Moreover, she and John Quincy knew some of the best doctors in America. Thomas had obviously not responded to any remedy, and remained in great distress and pain. Uneasily, perhaps with a sense of final choice, Louisa and her brother agreed to see a surgeon. The decision was difficult. In these medical times, doctors employed none of the sharp, delicate tools of modern surgery: no honed sterile instruments, no self-absorbing sutures — and no anesthesia. The patient lay conscious upon a table, often in excruciating pain, held down by attendants. The best surgeons, therefore, were those who could cut most rapidly. On June 21, 1822, Louisa (with Mary Hellen) and Thomas left Washington in the Adamses' carriage for Philadelphia. In that city lived and practiced America's most respected and eccentric surgeon, a doctor with the felicitous name of Philip Syng Physick.

Louisa and Thomas went immediately to Dr. Physick's office on Mulberry Street, near Third, where the doctor greeted them stiffly, coolly. Physick was fifty-four, of medium build with a high forehead that gave him a pale, marble-like appearance. He wore his hair "powdered and clubbed" in a queue that concealed enormous ears. He had a large nose, hazel eyes that penetrated the observer, thin lips and a wide mouth. Other physicians thought Philip Syng Physick a "cold, aloof, precise man," one who projected a "dignified and elegant" manner with an air of melancholy. The surgeon seldom laughed, and his rare smiles could be individually recalled by his students and patients.

Dr. Physick examined Thomas and diagnosed his case as "a dreadful one," Louisa said, "though we trust not hopeless." The question of "a painful operation" was postponed until Thomas could gain the strength to bear it. But his confidence in Dr. Physick gave Thomas "great courage, and he is determined to go through it, let the result be what it may. . . . The Dr. says he looks at him with astonishment for his sufferings are beyond description. All hemorodial complaints he says should be attended to early, and that he can assure me that nothing will do but the Knife, and it is only deceiving patients and prolonging their misery to pretend otherwise." Dr. Physick assured Louisa that he had never killed a patient in such an operation.

Louisa liked and trusted Philip Physick. She thought him "a very mild Gentlemanly man," and either his manner or his reputation made her bold, for she asked Dr. Physick to examine her hemorrhoids, too, "a complaint with which I have so long suffered." Louisa partially undressed, baring only that which was essential to the diagnosis, and Dr. Physick took a look. He concluded – as surgeons will – that she must have the same operation as Thomas, "performed sooner or later." But Louisa feared the knife. "I am however not in a hurry to do anything in so unpleasant a business," she wrote John Quincy, "and shall certainly take time to think about it. This is not pleasant news, but there is no choice when our doom is to suffer."

Dr. Physick ordered Louisa, Mary, and Thomas into a boardinghouse at 62 South Sixth Street, between Chestnut and Walnut, in the heart of Philadelphia. He lodged his paying patients at the house, where they lived comfortably, said Louisa, "at five dollars a week a head . . . and we propose to stay [here] as quietly as possible until he decides when the dreadful business can be done." Physick had personally selected the location, Louisa learned, because he "never knew it to be unhealthy in this part of the city." Other sections of Philadelphia Physick termed noxious – quite correctly – and forbade his patients from entering them. Nor could they leave the city without his permission, for Dr. Physick believed that the countryside contained bad air and fevers. Occasionally, he permitted a chosen few to scurry across pestiferous New Jersey to the salubrious sea baths along the coast. But the dangers were obvious. When one patient, a Mrs. Weston, disobeyed Dr. Physick and slipped out of Philadelphia without his permission, she got as far as Trenton, New Jersey, before suddenly dropping dead. The lesson impressed those left behind in the Sixth Street boardinghouse, who tsk-tsked and nodded in agreement at Dr. Physick's wisdom.

Louisa, Mary, and Thomas found the boardinghouse dull, but comfortable and spacious. A heavy "overpowering" summer heat settled upon the entire East Coast, unmoving through July, cooking everything. John Quincy complained of a succession of "roasters" day and night in Washington that reduced him "to the condition of a vegetable." Louisa and Mary took turns sitting by the open windows of their rooms, absorbing whatever breezes drifted in from the State House gardens across the street, and taking turns caring for the limp Thomas, but the task soon grew tedious, and Thomas whimpering. He got worse when Dr. Physick, who refused to cut in hot weather, postponed the operation until the temperature went down, whenever that might occur. In the interim, Dr. Physick prescribed a "rigid diet." For two weeks, Thomas could eat nothing but Iceland Moss, a lichen, "which is a powerful stomach-ice," Louisa wrote John Quincy, "and which appears to agree with him, although it is very nauseous to the taste." Louisa secretly delighted in Thomas's grimaces, and when the diet became too awful she gleefully wrote John Quincy about its potential in Washington, and recommended that two quarreling politicians "be condemned to Dr. Physicks Soups for six months if they are so fond of depletion." The diet, however, was so complicated and required so much preparation, including cooking for eight to ten hours, that Louisa and Mary became prisoners both to Thomas and the cookpot.

As they waited for the heat to lift, Louisa turned the postponement into a small holiday. She read all the newspapers she could find, and re-read Dr. Rush's *Treatise on Diseases of the Mind*. If her family was driving her, as she said, "raving mad," she wanted to know why; Louisa reached the comforting conclusion "that we all have a Crack." She also procured an old piano "to strum on," and wrote to George in Washington for her "large bound [music] Book with the Mocking Bird, your Uncle's delight." Soon the old boardinghouse filled with "By the Side of the Weeping Willow," "The Hunters of the Alps" (a "pleasing rondo"), and "Ah! Why Did I Gather This Delicate Flower?" Best of all, Louisa discovered the landlady, an unmarried relic named Miss Pardon, who loved to fret over Thomas, to his pleasure, and brag about Dr. Physick and his "*glorious* remedies." Miss Pardon was about sixty, "kindhearted and talkative," and a gentle, chattering soul who sported a strong mind tunneled with gossip and trivia that surfaced loaded with malaprops. Right off, Miss Pardon told Louisa her life history, and explained that in her youth it had been prophesied that she would be called an Old Maid, but she could bear that "asperation" very well. Louisa called her "our good Miss Malaprop," and when Miss Pardon's gentle blunders caught her off guard, she was forced to stifle an embarrassing burst of laughter by pressing her handkerchief to her mouth.

By far the most interesting and important work Louisa did during these hot and dull days of waiting involved politics. Some of the leading politicians of Philadelphia visited her almost every day, and in effect she created a salon with Charles Jared Ingersoll, a former Congressman and now U.S. Attorney in the city, and his wife; Rep. John Sergeant and his wife; Joseph Hopkinson, a former Congressman, family friend, and author of "Hail, Columbia," the national air, and his wife; and Robert Walsh, co-founder and editor of the *National Gazette and Literary Register*. They sat around Miss Pardon's and dissected President Monroe's Cabinet and appointments, and the upcoming election of 1824. They supported John Quincy, and Louisa urged her husband to come to Philadelphia "and show yourself if only for a week" and campaign. At first, Adams responded, with some humor, that he was like Prometheus bound to his rock, hard at work as Secretary. But as Louisa persisted — "Do for once gratify me, I implore you," she wrote, "and if harm come of it I promise never to advise you again" — John Quincy got furious. He would not go to Philadelphia "to shew . . . how much I long to be President." Other friends warned him, he said, that unless he made campaign excursions the office would not be his. "Well, and what then?" he wrote her. "There will be candidates enough for the Presidency without me." John Quincy declared his Macbeth policy: "If chance will have me King; why, chance may crown me. / Without my stir." He would remain in Washington, aloof, waiting.

John Quincy was afraid of the perils of campaigning; he thought intrigue and schemes faced him everywhere, and felt opposed by "all the leading members of both Houses of Congress, all the Editors of accredited Printing Presses throughout the Union, and all the caucusing managers of the State Legislatures." All of them were "crying me down, and disgracing me in the estimation of the People. — Meanwhile I have not a single active partizan in Congress. — Not a single Printing Press in pay, or in promise. — Not one member of any one State Legislature disposed to caucus for me, or connected with my interest by any stimulant expectation of his own." Who, then, would nominate him, put his name forward?

Louisa tried both to promote and protect her husband and his candidacy. "I can boldly stand and meet the rude shock of party clamour without a blush," she told him, but she knew that he — with his infamous temper — could not. When the *Columbian Observer* appeared in mid-August, for example, carrying, for want of anything better, the libel that John Quincy Adams did not wear a waistcoat or cravat, and went to church barefooted, Louisa jollied him out of his anger. When he wrote of these "lies" and "back-biters," she replied that her salon guests "asked if you really went to Church without shoes or stockings. I replied that I had once heard you rode to your office with your head to your Horses Tail, and that the one fact was as likely as the other." Louisa offered him good but unheeded advice: "Put a little wool in your ears and don't read the papers."

Walsh's paper, however, pulled John Quincy into a nasty exchange of letters with Jonathan Russell, which revealed JQA's fearsome overreaction to public attack. Russell, one of the American commissioners at Ghent, made charges in Walsh's *Gazette* about John Quincy's role in the negotiations, and raised doubts about JQA's motives and patriotism. Adams came out gunning, and in a series of long written assaults enfiladed Russell's position. He bragged to Louisa about how easy Russell was to defeat, but yet went on, and on. Louisa tried to calm her husband, and Walsh, a bit embarrassed, told her to inform John Quincy that there was "no dissenting voice" in Philadelphia. Adams had won. Even those in support of Russell conceded, Louisa wrote, that he was "*demolished.*" Yet John Quincy continued his attacks. So persuasive, so deadly, so unrelenting was he that for decades afterward when Americans wished to describe the complete pulverizing of an opponent, they used the transitive verb: "to Jonathan-Russell." It was, backhandedly, a tribute to Adams's ruthlessness.

6

Dᴜʀɪɴɢ ᴛʜᴇ ꜰɪʀꜱᴛ ᴡᴇᴇᴋ of August, rains washed the heat from Philadelphia. Dr. Physick deemed it cool enough to prepare himself and his surgical skills and instruments for Thomas Johnson.

Louisa and Thomas were well aware that surgery, no matter how elementary the operation or skilled the surgeon, carried great risks. The basic surgical tools consisted of several large amputation knives, chisels, hammers, and scalpels honed as best the surgeon could to some degree of sharpness. Doctors operated in street clothes, in homes or boardinghouses, on conscious patients. Sterilization was unknown, and infection a great killer. The certainty of fatal infection precluded major operations, and almost all surgery performed was limited to the surface of the body, superficial orifices, and the extremities. Yet surgeons like Dr. Physick sometimes performed daring operations to save patients. In 1809, Dr. Ephraim McDowell of Danville, Kentucky, removed a 22½-pound ovarian tumor from a woman who remained conscious during the entire operation, and lived for twenty years longer. In 1813, Dr. Wright Post of New York successfully corrected an aneurysm of the femoral artery, and Dr. John Ingalls of Boston amputated an arm at the shoulder joint. Both patients survived.

Before the sixteenth century, physicians had used for anesthesia the soporific sponge soaked in a mixture of opium, henbane, hemlock, lettuce, and mandragora dried in the sun; before operating, the doctor saturated the sponge with boiling water, and the patient inhaled the vapors. But this practice faded from medicine, and by 1500 anesthesia was almost unknown in surgery. Death from trauma, however, was not. By 1822, the prevailing attitude was that patients remained awake during surgery. To do otherwise was, somehow, unmedical. The author of a significant work on surgical anatomy wrote: "To escape pain in surgical operations is a chimera which we cannot expect in our time." Anesthesia would not be reintroduced to surgery until 1846, by a dentist using sulphuric ether. The best Thomas and Louisa might hope for from Dr. Physick, therefore, was thirty drops of laudanum and a glass of cherry bounce.

In 1822, Philip Syng Physick was the best surgeon in America, and he had stood at the head of his profession for almost a third of a century. He knew how to cut. He had studied medicine in Philadelphia, London, and Edinburgh, and at the height of his career he was both Professor of Surgery and Chairman of Anatomy at the University of Pennsylvania and at Pennsylvania Hospital in Philadelphia. Surgeons had to know anatomy. To expose and ligate an artery, amputate a leg at the hip or an arm at the shoulder, open the abdomen for excision of an ovarian tumor — and do it without anesthesia — called for speed, the precise knowledge of anatomical structure, and the "feel" of human tissue. Dr. Physick had that feel. He was decisive, quick and accurate — unlike a Boston colleague who, in his swift amputation of a leg at the hip, also severed one of his patient's testicles and two fingers of an assistant. No, Dr. Physick brought to the surgical bench "a correct, sharp and discriminating eye; a hand delicate in touch, dextrous in movement and of unswerving firmness; a perfect composure and self-possession." That, anyway, was his public image.

No region of the human body escaped Philip Physick's visit. He cut, probed, inserted, palpated, dissected, stitched, bled, and healed. He operated on the head, the eyes, the stomach and anus. He had a propensity, learned from Dr. Benjamin Rush, for phlebotomy. He was among the first surgeons to practice proctology; he devised the curved bistoury for treatment of fistula-in-ano. He bled the body for every disease, from cataracts to hydroencephalus. He won deserved national recognition as an opthalmic surgeon, and in his first recorded operation extracted the opaque crystalline lens from a patient's eye. He later described a daring opthamalic operation to his medical students:

> I once saw a case where the person had washed his face with urine whilst labouring under gonorrhea. Inflammation supervened and all the cornea became opaque. The patient called on me for his sight and from his anxious request, I consented

to operate on his eye, though with little hopes of success. I passed a knife thro' the cornea and cut off a piece of the iris. The eye was then closed and the patient put to bed. He can now see to read if the print be large.

In 1797, Dr. Physick performed his first lithotomy, cutting for stones in the bladder, and soon won an international reputation for developing new surgical techniques and skill in the operation. In 1831, at age sixty-three, Dr. Physick would perform his last and perhaps most famous operation, a lithotomy, on Chief Justice John Marshall, who was then seventy. Marshall selected Physick for his skill and reputation, and although the doctor, pleading age, first tried to turn the operation over to an assistant, Dr. Physick cut the Chief Justice in October, and removed more than a thousand stones from his bladder. Marshall lived another four years.

Dr. Physick also loved the instruments of his profession. He experimented and improved on them. He advanced the skills of surgeons by developing new methods of traction for dislocations, new treatments for hip-joint disease by immobilization. He won international recognition for splints of his design for major fractures of the femur and ankles. Here he employed the famous wood carver, William Rush, who built splints for Dr. Physick that reached from mid-thorax to ankle and wrapped around half the patient's body. The doctor immobilized his patients behind these embattlements for a year or more, during which he and Rush applied two to four new splints. Dr. Physick also injected his patients using new pewter syringes. He designed a large flexible catheter for the abdomen, which he forced down the esophagus as a stomach tube. He developed other catheters as well, preferring his waxed linen bougies to the metal and gum-elastic tools other surgeons employed, and he twisted, screwed, and pushed them into every human orifice. Dr. Physick relieved urinary obstruction from enlargement of the prostate by passing up the penis of his male patients a bougie-tipped catheter covered with the intestine of a sheep for softness and lubrication, distended slightly with warm water. It worked: His skills as a genitourinary surgeon were widely admired, and in demand.

One of Dr. Physick's most valuable contributions to surgery was the use of animal ligature. He first tried leather, impregnating it with varnish to lengthen the time before absorption; then buckskin, parchment, French kid, and catgut. For tying arteries after surgery, Dr. Physick perfected the practice of cutting animal ligatures short and permitting them to become imbedded in tissues and absorbed. He invented the needle forceps, which allowed him to pass a needle with a ligature beneath a deep bleeding vein or artery, and tie it. And he designed the guillotine tonsillotome for the removal of tonsils, and a form of wire snare, a double canula, to slough tumors — an instrument that would soon greatly interest Louisa Adams and Thomas Johnson.

Louisa called Dr. Physick "one of the great men of the age" — wisely leaving room for her husband — and a fellow surgeon proclaimed that the doctor "could even talk away disease." But Philip Physick inspired, along with admiration, feelings of dread. Dr. Physick treated patients and cadavers alike, and his medical students, denied access by his coldness to Physick's advice and counsel, believed that he actually preferred the latter. Patients who survived his surgery, however, made no such complaints, and praised him with amusing verse:

> Sing Physic! Sing Physic! For Philip Syng Physick
>   Is dubbed Dr. Phil for his wonderful skill;
> Each sick phiz he'll physic, he'll cure every phthisic,
>   Their lips fill with Physic, with potion and pill.
>
> *   *   *
>
> Lo! Physick! the college permits thee to work
>   In curing diseases the greatest of curses,
> Syng! dance then with joy when thou think'st at one jerk
> Physic can empty both stomach and purses.

Dr. Physick did indeed accumulate wealth, much of it from wise investments, and enjoyed an extensive income that enhanced the adulation. His patients thrived on his abuse, both surgical and verbal, no matter how corrosive or eccentric he became.

It would neatly tie Philip Physick's life together to write that his first love was not just his family, patients, cadavers, instruments, or inventions, but simply medicine. That would excuse his eccentricities: his direction, for example, that his close medical associate take the pulse of black men with a foot-long stick. He insisted upon strict, undeviating diets: he was, after all, also the first doctor to use carbonated water medicinally. He allowed, for example, a woman with breast cancer to eat only a piece of dry bread with a little salt and a glass of cold water three times a day. No one was certain whether the carcinogens or starvation got her first. Dr. Physick feared burial alive, and ordered that his body upon death be kept in a warm room, well wrapped, to insure early putrification, and that his grave be guarded to prevent his body's being disinterred and sold for necropsy — a peculiar request from an active morbid anatomist. Physick was dogmatic, arrogant, intolerant. He permitted no discussion of his treatments. When a patient complained of innumerable bleedings, Dr. Physick reached for his coat: "Sir," he said, "I must have my own way, or none at all; I bid you good day." Almost without equal, Dr. Physick knew his way around the human body. But he understood little of the human heart. In 1800, he had married Elizabeth Emlen, a Quaker woman, and they produced two daughters, two sons, and one of the earliest divorces in America. Philip Physick had insisted upon keeping the windows of their home tightly closed, even in summer, and always slept with gloves on his hands to improve his surgical feel. His behavior drove his wife to drink, and they separated two years before her death in 1820.

But, in truth, Philip Physick did not love medicine. It made him sick. It attacked him: He bore the scars of smallpox, and suffered from two separate yellow fever episodes caught while performing post-mortem studies of the disease in the field during the epidemics of 1793 and 1797. Philip's father had pushed him into medicine, after being impressed with his young son's surgical dressing upon the father's injured finger. At Pennsylvania Hospital, dutifully studying medicine, Philip Physick became so nauseated while watching the amputation of a leg that he fled the surgical amphitheater. Another time, the shock of seeing a cadaver boiling away in a pot, to remove the flesh from its bones so it could be used for anatomical study, drove the young medical student home, where he begged his father for permission to quit. But the older man insisted, and Physick returned to become the leading medical inventor and surgeon of his age. No, medicine was never Dr. Physick's passion, nor even his first choice of a profession. All his life, until he died of a heart attack in December 1837, Philip Syng Physick wanted to follow his maternal grandfather's path, and be a silversmith.

On August 7, Dr. Physick operated on Thomas Johnson "with the utmost success," Louisa wrote, "and giving great hopes of the recovery of our poor patient." During the ordeal, Louisa had paced her room, "sick of anxiety and dread, prey to the exaggerated terrors of a fertile imagination." But Dr. Physick was not only an outstanding surgeon, he was also quick, and he had left the boardinghouse fifteen minutes before Louisa knew he had finished. Louisa thought it "a slight operation," and concluded that "the suffering was not very great, but the soreness will of course be painful." Thomas suffered a few hours "of great anguish," and passed "a wretched night," Louisa said. But he ran no fever, and was soon more cheerful than he had been for a long time. There were still four or five tumors to remove, and on the seventeenth, Dr. Physick cut again. This time, Thomas suffered "great anguish" for two hours, and Louisa gave him a dose of laudanum — opium — which calmed "the irritation of his nerves." Dr. Physick, however, pained by rheumatism and "severely indisposed," postponed the third operation. Thomas, out from under the knife temporarily, improved, and by the thirty-first was allowed to eat meat and ride horseback.

Louisa, however, was soon bored by games of backgammon with Mary, and the endless nursing of Thomas, who, she said, "certainly wastes away in a wonderful manner." With his ensconced audience, Thomas enacted the dying male, and fancied himself "afflicted with every disease under the Sun." But Louisa, tiring of Thomas and Philadelphia, and wishing to "*operate* a change" in Mary's manners — the sixteen-year-old had taken to sulking — left with Mary by steamboat for a holiday up the Delaware River in Bordentown where Joseph Hopkinson, their escort and host, took vacations. This quaint New Jersey village, founded in 1682, was a spa attracting Philadelphians, with its own restorative mineral water. Bordentown's homes rose upward from the Delaware to a bluff, where the grandees built their mansions, it was said, so they could watch their own ships and barges hauling their own produce and merchandise downriver. In the windswept village, the pastel-colored wood and brick homes with shuttered windows, set flush with the sidewalks, hid gardens of boxwood and evergreens, of sycamores and maples. Along the streets, one-hundred-foot elms sheltered everyone who passed. Here, at 101 Farnsworth Avenue, Hopkinson showed them into his red-brick home, with its large shuttered windows and white doorway, which his family, among the fashionables of Philadelphia society, maintained for summer visitors.

At the Hopkinson's, Louisa found "a very merry party of young Ladies, mostly Carolinians . . . most of them wild as unbroken Colts." They formed a silly, playful group; Louisa at forty-seven was the oldest. Right off, out of sheer exuberance, they all weighed themselves, and Louisa complained to John Quincy that in these days, when fat was beautiful, "all the Girls" outweighed her, and even Mary had the advantage of Louisa by four pounds, 106 to 102. That evening, the women sang and danced together, and performed "imitations of acting," and ended their first evening uninhibited by men — almost drunk with happiness "with a ludicrously sentimental parting, something like an Irish howl." This was the first holiday of Louisa Adams's adult life, and a time of reassessment and gathering strength to overcome her illnesses. During the next four days, Louisa, Mary, and Elizabeth Hopkinson rowed out early on Crosswick's Creek to fish, without luck. Despite awakening the next morning "very stiff" from the workout, Louisa "determined to persevere in the same course by way of cure," and immediately after breakfast rowed out again to fish, ignoring her blistered hands. Louisa also walked around Bordentown, and with the rowing and walking soon found new strength.

Louisa and the other women were also invited by Joseph Bonaparte, exiled King of Spain and older brother of Napoleon, to tea at his estate. Bonaparte had fled Europe for the United

States in 1815 after the One Hundred Days, and would live seventeen years in Bordentown before attempting to return to the Continent. The United States was a friendly, neutral, prospering nation with several large French settlements which welcomed exiled French leaders. Bonaparte also held a lifelong dream of being a country gentleman, and in 1816, encouraged by his friends and advisors Steven Girard and Charles Jared Ingersoll of Philadelphia, he had purchased fifteen hundred acres at Point Breeze, near Bordentown, where he lived in elegance surrounded by a fortune in paintings and sculpture and, it was rumored, guarding Napoleon's crown jewels. Only his daughter lived with him (Joseph's wife refused to come to America), and he kept a mistress, Annette Savage, seven miles away at Bow Hill in Trenton, which wags renamed Beau Hill. While Napoleon served out his life confined to the bleak island of St. Helena in the South Atlantic, Joseph lived high above the Delaware, and one rode through the enormous parklike setting of lawns, shrubs, flowering trees, and statues of dogs and lions, of naked Greek gods and goddesses, to reach his villa. Louisa thought Joseph "very handsome . . . very much like Napoleon," but somewhat stiff in manner. For several weeks she regularly visited him and his small, pensive daughter, and they gossiped in French about Washington, Paris, bullfights in Spain; Louisa joined them for elegant French breakfasts, or rowed up the creek with small parties of her women friends and Bonaparte to fish.

Louisa filled her days with exercise and fun. It was as though she were young again, on holiday with her sisters, unencumbered by social dress or conformities. She walked to the spring for healthful drinks, and with the other women got out the Hopkinsons' boat and rowed down the creek from Point Breeze for an hour or two before dinner, then ate, and rowed back. They held readings in the evenings, or played whist "where we had as noisey a party as you can possibly imagine, absolutely shouting with laughter at every *jeu d'esprit* and puns which were uttered, and which fell with copious abundance from *our* lips." This was a special time for Louisa. She was free, away briefly from the demands of politics and society. She gained strength, muscles, and put her illnesses aside. She indulged the fun and intellect she so greatly treasured. Best of all, she shared herself with other women, which she had not done so freely for almost thirty years. When she was leaving, Louisa walked to the steamboat dock surrounded by new friends. She felt liberated and relaxed. "Nearly ten weeks of my time since I left home have been spent in pain and anxiety," she wrote John Quincy, "but this week has been one in which I have lived a year."

Louisa Adams needed her renewed strength. Immediately when she arrived in Philadelphia, Dr. Physick operated on her. Physick's approach, of course, was thorough, meticulous. "Stern and cold and almost callous" to his patient beforehand, Dr. Physick during an operation, Louisa said, was "soothing and kind." The doctor suffered also when his agonized patients screamed and groaned as he operated, and Louisa learned "that it takes him several days to brace his feelings or his nerves to his duty, but that once done he is immoveable." That was the mood Louisa discovered Physick in when she returned to Philadelphia. He had warned her that she needed the operation, and this was the time. Louisa, still in high spirits, went on with it.

Dr. Physick arrived at Miss Pardon's boardinghouse dressed, as he always did for surgery, in his dark blue coat with bright metal buttons, white vest (which he sometimes removed before going to work), and light gray pantaloons. Surgeons didn't scrub up before, or wear sterile gloves, hair nets, or face masks, or protect the patient on germfree linen upon a covered surgical table under bright light. Dr. Physick operated in his street clothes, his instruments pulled from their place in his bag as needed, with blood on blade and hands and white linen cuffs, and his assistant, Nathaniel Chapman, at his side. There is no evidence that Dr. Physick so much as washed his hands before working on Louisa Adams.

Dr. Physick ordered Louisa's hands and feet tied. He rolled her over on her left side. He elevated her pelvic area with a pillow and exposed it "to a clear light." He spread her perineum, revealing an orifice Dr. Physick knew much about. Concentrating now, peering down intently, he no longer saw an elegant lady of delicate breeding, the wife of a Presidential aspirant, but, starkly, an exposed anus with two large hemorrhoidal tumors in need of repair. He knew his way around down there. Dr. Physick, the proctologist, had been among the first to describe diverticula of the rectum; he had, in 1809, been the very first to construct and implant an artificial anus. He knew what he was looking at.

Hemorrhoids, then and now, presented little challenge to a physician of Physick's competence, but there was always the risk of a fatal hemorrhage. Louisa's hemorrhoids likely resulted from several things: low champerpot seats, which caused unusual stretching of the interior of her anus; the strain of twelve pregnancies; the constraint of tightly laced garments, such as the whalebone corsets that impeded the function of her liver, compressed her stomach (resulting also in indigestion), and forced her uterus, bladder, and rectum lower than natural in her abdomen. To remove Louisa's hemorrhoids, Dr. Physick employed the soft wire snare he had invented, the double canula. He selected a four-inch-long double canula, with short arms soldered to the side at right angles, forming a cross. The instrument looked much like a small pair of scissors, opened wide. Physick passed a double iron wire, fastened around one of the arms of the canula, across to and through the other arm, and then looped back, but left free and projecting four or five inches, to make a snare. This allowed him to increase or decrease the size of the noose formed by the double wires as he wished. Dr. Physick reached down to Louisa Adams's anus, where he placed the double canula and, opening the wire between its two arms to form a noose, secured it loosely about one of her hemorrhoids. He then used a pair of pliers to draw up the free ends of the wire, ensnaring the tumor and thus closing the canula, much as one closes a pair of scissors, tightly around the hemorrhoid. He twisted the wire about the closed arms of the double canula, making a neat package, like a tweezer squeezing an offending bump. He secured the second hemorrhoid in the same manner. "This gives momentary pain," he admitted, "but it is not in all cases so severe as might be supposed." Usually, Dr. Physick left the double canula in place, sometimes for twenty-four hours, with the patient resting comfortably, and it worked "marvelously well," he exclaimed. The hemorrhoidal tumor shriveled and turned black and fell off after a day or two, helped along by the continuous application of a "soft poultice of bread and milk." In Louisa's case, Dr. Physick left the double canula in place less than twenty-four hours, then removed the tumors by drawing the wire tight and cutting them free; he stitched the wounds, and covered them with caustic (arsenical) pastes. As painful as the extraction of the tumors was, the application of the caustic pastes matched it. Louisa suffered extreme pain, but neither she nor Physick recorded that she cried out, or fainted.

Louisa recovered quickly, and on October 2 wrote John Quincy: "Dr. Physick is unwilling to part with me as I have gone through the operation but he does not think it completed; as however I am very well, I did not think it worth while to suffer again, as it really reduced me to a shadow." Her brother, she said, was "a new man" and making a full recovery, too. Dr. Physick operated on Thomas one more time, but he decided that a second operation for Louisa was unnecessary, "and I am still at large." Indeed she was: Louisa entertained twelve guests at a levee, returned visits to Walsh and his family and the Sergeants, and went to see *The Forty Thieves*, a favorite entertainment of hers. She asked John Quincy to send a hundred dollars for Dr. Physick's bill, which he did. But the doctor had undergone a trauma of his own. His daughter eloped right after Louisa's operation, very much against Physick's will, and the physician took to his bed and was "quite sick."

Louisa and Thomas left Miss Pardon's in early October, and carefully made their way back to Washington as the leaves were turning. Thomas started his life's career as a valetudinarian wandering about Europe. Louisa was looking forward to December, when her sons would be home, the family together, and this bizarre Presidential campaign underway once again. She was healthier, and ready.

7

LOUISA DID NOT LEAVE Washington during the final sixteen months of the Presidential campaign. By January 1823, she proclaimed: "My health is so uncommonly good this winter [that] I am enabled to go through much more fatigue and my spirits are proportionately high." At one party that month, Louisa enjoyed "as complete a frolick as you ever witnessed, singing, dancing, playing and laughing. No one of the party was more jolly than myself and I doubt if the youngest of that party enjoyed it more." Louisa again opened her home every Tuesday during the Congressional session, and each gathering at the Adamses' now included dinner and dancing. One guest, however, wondered about the excellent quality of the Adamses' dinners, with four servants in waiting: "I dare say the President is right in thinking that $6,000 a year does not pay for all his hospitality. It seems to me the dinner giving system has increased very much since I first knew this great watering place . . . where amusement is a business, a need, to which almost everybody is given up from 5 o'clock till bed time — all the Secretaries give dinners & balls frequently, I fancy weekly, and many other persons who, I should think, can ill afford it."

Louisa renewed her commitment to her husband's success. At the start of the 1823 season, she wrote in her journal: "In a righteous cause, I dare both good and ill." She increased her visits around Washington, and rode into Maryland, where her relatives lived. "As my connections in this state are of the most respectable and distinguished," she said, "I am most solicitous to them in his interest. — Maryland, it is said, will be his. For myself, I have no ambition beyond my present situation, the exchange to a more elevated station must put me in a Prison."

During this campaign, and not insignificant to it, the Adamses bought a three-story house at 244 F Street.* They hired carpenters in 1820 and added a coachhouse and a stable, which made a separate, but attached, building. This allowed the Adamses to entertain grandly, and the style, one Congressman reported, was "very common . . . and is striking proof of the prevailing propensity to entertainment & gaiety." One room of the new addition was twenty-eight by twenty-nine feet, and served as a large drawing room and ballroom, which, said Louisa, "answered the purposes amazingly well." The new F Street house was often "crowded to overflowing," and Louisa found that six sets of guests could dance cotillions at the same time "with ease" in the new room. This house, and its large addition, made an excellent site for the culminating event of Louisa's campaign.

In December, the Adamses held an unusual family meeting and decided, together, to give a ball for Gen. Andrew Jackson on January 8, 1824 — the tenth anniversary of the Battle of New Orleans. They ordered five hundred invitations struck off immediately; theirs would be the largest party of the Washington season. For the next nineteen days, Louisa went out almost every morning paying visits and distributing cards of invitation to the ball; from the start, as word swept the capital, she was besieged for more. The Jackson Ball marked a major step in the political campaign: It recognized that with Crawford ill** and Calhoun trailing, Jackson and Adams were frontrunners. The Jackson Ball on the New Orleans anniversary repaid some small political debts, and projected the two men as leading Presidential candidates. The ball quickly took on immense political significance.

Louisa saw this clearly, and found her thoughts constantly focused upon "the great question." After the first of the year, she took over the Adamses' house, and directed Charles and

---

* Numbers 1333–5 F Street today, on lots eight and sixteen, square 253. This was the same house that James and Dolley Madison lived in during his two terms as Secretary of State. The F Street house remained in the Adams family until 1884.

** In September 1823, William Crawford had suffered a paralytic stroke that reduced his chances for the Presidency, but did not diminish his supporters' hopes. Crawford lived until 1834.

John (George now remained in Boston studying law), the young ladies Mary, Elizabeth, and Abby Smith Adams, and Louisa's sister Carolina Frye in the preparations. Charles bemoaned that his mother turned the house "topsy turvey." She hired carpenters to hammer twelve pillars into place under the lower floor to support the additional weight of the expected guests. She set the young men and ladies and Aunt Carolina to work weaving laurel wreaths, and sent Charles in the carriage with Mary to distribute invitations in Georgetown. By the sixth, the house was "all in disorder," and the Adamses had to dine in Louisa's dressing room. At first, they planned to open only four rooms, but as the number of invitations increased they soon needed eight. A pantry was temporarily removed, and Louisa shifted her own chambers upstairs to the third floor. She threw John Quincy out of his study, and moved him to John's sitting room. In the middle of this mess, Louisa opened the house to her regular Tuesday evening entertainments, welcomed a full floor of guests, and graciously played the piano for them.

The day before the ball, everyone in the Adams house except the Secretary of State, who stayed in his office as much as possible — and wisely so — was busily constructing wreaths, "and we all worked very vehemently," said Charles. Louisa directed the last-minute preparations, and got so excited that her son thought she might faint. On the morning of the eighth, with the ball just hours away, the Adamses' wreath-making went on in a frenzy; Louisa oversaw all the work, the placing of the wreaths, the hanging of decorations, the arranging of the dinner table. There would be so many guests, they would eat standing up. Doors were removed from the four lower rooms, and when it was ready by late afternoon, the house had a feeling of space and flowers and greenery and light. The Adamses ate at four, and by six were ready "except the lighting up."

The Jackson Ball was the largest and best of the 1824 season in Washington, and perhaps the largest of the decade. It was by far the biggest party the Adamses ever gave. Newspaper coverage had started several days before, and the *Washington Republican* appeared on the morning of the ball with a long poem in which the author listed the prominent guests expected at the Adamses' that evening. The second stanza:

Wend you with the world tonight?
Sixty gray, and giddy twenty,
Flirts that court, and prudes that slight
Stale coquettes and spinsters plenty.
Mrs. Sullivan is there,
With all the charms that nature lent her;
Gay M'Kim, with city air;
And winning Gales, and Vandeventer;
Forsyth, with her group of graces;
Both the Crowningshields, in blue;
The Pierces with their heavenly faces,
And eyes like suns that dazzle through;
Belles and matrons, maids and madams,
All are gone to Mrs. Adams.

By the end, Louisa had sent out more than nine hundred invitations, including one to every member of both houses of Congress except Alexander Smyth and John Floyd, who had managed to offend John Quincy Adams so badly that he placed hurt feelings before personal ambition, and refused to let them attend. Only President and Mrs. Monroe (whose custom it was not to visit private homes, and who did not wish to appear to favor any one candidate) and the ill Crawford stayed away by choice. Clay and Calhoun, and their ladies, arrived early. Jackson, said Louisa, was "a magnet so powerful as to attract not only all the Strangers but even the old residents of the City who never thought of coming to see us before." About nine, with the house already teeming, General Jackson pulled up in his carriage, having paused to offer a ride to the ubiquitous Senator Mills. The Senator liked the General, and although he considered Jackson "rash and inconsiderate, tyrannical and despotic," he also found him "very mild and amiable in his disposition, of great benevolence, and his manners, though formed in the wilds of the West, exceedingly polished and polite." Jackson was, said Mills, "as free from guile as an infant." As the General and the Senator pulled up to the Adamses' house, Mills exclaimed, "such a crowd you never witnessed!" Inside, eight large rooms were open, and literally filled to overflowing. The upper floors were packed "to suffocation," and the newcomers found the house already filled with "at least a thousand people." They pushed their way in.

The four lower rooms were hung with the patiently con-structed laurel wreaths, into which the Adamses had woven roses; they were arranged in festoons, in the center of which were variegated oil lamps. Garlands of evergreens had been wrapped around the pillars, and even John Quincy's precious bookcases, too heavy to move, were camouflaged with greens and forests of flowers in pots with small illumination lamps. The rooms were filled with flickering light, and the pungent smell of candles, oil lamps, roses, ladies' perfume, and gentle-men's sweat. In the large drawing room, converted to a ball-room, hung a chandelier woven with greenery, and where it joined the ceiling, evergreen garlands cascaded in cords to the pillars. It's a wonder the whole house did not go up in a roar of candle- and lamp-ignited evergreen blaze. On the floor, in the center of the ballroom beneath the chandelier, Louisa had directed a man from Baltimore in creating a chalk painting of eagles, flags, and military emblems, with the words "Welcome to the Hero of New Orleans" intertwined. The women were brilliantly gowned and jeweled, and all the men except John Quincy Adams "wore full dress attire — blue coats, gilt buttons, white or buff waistcoats, white neckties, high chokers, white trousers, silk stockings, and pumps." "In fact," gushed a *Harper's Bazaar* account "every body who was any body was there . . . and this, let it be known, was when *shoddy* was not — society was unmixed, and every one knew who was who, and was free to act accordingly."

Louisa Adams met Gen. Jackson at the front door, where she had stationed herself to watch for him, and she took him around the rooms, introducing the general to the ladies and gentlemen. Jackson was visibly impressed with this ornate pres-entation, and flattered, and Louisa shared the center of attrac-tion with him. She was, *Harper's* reported, "a very attractive woman," dressed in "a *suit* of *steel*. The dress was composed of steel llama; her ornaments for head, throat and arms were all of cut steel, producing a dazzling effect. General Jackson was her devoted attendant during the evening, and caused much comment by such assiduous attentions." There was dancing on the first floor, a supper and punch bowls on the third. When the table was opened at nine-thirty, Louisa took the general's arm and escorted him to a prime spot, where he would not be jostled too badly, so he might eat. Everyone pushed in behind them and, shoddy or not, elbowed the guest of honor aside to get at the tables laden with "natural and candied fruits, pies, sweetmeats, tongues, games, etc. . . . . prepared in French style, and arranged with most exquisite taste." The general managed to shout a toast to Louisa above the din, and most of the guests found space to raise their glasses, after which the general elbowed his way out from the tables to the air and safety of the hall. Jackson didn't stay long; there were also illuminations and bonfires and fireworks in his honor this evening: Americans still thought Jackson's victory in New Orleans had ended the War of 1812, and not Adams's treaty at Ghent. The general had to attend another, smaller ball, "where he expected to be greeted by the people with great joy," said Louisa, "but I believe he was disappointed and found very few persons there." Most of them were at the Adamses'.

Of everyone in the family, perhaps Charles had the best time. John was already taking a serious interest in Mary Hellen, and his mother watched them with the eye of one who understands the combustion level of passion and proximity. Charles, on the other hand, escorted a covey of young ladies up and down stairs to supper and dancing. One named Anne, who, as Charles told his diary, appeared "uncommonly beautiful this evening," was a plump and perfumed fantasy who made the dances seem too brief. By the time supper ended, and the music changed to reels, Charles barely had strength to walk, "for I was perfectly done up." He staggered to his room, passing the "picture of devastation" of leftover food, cups, and plates on the third floor, and "dragged myself to bed, complaining even of the trouble of undressing myself."

"The dancing continued until one in the morning," John Quincy wrote in his diary. He was thankful that Louisa had the extra supports installed. "The crowd was great," he noted, "and the house could scarcely contain the company." The last guest left before two, "all in good humour," said Louisa. She felt satisfied that they got through "this business" so well. The Jackson Ball was a smashing success, the culmination of her political work, and launched "the most stormy year of our lives. Let it end where it may," Louisa wrote George. "I trust there is not much of happiness in store for us away from the cabals and intrigues of public life."

V
Washington

1825–1830

1

THE ELECTION OF 1824 took from October 29 to November 22, as the states individually selected their electors. Jackson won ninety-nine votes in the Electoral College, Adams eighty-four, Crawford forty-one, and Clay thirty-seven. The top three men turned to the House of Representatives for a decision, and the weeks before that election were marked by backstairs wheeling and dealing. While John Quincy Adams, with his Macbeth policy, might wish it to appear that chance crowned him, he would leave nothing to chance alone. Realizing that the Presidency might not come to him, he went out and actively sought it. During these final days, Adams glad-handed those who might help him, dropped in at boardinghouses and hotels where Congressmen lived, and solicited their support. "To suffer without feeling is not in human nature," he wrote in his diary, "and when I consider that to me alone, of all the candidates before the nation, failure of success would be equivalent to a vote of censure upon my past service, I cannot dissemble to myself that I have more at stake upon the result than any other individual in the Union."

The most controversial event of this campaign, and perhaps of Adams's life, began on January 9, as the maneuvering for House votes got under way. On that day, a Sunday, John Quincy first went to church where he heard the Rev. Mr. Robert Little discuss Ecclesiastes VII, Number 23: "I said I will be wise, but it was far from me." The irony was not lost, and Adams later entered it in his diary: for that evening he and Henry Clay met, and what took place swung the election. Clay arrived promptly at the Adamses' house at six, and remained all evening. He could no longer win the Presidency for himself, but he was in a powerful position as House Speaker to help someone else win it. But in exchange for what? Clay, John Quincy recorded in his diary, wished to discuss "without any personal considerations for himself" the coming election. He assured Adams that "In the question to come before the House between General Jackson, Mr. Crawford and myself, he had no hesitation in saying that his preference would be for me." Clay also mentioned, with some apparent disgust, that friends of Crawford's had approached him with suggestions of impropriety, and he told Adams that certain friends, without Adams's authority of course, were also urging "considerations personal to himself." From John Quincy's brief diary account, it is clear that "personal considerations" entered their conversation twice that evening, and other historians have concluded that the two men at least reached an understanding, but perhaps stopped short of an outright exchange: that for his support of Adams in the House election, Clay would be appointed to the Presidential stepping-stone, Secretary of State. The words showing such an exchange of the Presidency for the State Department have not been discovered. But the transaction took place.

Such an agreement was essential to John Quincy Adams's victory. Clay controlled the Kentucky delegation, which had been directed by its state legislature to vote for Jackson, and he also strong-armed delegations from Missouri, Illinois, and Ohio. Word went out to Daniel Webster that if the Federalists of Delaware and Maryland marched into the Adams camp, the post of Ambassador to Great Britain, which Webster shamelessly coveted, might indeed be his after all. John Quincy himself also called upon Martin Van Buren and, in a desperate venture, mentioned that a young man whom Van Buren championed as Consul at Santiago "would be nominated, but perhaps not till after the election in the House." Adams was playing politics the way Clay, that "gamester," played. But John

Quincy had a troublesome inner voice that warned against satiating political ambition with moral compromises. He was a man whose New England background convinced him that every great success — especially one suspiciously achieved — would be followed by a righteous and compensatory failure.

The balloting took place in the House on a snowy afternoon, February 9, 1825. Everything that could be done, had been done. Webster, allured by the Court of St. James's, lined up the Federalists for Adams. Clay — in his own words transformed from "a candidate before the people, into an elector for the people" — became kingmaker, and delivered the votes of Ohio, Kentucky, even Louisiana. But the burden of the election, with all its wheeling and dealing, with Louisa's campaigning, finally fell in one cold moment upon Stephen Van Rensselaer of New York, "a kindly, upright, simple old Federalist gentleman." Reportedly, Van Rensselaer could not decide between Jackson or Crawford, but since he boarded at a roominghouse filled with Crawford supporters from New York, Delaware, and Georgia, he was thought to be a Crawford man. Clay had worked the New York delegation well: Seventeen were for Adams and seventeen under Van Buren's control. Adams needed to win on the first ballot, and he needed New York to win at all; other states would slip away if the voting went to a second round. His victory hinged, therefore, on the drowsy-minded Van Rensselaer.

At breakfast on the ninth, Van Rensselaer assured his fellow lodgers that nothing could persuade him to vote for Adams. But when he arrived at the Capitol, he was grabbed by Clay and taken to the Speaker's room where Webster, an impressive physical and political presence, confronted him; those two, Van Rensselaer later wrote, "could not be resisted." Still, he wavered. Martin Van Buren, in his autobiography, gave this colorful account of Van Rensselaer's decision:

> He took his seat fully resolved to vote for Mr. Crawford, but before the box reached him, he dropped his head upon the edge of his desk and made a brief appeal to his Maker for His guidance in the matter — a practise he frequently observed on great emergencies — and when he removed his hand

from his eyes he saw on the floor directly below him a ticket bearing the name John Quincy Adams. This occurrence at a moment of great excitement and anxiety, he was led to regard as an answer to his appeal, and taking up the ticket he put it in the box.

The first ballot, with Van Rensselaer's help, gave Adams the vote of thirteen states; Jackson, seven; and Crawford, four. Henry Clay rose from his seat and intoned: "John Quincy Adams, having a majority of the votes of these United States, is duly elected President of the United States." Light clapping in the gallery dissolved to loud hissing. Crawford supporters yelled "treachery and cowardice" about Van Rensselaer's vote, and later one said: "It's enough to make a saint swear!" That evening, Adams, the new President-elect, wrote in his diary: "May the blessing of God rest upon the event of this day!" But Senator John Randolph, who had watched the balloting, had his own opinion. "It was impossible to win the game, gentlemen," he said. "The cards were packed." And if they were, what remained was to play out the hand. Two days after his election, John Quincy Adams trudged through the snow to see President Monroe, and told him that Henry Clay would be his choice as the new Secretary of State. It was a suspicious capstone to this precarious election, for every President since John Adams had first served as Secretary of State. Monroe may have wanted the post offered to De Witt Clinton, but he remained polite, and silent, to the end.

Earlier, at noon on the tenth, Daniel Webster had led the Committee of Congress to Adams's F Street house to inform JQA that he would be President of the United States. As Adams listened to Webster's sonorous voice, he trembled and sweat appeared on his face and rolled down his cheeks. He read a prepared speech that sounded tragic and frightened, and he wrote that evening to his father, in his ninetieth year, for his "blessing and prayers." John Quincy admitted to his diary that he had been elected not in "a manner satisfactory to pride or just desire; not by unequivocal sufferages of a majority of the people; with perhaps two-thirds of the whole people adverse to the actual result." From this moment on, Adams and Clay would spend their lives refuting the accusation that "bargain and corruption" had won for them the Presidency and the State Department. Cries of bargain and corruption echoed in Washington as John Quincy Adams, the sixth President of the United States, rode by carriage weary and dark-eyed after two sleepless nights to his inauguration. His scolding conscience was telling him that what he had won by expediency he would pay for with adversity.

2

HOWEVER SHADY the leaves of destiny, John Quincy Adams had achieved his dream. He now set forth to prolong the Era of Good Feelings, and to unite this rapidly growing nation. Adams planned a Presidency that would take a strong step toward national unity and greatness, bind together the sectional differences, and undertake a national program of physical and moral improvements sustained by the Federal government. But this second Adams to attain the Presidency needed skills he never had. His plans proved too bold, and came too early in America's history. Instead of personal and national triumph, Adams's four years as President were marked by political miscalculation and personal sadness.

By the end of his first year in office, John Quincy Adams had made several fundamental political mistakes. He retained Monroe's Cabinet, with its squabbling members. He refused to employ political patronage to install his supporters; worse, he retained such men as John McLean of Ohio, the Postmaster General and an outspoken Adams opponent, who dispensed valuable patronage jobs to Adams's enemies. President Adams also misunderstood Congress and the American people, and this proved to be his most serious mistake.

In his first annual message to Congress, on December 6, 1825,

Adams proposed a national program of internal improvements. The concept was sweeping, daring, but needed a man who could overcome the weakness of the Presidency, convince a strong Congress, persuade a skeptical American people. The United States was a nation splitting into self-interested sections, and such a program required a man sensitive to its many voices. Congress had previously prepared and legislated similar national improvement plans, only to have two Presidents veto them. When President Adams suggested what Congress had twice passed, the rebellion of the legislative against the executive, of sectionalism against national unity, was evident, and final. Adams called for, among other things, the founding of a national university, the financing of scientific explorations, the establishment of a uniform standard of weights and measures, the building of astronomical observatories, the creation of a Department of the Interior, and the undertaking of a large-scale development program that included canals and highways. From today's perspective, this speech appears benign, but it met with hostility in Congress and among the American people. It came at a time when most Americans wanted less government, not more. It recalled Patrick Henry's warning of a Great Magnificent Government overwhelming the rights of the states, and it raised this specter just as men of the South were realizing that their "peculiar institution" might be in peril. Vice President Calhoun, in fact, suspected that Adams's inner desire was to abolish the twin evils of war and slavery. The President compounded this misreading of American sentiments by citing the example of "the nations of Europe and their rulers," an unfortunate echo of his father, who had been labeled a monarchist by some of the same men now listening to JQA. With this one speech, President Adams aroused a widespread animosity. The American people accused John Quincy of seeking power for himself, and greeted his ideas with mockery: His term for a series of national observatories — "those light-houses of the skies" — became a national joke. Far worse, Congress rejected every one of his proposals.

John Quincy Adams had not the talent or patience to be, as he wished, a Man of the Whole Country. From the outset, the factions that had supported Jackson, Calhoun, and Crawford combined against Adams (and Clay). The President further aroused sectionalism by stumbling over such obstacles as Federal land disposal in the West, Indian removal from Georgia, and the passage of a tariff so loaded with favors to key Northern Senators, and so damaging to the South, that it became known as the Tariff of Abominations. Halfway through his Presidency, with his national program in ruins, John Quincy faced a hostile Congress and people. With the elections in 1826, a new political party, the Democratic Republican Party, would capture a majority in Congress. In effect, Adams was a minority President, and to put together any programs at all — let alone one of imagination and high moral purpose — required the cooperation of his rivals. He never had it. "I fell," he wrote with sadness, "and with me fell, I fear never to rise again in my day, the system of international improvement by means of national energies. The great object of my life, therefore . . . has failed." His dream was becoming a nightmare.

Life in the White House, as it was coming to be called, quickly degenerated to a lonely existence. When the Adamses moved in, the north portico had not been added, and the building stood upon bare and unshaded open land. Sheds and stables leaned against each other; they housed eight horses, a small dairy, and farm tools. The White House had neither running water nor indoor plumbing. From his residence, President Adams could look north across Pennsylvania Avenue to the Square and farmland beyond it. From the south portico, formal gardens gave way to a long sweep of meadowland reaching to the river several hundred yards away, where Tiber Creek and the Potomac ran together into tidewater, near Adams's favorite rock and sycamore to which, even now as President, he frequently walked, peeling off his clothes, to skinny-dip. Monroe took much of the furniture with him, and the White House rooms were almost empty when the Adamses arrived. Congress had appropriated fourteen thousand dollars to furnish the mansion, and Adams moved in some of his old furniture, bought a chest of silver service from the departing Russian minister and a set of silver plate from Crawford — after carefully having it weighed and valued by an appraiser. John Quincy, unwisely as it turned out, also added a set of chessmen said to have cost $23.50 and a billiard table with balls and cues worth $61.

Louisa and John Quincy lived quietly in the White House. They were content to follow Elizabeth Monroe's precedent of seldom going out socially, and during the season gave dinners once a week, fortnightly levees, or an occasional ball, plus the traditional New Year's open house. Often, however, the Adamses' evenings were marked by loneliness, boredom, or the President's dozing off while reading. When Sen. Elijah H. Mills of Massachusetts visited, his account contained a hint of the isolation Louisa and John Quincy Adams felt in the White House. Sen. Mills said that he passed a hour with President Adams who "was very gracious and friendly," and urged the Senator "to call often – spend an evening; and added that they dined every day at five o'clock, and that it would give him great pleasure if I would come any day, and as often as I could, *sans cérémonie*, and dine with him *en famille*. So much for my standing at court." Senator Mills took Adams at his word, even though the Senator risked being known in Washington as "an Administration man," one "on the most intimate terms at the palace." He returned to visit the President one evening, "and while alone with him in his cabinet, the servant announced supper. I went with him to the supper-room, where we found Mrs. A. and her two nieces, and had a supper of roast oysters in the shell, opening them ourselves, which of course was not a very pleasant or *cleanly* process; but with whiskey and water with supper and a little hot punch after it, we had quite a frolic."

On such occasions, when President Adams relaxed, he enjoyed discussing literature, science, painting, classical poetry – even the vintages and qualities of wines. "My father," Charles wrote one evening, "was uncommonly eloquent after dinner today and laid himself out more forcibly than usual. When he does so, how immeasurably he rises above all others. There is no comparison." But too often, Adams remained his usual dull self, and after one guest encountered a bored and sleepy President, he wrote this doggerel which found its way into Louisa's notebook, perhaps because it caught a response in her as well:

Asked by the Nation's chief to take my tea
I hastened to him in surprising glee,
But when I got there, all my treat, by God,
Is just to watch his Excellency's Nod.

Gulian C. Verplanck found Adams a terrible host in the White House: "He himself is very dull and his neighbors at table when he gives formal dinners have a hard time of it." John Quincy continued to analyze his own feelings and shortcomings; behind his forbidding exterior lurked a man burdened with selfdoubt. "I was not satisfied with myself this day," he wrote in his diary after a dinner with Nicholas Biddle, president of the Bank of the United States, "having talked too much at dinner. . . . Nor can I always (I did not this day) altogether avoid a dogmatical and peremptory tone and manner, always disgusting and especially offensive in persons to whose age or situation others consider some deference due."

It is surprising how accessible President Adams was during other times. He kept an abridged diary of his day, which he mailed to George in Boston as a lesson in the regulation and wise use of time. From it we learn that John Quincy's presidential day divided into three parts: five to nine in the morning; ten to five during the day; and seven to eleven at night. He allowed himself an hour for breakfast, skipped lunch, and took two hours for evening dinner. Most of breakfast, however, he and Louisa read the newspapers, and during the two dinner hours they conversed or read, although he sometimes took a nap. He spent two hours in the morning exercising, which included the vigorous kindling of his fire and a four-mile walk or a swim. During the hours from ten to five, the President tended to business, and the heads of the departments called almost every day. The Secretary of the Treasury might confer on vacancies in the Custom House offices or questions of revenue law. The Secretary of War might place before him lists of promotions in the Army, courts-martial proceedings, reports of surveys by the Army engineers, Indian Treaties, correspondence with the governors of the states. The Secretary of the Navy might come by with voluminous dispatches from commanders at sea, more courts-martial, promotions, applications for midshipman warrants. Adams also read dispatches from the U.S. ministers overseas, State Department instructions, and other correspondence. There were also twelve to fifteen newspapers to read, and perhaps as many as ten letters to be answered; state papers flowed by so fast he complained of having only time to sign his name and move on. Intruding in all this was a steady stream of visitors, "supplicants of every denomination," soliciting favors or office. President Adams felt obliged to give an audience to everyone: passing vendors, special petitioners, wayfarers, the curious and the complaining. He had nowhere to go, and was home to all. One February day in 1828, for example, his visitors included the Russian ambassador delivering a letter from Czar Nicholas I announcing the birth of his son Constantine, various petitioners and guests, and an Englishman named Broadmeadow who showed the President "a small model of an improved and much simplified Steam Engine of his invention. He put it in operation, and shewed me its internal construction." Adams occasionally also sank into foolish posturing, sometimes conducting his Presidency like a European court. At least once, in January 1828, he gave an audience to a gentleman who requested it for his daughter, age two, and so closely re-enacted a similar audience given by Czar Alexander that Louisa was embarrassed. "I was forced to be a Spectator," she said, "but did not *take notice.*" Fortunately, for President Adams, neither did the opposition press.

The four evening hours John Quincy thought "the least effective of the day," when he was "usually weary and heavy laden." He disliked the weekly dinner parties and fortnightly levees, as he always had. Twice weekly there were evenings with Congressmen that promised a lively hour or two of political talk. He had little time to catch up on his letter writing or diary, left unfinished from the morning, or classical reading, before going to bed promptly at eleven, to rise again at five.

After the 1826 Congressional elections, President Adams lost all opportunity to lead; for the first time in the nation's history both houses of Congress contained a majority of members opposed to the President. One-fourth of the Congressmen even refused to pay courtesy calls on President and Mrs. Adams.

Just two years after taking office, John Quincy was a lame duck President. He confided to his diary: "My own career is closed." Rejected, he grew depressed and lost weight. He looked forward only to his annual trips to Quincy, between August and October. He traveled quietly and without display, and made only one public speech in his entire four years in office.* At the White House, Adams withdrew into office routine, gardening, and a vitriolic correspondence with George. Increasingly bitter, he awaited an inevitable second-term defeat. Adams would be the second President in U.S. history not to win re-election. His father had been the first.

3

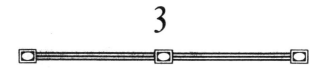

LOUISA ADAMS'S DREAM — of becoming her own person, of equality — ended, too. As she had predicted in 1823, her husband's election "put me in a Prison." Louisa had played an essential role in the social and political life of the nation, but her unique moment, her special status, ended with John Quincy's election. Now she had little to do, other than the traditional entertainments, and was shuffled back into her chambers until needed. Louisa spent four years psychologically imprisoned in the White House. Her personality changed: Charles thought his mother more sad and depressed after 1825, and said that she lost her "elasticity of character."

* Not counting Adams's farewell to Lafayette at his carriage before the White House. In his public speech, during a groundbreaking for the new Chesapeake and Ohio Canal (in which Adams's shovel first hit rock, which he dislodged, took off his jacket and dug again), the President claimed that this was the beginning of his hoped-for internal improvements. On the same day, Charles Carroll turned the first spade of earth for the B&O Railroad.

Slowly, painfully, Louisa peeled back the layers of her life, and re-examined her relationship with her family, and her husband. She hated the White House, which she considered a huge and impersonal mansion with vast state rooms, piecemeal furniture, and shabby living quarters void even of the comforts of "any private mechanics family." She even hated the tall cases of her husband's books stacked in his chamber, which depressed her every time she walked by them. In fact, she wrote George, "There is something in this great unsocial house which depresses my spirits beyond expression and makes it impossible for me to feel at home or to fancy that I have a home any where."

Shut up in this great house, Louisa reflected upon how much she and her husband differed, how much they disliked one another. They disagreed in sentiment, taste, personality. He was irascible, and by his own confession, harsh. She indulged in sarcasm. They argued, as they had for almost two decades, about how to raise their sons. She was easygoing and refused to press them to higher grades or achievement. He was anxious, demanding, unsatisfied. Louisa described herself as a "romantic enthusiastic foolish animal," still a lovely woman of delicate, well-drawn features with her light brown hair now showing gray; Charles thought his mother "the most pleasing woman" he knew, one whose affections for her children were "most powerful." His father, however, he found high-tempered, unpredictable. "He is the only man I ever saw whose feelings I could not penetrate. . . . He makes enemies by perpetually wearing the Iron Mask." Louisa, too, knew that her husband was impenetrable; only his fiery, explosive temper let her see inside the man. After her first summer in the White House, Louisa refused to accompany her husband to Quincy; she took her holidays alone, at the spas.

Louisa presented a paradox. She became a stereotypical bored and reclusive woman in the White House. Yet this change of role and importance aroused a troubling and persistent question planted in girlhood: What would her role, her purpose be? John Quincy, carefully guided since boyhood, had a clear call to duty. His destiny was obvious. But Louisa's?

Isolated, confined to routine and meaningless entertainments, an ornament at the White House, Louisa was now part of a self-fulfilling prophecy about American women. Small and physically frail, she continued to suffer from illnesses that originated in too many pregnancies, poor diet, lack of exercise. Contemporary attitudes depicted Louisa Adams, and all other American women, as weak, sickly, needing protection and confinement. A handful of women were aware that something was causing the appearance of widespread illness among American women at this time. One, Catherine Beecher, undertook a study. She herself suffered from "extreme prostration of the over-worked brain and nerves" — a common analysis of a woman's ailments — that forced her to walk with crutches. (Her sister Harriet, after marrying a carping man and giving birth to several children in close sequence, had became paralyzed on her entire right side.) Catherine tried all the popular remedies given to women of the day: rhubarb, iron and camphor, bleeding for "nervous excitement." She experimented with food cures, water cures, "electrical cures," sulphur baths, vapor baths, Russian baths, chemical baths, Turkish baths, sun baths, the Grape Cure, the Lifting Cure for "internal displacements," and various "breathing cures." Every time Catherine went to a spa for a cure, in every town she visited, she asked women about their health, and she concluded: "There is a terrible decay of Female health all over the land."

The principal cause of such widespread disease was the demand that women live as men willed. Confinement, lack of exercise, isolation resulted in illnesses corroborating the original belief that women were sickly. Confinement was the key word. Women suffered from physical, emotional, and sexual confinement. Every aspect of their lives enclosed them: Men controlled how they lived, where they went, what they said in public; even a woman's clothing restricted her. The sharp whalebone stays and pinching corsets and binding garments and shoes constricted a woman's movement, and the discomfort, or injury, of the pinching and lifting and lacing repressed her sexuality. Louisa's happiest moments, for example, occurred when she was released, free, running in loose garments in the relaxed summers of her girlhood, or rowing and fishing at Bordentown unencumbered with the demands of her husband's social and political life. Unlaced, unburdened, exercising, Louisa felt healthy. Not surprising, Catherine Beecher reached similar conclusions, and became one of the first advocates of physical education for women.

The issue, of course, ran deeper. But what started as a social fiction became a medical reality. Told she was sickly, a woman took to her chambers in confinement, which made her ill. Like other American women, Louisa Adams spent days, sometimes weeks, in her chambers: In 1827, for example, with the Adams Presidency souring, Louisa confined herself once for eight days and again for five days without leaving her room. Shut up in the White House, she complained that her health deteriorated, and "I am now always cross and unpleasant to myself and to everybody else." Louisa was expected to be sick, and she soon was, and her illnesses were both physical and emotional. For one thing, every winter during January, February, and March, Louisa developed coughs and a pain in her chest. The Adamses, like many other families, burned anthracite coal in stoves and open fireplaces for heat during this season. Louisa, in her unventilated rooms, breathed coal fumes for several months, and sometimes joked about having the "Lehigh Coal Catarrh." She was certain that she regained her strength with spring, when she could walk outside, "out of the atmosphere of the Anthracite Coal." The coal catarrh was an equal opportunity disease: and John Quincy also complained of its effect; and in 1836, Louisa would write that President Jackson was suffering from colds and illness. "The Lehigh Coal is supposed to affect him so much that his grates are ordered to be pulled down." Since women were confined far more than men, however, they suffered far more the ravages of isolated, poorly ventilated chambers that brought catarrhs, or worse, the neuroses of loneliness.

Louisa and other confined women also suffered what today would be called psychological aberrations. Excessive sentimentality and melancholia were two forms, and topics like grieving and death took on new interest among women. Their preoccupation with maudlin descriptions of death and illness filled diaries and seeped into newsprint and little gilt volumes. One of the most popular novelists of the 1820s, Lydia Huntley Sigourney, earned a national reputation by writing about dead children and weeping mothers. Women developed psychosomatic illnesses centering on "the nerves"; nervous exhaustion and nervous prostration became terms to cover a woman's inability to understand and deal with her own life. The symptoms today are well known – among both men and women – as manifestations of neurosis, hysteria, anger, anxiety: frequent nausea, dizziness, fainting spells, backaches, partial paralysis. Many women of the day, including Louisa Adams, escaped in "ailing," and they encouraged the creation of a new profession: the operation of sanitoriums and health resorts catering to their needs. Women with real or imagined illnesses were fleeing their homes, and their men, to the spas.

In a desperate and sad episode during her White House years, Louisa turned to her son Charles for help. She complained of being "almost a prisoner in my own house," with nothing to do, no one to "break the dreadful tedium of an almost entire solitude." She begged Charles for "some French book to translate by way of occupation as I cannot bear the loneliness of my life." It was a cry from a bright but isolated woman. Louisa was aware that other women also lived confined lives, on call for their husbands' purposes. "The habit of living almost entirely alone has a tendency to render us savages," she wrote Charles. "However sentimental you think me, I will say that *isolation* is an evil . . . and one likely to be productive of insanity in a weak woman." None of the Adams men offered Louisa understanding or comfort. Charles knew of no French book for her, and replied that hers "was the lot of every woman after she has attained a certain age in life." Her family was grown, she had less to do, he said, and added, "you are not alone in this feeling."

Louisa continued bored, isolated, and angry in the White House. She fulfilled society's expectations of her, and played with some skill the role of a sickly woman who could faint when she thought the occasion appropriate. Her husband and sons considered her a hypochondriac given to melancholia and "fits," but they never bothered to ask why. She was a woman. Their misunderstanding became a truth embedded in history. No longer needed, with little to do, Louisa Adams, once so strong and resilient, deteriorated in the White House to a reclusive, romantic, self-pitying woman. She stayed alone in her chambers, sometimes writing plays and poems, eating chocolate, and wallowing in outrageous descriptions of her own ill health, ending, as was fashionable for women at the time, with her glorious, widely bewailed, always untimely death.* Each part of her life revealed pieces of her emotional collapse, and displayed deeper feelings about herself and her husband, and about what was happening to her as a woman.

In the White House, Louisa Adams went on a chocolate binge. She spoiled herself with it, and became a child again, a self-indulgent symbol of her enforced withdrawal, a burlesque of society's woman. Louisa loved many things, but she loved chocolate best of all. She had started eating it as a teenager while learning to cook, and in Berlin renewed her taste because chocolate reminded her of home and soothed her. In the White House, with marriage and life tormenting her, Louisa devoured chocolate because it occupied time, and comforted her by recalling a childhood when she got what she wanted. Louisa never gained weight. She surrendered nothing of her physical beauty to chocolate, except perhaps her teeth: By adulthood, Louisa had few left, and carried dentures around with her in a bottle. False teeth did not discourage her from eating more chocolate. On the contrary, she found chocolate easier to eat with false teeth, and ate it almost every day during her White House years. In the vernacular, Louisa Adams was a chocoholic. She demanded it, devoured it, filled her days gorging on it. She rhapsodized in the flow of the thick, dark, melting deliciousness. She ended many of her letters

---

* An example, written to Charles in 1827: "I did not want to give you pain therefore I said little about my sufferings but tho' the *spirit* is still great the corporeal part is rapidly decaying and gradually sinking into its native element that to which all mortals are destined to return. – I do not mean to say that this change will be speedy on the contrary I look forward to long lingering pain ere I take my departure to a better world. . . . Today I am severely ill and the loud and constant beating of my heart will hardly permit me to write. Tomorrow perhaps the flow of spirits will ebb the other way and you will hear of my doing the honours of the Table."

to Charles and George and John Quincy with the fervent post-script that they send her chocolate from Boston immediately. Her sons and husband almost always complied, and mailed or carried home with them Louisa's favorite chocolate shells. Once Charles, a bit fed up with her requests, sent so many shells that he told his mother that she must remain in Washington all summer gobbling chocolate to diminish the supply.

One can picture Louisa Adams in her White House chamber, chocolate shells at hand, writing her volumes of poems, brief essays, letters to her sons and husband, to Mary, Thomas, and John Hellen, and to her sisters. In July 1825, Louisa started writing her autobiographical *Record of a Life, or My Story*, which formed one of the basic documents for this book. She made several versions of her translation of Marie Louis Alphonse de Lamartine's *"La Mort de Socrate,"* the fullest dated July 11, 1826, and dedicated to John Quincy. Louisa also continued writing short poems, sometimes exchanging them with George or John, and the titles convey their content: "To My Mother," "The Silken Knot," "The Last Request," and so forth. The poems revealed Louisa's conventional stylizing of romance and death. She also wrote prose sketches during her White House years, which included such short dramatic pieces as "Juvenile Indiscretions or Grand Papa a Farce in one Act" and "The Captives of Scio or The Liberal American. A Melo-Drame," which offered an example of that particularly saccharine form of play, the melodrama, which was popular at the time and which opposed passion and glorified female purity and blissful domesticity. It is likely that Louisa tried out her plays, and lightened White House evenings with amateur productions employing various young ladies and gentlemen staying with or visiting them.

Louisa wrote to entertain herself, to relieve her boredom, to live vicariously the lives of the people she created. This was an acceptable outlet for a woman's talents. Far more important, however, Louisa explored in these plays and poems issues and feelings that she could not, or would not, confront more directly. In December 1827, for example, Louisa worked on a play titled "The Metropolitan Kaleidoscope, or Varieties of Winter Etchings." (For a joke, Louisa used a pseudonym with an intended pun: Rachel Barb.) The play's characters are Lord and Lady Sharply, who live comfortably with their three sons in a large English mansion. These are, of course, the Adamses, and while Louisa's descriptions of the Sharplys' three sons offered no unusual insights into her own sons, her description of Lord Sharply revealed her perceptions of her husband. Lord Sharply, Louisa wrote, was a pompous but talented man of great position, a star "of the first magnitude." He had filled many high stations with glory to his nation and government. His vast knowledge of mankind, Louisa said, came not from direct encounter, however, but from books, and he showed a "natural coldness and reserve." Lord Sharply placed "morality in conduct, sobriety, unceasing industry and endless application" before anything, or anyone, else. "The good of his country was his constant aim," she wrote, and, perhaps thinking of Henry Clay, added, "but he sometimes staggered the Nation by the puppets he used to obtain his ends." He was "ardent and impetuous," and a man of violent temper with a "volcano that burst within," but which seldom vented. When it did, "the explosion was short and terrible." Louisa caught John Quincy between the eyes when she described Lord Sharply as "A Fond Father, a negligent and half-indulgent husband, and utterly indifferent to almost all the other branches of his family." Then she struck the theme of her antagonism toward her husband: "He was full of good qualities, but ambition absorbed every thought of his soul . . . and to the attainment of this object no sacrifice would have been deemed too great."

Lady Sharply, Louisa wrote, "had been a spoilt child!" — the exact words she later used to describe herself — and a woman of "strong affections and cold dislikes, of discretions and caprice, of pride and gentleness, of playfulness and hauteur." The only merit she had was "a desire to *act right* and to avoid all affectation, the odium of a deformed mind" (italics added). Lady Sharply also possessed "a too warm heart not understood by the cold and calculating world in the midst of which she lived," especially her husband and sons. Her life in the mansion was boring, and caused her to sink into bad habits of character. "With a temper soured, bad health, and an almost total indifference to life, or death, she was seldom roused to exertion, and knew little of enjoyment."

This poor woman, created from Louisa's imagination, matched another whose life was real. Together, they indicate an emerging theme in Louisa's mind of the right of women to be free from domination by men. Lady Sharply's warm heart and proper manners did her no good in the cold world inhabited by her husband and sons; her boring life corrupted her, and created in her an attitude close to suicidal. The theme of domination — or, if you will, suppression — began during Louisa's days as a schoolgirl in England, when her education was subordinated to her brother's, and was seen again at the spa at Töplitz in the battered countess, and again during the unilateral decisions about her sons before sailing to St. Petersburg. Louisa's sensitivity to "rights" was never far from the surface, and in September 1825, she boiled over when she read a newspaper account about a poor, uneducated Irish servant girl who had been seduced by her master. The occurrence was common, even in the Adams family, and servant girls often were unwilling sexual partners for the men who hired them. Louisa wrote George a long letter and two poems detailing the case. She conveyed in strong words her feelings about this girl who had been seduced by her master and then lived "in the constant hope that he would marry her." But when, "to the poor girl's utter horror and consternation," he married a younger and prettier maiden, the servant attempted suicide, was saved, then later drank quicksilver and "died in dreadful agony." Louisa overworked the death, pulling out all dramatic stops, and the poem is valuable both as an example of the popular melodramatic attitude about death, and of Louisa's emerging anger and "rights" theme. First, the death:

> The parching thirst, excruciat pain
> Seize on the chaos of the brain
> till Nature spent exhausted lies
> Pants, rolls in agony, and dies!!!

Beyond this histrionic gesture, the event truly angered Louisa Adams. Newspapers, then as now alert to titillating readers, portrayed the servant girl as dying for love. Louisa saw it differently: The woman had died without love, seduced and discarded by a man now "revelling in all the enjoyments of life" while the servant girl was "borne to the grave without a friend perhaps

without a pitying tear." Here, the anger and theme, too dangerous to be discussed directly in letters or conversation, emerge
in poetry:

> Am I then doom'd she wildly cried
>   Illusive hopes no more return
> He revels with his lovely bride
>   While I a wretch am left to mourn —
> Forlorn, deserted, lost, beguil'd,
>   In anguish must I weep?
> Become alas sad misery's child
>   Thro' sorrows path's to creep?

Louisa was not sympathetic to a master marrying a servant
girl; she and John Quincy remained aristocrats who preferred
the classes kept separated. But Louisa was indeed alert to women
as subordinates. Here she championed the right of a woman, even
a servant girl, not to be mastered, not to be seduced, betrayed,
and deserted. She was, within the boundary of socially accepted
form, making her quiet argument for a woman's right to freedom. This was not, as mentioned, a new concern of Louisa's;
constant acquiescence to her husband's demands had long forced
her to ponder the question, How can a woman control her own
life? Was she, Louisa asked, any different from the servant girl?
"That *sense of inferiority* which by nature and by law we are
compelled to feel," she wrote John Quincy in 1822, "and to
which we must submit, is worn by us with as much satisfaction
as the *badge oj slavery* generally, and we love to be flattered out
of our sense of our degradation" (italics added). Did not her
husband rule her just as the master ruled the servant girl?

Louisa knew that none of the Adams men comprehended this
injustice. When Charles, for example, misplaced some books,
Louisa was especially annoyed over the loss of "the 'Rights of
Women' which are rights he don't seem inclined to study or to
understand," she said. Louisa felt that, "as it regards women," the
Adams men she lived with were "one and all peculiarly harsh and
severe in their characters. There seems to exist no sympathy, no
tenderness for the weakness of the sex." Louisa felt like "a bird
in a cage," trapped by ridicule and indifference, an object only
for her husband's political benefit:

The more I bear the more is expected of me, and I sink in the efforts I make to answer such expectations. Thus sickness passes for ill temper and suffering for unwillingness and I am decried an incumberance unless I am required for any special purpose for a show or for some political maneouvre and if I wish for a trifle of any Kind any favour is required at my hands a deaf ear is turned to my request. Arrangements are made and if I object I am informed it is too late and it is all a misunderstanding.

How different was Louisa from the servant girl? In her isolation at the White House Louisa Adams slowly put together the connection: Were they not both women serving masters?

4

IN BOSTON, meanwhile, George, the outcast, had started a process of unraveling that lasted four years. It was marked by a constant series of small failures, most of them caused by his father, that left his parents increasingly frustrated and angry. George exposed the contrasting personalities of Louisa and John Quincy, and brought their tensions and bitterness into focus. George was their sacrifice to political ambition.

Gentle, never loved enough or needed at all, George viewed life from his floating island, his fantasy world. He shared his mother's interest in fiction, particularly Walter Scott, and developed a taste for stories and excitements, narratives of crime and depravity, mysterious horrors, that summoned fully his imagination. George loved his grandfather Adams, and wanted so much to be a hero like him to make the old man proud, that in his third year at Harvard he had joined the student rioting "convinced that he was gloriously resisting tyranny like his grandfather in 1776." But George was mere shadow. And as much as he loved his grandfather, George's fear of his father was so deep that Charles described it as "quivering." John Quincy permeated every moment of George's life. When George was attracted to a young woman during his freshman year at Harvard, for example, he quickly ended the romance after having a dream in which, as he kissed his love, his father suddenly appeared and scolded him: "Remember, George, who you are, and what you are doing."

By 1825, George had finished reading law for Daniel Webster, and although he preferred planning a great poetic work and Charles thought he would have enjoyed "the private life of a wealthy literary amateur," George opened a law office at 10 Court Street in Boston, and boarded with Dr. Welsh, the family friend. To get him started, John Quincy gave George a little business, and income, by placing him in charge of the family's financial accounts. But these accounts quickly became the focus for an oppressive relationship between father and son, and a symbol of George's failure. George soon fell behind in this work, and John Quincy started writing nasty, reproving letters to him.

The father tried every argument to improve his son. He continued instructing George, as he had since 1809, by letters (and poems with such titles as "The Garden of Virtues"), directing his son to study harder, rise early, attend church, be temperate. He demanded that George keep a diary, and in 1825, George dutifully took up his pen. But where John Quincy Adams's diary would stretch sixty-seven years, George kept at his only twenty-three days.

George began with strong resolution. In a print style of beautiful, clear, almost italic strokes, he made promises to do "what is right," improve his mind, and increase his knowledge. He divided his day into two parts: the morning for law and his father's accounts; the afternoon for reading. It was all in vain. George rose late, idled with his grandfather in Quincy, omitted Greek grammar and law books, and napped in the hot August afternoons. His indifference to his law practice deteriorated into incompetence. He stumbled about Boston on errands for his family, and a simple trip to the bank took on aspects of a comic routine:

George forgot the order form, returned to his office, and on the way back to the bank got a speck of brick dust in his eye. He found the eye so troublesome that "I determined to humour it and try to escape from the suffering by sleep. I slept two hours and for this do not feel any dissatisfaction or self reproach."

There was something wonderfully human about George Adams. His brief diary revealed a gentle, delicate, lost and bumbling soul open to his inner feelings, like his mother, while dutifully reciting the Adams litany of work and perseverance. Returning to Boston after a visit with his grandfather, George discovered that his horse was lame. This was commonplace; his father even had horses drop dead under him. George examined the animal, and because he had no choice but to continue, drove his chaise slowly, taking care not to hurt the horse. But the experience troubled him, and revealed George's emotional sensitivity. "It was impossible," he wrote into his diary, "to witness the animal suffering without becoming deeply depressed." George sought Dr. Welsh, and spent an hour talking to him about this troubling occurrence, and only then did his disturbed feelings settle down and resume "their tone." Another time, reading Dante's "Inferno" to a cluster of admiring ladies, George became so upset with the passages of "intense suffering" that he had to stop and step outside to breathe the evening air. Returning to his chambers, he stayed up beyond midnight conversing again with Dr. Welsh.

The entanglements inside George's mind created a rich fantasy world, marred by his own social impotence. A young man who could be moved to depression by a lame horse or Dante also soared to romantic heights fantasizing about women. During his visits to Washington between 1820 and 1823, George had awkwardly courted Mary Hellen. In his troubled mind, he found Mary's attentions flattering, and in the summer of 1823, during a visit home, he had asked his father's permission for an engagement to Mary. George assured him that the marriage would wait until his law practice had been established, "in perhaps four or five years." His father had reluctantly consented.

But during the next three years, George seldom traveled from his law work in Boston to see Mary in Washington. He wrote her infrequently. Worse, Mary proved to be, as Charles described her, "one of the most capricious women that were ever formed in a capricious race." She openly flirted with Charles and then John in Washington, and ignored George. Charles got badly snagged on this beguiling young woman; "George," he wrote in his diary, "would be in a perfect fever and sickness if he was to imagine that she had encouraged me in the least." Years later, Charles would confess that he had "too deeply loved the woman." After Charles, Mary turned her attentions to John, and he treated her engagement to George "as an utter absurdity." John was the best looking of the three Adams sons, and a self-centered young man who projected an aura of "affected mystery." His brothers thought John "artful," hot-headed like his father, a gambler and a horse-trader who indulged a fondness for carriages and horses. Mary thought John magnetic, a compelling force, and with George in Boston and Charles at Harvard, conveniently handy. As early as the summer of 1824, engaged to George for a year, Mary turned her flirtations upon John. In "dark and mysterious" letters from his mother and John, Charles perceived the end for George.

Charles and George took long and troubled walks in the gardens at Quincy, and stayed up late discussing Mary. George shared his fantasy of living with Mary on his father's property, but Charles already foresaw "a good deal of trouble" to George from this match. So did Louisa, and when the family gathered in Quincy in September 1824, for a dinner with old John Adams — already eighty-nine, yellow with age, weak of voice, and nearly deaf — she pulled Charles aside. No one wanted this engagement to go on, she said. John Quincy was now "tacitly opposed." Louisa could not keep John and Mary apart much longer. If the engagement to George could be broken, she told Charles, it should be. Later, she wrote Charles urging him to give George's engagement "a preposterous and ridiculous turn" when discussing it with him, and cause him to "terminate" the union "agreeably to our wishes." And so, by Louisa's conspiracy with Charles, George failed again. Sometime in 1826, the engagement to Mary ended, although George was never actually told so by Mary nor she by him. The whole thing simply melted, like an untouched wedding confection left too long in the sun.

After this episode, George had fantasies about almost every young woman he saw in Boston. Women were not his friends — with the exception of Harriet Welsh — and George admitted that he was both on his guard "against female power" and "painfully" mistrustful of "female fidelity." Well he might be; he had lost the only women he ever told he loved, and by his mother's wiles. Women of his own class now frightened George, and he dreamed of and imagined women he could dominate and conquer, women who were beneath him socially and therefore grateful for his attentions, or unable to repel them. One time, riding from Quincy to Boston, George became aroused by "an exceedingly beautiful girl" who boarded the stage at Dorchester. He studied the woman's eyes, the brilliant color of her cheeks, the shape of her mouth, "the dazzling whiteness of her teeth." This young woman pleased George in a new, different way. "She was slender, her limbs slight but very well proportioned; her skin of the purest whites marked by the brilliant blue of the veins which were visible; without color but looking [in] perfect health; delicate to a degree that inspired the idea of fragility." George imagined her "in the third or fourth class of society," perhaps a mechanic's daughter or a shopkeeper's, "yet so aristocratically beautiful!" He never spoke to her, but let his fantasy roam over her until they arrived in Boston. This was the kind of woman George sought: a woman "poetically beautiful," but also not of his class, and perhaps most important, fragile. He hurried to his office, and wrote a detailed description of his trip and the young woman into his journal.

George stopped his daily journal on August 24. He had accomplished little. He preferred weekends with his grandfather in Quincy, smoking cigars and staying up late with Cyrus Briggs, and whole days with friends "walking on the beach and the fields, eating chowder, smoking and talking." The words "dejection" and "much depressed" now appeared in George's diary. Like his father and uncle, he spent days "in the blues." George made a final entry on December 31, 1825. He regretted that keeping a regular diary was beyond his ability or desire, and lamented the distractions that diverted him and past irresolution that "has recently alarmed me by its gradual expansion." These characteristics also alarmed his father, and George prayed to be delivered —

somehow — from his tyrannical parent. "I close the year in melancholy feeling," he wrote. "Its course cannot meet approval from a strict and scrutinizing conscience." George had failed at love; worse, he had also failed at regularity, temperance, duty, and controlling his passions. He concluded with a certain Adams tone: "I feel that my life has been wasted and my time misapplied." So did his father.

Instead of easing pressure on George, however, John Quincy increased it. He left no part of George's life untouched, and like the ubiquitous figure in George's Harvard dream, the father forced his presence into every corner of the son's existence. In the spring of 1826, George won election to the Massachusetts state legislature, a brave first step into what Charles, in a haunting metaphor, called "the ocean of political life." John Quincy, after congratulating George, began issuing a list of warnings and advice that continued all summer and into the autumn. "Arm yourself," the President told his son, "with fortitude — prepare and discipline your mind for disappointment. Consider the station to which you are called as a Post of *danger* and of *duty* and think as little as you possibly can of it as a post of honour." Adams might have been describing his own Presidency. His list, as it always did, went on, and on: Read Plutarch, acquire knowledge of politics, know the laws of your state, cultivate the governor; employ "all the Stoic virtues — Prudence, Temperance, Fortitude, Justice" and the Christian graces of "Benevolence, Charity, Humility, Courteousness, all tempered with inflexible perseverance and firmness." George would find time, his father said, by rising early and avoiding procrastination. As this list grew, John Quincy added other lists, and never let up. No one could have filled the father's requests: forms from the family insurance company, inquiries about stock for sale, questions concerning the operation of the farm in Quincy — which even included how the hay would be cut and used, and how the manure distributed.

But George, who liked to nap and smoke cigars and visit, slipped behind in his accounts and replies. He sent no list of deeds or vouchers, as his father requested, and made a thirty-one-cent error on a bank statement, which sent his father into a rage. To John Quincy's repeated inquiries about stock companies,

George replied with silence. Only during sessions of the state legislature, which George attended faithfully, did the father fall silent, waiting. When it adjourned, he demanded once more "with some impatience" his accounts, soon two quarters behind; the lists of vouchers, securities; the mortgage deeds to be recorded in Boston and Dedham, the accounts of the farm and house in Quincy, the payments of interest to Thomas Adams — and on and on. George remained silent.

It was these demands, and this tension, that now created the most revealing episode of George's young and fragile life.

5

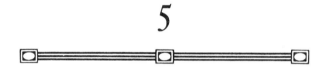

THE DEATH OF JOHN ADAMS, and the settlement of his estate, set off a sequence of events that tore apart his son's family. In his last days, the old patriot had wished nothing more than to survive to July 4, 1826, the fiftieth anniversary of the signing of the Declaration of Independence. Feeble and ninety-one, too old to travel into Boston, he had sent by courier a feisty toast for the town's celebration: "Independence forever!" On the morning of the Fourth, when his granddaughter bent to his pillow and told him the date, Adams had rested peacefully all morning, serene in that thought, and about one o'clock whispered, "Jefferson still survives." These were his last words.

When George learned that his beloved grandfather was ill, he hurried from Boston to Quincy to be with him. The old man recognized his favorite grandson, and their eyes conveyed their love. He treasured George. They had exchanged books, and he had encouraged George to poke around his library. George had come to Quincy almost every weekend these last few years to read to him. The old man had chuckled over George's letters, especially the descriptions of Congress, which were nasty like his mother's, and he had preserved them all, tying the letters neatly in bundles, for re-reading. Grandpapa Adams loved this forgotten, rejected son; he always signed his letters to George, "Your affectionate grandfather," and he meant it. And so they touched and waited on the Fourth of July, fifty years after Philadelphia. George stayed with Grandpapa, the man who had raised him and loved him most, until the old gentleman died at six-thirty that day, "as calmly," George wrote his father, "as an infant sleeps."

In Washington that July 4, the second President Adams walked to the Capitol and spent the day listening to commemorative ceremonies. Unknown to him, his father lay dying in Quincy and Thomas Jefferson was slipping into death in Monticello, Virginia. At one o'clock, as John Adams spoke his final words, Jefferson died. The details of these deaths — Adams and Jefferson together on the fiftieth anniversary of the Declaration of Independence — enthralled the romantic nation, and seemed to reach beyond mere coincidence. Adams and Jefferson had been colleagues in Philadelphia that hot July fifty years ago, then Presidents, political opponents, and in their final years, friends once more. That their deaths fell on this anniversary, and that each in his final hours had this great day in mind, made the event more dramatic. John Quincy Adams later wrote in his diary: "the time, the manner, the coincidence . . . are visible and palpable marks of Divine favor."

For Louisa, John Adams's death was "painful." She felt for him "the love and duty of a daughter"; in the years since her marriage they had become friends and he never said a harsh word to her, "and on this fact my memory will *feast* till I like him am gather'd to my fathers." In Massachusetts a week later, as John Quincy entered his father's empty bedchamber, the loss struck him like a blow. "That moment was inexpressively painful," JQA wrote in his diary. In this room the two men had shared opinions and political news and strategy; here they had said goodbye for the last time. The wisdom, the counsel, the sage advice would be heard no more. In this house John Quincy had learned to read, had recited poetry to his mother, listened to the thunder of war, complained of his first diplomatic appointment, and returned from his last overseas post. The old house was full of the two generations. Now, he wrote Louisa, "Should I live through my tour of service, my purpose is to come and close my days here, to be deposited with my father and mother."

When he attended church the next Sunday, Adams sat in his family's pew. Here he had prayed as a child, and his parents had worshipped in times of peril and in times of peace, with hopes and fears for their country. His eyes flooded with tears. Where were they now, the leaders of yesterday? The Braintree elders, the stern deacons of the congregation, the thin, eagle-like Mr. Wibird who had baptized him? Gone. The church now filled with men and women who had been children with him, and they brought their children, and their children's children. The generation of the Declaration was gone. John Quincy was, he realized, the elder these children would recall.

Generations of his family reaching back almost two centuries had belonged to this congregation, now the Unitarian Church of Quincy. But John Quincy Adams had never joined. The wars, his absences, his feelings of Christian unworthiness had been excuses for putting off what should be done. Here, in his parents' church, he collected the loose ends of his life, and resolved to return to home and God. Adams informed the Rev. Whitney of his desire to make a public witness of his Christian faith and hope. On October 1, when the pastor asked who wished to come forward in the divine mission of Christ to live forevermore according to the rules of his gospel, members of the congregation slowly rose to their feet, the President of the United States among them, to partake of the solemn communion ritual. John Quincy Adams became a born-again Christian.

John Quincy's emotional homecoming embroiled him in a fight with his wife, and then his son. During the Adams/Jefferson funeral orations, Louisa had been "shocked" to read in the newspapers of Jefferson's poverty. She and John Quincy had argued since the end of their honeymoon about money, and the financial burden of public office. Here was startling evidence of its result. Even as Thomas Jefferson had lain dying, a subscription for his financial relief was being proposed to members of Congress gathered to celebrate the Fourth. After a reading of the Declaration of Independence, a hat was passed among the Congressmen and visitors for this great document's author. "Not more than four or five contributions went in," said a visitor, and Jefferson "died in want."* "Shame on Virginia!" Louisa wrote John Quincy. Never, she warned, let your family become burdens on this nation.

The disposition of John Adams's will opened this old wound, and set off a snapping, summer-long feud between Louisa and John Quincy. The old gentleman had been generous, and among other bequests left JQA the old house and 103 acres of land surrounding it. But Adams would have to pay the estate twelve thousand dollars to possess the property. Further, he would have to pay Thomas half the value of the old President's library of books, manuscripts, letters, papers, and the family portraits. John Quincy faced a difficult choice: He could put up for sale the home of his mother and father, or he could somehow meet the conditions of the will, "though it will bring me heavily into debt." The money, with interest, was to be paid within three years. John Quincy wrote Louisa all summer about his choice, but in fact he had decided almost immediately: "I can not endure the thought of the sale of this place."

Louisa vehemently opposed John Quincy's going into debt — "God forbid!" — or leaving the Presidency in poverty. "That you should be desirous of owning the House that was your Fathers is natural," she wrote him, "but that you should waste your property and burthen yourself with a large unprofitable landed estate, which nearly ruined its last possessor, merely because it belonged to him, is scarcely prudent or justifiable, and

---

* Jefferson fell into debt during his retirement. His crops failed and he suffered losses every year during the decade 1810–1820 when farm prices dropped to unprecedented lows. The financial failure of a close friend, whose note for $20,000 Jefferson had endorsed, brought the ex-President to bankruptcy. He sold his personal library to Congress for $23,950, and a public lottery of his farmlands was conducted to help him out. But the lottery was undersubscribed, and private donors had to rush to his aid. The author of the Declaration of Independence died $40,000 in debt; even his personal home, Monticello, eventually had to be auctioned to settle his estate.

the Jefferson family afford too gloomy an instance of its folly to render such an act excusable." John Quincy reacted in anger: He planned to inventory his father's estate, he told Louisa, and survey the lands; he would employ George in matters pertaining to the will, and John with the business of the Presidency. She could do what she wished.

Louisa, embittered by this rebuke, quickly left Washington — not for Quincy, but for the spas. She put Johnson Hellen in charge of the White House — she did not wish to leave "publick property" in the hands of servants — and headed for Lebanon Springs and Saratoga Springs, New York, departing so fast that she forgot the bottle containing her false teeth. For two weeks she dragged an entourage that included three servants, Elizabeth, and the irritable adolescent Charles around the crowded springs, where so many people raised so much dust that the baths were gritty. Charles, who considered his mother melancholy and dull, played billiards, and drank too much champagne on his nine-teenth birthday. Louisa and Charles argued continually about where they would go and what they would do, and she soon de-clared, "I am so tired of Springs of every sort." Back in New York City after five tedious weeks, Charles deposited his mother in her hotel room, and went downstairs for a drink. In the bar, he discovered Thomas Hellen "as if dropped from Heaven for my relief." A few drinks, and Charles had convinced Thomas to take over the escorting of Louisa, and "jumped on board the Steam Boat, thanking Heaven, that I had some prospect of re-lief" from his mother. After five days of rest, billiards, cigars, and riding in Philadelphia, Charles went on to Washington and spent six weeks "with but little stir," a proper compensation, he thought, "for my sufferings on the journey."

In New York, however, Louisa received a letter from her husband that terrified her. John Quincy had started surveying his father's land, and, while employing George and John in paperwork, also demanded that they assist him in the heavy, exhausting survey project. It rained and they trudged through waves of mosquitoes, "over tangled brakes and Rattlesnakes," and felt "everything of heroic fatigue but the glory," he wrote. John had quickly announced his displeasure, and quit. George, too, lasted but half a day, and retreated back to Boston. In this small exchange of news, however, Louisa correctly read great peril. John and Charles rebelled against their father; they were flexible and strong. But George was weak, unable to perform as a first son ought, and unsturdy beneath the increasing burden his father placed upon him. If he had quit after only half a day's work, especially if he quit in front of his father, the vituperation must have been severe. Louisa was convinced that George had been shattered, and she rushed to Quincy.

Louisa found the old house empty, without furniture, and cold for late August. Around the patriarchal home, caterpillars were ravishing the trees, which stood as barren as though winter had cut across the farmland. In this foreboding scene, as Louisa suspected, George had battled his father for two months, and their conflict had reached its worst moment during the land survey. Unable to keep up, slapping at mosquitoes, complaining about the rain, George had been "lashed and sneered" at by his father. John Quincy Adams's frustration with his son, with his own life, had erupted.

George could not shoulder the demands, the cutting humiliations. He could not play all the roles his father required: lawyer, dutiful son, legislator, correct young man. Worse, he could not handle the weight of being the firstborn son of a firstborn son, nor satisfy his father's endless lists, the calls for perseverance, fortitude, temperance, resolution, industry that went beyond his reach, even if he intended to grasp them. In his grandfather's fields, under his father's whipping tongue, George had failed once again. The son had fled his father's cruelty.

All around him this summer there had been death. The barren trees, the empty house, spoke of its harvest. When the old man died, George had been sick for several days. Then, on the fields of his beloved grandfather, scarred more deeply than anyone knew, George had been ridiculed and laughed at by his unquenchable father. He could neither survey nor measure up. He had failed in every way. Emptied by death, George was devoured in life. His spirit died.

When Louisa reached her oldest son in Boston, she found him huddled alone in his chamber, crumpled, curled against the chill like a fallen autumn leaf. Louisa was barely able to comfort him, and reported that George was "in very bad health. . . . The state of his mind is by no means such as I would have it." She told Charles, "The scenes in which he has been called upon to become the principle performer . . . have now produced a state of painful dejection, which will require the greatest tenderness in his friends to remove and have impressed him with an idea that he is unfit for this society or the duties for which other men are born." Louisa stayed in Boston to comfort George as best she could; she did not return to Quincy. When John and President Adams left for Washington in mid-October, Louisa reluctantly departed from her oldest son, and arrived in the White House two days after her husband, "dispirited and unwell." With the family together, and only George missing, Charles felt "a creeping dread."

Louisa and John Quincy had no tools, no special knowledge of therapies for dealing with their oldest son and the complaints he made, or his actions. Doctors had enough difficulty healing the physically ill; vague discomforts, lethargy, procrastination, ignoring a father's terrifying demands, feebleness, "moments of despondency" (as George called them) had few labels and no treatment. The Adamses, without guidelines, suggested a wide range of cures. Louisa urged the benefits of sea air and a Washington visit. She suggested optimism: Life was "a perpetual ascent toward perfection," she insisted, and "we ought always therefore to look up rather than down." She advised her son to have "steady attention to business" and "to the Graces." John Quincy clipped and sent a letter from the *National Intelligencer* about organizing time, listening to sermons, and working on business; he told George to read it and place it under his pillow before going to bed. He instructed his son to rise early, make his own fire (for exercise), read the Bible, "burst the bonds" of "licentious life," and "return to the laws of unsullied temperance." He extolled the benefits (again) of keeping a diary, "the Time piece of Life" and "one of the best preservatives of Morals." Regular attendance at church, he told George, would improve "your heart and mind," and induce "meditation, self-examination, modesty — to soothe the angry and turbulant Passions." Prayer and regularity would "Methodize your *Mind*,"

But while full of suggestions for George for controlling his erratic behavior, the Adamses remained insensitive to its warnings, and unsympathetic. When Harriet Welsh kindly wrote them detailing the impact of their demands upon poor George's behavior, and warning them that "the excessive idea of duty to the whole family is dangerous," Louisa ignored it. She replied that the young woman's letters always gave them pleasure, "altho' they are a little on the harum scarum line." John Quincy believed that George could save himself by better occupying his time, that he could overcome his "dejection and Low Spirits" with attention to duties and resolutions: There were, the father told the son, "no desponding fits which you cannot completely cure by going to bed at nine and rising at five o'clock." A good night's sleep, and useful occupation during the day, were "Specific and infalluble remedies for all the *blues*." When George still wrote of a "gloomy turn," his father replied sharply: "You must not indulge mere melancholy humours." Denial he thought, was the best cure of all.

6

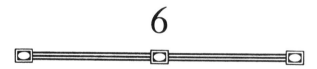

WHILE GEORGE was sliding downhill, Charles was rising into prominence within the Adams family. Charles was all George wished to be, but wasn't. He did not fear his father, as George did. Charles had stayed close to his parents, never separating for long until he was almost fifteen. George had spent most of his youth living with aunts or grandparents. He was the rejected son, Charles the favored. Charles had learned how to handle his parents, and best of all, he knew how to take care of himself.

For about eighteen months, Charles lived in the White House, growing bored with his mother's neuroses and his father's gloom, and trying to read law. He shared Louisa's romantic blood, and devotedly read poets and novels — so much so that at one point his grandfather had written him, scolding: "Mathematicks and Law are the true rocks on which a man of business may surely found his reputation. . . . It is not novels or poetry. It is neither Scott or Lord Byron who make useful men." But Charles was rebellious. He replied that studying law, and little else, lacked "brightness," and that while law was indeed "an exceedingly *useful* study" it was also very, very boring and threatened "to make us mere machines." John Adams, however, had replied: "Study, dear Charles, makes the man." Charles wasn't so sure. He also loved "Segars," wine, champagne, the Old Punch Bowl Tavern in Brookline, billiards, and the ladies. Wearing his royal-blue coat with high silk choker and his jeweled stickpin, Charles, a handsome and fair young man, enjoyed strolling Pennsylvania Avenue appreciating the ladies who came out in large numbers during sunny weather. Charles was wise enough to control his passions, or at least hide them well; unlike George, he recognized what was worthwhile, and what was not. He also kept his biting edge, his wit, and a fresh perception of his family that saved him.

Charles was also wise enough to know when to act. He very clearly understood the impact on his family of the political life, and witnessed the internal dissension it caused between his mother and father. He wished to avoid it, and had written his grandfather in 1826: "God knows I am a little disposed to pass through the stormy, violent lives of my Father and yourself. The sacrifice is so great." He saw his family "destined to live in storms," and wanted nothing of it. "A political life is after all a very disagreeable one. In quiet times there is little room for distinction, and the profession sinks; in violent times, all the rest of life is sacrificed. A family is a dangerous thing, for it may be dragged into the political arena to be vilified and overthrown. It is every instant exposed to the risk of losing its head. And what's all this for? A name." Charles was unwilling to sacrifice himself for the Adams name, or tradition. He understood that his freedom, his youth would soon end, and adulthood and "female ties" restrict him. Rather than despair, Charles acted. Disgusted by his mother's melancholia and isolation, kept at a distance by his tormented father behind the iron mask, quarreling with John over his bad manners and "insidious and malevolent conduct," Charles fled the White House for his friends.

On June 22, reading Samuel March Phillipps' *Treatise on the Laws of Evidence*, Charles received a letter from John Hancock Richardson, Harvard '25, announcing that he and Henry Samuel Tudor, Harvard '24, were gathering in New York for a bit of celebrating. The three were close friends, college pranksters, and drinking buddies who had often been known to spend an entire day (or night) with "our old companion, a bottle." Charles tossed Phillipps's *Evidence* into a corner and ordered his trunk packed immediately. The next stage for New York left early in the morning. He was on it. "I had been wishing for something like an absence," he wrote in his diary, "as our family had become exceedingly disjointed and uncomfortable. Indeed I never saw a family which has so little of the associating disposition."

In New York, Charles found Richardson at the new National Hotel at 112 Broadway, on the corner of Cedar Street. It was a rainy Sunday, without temptations outside, and the two opened a bottle and spent the afternoon leisurely drinking it. They were joined that evening by John Howe Boardman, Harvard '26, who had been one of the great dunces at college but was maturing to an agreeable companion, and the next morning Tudor arrived bringing clear weather and the opening of bachelor festivities. Tudor was "a little more boisterous than I liked," Charles said, and he could "set us off as well as himself." Right away, Tudor reminded Charles that he had a debt to settle. In 1824, the youngest Adams had bet his friends — in addition to his bet with Johnson Hellen — that his father would not win the Presidential election. Charles now found himself paying for an "afternoon with Champagne wine" to celebrate a victory he detested.

For the next week, the four young men never endangered sobriety. They went to the theater, parties, fancy restaurants, taverns, celebrations, and levees. They strolled the Castle Garden, and sailed to Staten Island for wine and "delicious oysters."

Charles even visited the mayor and other New York politicians who supported his father for re-election. The four young men met every day for "the ritual routine of Turtle and wine" lunches. One evening, Tudor started "a wild harum scarum scrape" between Richardson and Boardman that resulted in shouting and pushing, and could only be settled by five hours of champagne drinking. After another rowdy day, back in the National Hotel at eleven, Tudor called for champagne, "and," said Charles, "I nothing loth ordered it to our bed room." Boardman, Tudor, Adams, and Richardson spent the next three hours drinking all the champagne in the hotel, and by two in the morning, having reached "a condition to be outrageous," they set forth from the hotel boisterously declaring their intentions to buy more. "After a variety of ludicrous incidents, imminent risk of transportation to the Watch House," they settled for supper in a cellar tavern, where they purchased more bottles and brought them back to their rooms for another hour of drinking. They went to bed at sunrise, Charles declared, after "a most ludicrous and agreeable evening."

By the end of the week, the champagne, the turtle soups, the oysters, the wine, the New York water all "had the effect of quite breaking us up. . . . I among the rest could hardly hold up my head." Before separating, the young men consumed a final luncheon of turtle and champagne, followed by an afternoon of burgundy, and then the theater. "The evening passed soberly," said Charles, "even by Tudor." Charles left at five the next morning. He reached the White House "feeling somewhat rusty," flat broke, and pleased beyond measure. He had briefly defied "the melancholy thought" that now intruded, that this might have been the last time he could enjoy the unfettered society of his young male friends. He had "made merry," but as the end of these days arrived, Charles sensed that the occasion would not come again. Hungover, bothered by diarrhea, his money exhausted, Charles savored the memories even as they started to fade, replaced by the reminder "that more troublesome times are coming."

Charles proved as calculating in love as he was in revelry, and as prescient. He had met a beautiful young woman at the

French ambassador's ball, and had decided that this was the person he would marry. Abigail Brooks lived in Medford, Massachusetts, outside Boston, but traveled to Washington during the winter for the society and a visit with her older sister, Charlotte Gray Brooks, and her husband, Edward Everett, a member of Congress. At another ball a year later, in February 1827, Charles made the accepted, overt social signal of continuously dancing with Abby Brooks, and she reciprocated by taking his arm and walking the room – the same signals Louisa and John Quincy had exchanged in 1795. He formally asked if she would permit his attentions in the future, and Abby, much embarrassed, replied that she would have to ask her father. What followed further emphasized the special place Charles occupied in Louisa's and John Quincy's lives, and their possible awareness that their youngest son had been more sexually active than his brothers. Charles, it turned out, was not only putting aside the things of his youth, but also shifting from loving a mistress to selecting a wife. Paramount in all this was his keen sense of maintaining a high level of comfort for himself.

At first, Abby's father, Peter Chardon Brooks, refused to give his consent to his daughter's engagement. He was an affectionate and indulgent father, somewhat similar in attitudes and position to Joshua Johnson, and he wished to keep his "pet" child at home a little longer. Abby was just nineteen, and Charles not yet twenty. Charles had no prospects for employment, and had only started law studies. In a series of letters between the Adamses and Peter Brooks, Charles was described in glowing phrases by his father, and Brooks' objections were slowly overcome. Their son's choice of Abby, John Quincy wrote Peter Brooks, could not have been more agreeable to him or Mrs. Adams. Charles was preparing himself for the law, he wrote, and would be admitted to the bar in August 1828, about the time he came of age. Adams suggested to Brooks (the idea originating with Charles) that the two young people contract an engagement, but postpone marriage until Charles reached twenty-one. John Quincy wrote a flattering endorsement of his son: He was "sedate and considerate – his disposition studious and somewhat reserved – his sense of honour high and delicate; his habits domestic and regular, and his temper generous and benevolent. An early marriage is more congenial to a person thus constituted, than to youths of more ardent Passions, and of more tardy self controul." With such a strong recommendation from the President, Brooks gave in, and granted his consent. He even apologized to the Adamses for withholding it at first. But he proved to be more tenacious with his daughter than anyone expected.

To describe the Adamses as enthusiastic would understate their reaction. Louisa spoke for her husband when she told George that "Miss Brooks is a great belle here and a wonderful favorite with the family." Why were the Adamses so eager and pleased? Abby was indeed young and lovely, and Charles by marrying her would guarantee a start on an heir for the next Adams generation. But more than that, Charles had taken to heart his father's warning not to "linger through his days in torpid inaction or to depend upon anyone but himself for his future support, and his condition in the world." Charles would not be harassed by politics, or threatened by poverty. While they might exaggerate his prospects, neither Charles nor his parents could overestimate Abby's fortune: Peter Brooks was the wealthiest man in New England. "Both her fortune and my own prospects," said Charles, "are such as to prevent any uneasiness as to our condition in life." Unlike his parents, Charles would never worry about money.

It is also likely that John Quincy and Louisa had a third, and very private, reason for giving their consent so quickly to Charles's selection. Charles was a passionate young man. Early in his youth he had learned that "There is magic in a Petticoat to a young man," and he discovered — or at least fancied — fiery Southern (Maryland) passions in himself "not . . . to be trifled [with]." These were feelings Charles refused to suppress and, like his father in Newburyport and Boston, actively pursued. Women stirred Charles "by a voluptuous manner, to which I am unfortunately peculiarly susceptible." For at least a year, and probably since he returned to Washington from Harvard in 1825, Charles had been keeping a mistress, a comfortable and acceptable outlet for his sexual passion. Her name is lost, or destroyed, but it is likely that she came from the lower classes and lived in Washington. If she were a mere servant girl, the entanglement would have been less binding and ending it less painful. But if she were a woman such as George fancied, perhaps a mechanic's daughter, the relationship would have been deep enough to have roots, however fragile, that would leave scars when extracted. Moreover, that Charles would keep a mistress indicated several things: He very likely experienced sex with prostitutes early in his adolescence, and sought a different, if not more dependable and interesting, relationship; he had, at eighteen and nineteen, the sexual maturity and the extra cash to maintain a mistress; and, most of all, he had the sophistication to keep the knowledge private at a time when such information might have destroyed his father's ambitions.

Did his parents know of this liaison? It is very likely that they did. Washington was a small and gossipy society filled with Adams relatives and friends — and in 1827 teeming with President Adams's political enemies. With the Presidential election less than a year away, and its low tone already being sounded, no member of the Adams family was free from attack.* Louisa and John Quincy, by their swift acquiescence to Charles's request for an engagement, may have been extracting him from a relationship before it became embarrassing to the family.

Within two months after his engagement to Abby Brooks — four weeks after the Adamses got Brooks' final approval (revealing Charles's caution) — the youngest Adams made his difficult choice. He went about the delicate task of ending his liaison with his mistress. Charles knew that his engagement would last two years, and that he was now watched closely in society. Any continuing dalliance risked breaking the precious thread between Charles and his future comfort and security. The danger was too great, and on April 24, 1827, Charles entered in his diary:

> In the evening I went through one of those disagreeable scenes which occur sometimes in life. No man of sense will ever keep a Mistress. For if she is valuable, the separation when it comes is terrible, and if she is not, she is more plague

* Even Louisa felt compelled to defend herself and her father and wrote an account of her marriage for *Mrs. A. S. Colvin's Weekly Messenger*, June 2, 1827.

than profit. Ever since my engagement, I have been preparing for a close of my licentious intrigues, and this evening I cut the last cord which bound me. What a pity that experience is always to be learnt over and over by each succeeding generation.

His father could not have agreed more with that last sentence.

Charles put aside the Maryland passion; he had acknowledged his weaknesses, and had indulged them, but retained his reason and control. He now assumed the traditional role of the engaged male. Women of this period were sexually divided into two categories: good and bad (pure and impure). Bad girls responded sexually, while good girls remained pure of mind and body — if not of spirit — and unclouded by the shadow of vulgar thought or deed. Society reinforced this idea. The heroines of the novels Charles and his mother read were always fair, chaste, docile, loyal, uncomplaining. Their opponents were women of depraved character, dark and, in the favorite negative description of the time, "voluptuous." The perfect heroine, therefore the perfect woman, was delicate, accomplished in art and music, and never vain; she was melancholy, given to weeping, and occupied to distraction with her own death and the deaths of other women and great men. Abby and his mistress were like the women in these novels, and while Abby had a "high" temper and sometimes collapsed into "unmeaning and loud nonsense, on the whole," he reported to his diary, "I think her calculated to make a person happy, provided he is aware of the duties which befall upon him." With the cold eye of his father, Charles concluded: "I do love this girl as I think a woman ought to be loved. Sincerely, fervently and yet with purity and respect." The advantages outweighed the disadvantages of the union, he calculated, like a balance sheet showing a pleasing surplus: Poor, sexually-exciting mistress for docile, rich wife; the sacrifice was worth it.

But Charles's engagement to Abby Brooks did not progress smoothly.

7

BY JUNE 1827, the fissures in the Adams family had widened substantially. President Adams had failed to implement any of his plans, and after watching the defeat of his party in the previous autumn's elections, which completed control of Congress by the opposition, he now fended off public attacks on himself. Not surprisingly, President Adams began complaining of nervous symptoms, aches, and fevers. He had a soreness and pain in his right side that troubled him when he swam, and he feared that cramps would drown him. He worried about chronic constipation, indigestion, and catarrh. He slept fitfully. He sometimes lost his appetite. He thought he was developing erysipelas, like Louisa. His spirits drooped. John Quincy wrote word pictures of his miseries in his diary, and they sounded similar to Louisa's and George's: "uncontrollable dejection of spirits, insensibility to the almost unparalleled blessings with which I have been favored; a sluggish carelessness of life, an imaginary wish that it were terminated, with a clinging to it as close as it ever was in the days of most animated hopes." John Quincy Adams knew what was really troubling him. "My own career is closed," he wrote. "My hopes such as are left me, are centered upon my children."

Defeat also piled upon defeat for George. In May 1827, he ran for re-election to the Massachusetts legislature on a pro-administration ticket, and received 1,430 votes. But he needed 1,585 to win in a field of five candidates. Promptly renominated, he failed in a second election. John Quincy wrote George that his loss "was a mis-fortune," and then added: "Shall I say that it gives you time to redeem the arrearages of your promises to me? No — I leave you to say that to yourself." To George, he sent instead the wisdom of Solomon: "In the days of prosperity, rejoice; but in the days of Adversity, *consider*." In these days of adversity, George had much to consider. He promptly took sick, wrote his mother, and when his letter reached Washington "whining about his general health as an excuse for neglect of writing," Charles said coldly, "this put Madame into a fit of tears." George complained of an abscess, and since infections of any sort were serious, Louisa rushed northward with only a household servant and Elizabeth with her. "I," said Charles, "certainly felt most prodigiously provoked by George and his nonsense."

The entire incident — illness and trip — was suspicious. The Adamses seemed to flee the White House for any reason: Charles to New York, Louisa to the spas and now to Boston, and the President every August and September to Quincy; only John stayed home, busy with Mary Hellen. Once out of the White House, Louisa slowed her journey in Baltimore, then Philadelphia and New York. Immediately her letters became filled not with concern for George, but with political news for John Quincy. Supporters serenaded the First Lady at her hotel rooms, and in Philadelphia she parried requests from Pennsylvania politicians who crowded into her chambers to be presented. When Louisa boarded the stage in Bordentown, her friend Joseph Hopkinson leaned into the window and told her that John Quincy would "have Pennsylvania" in the coming Presidential election, if he would campaign. Louisa, in an echo of her visit in 1822, wrote her husband urging him to leave the White House and journey among the people of Pennsylvania. But Adams was stubborn, and in his own 1822 echo replied: "I shall not go upon any electioneering mission to Pennsylvania or anywhere else. My journies and my visits wherever they may be shall have no connection with the Presidency." Louisa, however, ignored his disapproval and repeated her request. Campaigning, she said, would get him out of the heat of Washington and away from the swarm of people who "tease and embarrass you." His appearance would repay those politicians who had supported him, and lift his spirits. He would enjoy "that tribute of respect" he was entitled to, she said, and allow the people to become "personally acquainted with your manners." Louisa's argument was the classical political axiom: Go into the countryside, dispel your critics, return political favors, soak up adulation. She even determined the best route for her husband to take through Pennsylvania for maximum political exposure. But John Quincy remained firm. "I go as straight and as quick as possible to Quincy," he told her. His plan, she replied, "embarrasses me very much."

Louisa continued arguing with her husband about campaigning, and when she reached Boston, she argued with him about George. She found their oldest son mending, and during the month she nursed him back to health she wrote John Quincy trying to get him to see George as she did. His personality, she said, went through "twenty changes in a day,"* and it was "of the utmost importance that he should not be harrassed with business or care." John Quincy replied that George's illness was a sham, an excuse to avoid overdue work. He merely needed "bolstering," like a sagging piece of furniture, and wanted only to adhere to the principles of temperance, fortitude, perseverance, to recover. Louisa, strongly interceding in George's behalf, saw deeper into his troubled soul. She thought he needed to stop "his too stimulating habits" — snuff, alcohol, and a little opium to sleep — and seek "new objects to remove him from *des liaisons dangereuse*, otherwise he will take some rash and ridiculous step which may lead to his ruin." Ten days later, she repeated the warning to John Quincy. George, Louisa wrote, "is an uncommonly fine young man" who needed "kindness blended with firmness to prevent his taking some rash step." He was filled with dread of seeing his father again in August.

In late July, Louisa and George headed south, and John Quincy, John, and Charles started north; on August 2, the entire Adams family met for the first time since March 1825, at the City Hotel in New York. Louisa and John Quincy hardly spoke to each other. "My mother," Charles wrote in his diary, "does not appear either in good health or spirits. My own feelings inclined to great melancholy on seeing what I think to be the future prospects of our family. My father seemed excessively

---

* Louisa worried: "He is in all respects the same old exaggerated conceited timid enthusiastic negligent cold and eccentric being that he has been ever since he was born. . . . He surely is one of Shakespeare's fools for tho' full [of] capacity and intellect he is constantly acting like one divested of understanding."

depressed and in all appearances from the same cause. . . . George's manners struck me in a very strange way at first, and it has taken some time to become familiarized with them." The Adamses parted the next day, with the men all going to Boston, and Louisa and a servant visiting Saratoga Springs and the beach spa at Long Branch, New Jersey, for the sea baths,* before reaching Washington. "The shocks and agitations I went through" with John Quincy, Louisa said, convinced her that "the unfeelingness which was exhibited towards me can be forgiven but never forgotten." She wrote Mary Hellen that the Adams men were "harsh and severe" and showed "no sympathy, no tenderness" toward women.

For the remainder of the summer, Louisa and John Quincy wrote infrequently, and briefly. He addressed her as "Mrs. Louisa C. Adams" or "Mrs. Louisa Catherine Adams" — not as "My dearest Louisa" or "Dear Louisa" — and sometimes put no greeting at all on his letters. He was more angry with her than he had ever been, and frustrated with George, who avoided his father for two weeks. In September, John Quincy wrote that "George's health is as it was, and is likely to be — depending entirely upon himself. — He is to me dutiful, and affectionate, and wants nothing but a firm purpose, to be all that I could wish." It was this firmness that Louisa sought to avoid, and she remained convinced that her husband's pressures on George would harm him. When she finally wrote John Quincy, she addressed her letter to "The President," and signed it "Love to John and Charles from your Wife, L.C. Adams." She, too, remained angry.

---

* At Fish Tavern on the high bluff above the beach, a thin flag at the top of the stairs leading down to the water signaled who could use the beach: At set times a red flag hoisted on the pole indicated that gentlemen only were permitted, and then a white flag replaced the red, which cleared the beach for the ladies, who wore long shifts and oilskin caps and waded kneedeep into the Jersey surf holding fast to a stout rope.

8

PRESIDENT ADAMS spent eleven weeks in "idleness" in Quincy. He got Charles settled at Mrs. Ann Wilson's boardinghouse at 3 Cambridge Street near George's chambers at Dr. Welsh's, in Boston, preparatory to studying law under Daniel Webster. He took in chowder picnics and fishing parties below Boston light, and went sea bathing. And he began the slow and painful process within himself of putting aside his oldest son, and placing his hope in the youngest. Charles himself feared that George had changed "almost immeasurably for the worse," and he felt himself growing closer to his father. They shared a common awareness: If the Adams tradition of service to God and Country was to be preserved, the burden would fall upon Charles.

Adams left Quincy in October, and on his way to Washington stopped for several days at the farm of an old friend, Ward Boylston, in Princeton, Massachusetts. He slept in the same room he and George had shared in 1825, and the memory, and the knowledge of what he must now do with his sons, moved him greatly. He understood that the failure of George was his failure, too, and he wrote his oldest a letter of lost hope and missed opportunity:

> I am writing by morning candlelight in the little room where just two years since, I gave you a pair of sleeve buttons and a copy of verses, as tokens of my affection and hopes for you. This room contains as you remember a singular picture, which as you pass before it changes its aspect and character so as to present the portraiture of three different persons. Can you imagine the feelings which this combination of trivial incidents has excited in my bosom? In the first letter you write me, let me know whether you still possess the sleeve buttons and the verses and whether they ever excite any reflections in your mind.

Adams's sad letter conveyed his feeling of a moment of close-ness, even friendship, with his son in this room — but a moment lost forever. Did George still have the verses or the buttons? His reply, if he wrote one, has been lost. But his father's touching in-quiry remains, with its haunting combination of remembrance and farewell, and its symbolism. Two years earlier, John Quincy had shown with a small gesture his affection and hope for George. He had recognized by his gift of verses his son's love of poetry — perhaps the one thing they truly shared — and his gen-tleness, his taint of Maryland blood; George was more Johnson than Adams. And the buttons? George probably needed them, for he was careless of his dress, like his father. Verses and sleeve buttons: one gift poetical, the other useful; one romantic, the other practical; one Johnson, the other Adams. In those few hours together in this room, John Quincy had prayed that his son might turn out to be both verses and sleeve buttons: that George would live up to the best of both families. But now that image had changed, like walking across the room before the portrait; George was no longer the person he had seemed to be then, but had shifted slowly with the passage of time from one character to another and a third, until he had become a distorted portrait of neither verses nor buttons, neither Johnson nor Adams.

Leaving this room, and all that it meant to him, John Quincy Adams rode southward deep in thought. At Hartford, he wrote Charles one of his fact-filled letters detailing the events of the journey, and he suggested that they start a regular correspon-dence; Charles had asked for some fatherly advice about law and other matters, "with the intimation that if I would give it, there should be some attention paid to it." On the steamboat *McDonough* churning down the Connecticut River, Adams ad-vised Charles to start rising at six, "still better at 5 o'clock," and he would have plenty of time for study and courtship. John Quincy was cautiously reaching out, transferring his role as teacher, counselor, father from his oldest to his youngest son. "If you write me once a week," he tested (seeking regularity), "I shall give you more advice."

Charles replied to his father promptly, and they started a

correspondence that reached more than forty letters before it was suspended by Presidential business, and an argument, in July 1828. The exchange shows us much of John Quincy and Charles Francis Adams. At this time, Adams was still communicating with George, and his treatment of the two sons in these letters offers haunting insight into the mind of the father. Often letters of diametrically opposite emotion were written the same day: an uncompromising list of demands to George with details of the father's displeasure; then a long, kind letter to Charles praising or gently lecturing this chosen son. The letters to Charles blossomed into a brief intellectual exchange, reflecting the father's growing admiration, and the son's willingness to stand up to and even challenge the father. Those to George, however, remained dunning letters until they, too, ceased in late 1828.

John Quincy intended his letters to Charles to be guides for his son's success. He believed that Charles would follow in the Adams footsteps and seek a public career. He urged his youngest to improve himself, to budget his time by rising early, which was "indissolubly connected with many of the most active virtues." He estimated that Charles had two or three hours every day before breakfast, and should use his free evenings to retire early: "One hour of the morning lamp is better than three of the evening taper," John Quincy advised. The time thus gained Charles could spend in hard work, remembering that "Genius is the child of toil." As Louisa already knew, John Quincy believed that the more arduous the task, the more praiseworthy the achievement; small pleasures came only with great pain. Regularity, perseverance, early rising were the path to follow. He sent Charles a short poem:

> Six hours to sleep and Six to Law
> And four devote to prayer
> Let two suffice to fill the Maw
> And six the Muses Share.*

Adams directed Charles to write regularly. "Observe, read, practice." Observe the style of others; read newspapers, Cicero's

* John Quincy Adams adapted his version from Sir Edward Coke's, written in *Institutes of the Laws of England:* "Six hours to sleep, as many to righteous law / Four to your prayers, and two to fill your maw."

familiar letters and his letters to Atticus (and "read them in Latin"); compare Pliny's letters to Cicero's. Read Voltaire, Pascal, Bacon, and American history. For examples, Adams included historical and critical essays on Cicero's orations, thus giving himself exercise in reading and the practice of writing.

Charles was nimble enough not to take his father too seriously. He frequently disagreed with him, and spoke his mind. He could never, he wrote, rise early in the morning no matter how much time it might save him. He got up at seven and doubted that he could improve. His father admonished Charles's "sensual indulgence" and ridiculed his inability to overcome it as a "scantiness of will." Charles, in turn, pointed out with some glee that when his father rose at five, exercised, and conducted business for twelve hours, he frequently fell asleep at the dinner table. John Quincy admitted that was true, but two hours' extra sleep in the morning would not spare him "this involuntary siesta" in the evening; a laborious day logically ended in fatigue. Charles pressed on: Early rising was "in fact a hardship." John Quincy, defending his favorite maxim, challenged Charles to name anyone, anywhere, who had risen at five in the morning for the last five years and was now unsure of his direction or prospects. Charles immediately indicated a lad named Kimball, known to them both, who "seems not a bit advanced to reputation or standing than when he first started" rising early. John Quincy fell silent on the subject.

Charles also disagreed with his father's recommended reading list. He said that Cicero, "the individual whom you have pronounced your favorite," lacked "firmness of character" and was inferior to Cato. Charles brazenly went on to call his father's political life a shackle to "independence of mind and feeling," and he brashly mocked his father's definition of office holding as a "call to duty" when the true motive, Charles told him, was raw political ambition disguised as patriotism. Finally, he said his father's letters were degenerating into sermons.

So testy did this exchange become that Louisa had to step between father and son. She warned Charles that "even if his deductions are not entirely like yours on points of moral character, respect prejudices acquired by favorite studies and . . . do not harshly and positively condemn them." Adams said he would stop writing, and give his son "a respite from further superfluous Counsel." As for Charles's comments on politics, which the President rightly took as a slur on his life, Adams wrote: "If you *prefer* to remain in private life, stand aloof — you may be sure not to be disturbed in your privacy."

Still, the exchange did not end there, and both continued to enjoy it. Charles felt closer to his father, and thought he saw glimpses through the iron mask. John Quincy told Charles how much he enjoyed the correspondence, too, and was pleased with his son's regularity. He even found his youngest son's combative letters and assertiveness a welcome contrast to the gloomy political view outside his windows in the capital. "Your letters," he wrote Charles, "are becoming a necessary of life to me. I have not in seven years read so much classical literature, as since I began these letters to you. And I might add I have not in seven years enjoyed so much luxurious entertainment."

The collapse of this brief closeness came over love and money. When Charles reached his twenty-first birthday, he had not been admitted to the bar. Without steady income, he could not marry, and he first sought out his father, and then Peter Brooks, to fill the financial gap. This led to a long argument between father and son, and the termination of their correspondence. Charles had already pestered the President for a raise in his allowance, and John Quincy had increased it from eight hundred dollars a year to a thousand. But Charles had always counted upon Peter Brooks and John Quincy Adams to support him and Abby until his law practice provided sufficient income; better yet, Brooks had promised his daughter a twenty-thousand-dollar dowry, and Charles figured that, once married, he could live off the interest. All he needed was his father's initial financial support. With that in mind, Charles made a special trip to Quincy in August 1828. After taking a saltwater bath with JQA, he approached his father about another allowance increase. The discussion quickly became an argument between them. No mention of it now exists in John Quincy's meticulous diary, but the topic was so painful to Charles that he returned to it repeatedly during the next six months, and wrote in his diary that his feelings "were cruelly hurt, and in a manner which no subsequent kindness can remedy." John Quincy, foreseeing retirement from public office and without resources to support his expanded family, replied to Charles's request with a heated warning against extravagance, and a reminder that Charles was, after all, "a beggar, living on charity." If Charles would practice "self control," and rise at five, "this fund of three hours a day before breakfast," he lectured, would "be worth more to you than an income of ten thousand dollars a year. . . . It will certainly be worth more than all the mines in Mexico, in *Virtue*. . . . Give me an early riser, and I will give you a virtuous man." But Charles was far more interested in money than virtue, and parted from his father with mutual recriminations. Charles thought him not merely parsimonious, but cruel. The least he expected was "an active kindness. . . . Not in deeds if he was unable to assist me, but in words and manner." He got neither.

Charles unwisely took his case to Peter Brooks, and wrote that the thousand-dollar allowance a year from John Quincy and the twenty-thousand-dollar dowry might "barely suffice to support us." Nothing would change this financial equation in the immediate future, Charles argued; it would be years before he earned anything practicing law. Brooks wasn't impressed. When Charles rode out to Medford to press his case, Abby's father told Charles that he wished the marriage deferred a year. It was an "unexpected blow," and Charles, hedged in by the two older men, felt his spirits "prostrated." In his diary, Charles attacked Brooks for his "miserly timid policy. He could provide for his daughter's comfort, rolling in wealth as he is."

Charles remained angry over his treatment. After a visit in Washington — when John Quincy kindly gave Charles two shares of Middlesex Canal Company stock, worth $250 each — Charles deliberately refused to say goodbye to his father, who was "cruelly disappointed," Louisa wrote, and "went all about the rooms to look for you." But money had always created problems with John Quincy and Louisa, and now was embarrassing them. Louisa wrote Charles: "When you were engaged to Miss Brooks you were in every way her equal; as far as money goes you may not be thought so now. Real greatness is but little appreciated but the penny turns every thing." Then she added a little fib: "I never coveted any body's money and I never shall."

One major reason for John Quincy's saying a firm no to Charles was George. Not long before, Adams had learned that George had plunged himself into debt, and this was a time when indebtedness led to imprisonment. George had not paid his board at Welsh's, and he needed money for expenses. Worse, he had borrowed one thousand dollars from Henry Wood, a Quincy tomb maker. When John Quincy found out, he lacerated George. "What is Henry Wood?" he wrote, "and What are You? By what properties was it that he had a superfluity of 1,000 dollars to put out at interest, while you was plunging up to the ears in consuming debt . . . and was running in arrears for your daily bread besides?"

Angry as he was, Adams devised a very kind offer to George, but one which made Charles's plea impossible. John Quincy proposed to buy George's books for two thousand dollars. All George had to do was to make a list of the books and the value of each, draw up a bill of sale, and write or paste his father's name into each book "to authenticate the property as mine." George could retain possession of the books as John Quincy's agent until he needed or called for them, which both men understood the father would never do. This was simply a bail-out for George, a disguised gift. The plan would relieve George of his debts, and leave his quarterly allowance of $250 unencumbered to defray current expenses. John Quincy implored his wayward son "nevermore to burden yourself with shameless expenses and senseless debts. — As to Books — debts for Books! of what earthly use to you are, or can be Books, with such life as you have led?" The President sent his son the money, and asked that he reply by next mail that "you are persevering in your course of reform" and show "punctuality . . . frugality . . . industry." And, his father prayed, "may a merciful God redeem you from the very verge of ruin."

It is not difficult to understand John Quincy Adam's despair. His Presidency, his long-sought dream, had now diminished him to "toil and distemper." His mental and physical ailments persisted: "My eyes complain of inflammation and my heart is sick," he said. "I write this evening with a heavy heart." His sons, too, seemed determined to fail, or embarrass the family. Desperate for continuity, and with little else to do, President Adams turned to a symbolic occupation: horticulture. The President and the White House gardener, Owsley by name, planted Spanish cork, walnuts, shagbark hickory, persimmons, tulip trees, chestnuts, and honey locusts; they put down vegetables, berries, and fruits in season. Adams planted catalpa and fruit trees around his F Street house. He placed, with Owsley's help, a border of oaks and a grove of walnuts around the White House, and hoped that the trees would survive into the next century. Adams gathered nuts, seeds, vines, and shoots during his rides and walks, and watched for their tiny sprouts and fondly measured their growth. Within a year, the President had seven hundred trees of twenty varieties, including three hundred oaks grown from acorns, in the White House grounds; he instructed each U.S. consul abroad to send seeds, and put in those. John Quincy wasn't only planting for his nation's future. He also believed in the symbolism of that planting: that a man should raise a son and grow a tree. Both gave a sense of regeneration and continuity. While his sons might fail, his trees would not. Or so he thought. When George visited Washington for the last time, John Quincy went for long walks with him, and showed off his seedlings. George promised to write regularly and bring his work up to date. John Quincy sent his son home with a tin box of sixty oak acorns for planting around the old house. But George never compiled the list of books, or wrote up a bill of sale, or entered his father's name in any book. Nor is there any evidence that the two thousand dollars settled George's debts. Nor did he write regularly to his father, or plant the acorns.

In Washington, President Adams tried to protect his tender shoots against hailstorms, the heat of sun, drenching rain, devouring insects, the unexpected bite of frost. He started a government plantation of thirty thousand acres in Santa Rosa, near Pensacola, Florida, where workers set out a hundred thousand live oak saplings for future naval ships. But all his little seedlings — symbols of Adams's determination to leave something to the next century of America — would be abandoned and trampled when Andrew Jackson moved into the White House. "A planter," John Quincy Adams said defining both his Presidency and his fatherhood, "must make up his mind to endure many disappointments."

9

FOR TWO YEARS, 1828 and 1829, the Adamses encountered an almost continual series of private disappointments from their sons, and public attack from their opponents. No other period of their lives was so troublesome, or tragic. The 1828 Presidential campaign between John Quincy Adams and Andrew Jackson was developing into what historians would later describe as the "dirtiest" political contest in the nation's history. And while Charles and George created private anguish upstairs at the White House, John caused two public embarrassments during the campaign. At the end of these two years, John Quincy Adams would look back, and write Charles: "Woes cluster — rare are solitary woes."

John piled woe upon woe by being not only handsome and hard-working, but also flawed and careless. He served as his father's private secretary, and his bungling drew the President and Louisa into one of the major scandals of the 1828 campaign. His loud mouth and temper almost got him a duel, saved only by his father's clever ploy.

Shortly after Adams became President, he had purchased a second-hand billiards table from a Washington merchant. The table came with new green felt cloth, cues, and balls, and Adams installed it in the White House for his "exercise and amusement." John Quincy actually played little, but John and Charles wasted long hours with the chalking of cue stick and clacking of billiard balls. In March 1826, John, as Presidential secretary, had forwarded to the House committee concerning public buildings an itemized inventory of furnishings purchased for the White House from the Congressional appropriation of fourteen thousand dollars. John prepared the list himself, and carelessly included the billiard table, felt cloth, cues, and balls. When the report was published, it appeared that the President had used public funds for private pleasure. President Adams immediately notified the House that the "inventory so far as it related to the billiard table, &c. was entirely erroneous; and that no part of the public appropriation had been, or would be applied to any such purpose." But the damage was done.

John's mistake brought the opposition press into full howl. Among most Americans, the term "billiards" evoked images of loungers in dark rooms, cigar smoke, wagering, liquor, and stories that would offend the purity of decent women. Duff Green, pro-Jackson editor of the Washington *United Telegram*, protested such a purchase "out of the *public purse*," and warned that young men enticed by the click of ball and smell of cigars would now tell their frowning elders: "Why, the President plays billiards!" Rebuttals by the pro-Adams press appeared too late, and too weak. The table, said one newspaper, was placed there for General Lafayette's visit; no, said another, the billiards were for Mrs. Adams's exercise. Robert Walsh of the Philadelphia *National Gazette* helped not at all when he wrote that a billiard table was "a common appendage in the houses of the rich and great in Europe, and by no means uncommon as such in the United States." Now Adams enemies said he was not only extravagant with public funds, he was also aristocratic in private tastes.

By 1828, the outcry over the billiard table had set the tone of the Jackson campaign against Adams. The protests of "gambling furniture" in the "President's Palace" encouraged other charges: that the Adamses lived in "regal magnificence"; that John Quincy had waxed fat throughout his career on public funds. The Adams press replied with innuendo about Andrew Jackson's marriage to Rachel, implying an adulterous relationship, and one paper called Jackson "adept at billiards, cards, dice, horseracing, cock-fighting, and tavern brawls." One of the low points of the campaign was reached when Russell Jarvis, a former Adams supporter turned snappish, published a libelous attack in the *Daily Telegraph* saying that Adams, when minister to Russia, had "pimped" Martha Godfrey, the nurse-maid, to the lust of Czar Alexander I. Louisa felt compelled to write a letter "to all my Children" explaining the single en-counter of Alexander, Miss Godfrey, Charles, and the Adamses in the royal nursery. She also wrote and published a full account of her life, with this incident clarified in it, in *Mrs. A. S. Colvin's Weekly Messenger*, a pro-Adams paper.

To compound matters, Jarvis appeared at a White House drawing room soon after the attack,* and when he and his wife entered with a cluster of friends, someone asked John, "Who is that lady?" John glanced over, saw Jarvis and lost his temper.

"That," he said loudly, "is the wife of one Russell Jarvis. *There* is a man who, if he had any idea of propriety in the con-duct of a gentleman, ought not show his face in this house."

Jarvis had clearly heard John's words. He and his party im-mediately took leave of Louisa Adams, and went home. But sensitive gentlemen required apologies for insults, or took satis-faction in an engagement of pistols on a "field of honor." Al-though illegal, dueling was immensely popular during the Adams administration, and not to fight a duel meant yielding to charges of cowardice. Alexander Hamilton, Aaron Burr, Andrew Jack-son, Henry Clay, John Randolph, William Pitt, George Can-ning, Lord Castlereagh, and even the Duke of Wellington while still Prime Minister of England had all fought duels. The weap-ons were usually long-barreled, large-bore pistols or heavy muskets, fired at a distance of six to nine feet; the shells, if they struck, killed or maimed. John Quincy Adams regarded dueling as a barbarism, yet believed it could not be stopped by law. That he himself avoided dueling during his long and conten-tious public lifetime may be attributed to the fact that he had poor vision, a trembling hand, made a small target, and — far

---

* The Adamses' drawing rooms were open to any well-dressed gentleman or lady.

more likely — kept his ulcerous comments confined to his diary. Not so John Adams 2d, whose verbal slap at Russell Jarvis was foolishly made in public, in the White House. This could not go unanswered.

Jarvis mulled over the insult for a few days. Here was a splendid chance to embarrass the President, by challenging his son to a duel. If the young man avoided the confrontation, or hid behind his father, the word coward would echo in the South and West, where dueling was the gentleman's response. But Jarvis needed to provoke the challenge. One day as John was walking across the Rotunda of the Capitol carrying messages from the President to Congress, Jarvis jumped him. He pummeled the President's son, pulled his nose, and slapped one side of his face. John tried to spear Jarvis with his walking stick as bystanders separated them.

But Jarvis's attack did not provoke a duel, as planned. Instead, President Adams sent to Congress — after Clay had carefully measured its mood — a message that his private secretary had been "waylaid and assaulted" in the Rotunda by a "person," and that Congress should consider legislation that would secure the official avenues of exchange between White House and Capitol and prevent such disorders. Newspapers quickly took sides, and the *National Journal*, an Adams paper, called the "assault within the Capitol" an "outrage," while the *Telegraph*, protecting one of its own, considered "the pulling of the Prince's nose" a "signal chastisement" of the "Royal puppy." Congress investigated, and both antagonists were cross-examined. Finally the whole matter was put aside, and the scuffle in the Rotunda passed slowly from the public mind. Attempts to censure Russell Jarvis failed, and Louisa Adams long believed that the nose-pulling in the Capitol ruined her son's career. John Quincy, perhaps overwrought, wrote Charles that "Slander and Assassination are working hand in hand against us. . . . The assault upon your brother . . . was the act of an Assassin."

Between the embarrassments over billiards and the insults, John Adams 2d, much against his parents' wishes, became the first President's son to be married in the White House. In November 1827, Louisa had asked John Quincy to consider the engagement of John to Mary Hellen, but the President refused. As a result, a strange charade got underway: For the next ten weeks, the President silently ignored a romance that noisily filled the White House. At one point the couple announced that they had broken up, and another time Mary loudly threatened to pack and march out — although as a single, unescorted female she would not have gotten very far.

On February 1, 1828, John told his mother that his marriage to Mary Hellen would take place in twenty-five days. The President refused to believe it. Louisa wrote Charles: "I have declined having anything to do with it, therefore can give you no further information." Inside the Adams family, the days turned sour. Mary Roberdeau, a guest from Philadelphia, talked of nothing but her dyspepsia. Abby Adams ate too much ice cream, and became loudly sick for two days. George hadn't written for six weeks. Johnson Hellen and John were thrown off the family carriage when it overturned, receiving bruises and a scare that sent Mary to bed "with one of her usual attacks." One servant lost the use of his eye, and another was expected to die any day (and did). The President said that Gen. Jacob Brown, commander-in-chief of the U.S. Army, was "at his last gasp," while Abby Brooks' brother "will probably not survive this week" (he did). Louisa also took to her chambers, and reported that everyone was as low-spirited and uncomfortable "as a parcel of caterwauling cats." It didn't cheer the family when one evening at the theater some members of the audience, despite the President's presence (or because of it), called for "Jackson's March," a political air, before the curtain. When they were hissed down, a young woman seated near the President and Mrs. Adams said loudly: "Never mind, we will have this march often enough in '29." John Quincy returned home and wrote of "the *fears*, the *envy*, the *calumny* and *contentions*" of politics. "I do say to all my Sons, never seek the Path of public life directly or indirectly. I say pursue your profession — devote your time faithfully to your private duties. Your first labour is for subsistence — Till you can secure that, let nothing divert you from the pursuit. — Be ready at the Call of your Country — but never go in search of it. . . . Above all, be parsimonious of time — Make sure every day of doing some thing, the recollection of which on the pillow may soothe you to the Slumber of the Night."

In this atmosphere the preparations for John and Mary's wedding went so quietly that, said Louisa, "you could never imagine that any thing of the sort was dreamt of and strange to say neither by word or look has your father intimated the idea of such an event taking place. . . . He had never said a kind word to the young Lady to give her courage for the occasion." The President appeared thin, and complained a lot. "John looks more as if he was going into a consumption than if he was going to be married." On Monday evening, February 25, twenty-three guests gathered quietly in the Blue Room of the White House; Charles and George remained in Boston. The candlelight flickering on the elegant crimson satin-covered furniture and the bronze-doré Minerva clock on the long mantelpiece gave the room a subdued but rich tone. Four bridesmaids — Abby Smith, Mary Roberdeau, Elizabeth Cranch, Matilda Pleasonton — attended Mary, and four groomsmen — Edward Everett, William Smith, and Johnson and Thomas Hellen — attended John. The Rev. William Hawley of St. John's Episcopal Church across Lafayette Square, wearing old-fashioned knee breeches and silver shoe buckles, conducted the wedding at Louisa's request. The whole ceremony went forward heavily, but by the time the company sat down to supper, and the bride "passed the cake through the ring" and cut slices for the guests, President Adams, perhaps loosened by repeated champagne toasts, danced a Virginia reel "with great spirit," to the surprise of his wife. At the end of the evening, he wrote: "The company retired about midnight. May the blessing of God almighty rest upon this union." The next morning, he sent Charles an account, concluding with a kind reference to Charles's own long-desired wedding. Louisa, however, did not reconcile herself so easily, and took to her chamber "quite unwell." Dr. Henry Huntt, the family physician, gave her an emetic and bled her three times. She, too, wrote Charles: "I am not much in a humour to write, I shall therefore only announce to you the fact that the wedding is over, that Madame is as cool easy and indifferent as ever, and that John looks already as if he had all the cares in the world upon his shoulders, and my heart tells me that there is much to fear." Since Gen. Brown had died on Monday, his body now lay in state in the White House. John and Mary could not receive company for three days. "And," Louisa wrote, "I am very glad of it as John looks quite sick." She mailed Charles a piece of wedding cake "as is the fashion" and urged him to come to Washington, "for your mutual visit will restore harmony to the family and we shall all be happy and none so much as your affectionate mother, L.C. Adams."

By the twenty-eighth, General Brown's body had been removed from the White House, and the "cool" bride and "sick" groom opened the President's doors to company. Many of the wedding guests returned to dine and dance that evening in the yellow drawing room (now the Red Room). Even John Quincy joined them, and Abby Adams remembered, "It was one of the pleasantest days I ever passed." Upstairs, however, Louisa remained in her chambers. Dr. Huntt paid three calls, and she saw eighteen visitors, but no one from the wedding party called on her except Catherine Johnson Smith, who stayed all day and all night. There was no dancing for Louisa Adams, no toasts, no merriment for the stubborn son and his impulsive bride. Until Louisa's death, she considered her daughter-in-law one of the most slothful, indifferent, but companionable women she ever knew. Louisa both loved and disliked Mary, and beyond these emotions, she was certain, as Abigail Adams had been before her, that her daughter-in-law was unworthy of her son.

Mary and John settled into the White House, where they lived until 1829, when the entire Adams family moved out. Their first baby, and Louisa and John Quincy's first grandchild, Mary Louisa Adams, was born in the White House on December 2, 1828. Within two years, Mary again gave birth, to Georgiana Francis Adams — named after her two rejected uncles — in Quincy.

10

ON A SUNDAY EVENING in March 1828, President Adams sat at his writing desk in the White House. Suddenly the board under his hand started trembling, the floor rolled, and the windows and shutters rattled. The room, he thought, felt like a steamboat underway. The sensation lasted two minutes — Adams timed it — and the President recognized it as an earthquake. It was simultaneously felt by Americans in New York, Pennsylvania, Virginia, and westward to Kentucky. Adams, who like his wife always looked for meaning in such events, wondered if the agitation was filled with hope, or dread. He was already feeling, as his father had before him, political earthquakes in the White House, and all the American states were now shaking under the trampling cohorts and the political upheaving of Andrew Jackson.

In the election, held between October 31 and November 14, President Adams carried New England, New Jersey, Delaware, and Louisa's Maryland. The rest of the nation went overwhelmingly for Andrew Jackson. Louisa tried to cheer the family: "It has never been possible to make me believe that defeat is disgrace," she wrote Charles. After the returns were in, she said that "we are all in good spirits." Charles replied that everyone in Boston was angry for two days. "Much now depends upon the family sticking together," he wrote his mother. "We are now attacked on all sides. . . . My hope is that the courage of the family will rise with the storm. . . . It is no time for gloom or despondency." The Adamses refused to shut themselves in the White House in defeat, but opened up the mansion and went out in glory. Some twelve hundred people attended Louisa's last drawing room, "and I can positively assure you that there was no wailing or gnashing of teeth." The party broke up at two.

But once again there was a warning sign. Alone in his room

at the first of the year, President Adams wrote: "The year begins in gloom. My wife had a sleepless and painful night. The dawn was overcast, and, as I began to write, my shaded lamp went out, self-extinguished." Was it an omen? In John Quincy's troubled mind such trivial events took on meaning. He prayed, and reached for that firm support upon which he always depended, his Bible. He read the first Psalm, which affirms that the righteous are, and shall always be, blessed. Adams assured himself that he would be vindicated. He had tried to lead the nation in the right path, to teach it scientific laws that he believed manifested God's will for America. But the people elected Jackson, whom Adams considered less than God-fearing, unscientific, and lawless. Had Adams failed his Creator? Or had his Creator ignored him, His servant? Questions floated everywhere, and John Quincy fell prey to "involuntary but agonizing doubts, which I can neither silence nor expel."

In February, the people of Washington greeted Andrew Jackson's arrival with cannon salutes. Daniel Webster couldn't recall a larger outpouring: "Persons have come five hundred miles to see General Jackson and they really seem to think that the country has been rescued from some dreadful danger." The new President had at his disposal some eleven thousand government jobs, and the taverns and boardinghouses overflowed with eager Jackson supporters. When Jackson entered the capital he was a tall and sad man deep in mourning for his wife, Rachel, who had died a few weeks before (a victim, Jackson believed, of the campaign abuse), and he had to struggle through noisy supporters preening for patronage.

The Adamses moved out of the White House on March 3, and the next day, after the inaugural ceremony at the Capitol, President Jackson and his followers marched down Pennsylvania Avenue to the mansion. They burst into the White House rooms, bounced upon the beds, looked in the closets, and turned the furniture over. "Orange punch by barrels full was made," Henry Clay later reported, "but as the waiters opened the door to bring it out, a rush would be made, the glasses broken, pails of liquor upset, and the most painful confusion prevailed. . . . Wines and ice creams could not be brought out to the ladies, and tubs of punch were taken from the lower story into the garden, to lead off the crowd from the rooms. On such an occasion it was certainly difficult to keep any thing like order, and it was mortifying to see men, with boots heavy with mud, standing on the damask satin chairs, from their eagerness to get a sight of the President." Like Jefferson, Jackson represented a change toward a broader democracy. And as had happened with Jefferson, the President he succeeded, an Adams in both cases, refused to attend the inauguration or White House ceremonies. Instead, John Quincy Adams went horseback riding far from the boisterous Jacksonians.

Since their F Street house was rented out, and Louisa refused to move on to Quincy that winter,* the Adamses had rented a farm from Commodore David Porter (over Mrs. Porter's political objections to the Adamses). The farm, called Meridian Hill, was both a convenient and symbolic location for Louisa and John Quincy. It stood about a mile and a half from the White House on the original center line of the District of Columbia; the meridian line ran due north–south through the front portal of the White House to the entrance of the Porter farmhouse and onward to Massachusetts. From Meridian Hill the Adamses connected back to the political past, and ahead to their uncertain future. ,

The Meridian farmhouse was so designed that it formed two separate residences, with room for John,** Mary and "little rosebud" Mary Louisa, and a study for John Quincy that overlooked a flower garden and a nursery of young trees. Adams entertained a steady flow of visitors, and read and wrote, and, with a daily walk or horseback ride of two hours, soon declared that he was more occupied than in the White House. Even the bubbly intrusions of "Mademoiselle Louisa," her grandmother said, "contributes very considerably to his enjoyment."

For the first time since 1809, the Adamses did not have a

* She and John Quincy had fought about this until he had become, Louisa said, "entirely unwilling to speak upon the subject." She thought the matter might drag on until she was forced to be "carried there [Quincy] to become a boarder in the family."
** John was employed by his father.

houseful of relatives, or servants. Of their White House servants, Pomphrey and Susan had left "dejected" because they could not find work. Jane Winnull had given notice that she would not travel north; her reason, unknown at the time to the Adamses, was her love for Johnson Hellen. John Kirk and his wife remained, and would torment Louisa and John Quincy in the years ahead with drunkenness and defiance. Louisa fired John Kirk several times, but insisted on retaining his wife, an excellent cook. For almost two decades, the Kirks, fired by Louisa and re-hired by John Quincy, appeared and disappeared in the Adamses' life; one winter, after being dismissed again they occupied the empty Old House while the Adamses were in Washington, and Charles and Louisa despaired of ever being rid of them. They never were: the Kirks attended the Adamses' funerals.

The greatest loss, however, was Antoine and Mary Guista. Antoine had been John Quincy's personal valet, whom he had first hired in Amsterdam, when the young man had deserted Napoleon's army. In London, Antoine had married Mary Newell, who had worked for the Adamses at Ealing. Both had served them since, Mary as cook and often head of the household servants. But John Quincy could no longer afford them when he left the Presidency, and with his recommendation they found employment with President Jackson, who, in a display of pique, refused to allow Antoine and Mary to visit the Adamses. Within two years, the Guistas would leave the White House, and with money they had saved, would open an oyster and coffee house in Washington and earn a very comfortable living. In a twist of fate, and a comment upon the American Dream, within five years Antoine Guista, former servant turned entrepreneur, would loan ex-President John Quincy Adams money during his impoverished years.

While the Adamses rested comfortably at Meridian Hill, Charles, in Boston, reported to them of George's health. His parents insisted that he check on his older brother, and Charles did so as infrequently as possible because of his disgust: George lived "like a pig." Charles, on the other hand, lived as his parents wished, with a certain neatness and sacrifice. He had a small and promising legal practice (he had been admitted to the bar on January 10, 1829), and a tiny law office, just ten by twelve feet, at 10 Court Street, rented for seventy-five dollars a year, which did not include heat. Charles purposely denied himself a fire in his north-facing room, and claimed he never enjoyed better health during any winter, although he confessed to his mother that "the toughness of the experiment rather tries me." It was unpleasant, he said, to pour a tumbler of water and have it come out ice. The whole business, from law to cold-room experiments, made Charles grit his teeth and say, with his father's tone but his mother's attitude, "You know that among these snowbanks it is well to have a granite character."

One evening late in March, Charles walked through the quiet streets of Boston to visit George in his cluttered and filthy room. In his diary this month, Charles had described George's "indolence and inactivity, mental and bodily." He knew, although he never wrote his parents, that George stayed alone in his room, and sometimes didn't bother walking to his office at all. This evening, Charles found his brother "in a state which I do not much admire though I have often known it and experienced it myself last spring." He decided to alert his mother, and the next day wrote what she already knew, that George complained of "dejection, low spirits, and inability to occupy himself — and this acts upon reflections of a melancholy kind in regard to Father and himself." Charles's report to Louisa was cool, objective. He shared his father's harshness toward George, and like his father Charles attributed George's difficulties to a lack of discipline. His brother, Charles said, "wants training and enlivening."

But Louisa was alarmed. She realized that George's indolence, solitude, and depression had not responded to her remedies or those of her husband. George would not rise early, exercise, work diligently, eat properly, or keep regular hours. Louisa still thought sea travel and being home would help, and in early April, responding to Charles's letter, she wrote George suggesting that he come to Washington "to escort your father and myself on our way home." Louisa wrapped her request in an obvious fib: "You know that we are neither of us famous travelers," wrote the woman who had crossed Europe in a carriage in winter, "and your assistance for me will be absolutely necessary." She employed every argument. George's health, she told him, would benefit by a change of air. His presence would be "most delightful" to her, who had little to do. Once back in Quincy, George would live with them, and his father would keep a horse and a gig "and you will always command the use of it." As a final and most revealing inducement, Louisa promised that she would keep his father from persisting in his demands upon George. She portrayed John Quincy as mellowing, busy with writing and reading. Louisa urged George to reply "immediately" to her request, and added a final enticement: "P.S. If you come you will see our pretty Baby."

What chaos filled George's life. He had failed his father. Charles was the favorite son, with a law business and engagement to a promising woman. George still depended upon his father for a small income, and had little law work. But as bad as George's public life and appearances were, his private life was far worse. He could in no way comprehend the impact of it upon his mother and father, had they known; George could only understand that if they discovered all that he actually was, or was not, he would be destroyed.

Sometime toward the end of the previous year, George had seduced a young chambermaid at Dr. Welsh's, Eliza Dolph. He was still seeing her. The fact could not have been unknown to Charles. He and the Welshes were close friends, his office was nearby, and he spent time visiting George or Dr. Welsh and Harriet. Charles also alluded to such a liaison in his diary in April, when Johnson Hellen, his cousin, announced his engagement to Jane Winnull, Louisa's servant. Here was, as Charles said, "a sad blow," and one bristly with danger. Louisa was shocked by the engagement, and when Johnson and Jane married only five days later, the entire Adams family in Washington took to chambers and smelling salts. Charles remained silent in Boston. He was in a trap. He knew something about George and Eliza; his diary during this time records conversations with the watchful Harriet. When Johnson and Jane married, Charles wrote in his diary: "May a similar misfortune never come nearer

home in the family. I have not design to forebode." His wish
not to predict, or foretell, was clearly a wish that something he
knew about not happen.

Charles, therefore, had a motive for getting George out of
Boston: keeping him away from entanglement with a chambermaid. Seen from this perspective, Charles's letters to his mother
take on another meaning. The spring reports on George's failing
health, his living conditions, his indolence and attitudes, may
have been designed to elicit letters from Louisa urging George to
come to Washington – precisely what Charles thought best for
his brother. Charles and Louisa held the same perception of
what was best for George: a trip, closeness to his family, his
mother's care. But while Louisa thought these things would
benefit George's physical and mental health, Charles hoped they
would also divert his older brother's sexual attentions. And so
Louisa also wrote Charles, asking him to "persuade George to
come on immediately." But George vacillated.

The impact of these requests on him must have been formidable. Turn these events around, and see them from George's
perspective. George knew he was in debt to his father for past
accounts, lists of books, letters; that his law practice was a
mockery, and his primary means of support the father to whom
he already owed so much. The enticements that his mother held
out were actually threats. His father could not have mellowed
or become so indulgent as to forget past promises and overdue
listings. He would surely repeat demands for George's improved
behavior, and see that they were carried out. He could not move
in with his parents, George knew; a horse and gig would only
take him from Quincy to Boston, and trouble. And as for seeing
John and Mary's new "pretty Baby," that held danger for
George as well. He, too, was a father: Eliza Dolph had given
birth to their own pretty baby in December 1828.

In January, George had moved Eliza, under circumstances
that would create yet another scandal, from the Welshes' to live
with another family elsewhere in Boston. He hoped "to restore
the mother to her friends and society again." Perhaps aware of
the net around him, George had previously addressed to Charles
a confidential letter detailing his entanglement with Eliza, and

stating that if he should die within the year 1828, he wished his debts to be paid and the balance of his estate given to her. George had placed the letter deep inside his trunk, and told Charles during one of their visits to search for the document should anything happen to him.

On April 20, 1829, George received a direct appeal from his father: "I wish you to come on immediately upon receiving this Letter, to return to us." George dreaded facing his father. He had broken every rule his father ever made. He was in debt, intemperate, immoral, slothful, frozen into inaction by fear of John Quincy's retribution, depressed. Charles thought George "seemed very much disarranged." Wobbling along the edge of reason, facing a journey with immense consequences, George began hallucinating. He heard birds speaking to him, and two nights before taking the stage to Providence, he thought someone tried to break into his chamber. He scrambled out of bed, wildly tossing sheets and pillows, and searched throughout his room. He found no one, but remained convinced that someone lurked nearby.

Early Wednesday morning, April 29, George Washington Adams loaded his trunk on the stage in Boston and rode to Providence, where he boarded the *Benjamin Franklin*, a luxurious new steamboat bound for New York under Capt. T. S. Bunker. That afternoon, as the steamboat rounded Point Judith and headed down Long Island Sound, George appeared well and cheerful, and gave a donation to a missionary on board with some Indians in his care. But as evening came on, George complained of a headache, and mentioned to a fellow passenger named Keep, who struck up an acquaintance, that he wished the motion of the boat would either ease, or increase and make him really seasick. As it grew later, George became more troubled. He thought he heard voices in the steamboat's engines: "Let it be, let it be." The deep and rhythmic sound repeated "Let it be," and the twin paddlewheels churning the sea drummed "Let it be, let it be." When George retired to his berth below deck, the sound followed him, pounding the side of the ship; "Let it be, let it be." He went to bed, but got up almost immediately. He awakened another passenger and accused him of spreading rumors against him among the travelers. When the gentleman denied the charges, George backed away and returned to his berth and lighted a candle. He walked menacingly from berth to berth staring at each occupant before once again going to bed.

George slept fitfully, and about three o'clock the next morning, Thursday, April 30, he rose once more, dressed, and climbed to the deck. He found his way onto the bridge, and confronted Capt. Bunker. He demanded that the captain stop the steamboat and put him ashore. The *Benjamin Franklin* was then cutting through the lower reaches of the Sound at about sixteen knots an hour. Capt. Bunker, a man fastidious about his schedules, knew he was on time and would not be delayed. He asked George: "Why do you wish to be set ashore?"

"There is a combination among the passengers against me," the young man replied. "I heard them talking and laughing at me."

Capt. Bunker waved George away, and a few minutes later George encountered John Stevens, a Bostonian and Jackson partisan belatedly hurrying to Washington in search of a job. The two men held a brief, blurred conversation. Stevens continued his walk upon the upper deck; perhaps ten minutes later, he happened to look over the rail and saw George's hat near the stern. He shouted for the captain, and the ship was immediately searched, but in the pre-dawn darkness with only the light from a scattering of stars like sparks at sea behind the ship, all they found was George's cloak, near his hat. He had jumped or fallen overboard.

Two days later, about one o'clock on Saturday afternoon, Louisa Adams's brother-in-law Nathaniel Frye slowly rode his carriage up the long, dusty road to Meridian Hill. The Adamses were expecting George, and at first mistook Nathaniel's dusty plume as a sign of their son's arrival. Instead, Frye wearily climbed down from the carriage and walked solemnly into the house; gathering Louisa and John Quincy in the parlor, he showed them a copy of the *Baltimore American*, dated that morning, May 2, which carried a small notice of George's disappearance. Louisa and John Quincy denied the shock and fear they felt: He was missing, but perhaps still alive; no body had been found. But shortly, Judge William Cranch, John Quincy's cousin, also rode his carriage out to the Meridian farm. He brought letters from New York, and from the firm of Davis and Brooks, undertakers, who had George's trunk and possessions. George had boarded the *Benjamin Franklin*, but had not disembarked; while no body had yet been recovered, no hope for him remained.

In Boston on May 2, Charles left his office to attend court, and returned to find Peter Brooks waiting for him. Gently, Brooks told him of the accident, and showed Charles newspaper accounts. Charles suddenly felt chilled all over his skin, and weak. But his concern turned almost immediately to the impact of George's death on his parents: "My father almost lived in him and the loss will to him indeed be dreadful."

The news, Louisa wrote, wrung John Quincy's heart "almost to madness." He remembered now a sermon he had heard the previous Sunday, taken from the Book of Job, which had troubled him all week until it struck with a sudden, direct impact on his heart and mind. Here were his fears made manifest. This was his retribution, the punishment of Heaven for the father's mistaken zeal in pushing the oldest son too hard, for demanding more than George could meet. Both John Quincy and Louisa, together, now feared that they had urged George beyond his strength "to exertion foreign to his nature." They reviewed and detailed their errors as parents, and both suffered great feelings of guilt. Louisa, who would never forget the joy of her first son during those bleak days in Berlin twenty-eight years ago, now wept over leaving George and John alone in the care of others during the boys' youth. If only she had been stronger, she thought, and had insisted that the boys come with them to Russia, perhaps their days together would have been more like those at Ealing when George was growing and full of promise. John Quincy, too, recalled that "lottery ticket" of a lad "as he was, all goodness and affection." He remembered George's last visit, and their walks in Washington, and his hope that George would plant his oaks and thrive with them into the next generation of the family. But now the tree had felt the lightning.

In death, George did something he could not do in life: Louisa and John Quincy, in their sorrow, guilt, and self-examination, reached toward each other. While death may exit through ten thousand doors, George's exit was for Louisa and John Quincy an entrance into something else: In his death, they began their own lives together. They prayed for each other. They asked Heaven's mercy upon their errors as parents, and strength upon their weaknesses. They turned to each other and their religion for God's revelation in this affliction. "We are in great distress," John Quincy told Charles, "but I write to inform you that the first Shock of this heavy dispensation of Providence is past, and that your Mother and myself, relying on him who chastiseth in Mercy still look for consolation in the affectionate kindness of our remaining Sons." John Quincy, who had been so harsh, was tender and close to Louisa, "a ministering angel always at my side," she said. Louisa, in turn, worried that the agony in her heart might cause her to speak to her husband in reproachful terms, adding to his misery. He read to her, and she to him, their most comforting passages from the Bible, and at her request he read to their assembled family the service for the dead from the Episcopal Book of Common Prayer. They drew strength from each other. Within a few days, he could write that she was "composed and exhibiting that fortitude that comes only from on high." Louisa was so strong, in fact, that she refused the traditional woman's confinement, and did not keep to her chamber. Instead of rejecting life, Louisa and John Quincy searched it for new meaning and direction. They sought forgiveness, and a sign.

John Quincy Adams walked alone, praying, through the Rock Creek woods and along the familiar paths of the District that he and George had walked together two months earlier. "May we humble ourselves in the dust," he asked, "and be conscious that thy chastisements have been deserved." During one of his walks, Adams took shelter against an old oak tree and watched a solitary May shower slowly wash through patches of spring sunshine. The rain momentarily quieted the woods, cleansing it, brightening bark and leaves, releasing from the earth small patches of mist and the rich odor of wet soil and, everywhere, the insistent promise of life. As the shower passed, it left above him, arched across the May sky, the sign John Quincy Adams had sought: a glorious rainbow that touched his heart with the message of God's goodness and mercy. It was right, he thought, that the sign had come this way: in nature, in the spring, on a walk in the woods reminiscent of his last hours with George.

Louisa, too, prayed and watched. She asked God's forgiveness, and implored Him to grant her fortitude. Louisa and George had expressed their closest feelings for each other in poetry, which filled their letters. They had used poems to communicate their thoughts and love. Three weeks after George's death, the *National Journal* of Washington published one of his poems, titled "The Spark at Sea," and Louisa Adams read it for the first time.

> There is a little spark at sea
> Which grows 'mid darkness brilliantly,
> But when the moon looks clear and bright,
>   Emits a pale and feeble light,
> And when the tempest shakes the wave
>   It glimmers o'er the seaman's grave.
>
>   *   *   *
>
> Such friendship's beaming light appears
> Through the long line of coming years
> In sorrow's cloud it shines afar,
>   A feeble but a constant star.
> And like that little spark at sea
>   Burns brightest in adversity.

The poem renewed Louisa's tears, but she also embraced it, as John Quincy had the rainbow, as a sign. Here was George's message to her. His love was eternal, like the little star-spark at sea marking his grave, and even shrouded in sorrow would always burn brightest, a feeble but constant light. Every year after her son had stepped out to his death at sea, Louisa paused on his birthday to remember him with a poem.

The Adamses delayed their journey northward for a month. Louisa claimed to be "impatient" to get started, but in truth she was reluctant to leave Washington and the precious new life of her granddaughter for the emptiness of New England, now bereft of her oldest son. John and William Smith had gone to New York, and brought back George's trunk and personal items left on the steamboat. As May gave way to June, the Adamses released their hope that George might somehow be alive. Slowly, in sorrow, John Quincy and John left for Massachusetts on June 10. In Baltimore, John Quincy wrote a gentle letter filled with love to his wife, "my dearest friend," telling her of his trip and closing, "May the blessing of God rest upon you till we meet again. Love to Mary and a kiss to Baby. From your affectionate J. Q. Adams."

Father and son traveled the New Line through Delaware "by the Canal" — the internal improvements seemed agreeable to John Quincy — and despite John's sunburning his balding head they arrived swiftly and in health in Philadelphia. But on the steamboat *Swan* the next day between New Brunswick, New Jersey, and New York City, Adams read in the June 13 *New York Herald*, that his son's body had been found three days earlier. It had drifted in with the tide on City Island. "May it soothe you to learn," he wrote Louisa immediately upon landing in New York, "that the person was entire, without mark of violence or contusion. — His watch and small pocket book were still in their places, and his name was yet legible within his boots. . . . My most beloved friend, may you receive this as a dispensation of Mercy of Heaven in its severity." In Washington, Louisa also learned from newspaper accounts that George's body had been found, "and all every hope which had lingered in my heart is extinct," she wrote John Quincy. She asked that George's personal belongings be returned to her.

In New York, Adams's friends told him the details. A coroner's inquest had been held — death due to drowning — and the body placed in a tomb in East Chester, near City Island, about sixteen miles northeast of the city. On that Sunday, John Quincy and John rode to East Chester and dined at the home of a young physician, who gave John Quincy George's personal things. Afterwards, the father descended into the crypt and saw his son's coffin, but did not ask to have the cover unscrewed to view the remains. With an Episcopalian minister, he said a brief service, and after making arrangements to have the body sent on to Quincy in the autumn, he and John returned to New York City. Alone in his hotel room, John Quincy took George's things from his own pocket, and spread them one by one upon the bed. He looked closely, sadly, through his son's last chosen items: eight five-dollar bank bills, several receipts and notes of accounts, a purse with two dollars in silver change, a penknife, a watch, a cypher-seal, a silver pencil, George's snuff box, a comb, and the key to his trunk. And there among them John Quincy Adams found the sleeve buttons that he had given George four years ago as tokens of his love and hope. Verses and sleeve buttons. Tears welled in the father's eyes. Verses and sleeve buttons. He had demanded that George write an explanation of what he had done with them, but the son never did. Instead, George had always carried the sparkle of verses in his heart, and the sleeve buttons in his pocket. At last, they both were fully accounted for.

11

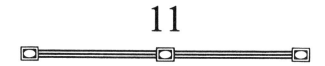

IN BOSTON, Charles Francis Adams's mourning for George took a more practical turn. While saddened by his brother's death, Charles was also determined that the family name not be further tarnished, and that all debts be settled. The more he poked through his brother's papers, the harsher his reaction: "How unfit my brother was for active life appears to me more striking every day," Charles said. The disorder of the family accounts was such that Charles declared that they "cannot be unravelled and all that can be done is to begin anew." He urged his father to come to Boston to take into his own hands the family finances. When John Quincy arrived in Boston, he appointed Charles his agent. He wanted the family property in a condition where he could live without encroaching upon his capital, and he wished to build a stone library for his and his father's manuscripts and papers. Charles, rather coldly, saw the opportunity as "a trust I undertake in order to benefit myself. It may be the means of giving me some business in my profession." But he actually spent most of the summer in his brother's hot room at Dr. Welsh's going through George's papers, which showed "great irregularity and disorder," and appraising and listing George's law books and possessions. Charles also burned George's papers to keep them from the rest of the family.

There was one item that Charles sought immediately. The letter that George had addressed to him turned out to be a will of sorts, settling George's debts and providing for Eliza. Charles was not surprised by it, and probably knew the outline of this account. George, the oldest son of a prominent Massachusetts family and (at the time) of the President of the United States, could not have moved a chambermaid and her eight-week-old baby into a new residence without Charles's and the Welshes' knowing. Charles's cool reaction to the letter, therefore, was understandable: He already knew about Eliza and the baby, and his principal concern, as he wrote in his diary, was "to get possession of this paper, as it might pain my father."

Since the provision upon which the will had been based— George's death in 1828, not 1829 — had not occurred, Charles felt no legal obligation. George's debts to his father would wipe out any balance for Eliza. Charles decided to do what he could in the spirit of the request, to "preserve her, if possible, from destruction," although he considered the whole shabby matter the result of "a foolish effusion of a thoughtless moment." Just the same, he destroyed the letter, "it being in itself of no value."

Nothing, however, could hold back the scandal. During the morning of May 28, as he worked in his office, Charles had a visit from Miles Farmer, who looked after Boston real estate on Hanover and Mechanics Streets for an Amherst gentleman. As partial payment, Farmer, his wife, and their four children lived rent-free in one of these houses. It was into this family that George brought Eliza and their child. In January 1829, George evidently persuaded Dr. David Humphreys Storer, a Boston physician who had cared for Eliza during her pregnancy and delivered the baby, to see Farmer and ask him to take Eliza and the child into his home. Farmer agreed, but complained that George Adams kept coming around the house to see Eliza; his attentions aroused the suspicions of the tenants and endangered, so Farmer thought, his own position. Farmer worried that his employer might think him harboring a tart or scullion, or, worse, accuse him of fathering the child. He told George of his fears, and George, to protect Farmer's reputation, had promised him a hundred dollars should he lose his job; it was money intended to keep Farmer silent. After George's death, Farmer did indeed lose his job — for other reasons — and went to Charles. George's untimely demise, Farmer lamented, had deprived an honest man of both his character reference and his financial backing, and he hoped that the Adams family might set things right. "I was a little shocked by what he told me," Charles confided. The groundwork for a blackmail attempt was laid. Farmer wrote demanding letters, and once sent a woman to Charles's office making inquiries. In late June, when Dr. Storer billed the Adamses for medical care for Eliza Dolph — a more sophisticated form of blackmail — Charles got angry. He wrote Miles Farmer that he would not be blackmailed. Eliza, he said, "must work for herself," although "she shall be in no worse situation then she was before this occurrence, so far as demands upon the money she may earn will go." In fact, Eliza soon went to work again as a domestic. As for the child, whose name and sex were never mentioned in the Adamses' writing, Charles wrote Farmer that "I will make some provision probably similar to what it would be entitled [to] by law." Charles offered Farmer a *quid pro quo*. If Farmer would forget blackmailing the Adams family, Charles would overlook "a considerable debt" that he discovered Farmer owed George.

But Farmer was in no mood to be conciliatory. He replied to Charles that if the Adamses did not pay him, he would reveal everything with "a public statement." The ploy was a classic blackmail threat, and Charles to his credit stood firm against it. "Whatever I might be disposed to do as Charity," he wrote Farmer curtly, "I certainly will be *forced* to do nothing. You are welcome to all the benefit a disclosure will give you." But if Farmer did disclose the scandal, Charles warned, payment of his note to George would be demanded immediately. Farmer called on Charles personally, but when he found "that I was not like to give way to extortion," Charles said, "he changed his ground and tried apology. I told him I wished to be rid of the business as soon as possible." Though he thought Farmer "a troublesome and dangerous animal," Charles knew time was on his side.

Farmer was convinced that money could be made from George's misfortune, and he next tried to extract some from Dr. Storer. Their conflict reached the Massachusetts courts in 1830, and in March 1831, the case went before three referees, who awarded Farmer two hundred dollars in damages. But Farmer, still unsatisfied, thought he should have received more, and in retribution he published his version of the affair in a forty-four-page pamphlet that attacked both Dr. Storer and, obliquely, the Adams family, and encouraged small gossip about the scandal across New England. As for the doctor, Charles thought him as great a scoundrel as Farmer, deliberately inflicting "infinite pain," and refused to deal with him. Charles rejected the doctor's bill of June 20 on the grounds that it did not detail the number of visits made to Eliza. On October 14, 1829, however, Charles did pay to Dr. Storer thirty-seven-dollars for his services to the young chambermaid. As the episode slowly faded, Charles wrote of George with exasperation: "There is much to tease and perplex one in this business and the more I progress the more I feel it. Poor fellow, he had wound himself nearly up in his own web."

Charles continued sifting through George's papers, and burned most of them. He worked on the family accounts late at night, illuminating his work with his Astral Lamp, an ingenious device that burned oil in a flattened ring that threw uninterrupted light upon the table. "Much money has been lost," he concluded, "by George's total neglect of books and accounts." Charles went through all of George's private letters, and enjoyed a leisurely hour in an August afternoon reading copies of his brother's love letters to Mary Hellen, who "was the flower of his life." Charles noted that while the letters were "affection-ate," they had been written only once a month; Charles wrote Abby Brooks twice a week. This was George's mistake, Charles concluded, for it allowed Mary's affections, "at all times vola-tile, to become perfectly cool." The tangled family accounts, the jumble of books and letters, the blackmail all led Charles to a rough judgment about George: "George's fate was melan-choly but on the whole, I have been forced to the unpleasant conclusion that it was not untimely." Had he lived, Charles thought, George probably would have caused more misery to himself and to his family.

In some ways, this summer was two seasons for Charles. It was a "season of suffering," and a season of joy. Charles and Abby planned their wedding, at last; when Abby turned twenty-one in April, her father purchased a house for his precious daughter at 3 Hancock Avenue in Boston, where she and Charles would live. Charles visited Abby every moment he could; he bought her a blonde lace veil, "a little extravagant but I could not avoid it." He directed the building of bookcases in his new unoccupied house, and hauled George's heavy wooden shelves out of his room at the Welshes' and into his own chambers. He rose early, and bathed regularly in the Charles River. And he learned one important lesson from George's wasted life: Leave nothing incriminating. The "high spirits" and liaisons of his youth were now behind him; "I am sobered down," he said. That summer, in addition to destroying George's records, Charles carefully weeded the "follies" from his own journals and diaries, and burned them as well.

VI
Washington

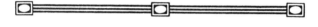

1830–1852

1

THE DAYS OF DARKNESS lifted slowly. For more than six years, from 1828 to 1834, joy and tragedy accompanied the Adamses as regularly as the seasons. Just after the Presidential defeat, for example, had come the birth of their first grandchild, Mary Louisa Adams, whom they fondly nicknamed "Looly." After George's death, Georgiana Francis — "Fanny" — was born. The year that started with John Quincy's lamplight's snuffing out closed with Charles's wedding.

John Quincy spent the summer alone in the old house trying to gain strength from the simple repetitions of life. He rose at five, and before breakfast read as many as fifteen sections of Cicero's orations — for tone of oratory — and three chapters of his Bible — for comfort and as "a guide through the darksome journey of life." He would need the strength: In November, in the days of waning sunshine and nighttime frosts, the coffin with George's body would arrive in Quincy, and John Quincy Adams would place it in the family tomb alongside his sister, Nabby. These were months of taking measure: Adams was sixty-two years old, alone, beaten, and saddened. He had no way of knowing that the most important work of his life lay ahead of him.

Louisa remained in Washington, alone in her own pain. She was fifty-four that year, and suffered from angina pectoris, as well as erysipelas. To mitigate her sadness, Louisa wrote poems about George's death, creating dozens during the next four years; she never forgot his birthday, and the remembrance always prompted an outpouring of guilt for the son she felt she had abandoned. The poetry served as therapy, and helped Louisa relieve some of her anguish and understand much of her loss. But she could not overcome her grief to ride the dreaded steamboat and stages to Massachusetts. She tried, but got only as far as New York City before suffering, in the City Hotel at midnight, "one of those violent attacks which she is subject to," said Charles, "with all the family and servants up and trying to assist her in her distress." To continue to Quincy meant riding the steamboat that had carried George to his death; unable, or unwilling, to go on, Louisa returned to Washington.

Charles married Abby Brooks on September 3, 1829. Only twenty-one guests attended the wedding, which was held at the Brooks' home in Medford. Louisa stayed in Washington, but John Quincy was there. By midnight, wrote Charles, his bride and future secure, "we were on our road to town, took possession of our house and there consummated the marriage." After three weeks, however, Charles felt as though nothing much had changed. He was, he wrote John, about as he had been in all respects, "excepting a marvelous change for the better in the acquisition of a perfectly comfortable home, the object of my earnest wishes for many months past." The fact that Abby occupied it with him appeared secondary; she came with the new furniture.

Abby would prove a docile, obedient, and fecund wife. She had been raised in the traditional manner to serve and obey her husband, to bear and raise his children without question, to run his household, and nothing more. She had been trained in servitude, to live as someone of the second class, neither a citizen nor a person, merely a servile woman. Charles liked her because she was "easy and obedient." Abby would be pregnant at least eight times in the next eighteen years, and miscarry a ninth pregnancy. In 1831, she would give birth to Louisa Catherine Adams 2d, "as bright eyed and sprightly," John Quincy would proclaim, as his other little granddaughters "of whom I am sorry to say we are so foolishly proud." John Quincy Adams 2d, would arrive in 1833, assuring the continuity, Louisa would write, of the "direct Male Line in our persecuted race." He would be followed by Charles Francis Adams, Jr. (1835), Henry (1838), Arthur (1841), Mary (1845), and Brooks (1848). As the babies kept arriving, little Louisa 2d spoke for all grand-daughters when, told that the fat nurse had just left another boy (Arthur) at the house, she replied: "She could have left it somewhere else."

The summer of 1830 was dry and hot with only occasional thunderstorms breaking the spell. Charles and Abby, married almost a year, joined Louisa and John Quincy, and Mary, Looly, and Fanny, in Quincy, to escape Boston's roasting. The old man enjoyed napping away these afternoons until five, ris-ing in time for tea, and perhaps, in the cool of evening, a horse-back ride, a clambake or chowder supper along the shore with friends. If not, the Adamses' dinner bell rang promptly at nine, followed by an evening of writing or conversation, and bed at eleven.

On September 30, 1830, the *Boston Daily Courier* published an anonymous paragraph suggesting John Quincy Adams as a candidate for the House of Representatives from the Plymouth District, into which the town of Quincy had been gerryman-dered by the Federalists. The letter was a ruse by the editor, who supported Henry Clay and hoped, by having Adams elected to Congress, to clear the way for Clay's nomination for the Presidency by the National Republicans. Soon the Na-tional Republicans from the Plymouth District approached Adams and sounded him out. They feared that the district might be unrepresented in 1831.* Adams's candidacy, therefore, would answer two needs: Clay's and Plymouth District's. Adams, however, remained firm in his belief that public office should seek the man. Even when the *Hingham Gazette* sug-gested his name and two readers supported the proposal, John Quincy still told his supporters that his acceptance would wait until the people had voted.

---

* The Massachusetts constitution required an absolute majority of the votes cast to elect a district's representative, or none would be elected. Three districts in that state during the next session of Con-gress would in fact lack representatives for this reason.

As the people of Plymouth District rallied to Adams, however, his family withdrew its support. Charles felt that his father had already devoted too much time and energy to public service, and not enough to his family. He was too old and too poor. While Charles tried to dissuade his father with lawyerly argument, Louisa simply exploded in anger. She had charted a quiet retirement for her husband, and was even willing to remain in New England herself a winter or two, both to test her will and to prove her spirit. When John Quincy declared to his family his willingness to accept election, Louisa was furious. If she were to be "dragged forward" again, she announced, "it should be for something respectable and worthy." Her husband had once again placed personal ambition above her wishes. "Family is and must ever be a secondary consideration to a zealous Patriot," she wrote with a touch of sarcasm.

Louisa announced that she would not return to Washington. Even a Quincy winter was more attractive than another round of "Bull Bait politics" in the capital. Charles, dismayed at "Madame's" plans, wrote John asking him to write his mother a mild letter approving their father's choice and requesting Louisa's company in Washington. John did, and Louisa turned all her frustration and anger upon him. Her response is illuminating for its intensity and for its restatement of Louisa's continuing examination of the relationship between men and women. The inequality evident by her husband's unilateral decisions troubled her; the fact that such a series of discussions had forced her to "abandon" George, exacerbated Louisa's concern.

Hadn't she suffered enough for her husband's career? Louisa asked John. Where was her reward for this? Was it in George's grave, or in the grave of her lost daughter in Russia? Was it in the closeness of their family after years of political turmoil? Louisa said that she was being asked once again to sacrifice herself for her husband's "grasping ambition which is an insatiable passion swallowing and consuming all in its ever devouring maw." But such sacrifice was not her interpretation of marriage. She would not be a cipher, a pawn to be pushed about the marriage board as her husband wished. "In the marriage contract," she told John, "there are as in every other *two parties,* each of which have rights strictly defined by law and by the usages of society. In that compact the parties *agree* before the face of heaven to promote as far as in their power the welfare and happiness of *each other.*" But where was this mutual cooperation, this mutual happiness in Louisa's marriage? More importantly, Louisa believed that the marriage contract gave her a right to disobey her husband, and a right, as a co-equal, to express her opinion.

The election took place November 1, 1829, and Adams held firm to his Macbeth policy. Reading the final tally in a local newspaper five days later, John Quincy noted that in the twenty-two towns of his district, he had received 1,817 votes, his nearest opponent, 373. He had won in a landslide. Far sweeter, this election marked the first time in John Quincy Adams's long public career that he assumed office as the result of popular vote; all his previous posts had been gained by appointment, or election in the House. This was the first of eight elections he would win — Adams would serve in the U.S. House of Representatives for seventeen years (less ten days) — and the best. He wrote elatedly into his diary that evening: "I am a member-elect of the Twenty-second Congress. My election as President of the United States was not half so gratifying to my inmost soul. No election or appointment conferred upon me ever gave me so much pleasure."

John Quincy had several reasons for accepting the election. He was, obviously, very flattered. He also missed politics, and felt himself sinking into passivity away from the arena. Further, accepting would set an example for future American Presidents to continue in service to their nation. "For myself," he wrote Charles, "taught in the school of Cicero, I shall say, '*Defendi respublicam adolescens; non deseram senex.*' — 'I will not desert in my old age the Republic that I defended in my youth.'" Finally, however, John Quincy Adams accepted the election as Representative because he needed the income. The Adamses, like Presidential families before them (and despite Louisa's warning), were threatened with poverty, and Charles, looking over the family accounts, thought his father at the very edge of financial ruin.

Louisa, fully aware of her husband's financial and political future, and her own impotence before his wishes, gave in. Unwilling to face alone the test of a Quincy winter, she set off for Washington after Thanksgiving by herself. She took the overland route, riding "smart and steady" with John Kirk, but her carriage was "buried" in snow in Connecticut and she had to walk a quarter of a mile "clinging to the bushes for support. . . . It is strange that I should have gone this distance and suffered so much to avoid Steam Boats in the night."

John Quincy preferred the steamboats. He took just ten hours from Philadelphia, crossing the Delaware peninsula by canal boat, and riding the new and frightening horse-drawn railway cars to reach Baltimore. Although he had left five days after Louisa, and visited railway directors in Maryland, John Quincy arrived home in Washington only an hour behind his wife.

2

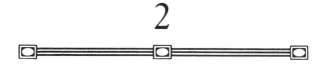

THE LOCATION in the capitol building of the old House of Representatives, now known as Statuary Hall, was a beautiful and spacious room, semicircular in shape, with massive marble columns. Its designers envisioned a contemporary chamber, with ornate sconces, two fireplaces, a handsome crystal chandelier hanging from the high domed ceiling, and red brocade draperies encircling the amphitheater of galleries. There, ladies wearing wide skirts, billowing arm sleeves with shoulder ruffles, tight corseted waists, and enormous, soft broadbrimmed hats, sat in the front rows or came and went, as at a play. The focal point was the Speaker's chair, elevated well above the floor, with its canopy of rich crimson silk trimmed with a bright fringe. The canopy resembled a spread um-

brella supported by four posts, and the silk fell to the floor behind the chair in copious folds. The members, made comfortable
not by the decorative fireplaces but by two great, humming
coal furnaces below, sat in a semicircle around this throne, one
behind the other in rows to the entrance. Each enjoyed a plush
mahogany easy chair "of the richest fashion," and a mahogany
desk with drawers and a place for ink, pen, and papers — an
excessively comfortable and injudicious arrangement, some ob-
servers thought, encouraging long sitting and windy speeches.
Within this rich and silken chamber raged the rending debate
about America's poorest and least powerful outcasts, its enslaved black men and women. The contrast was not comforting:
white men, powdered and groomed, often uncouth and stupid,
exercising rights and power few outside this chamber understood or enjoyed. Moreover, as an arena for such a skirmish,
this marbled hall was imperfect. "It is an elegant chamber to
look at," Charles Dickens wrote, "but a singularly bad one for
all purposes of hearing." Into it marched John Quincy Adams,
a bald little old man with a high-pitched voice that didn't carry
well, but who would make the slaveholders and their friends hear
him all too clearly. And in turn, from his desk in this strange
chamber, Adams could hear every syllable of the whispers of
his opponents across the room. It was an advantage he would
soon need.

In 1831, when Louisa and John Quincy returned to Washington, the coming struggle between the Union and the slave
was taking shape. Adams, who as a boy had watched the nation battle for its independence, would now as an old man
fight to ensure its survival. The issues surrounding slavery
were complex, but the human tragedy was all too clear. The
expansion of cotton planters into rich bottom lands, and rising
world demand for the fiber, had made slave labor widespread in
the South. Southern slaveowners dominated the region and the
House of Representatives, where the "Federal ratio" gave
them a strong hand. The Constitution provided that the slave-
holding states could count five slaves as being equal to three
free white men, and the number of Representatives in the House
was based upon this confected population scheme. Slaveholders,

therefore, enjoyed not only almost unlimited land, cheap labor, and political influence at home, but also immense power in Washington.

The issue of slavery was not, at this time, neatly defined and categorized in the minds of Louisa and John Quincy Adams. They did not abhor it with all their souls, as the abolitionists did. Nor were they ready to commit themselves without hesitation to its demise. Both agreed, in diaries and letters, that the question of being slave or free posed the gravest threat to the nation. But both also viewed slavery in the abstract, and John Quincy seemed never to personalize this "peculiar institution." Louisa did; the single most important act of her life was humanizing this most inhuman condition.

In 1820, during the Missouri Compromise debates, John Quincy had written in his diary: "I take for granted that the present question is a mere preamble — a title page to a tragic volume." President Monroe thought that the issue could be "winked away by a compromise," but Adams did not. "Much am I mistaken," he wrote in his diary, "if it is not destined to survive his political and individual life and mine." Adams saw slavery as "the great and foul stain upon the North American Union."

Preserving the Union was the heart of this issue for him. The nation, he thought, needed time to solidify itself. Adams had privately argued that the abolition of slavery should be left to the people of the states. As Secretary of State he had negotiated for indemnity from Great Britain for slaves carried off by British forces leaving the South at the end of the War of 1812, and sought the return of slaves who had escaped to Canada or Mexico to their Southern slaveowners. For Adams, the issue was best articulated by Daniel Webster, during his debate with Robert Y. Hayne of South Carolina defining states' rights and nullification, when Webster said: "Liberty and Union, now and forever, one and inseparable." John Quincy wrote into his diary: "The two doctrines are now before the nation. The existence of the Union depends, I fully believe, upon this question." On July 4, 1831, when John Quincy spoke before a large gathering in Quincy, he set forth his own rallying cry — in an echo of his father's last toast "Independence Forever" — with the stirring words: "Independence and Union Forever!" That was what he was fighting for.

The Adamses, as residents of Washington, saw slaves around them all the time. There were few free blacks, and it was common practice for householders to employ hired-out slaves as servants; a few lucky and hard-working slaves were even able to buy their own freedom in this manner. While the Adamses never owned a slave, they frequently hired one or two from slaveholders, usually residents of Maryland or Virginia, as cooks or house servants. Such employment did not conflict, as we shall see, with Louisa's or John Quincy's position on slavery.

Anti-slavery and pro-slavery feelings collided in the District of Columbia. Slave trade — the buying, selling, transporting, hiring, imprisoning of black men and women — thrived in the District, and some Washingtonians were troubled by the sight of long lines of slaves, in chains, shuffling through the capital to Alexandria on their way to market. The pages of the *National Intelligencer*, which the Adamses read carefully, also contained advertisements for runaway slaves. Each was a brief paragraph, a short story, of human misery: a mother with two children, ages five and eighteen months, fleeing to Pennsylvania; she wearing a faded cotton dress, no shoes, and the children in rags. Or Clem, twenty-two, and Sophy, eighteen, and six months pregnant, running north together. The description of the slaves detailed the reasons one human being would flee another: identifying scars from beatings, crippled feet from chains, scalding "wounds," brands; or the inner scars, the *plans* of the owners to sell the children, or separate a man from his woman. The rewards made hunting down these runaways worthwhile: twenty-five dollars if captured in the District, Virginia, or Maryland, and up to two hundred dollars if caught in Pennsylvania, and returned. By contrast, the Adamses paid their white coachman three dollars a month. A common laborer, by capturing a slave in Pennsylvania, could earn more than five times his yearly salary.

Petitions to abolish slavery in the District met strong opposition. Washington was surrounded by the slave states of Maryland and Virginia. If the District became free, its residents feared, it would attract, and perhaps encourage, runaway slaves. Washington would be a black island in the middle of a hostile white ocean. Worse, said the opponents of such petitions, Washington might become a base camp for insurrection in the nearby slave counties. Nevertheless, by 1831, the vanguard of petitions to rid the District of Columbia of the shame of slavery started trickling into Congress; the first carried only a few hundred signatures. But the flood was coming.

It would be an error, as mentioned, to say that Louisa and John Quincy Adams were eager from the start for the emancipation of black slaves. That was not true. Adams saw the issue always first in terms of preserving the Union; it was the nation he wished to save, not black men and women. On the eve of the Adamses' departure for Washington in 1831, Alexis de Tocqueville recorded his conversation about slavery with the new member of Congress, during which John Quincy Adams made this shocking statement:

> I know nothing more insolent than a black when he is not speaking to his master and is not afraid of being beaten. It is not even rare to see negroes treat their masters very ill when they have to do with a weak man. The negresses especially make frequent abuse of the kindness of their mistresses. They know that it isn't customary to inflict bodily punishment on them.

Louisa, on the other hand, saw slavery largely in human terms, although she also shared her husband's concern for the destruction of the Union. In 1831, as a resident of Washington with relatives in Maryland, she feared the retribution of the slaves, and the surliness of the free blacks. It would take time and an awakening for Louisa to remember her feelings toward her dark-skinned roommate in England and the slave-girl in London. More than forty years later, Louisa now harbored shameful prejudices. In February 1831, for example, she reported that President Jackson had closed the social season in Washington "with a grand Negro Ball" in the White House. Louisa was offended by these guests' presence in the drawing rooms using the President's china and silverware, and she wrote an embarrassing poem. Two stanzas reveal its tenor:

> Says Coffee to Sambo, d'ya go to the ball?
>   Yes! I was invited today
> And dey say we to dance in the great dining hall
>   Dey be taking de Carpet away.
>
>   *   *   *
>
> And dere's cake and dere's wine and all sorts of tings
>   Jist what at the Draw Rooms we see;
> When the company comes and the waiters we brings
>   With the punch and the coffee and tea.

This was Louisa at her worst, and an attitude that would gradually change as she and her husband were drawn into the vortex of abolitionism. Neither Louisa nor John Quincy entered this struggle with enthusiasm. Both were too old, and radical politics — for that's what abolition of slavery was — too outside their character and beliefs. John Quincy joined the struggle for no political benefit; he sought nothing from the abolitionists. But he greatly feared the destruction of his Union, the nation he loved more than anything else on earth. Louisa was more complex. Her interest in women and their traditional roles in society, her contacts with such abolitionists as Sarah Grimké, would slowly lift her vision to see, even as a woman in her sixties, that slavery and women's rights had similar roots. Was she indeed any different from the servant girl?

John Quincy Adams began his term in the House of Representatives without a widely-known public position on slavery. But he stepped out front — Louisa thought as a sacrificial stalking horse for the abolitionists — and was one of the first, and loudest, voices crying out against this institution. Adams complained that he wished to speak on other issues as well, but from the start he was irrevocably drawn by "the Slave and Abolition whirligig."

3

As the Adamses embarked on this great cause, personal tragedy visited them again. At their ages, Louisa and John Quincy thought much of death, and sensed its presence. To ward off a cholera epidemic that swept along the East Coast in 1832, John Quincy wore his flannel undergarments all summer; Louisa forbade anyone in the family to eat corn, and ordered all cucumbers pulled from the vines in their garden. Everyone came through safely, but the presence was felt. In November 1833, while riding across New Jersey toward Washington, John Quincy was nearly killed in a railroad accident. A fire in the woodwork around a wheel caused the wheel to break off, which sent the passenger cars jack-knifing and careening off the tracks. Adams's car stayed upright, but the car behind his overturned; two men were killed immediately, fifteen people injured, and a woman and her child "mutilated beyond expectation of recovery." For more than one hundred feet, the ground was covered with "mangled and bleeding" men, women, and children, and "limbs in frightful varieties of distortion." After proceeding to Philadelphia, John Quincy wrote Louisa that he was safe and unhurt, but he realized that only chance had saved him, and that Louisa and Looly might have been in that woman's seat. Adams felt a mingling of terror and gratitude to God. He continued on to Washington by railcar, however, not wishing to show his fear, and he was pleased to note that he left Philadelphia at seven-thirty A.M., reached Baltimore at two-thirty, visited until five, and took the railcar on to Washington, which he reached at nine the same day. John Quincy thought eleven hours of railcar riding "very tedious"; he liked the precision of the new lines, but not the speed or the sparks.

Age, and chance, brought a sense of helplessness, and the surrender to a greater power. The previous year, in 1832, John

Quincy's brother had died, at age sixty. Thomas, a lawyer and judge, had started life with such promise, but he had struggled as a young man "with some earnestness, to keep off the Blue Devils" of depression. Like other Adamses, Thomas sought relief in a bottle. He married a woman the Adamses considered beneath him — and them — and Charles once described her as "ineffably coarse" and "cunning and deceitful, hypocritical to a degree beyond belief and malicious as a serpent." Thomas would take off on drunken sprees that lasted for days, after which he would return and threaten his wife and children, who fled to their aunt and uncle's home in Washington. Thomas could not break the vice — old John Adams thought the "affliction" was visited upon his family to check its pride — and often Charles found his uncle "roaring" and his family "in a flutter." More than once someone had to bring the poor drunkard Thomas back from a tavern in Dedham or Boston "raving" in a chaise. By 1831, Thomas had degenerated into a frail man of nervous spasms, which kept his arms in constant motion and jarred his whole body, said Louisa, "with an almost constant delirium." The sight of this "always kind and affectionate" brother-in-law saddened her. In March 1832, Thomas Adams died — as his brother Charles had years earlier — from alcoholism.

The Adamses' middle son, John, also had difficulty with drinking. He worked hard at the Columbian Mills along Rock Creek in Washington, and he knew that his father's financial security rested in part upon their success. In 1923, John Quincy had purchased the mills from Louisa's cousin George Johnson, after a cursory inspection; as Charles later said of JQA, "He is a singular man with regard to the management of his property. Investments with him are chance things." To pay for the mills, John Quincy had transferred nine thousand dollars in U.S. 6-percent bonds, and had taken a second mortgage on his F Street house. The mills were set up to grind wheat and corn into flour and meal, which was then sold in Washington or shipped by schooner down the Potomac to Atlantic coastal ports. Adams hoped they might support him and his family as soon as 1825, but in fact the Columbian Mills troubled him for the rest of his life.

In 1829, John Quincy had placed his son John in charge of the mills. John went after the job with enthusiasm and dedication, but the task was overwhelming, and solutions out of his reach. He could not control drought on the farmlands, or an abundance of wheat one year and a dearth the next, or the fluctuation of flour prices in Europe. Flash floods from summer thunderstorms roared down Rock Creek, damaging the mill and the roads leading to it. Competing flour and meal arrived from western farms on the new B&O Railroad, and one mill after another in Washington went bankrupt. Still, John had enthusiasm, and his mother reported to Charles that he was "active, steadily industrious and much more cheerful than for years." He started rising at five, working at the mill for several hours, then home for breakfast, returning to work until dinner, then back until eight at night.

But the mills ground John down as well. His health deteriorated. Louisa worried about his exposing himself so much to "the evening damps of that unhealthy Creek." John began drinking. He suffered from stiff joints and limbs, fevers, loss of memory. He periodically lost his eyesight. "Poor John," Louisa wrote one time, "is seldom able to get out of bed until twelve o'clock and then shuffles about the house wrapped in his wadded coat." For two years, John lingered in pain and sickness, growing weaker and weaker, and by 1834 Louisa was convinced that his illness was owing to "the dreadfully debilitating" climate around the Mills. She exhorted John Quincy to find "some lucrative and advantageous scheme of business" in Quincy for John. In a touching, quietly desperate series of letters, John Quincy wrote his son trying to persuade him to move with his family to Massachusetts. There was plenty of work at the old house, his father promised, where he could "be useful to me and may if you so desire make yourself a comfortable and independent existence." But Adams's kind, loving offers could not help John. In early autumn, a letter arrived telling them that John was gravely ill. John Quincy left quickly, carrying with him Louisa's desperate admonition to feed John "good soups which you must take care to give a half an hour before the times at which he has been accustomed to take his *refreshment.* Meat jellies would likewise prove efficacious." Their love and concern for John, however, did no good. When John Quincy arrived in Washington on October 22, his son lay unconscious in a coma. He died the next morning at four-thirty, with his father at his side.

In a sense, John had sacrificed himself for his father: The family misfortunes had become his intolerable burden. As with George, the father's financial worries interlinked with the son's opinion of himself, and with his death; but where one had been abused by the father, the other had abused himself. While John could please his father — which George never could — he could not please himself. His father called John "a kind, tender, affectionate Son, who had devoted his whole life to me. . . . A more honest soul, or more tender heart never breathed on the face of this earth." Both John Quincy and Louisa were shocked into collapse by their second son's death. They turned all their love to Charles* and their grandchildren, and their commitment to the issues ahead.

Mary and her two young daughters moved in permanently with the Adamses. The Columbian Mills, impossible to lease or sell without a loss, continued a burden until John Quincy hired Nathaniel Frye, Louisa's brother-in-law, to manage them. Adams was financially strapped, and could barely meet his daily living expenses or pay the interest on his debts. He turned to his old servant, Antoine Guista, who kindly loaned John Quincy thousands of dollars and renewed the loans without hesitation, or collection. Adams survived for the rest of his life on the rentals of his Washington property, a scanty income from the Mills (Frye proved a genius at grinding out flour and profits), his mortgaged Boston real estate, investments watched carefully by Charles, small lecture fees, and Guista's loans. Both Louisa and Charles accused John Quincy of sacrificing his children and financial security to his political ambition. But Adams saw the larger issues on the horizon: "From our sorrows," he said, "let us turn to the consideration of our duties."

---

* After the death of his brother John, Charles wrote in his diary: "I cannot regret the loss of either of my brothers as a calamity either to their families or to themselves."

4

THE ABOLITIONIST MOVEMENT was part of the great religious awakening overflowing the land. Education, temperance, penal reform, international peace, aid and care for the needy, social responsibility for the poor, orphaned and widowed were humanitarian measures that increasingly concerned many Americans. The abolitionist movement was in part a religious crusade to free the enslaved black people of this land, and its members aroused fellow Americans with moral outcry. The abolitionists were the radicals of their day. They advocated nonviolence, integrated their meetings with free black men and women, faced threats and stonings from hostile mobs. Some of them also embraced bizarre and unpopular ideas: unstructured child-rearing techniques, the boycotting of Southern goods by a Free Produce Society,* and vegetarianism. Abolitionists were determined to eat right, raise correctly, boycott, and liberate. And within the heart of this movement arose the most radical thought of all: the liberation of women. The American Anti-Slavery Society, with hundreds of local chapters across the North, agitated on a wide front. Its members mailed pamphlets to the South, and petitioned Congress for the abolition of slavery. The circulation of these petitions had a surprising effect: It organized Northern communities, educated large numbers of Americans to the plight of the slaves, and created a rallying point around which women organized.

By mid-decade, these petitions were pouring into John Quincy Adams's office; only one came from his own constituents. Angry Southerners had sought to stop the abolitionists from spreading their views by changing the postal laws, preventing abolitionist speeches in the South, and banning anti-slavery litera-

---

* The Free Produce movement held that slavery could be weakened by boycotting slave-made goods and produce grown in the slave states. The movement had little impact on the South.

ture, such as William Lloyd Garrison's radical *Liberator*. Next, they sought to halt all discussion of slavery in Congress by blocking the presentation of abolitionist petitions. Member after member rose in vitriolic wrath against these divisive petitions. After several days of listening to the Southerners' views, Adams sat at his desk on the House floor and wrote Charles: "The voice of Freedom has not yet been heard, and I am earnestly urged to speak in her name. She will be trampled under foot if I do not, and I shall be trampled under foot if I do. . . . What can I do?"

By January 1836 Adams was rising from his desk every day and speaking out. He debated points about slavery, and read petition after petition calling for its abolition. "Over head and ears in debate," he wrote enthusiastically to Charles. "I have taken up the glove in the House. I had no alternative left." In joining the battle, Adams discovered new vigor and purpose. He loved the rules, the language, the verbal rolls and thunders that trapped or exposed an opponent. Each day now seemed worthwhile: "A skirmishing day," he wrote with glee; he had presented three petitions, reading each one to the squirming House members, followed by "a sharp debate," and a rebuttal against him that Adams found "warmly personal but without abuse." Nothing stopped him — not his age, health, weaknesses, and certainly not the opposition. Nearing seventy, Adams was hardly the heroic figure the abolitionists might have chosen. He (and Charles) feared speaking in public, and prepared each speech arduously. Adams was longwinded, and tended to verbal flourishes: More than once Louisa had to warm him to control "the winged griffins of your imagination." He was shaky with age, shrunken,* ill much of the time, and always aware of death. His voice sometimes failed him. Louisa said he was more stubborn than ever, easily distracted; Charles thought his father's "whole system of life is wrong — that he sleeps far too little, that he eats and drinks too irregularly."** The pain of lumbago

---

* Adams measured himself regularly, and in his youth said he stood five feet, seven inches, but now was only five feet, six inches.
** Adams ignored Dr. Physick's advice in 1832 to cut back on drinking. He took two or three glasses of Madeira wine after dinner. He also knew wines better than anyone. During one memorable din-

and sciatica discomforted him, and Dr. Huntt prescribed warm baths, and "Burgama Pitch Plaister, which I took," Adams said, "and Lauclamma in Castor Oil, which I did not take." Told to remain in bed, Adams got up, wrapped himself in his trusty flannel waistcoat (in May), and walked to the House for the debates. He also read Psalm 90, verses nine through twelve: "For all our days are passed away in thy wrath: we spend our years as a tale that is told. The days of our years are three score and ten; and if by reason of strength they be fourscore years, yet is their strength labour and sorrow; for it is soon cut off, and we fly away. . . . So teach us to number our days, that we may apply our hearts unto wisdom." It was a good prayer for that year. As Louisa warned, "The Battle of the Grugs is raging."

Old, ill, infirm of voice and body, Adams measured his days carefully, and applied all the wisdom of his heart to this battle. The forces against him were young, powerful, and many. "One hundred members of the House represent slaves," Adams would later write, "four-fifths of whom would crucify me if their vote could erect the cross; forty members, representatives of the free, in the league of slavery and mock Democracy, would break me on the wheel, if their votes or wishes could turn it round; and four-fifths of the other hundred and twenty are either so cold or so lukewarm that they are ready to desert me at the very first scintillation of indiscretion on my part. The only formidable danger with which I am beset is that of my own temper." With each debate, with each presentation of petitions, with each new step of the slaveholders into new American terri- tory, Adams and a handful of men in opposition found them- selves engaged on the House floor in "angry discussion." John

---

ner party at this time, given by Roswell Colt, a New York socialite whose wine stock received well-deserved acclaim, Adams and other guests drank Madeira, adding a single glass of hock taken with the oysters on the half-shell, and a glass of sherry with the soup, followed by champagne with the meats. When the cloth was removed, Colt sum- moned from his inestimable wine cellar fourteen different Madeiras, and as the host filled the glasses and passed them, unnamed, around the table, John Quincy Adams delighted and surprised everyone by sip- ping and correctly identifying eleven of the fourteen wines. That kind of delicate taste came only after years of practice.

Quincy realized he would soon "be under the necessity of making some remarks offensive to the Slave holders, and in no wise pleasing to the *Northern Men with Southern principles.*"

The battle began on May 18, 1836. The slaveholders and Northern sympathizers sought to cut off all debate, all presentation of these troublesome petitions. They wished to limit, in effect, the right of some members to speak freely in the House, and, far worse, they determined to halt once and for all the right of Americans to address their government, through petitions. In a phrase, the slavery sympathizers planned to limit freedom of speech. What they did, however, was stir old John Quincy Adams to long battle, and awaken the American people to the very issue they sought to suppress.

That May, a committee headed by Henry Laurens Pinckney of South Carolina presented to the House three resolutions. The first stated that Congress had no constitutional power to interfere with slavery in any state. The second said that Congress ought not meddle with slavery in the District of Columbia. But the third resolution was more basic, and dangerous: "All petitions, memorials, resolutions, or papers," it said, "relating in any way, or to any extent whatsoever, to the subject of slavery or the abolition of slavery, shall, without being either printed or referred, be laid on the table, and that no further action whatever shall be had thereon."

The first two resolutions did not differ from instructions by the House which Adams himself had voted for a few days earlier. But the third resolution destroyed any chance for compromise, and opened the battle between slaveholder and opponent, between much of the House and Adams, that lasted eight years. The resolutions were clearly a violation of the U.S. Constitution, but the Speaker, James K. Polk, a Tennessee slaveholder, shut off any argument against them. For the next two days, during discussions of other questions before the House, the irascible Adams rose to make his points against slavery, and warned that the nation was being slowly led to a war that threatened the Union. The nation was now too weak to come through such a war intact. His duty, Adams wrote a friend, was to speak out and delay the coming civil conflict. His positions may have seemed uneven, but his goal was always firm: preservation of the Union. "This is the cause upon which I am entering the last stage of my life," he wrote, "and with the certainty that I cannot advance it far; my career must close, leaving the cause at the threshold. To open the way for others is all that I can do. The cause is good and great."

On May 26, 1836, the House took the final step against Adams and the petitioners. The Clerk of the House called the roll on the third question — that of silencing all discussion of slavery in the House. When John Quincy Adams's name was called, the old man rose and shouted above the cries of the opposition: "I hold the resolution to be in direct violation of the Constitution of the United States, of the rules of this House, and of the rights of my constituents." But he went unheeded, and the resolution passed, 117 to 68. Pinckney's third resolution became known as the "Gag Rule," and the House, supported by Southern slaveholders and Northern Democrats, renewed the Gag Rule in more and more stringent form with each session of Congress, until 1840, when it became a standing rule of procedure, known as the Twenty-first Rule.

Defeated, Adams wrote to Charles that opponents in the House were seeking "my ruin as a Public man, and the ruin of my character as an honest man." Adams battled them without pause; he once remained at his desk for twenty-four hours before returning home exhausted. "They hunt me like a Partridge upon the mountains," he said. "Well — be it so." They could not silence him. The old man, rather than withdrawing, stepped forward to the struggle. "I am aware," he wrote his son, "that my severest trials are yet to come."

As Euripides taught, Whom the gods wish to destroy, they first make mad. The Gag Rule soon become a rallying point for an ever-widening cause. It nullified the right to petition, but could not destroy it. Instead, abolitionists attacked the House with petitions, and in the next two years, the American Anti-Slavery Society alone sent 196,720 petitions opposing slavery and another 32,000 against the Gag Rule. By April 1838 the petitions filled a room in the Capitol building that measured twenty by thirty by fourteen feet. Not a single petition was heard by the House. The controversy spread beyond the radical abolitionists. Other Americans joined the struggle. Where at first the issue had been the abolition of slavery, it soon became the right to petition, then the cause of freedom of speech. More and more white men and women — few of them abolitionists — became concerned about their Constitutional rights. If the House could refuse petitions concerning slavery, they reasoned, it could refuse petitions on any issue it wished: Indians, a national bank, internal improvements, Antimasonry. For the first time, white and free Americans saw their freedom interwoven with that of black men and women slaves. For the first time they asked: If any among us is enslaved, are we free?

5

IN 1837 AND 1838, Americans became political activists. The most radical joined the anti-slavery societies and petitioned Congress, while others, frightened by the Gag Rule, acted to defend against threats to their own freedoms. No two years since 1814 contained more turmoil. Those who were free demanded freedom for others, and those who were women realized, in their pursuit of freedom for others, that they themselves were enslaved. Not since the Revolution had women in such numbers spoken out in public, and never before had they argued with such strong language for their rights and those of slaves. The "lowering clouds" of 1837–38 warned of the coming storms, and foreshadowed the struggle for equality that continues in America today.

"The Cult of True Womanhood" was the cultural expression of the stereotypical woman of this time. An entire industry had grown up around the ideas of women as pious, pure, domestic, and submissive, and with the invention of inexpensive printing machinery in 1830, made womanhood a distinct and popular topic in novels and women's magazines. Most illustrative was *Godey's Lady's Book*, which celebrated Queen Victoria's ascension to her throne in 1837 by extolling her as typical of "all that is majestic, all that is soft and soothing, all that is bright, all that expresses the one universal voice of love in creation." Women, *Godey's* showed, were invested with love and gentleness, not the masculine power and energy of the abolitionists. As Ralph Waldo Emerson wrote at the time, woman was the "civilizer of mankind."

Society idealized the religious wife who sacrificed her ambitions to her husband's. No church except the Society of Friends (Quakers) allowed women a voice in church affairs or the ministry. Men believed that a woman's name should appear in print twice: when she married and when she died. Social convention ruled that political involvement was inconsistent with female submissiveness. Political activism, society feared, would lead to neglect of the home and family.* Men, and most women, feared female "notoriety," and told activist women that they should stay home, be silent, protect the family, and become "the grace, the ornament, the bliss of life." A woman's skill was in household matters, and culinary surprises. Any excess energy she might have could go to caring for the community poor, orphaned, or widowed.

Pulpit and press extolled a woman's proper role, and courts hardened it into law. A woman could not vote or stand for public office. She had little influence outside the bedroom upon American politics. She still received an inferior education, if any, and was excluded from higher institutions of learning. A married woman had no legal rights to inherited property or her earnings; she could make no contracts, sue nor be sued, nor claim her own children in case of marital separation. Some premarital contracts softened the harshness of these laws, yet the concept

---

* An argument popular in the 1980s: The theme that the active woman would neglect her home and family has persisted from abolitionist days through suffrage to the debate on the Equal Rights Amendment.

of a woman's inferiority was firm in the law and, perhaps more importantly, in the public mind. Women were secondary creatures. As late as 1850, *The Public Ledger* of Philadelphia contained an article ridiculing the advocates of equal rights for women. "A woman is a nobody," the article stated. "A wife is everything. A pretty girl is equal to 10,000 men and a mother is, next to God, all powerful. The ladies of Philadelphia therefore . . . are resolved to maintain their rights as wives, belles, virgins and mothers and not as women."

Early in the century, a few women had met together in home parlors for charitable, religious or educational work. Gradually, these gatherings became social forums, and the smallest units of power women had. From them grew such organizations as the Washington Orphans' Society, to which Louisa Adams belonged, or the Female Missionary Society, which by 1818 was active in forty-six New York towns. Women in Philadelphia, Charleston, New York, Washington, Baltimore met in their homes and churches and formed associations to help the poor, orphaned, widowed. By 1838, Boston women had aided ten thousand families and distributed more than twenty-two thousand dollars in charity in that city alone. Raising money for the poor, or food for the indigent, gave American women skills in meeting together, working toward a goal, mastering the collection of money, developing a wider-ranging organizational network, and speaking — softly, among themselves at first — about their lives, politics, and the barriers they encountered.

These, of course, were precisely the skills the anti-slavery movement needed. Women who could organize, attend or chair meetings, debate issues, raise money, and form a wider network of help for orphans or the poor, could organize, gather signatures, and distribute petitions for the enslaved. Petitions, therefore, focused the emerging political awareness and concern of American women. Petitioning the government was not a new device for redress of grievances. Individual slaves and voluntary societies had petitioned since colonial days, but the petitions were then little more than random personal letters to which a list of signatures was affixed. By 1830, petitions were reaching the House in larger numbers, and dealt with the tariff, currency, the Bank of the United States, abolition of Sunday mail delivery, support of the Cherokee Indians and the ten-hour work day. Petitions gave the ordinary person a sense of participation in the democratic process. They provided a means for those outside political power to make their opinions felt. They were, therefore, a perfect weapon for women and the anti-slavery societies, who used them in a systematic way as a means of agitation and a basis for organizing.

When the American Anti-Slavery Society (A.A.S.S.) temporarily united three radical wings of abolitionists in one organization, custom and the prevailing notions of "propriety" made participation by men and women together difficult. Lucretia Mott and twenty women formed the Philadelphia Female Anti-Slavery Society, the feminine counterpart to the all-male A.A.S.S. By 1837, the abolitionists had created 1,006 anti-slavery societies in New England and the Midwest, with a combined membership of more than 100,000, half of them women. Petitioning now became a major form of anti-slavery activity. Women took to it with enthusiasm, and saw petitioning as a way of testing their embryonic political power. Earlier in the decade, British abolitionist women had swamped Parliament with tens of thousands of petitions, and were credited with the final push of militancy that brought the British Emancipation Act of 1833 into life. British women had set an example of power for their American sisters.

In May 1837, abolitionist women decided to organize and unite. They called an Anti-Slavery Convention of American women, and some seventy-one women from eight states met in Philadelphia for what was basically a political meeting. Never before had so many American women met primarily to organize, design, and launch a major political attack. This was the first wave of women's political activism. The Convention women set as their goal the organizing of women in New York, Boston, and Philadelphia, and the gathering of one million signatures on petitions before the opening of the next session of Congress.* Their

* By the third session of the Twenty-fifth Congress in 1838, the women had five hundred thousand signatures on petitions. Whether or not they reached their goal is unclear, for the above number covered

organization was unprecedented, and incredible. Instructions and sample petitions went out to all affiliated societies, and each local female anti-slavery group appointed a petition chairwoman for every county, set signature goals, and followed up on results. The anti-slavery convention stressed that petitioning by women was their primary goal, but they also understood that petitioning itself would create an excellent grass-roots women's organization.

The anti-slavery societies became the most important political organization for women in the nation's first sixty years. Yet the majority of American women remained outside them, and completely ignorant of the issues of slavery or women's rights. Juliana Tappen of New York, for example, spent months knocking on doors, and discovered to her dismay that few women had ever heard of slave trade in the District of Columbia or Texas, or knew where those places were. Fewer still understood the idea of emancipation, or considered themselves enslaved.

Louisa Adams was lucky. She was well-read, and exposed to the full impact of these petitions and ideas. By 1832 anti-slavery petitions filled her home. Many were written and signed by women. At first they sought the abolition of slavery or slave trade in the District of Columbia, but gradually, during the years 1837–38, they turned to the deeper question of human freedom. Within these two years, women who petitioned for the freedom of the slave began to petition for their own freedom, for the freeing of all enslaved people. This made interesting reading inside the Adams household.

The regular petition day in the House was Monday, and on January 9, and again on January 23, 1837, John Quincy Adams rose to present petitions from women. The Gag Rule had not yet been renewed for that session. One can imagine the rheumatic Adams getting up slowly, painfully from his mahogany seat, knowing that he faced the hostility of his colleagues, reading the

---

only those petitions sent through the A.A.S.S. A large number also went to sympathetic Congressmen. By 1840, anti-slavery petitions were no longer even received by the House, and no complete record of them survives. But during that session, John Quincy Adams noted that he received "a greater number of petitions than at any former session." The women hadn't quit.

names and demands of these brave women, shouting over the cries of "Out of order!" and "Silence him!" that filled the chamber. On these two Mondays, Adams presented forty-five petitions before the House voted — as it did at the start of each session — to again enforce the Gag Rule. One can hear Adams, his old man's voice cracking above the din of the House, intoning the names of these anonymous women:

Lydia Lewis and 150 women of Dorchester "praying for the abolition of slavery in the District of Columbia"; Rachael Newcomb and 130 women of Braintree; Mary Perry and 82 women of Plymouth; Abigail M. Emmons and 315 women of Franklin; Phoebe Weston and 156 women of Westminister. . . .

"Point of order! Point of order!"

. . . Ann E. Hildreth and 95 women of Derry, New Hampshire; Eliza Tower and 17 women of Waterville, New York; Esther Chase and 64 women of Kirkland, New York; and on he read, petitions with just 2 names, some with 6 or 7, others signed by as many as 575 men and 295 "female citizens" from Westmoreland County, Pennsylvania.

As he spoke, the House members acted. Adams presented the petition of the Dorchester women — tabled — and the women of Plymouth — tabled — and South Weymouth — objection! — and, reading from the petition: " '. . . impressed with the sinfulness of slavery, and keenly aggrieved by its existence in a part of our Country over which . . .' "

"A point of order!" Pinckney jumped to his feet. "Has the gentleman from Massachusetts a right under the rule, to read the petition?"

Speaker Polk replied that Adams had "a right to make a statement of the contents" of the petition. He overlooked the fact that the Gag Rule had expired with the last session, and had not yet been renewed.

"It is a privilege I shall exercise," Adams said, "until I am deprived of it by some positive act."

Adams pressed on, reading the petition: " '. . . keenly aggrieved by its existence in a part of our Country over which Congress possesses exclusive jurisdiction in all cases whatever . . .' "

"Order, order!" the other House members shouted.

" '. . . Do most earnestly petition your honourable body . . .' "

"Mr. Speaker!" John Chambers of Kentucky shouted. "Mr. Speaker, I rise to a point of order."

Adams read faster: " '. . . immediately to abolish slavery in the District of Columbia . . .' "

"Mr. Speaker!" Chambers screamed, "A call to order!"

Polk shouted at Adams: "Take your seat!"

The ex-President slowly eased himself into his chair, still reading loudly from the petition: " '. . . and to declare every human being free who sets foot upon its soil.' "*

House members immediately tabled the obnoxious documents. Adams bounced up to tell them that the good ladies of Massachusetts had vowed to renew their petition every year "in the holy cause of human freedom." The members reacted to the warning by renewing the Gag Rule for the remainder of that session.

Petitions continued to tumble into Adams's office and home, where Louisa and Mary helped him carefully list each one. The two women compiled the objectives of the petitions, the petitioners, and also copied John Quincy's letters to them. Adams continued bringing the petitions to the floor of the House, and the House was stormy for days after one of his presentations. John Quincy thrived on the adversity. Louisa told Charles: "Your father [is] *exuberant in toil*." Suddenly, at seventy, Adams felt "uncommonly well," his health invigorated by his talent for needling his opponents to exasperation. The slaveholders and Northern sympathizers regarded him as incendiary, and dangerous. Calhoun called Adams a "mischievous old man."

By the end of February 1837, Louisa's list of petitions had grown so long that John Quincy stopped describing their details. In a six-week period, she had recorded 3,509 signatures of women petitioners. In part, these petitions became a roll call of courageous women: 60 women in Duxbury, 29 in Hingham, 65 in Needham, Massachusetts; 164 in Walton, and 1,265 "ladies" in Herkimer County, New York. These were the brave and

---

* Samuel F. Bemis, *John Quincy Adams and the Union*. New York: Knopf, 1956, pp. 341–342.

outspoken, putting their names first on the petitions and gathering the signatures: Lucia A. Bradford, Lydia R. Beck, Emily A. Gilman, Elizabeth B. Sergeant, Rachael Rich, Caroline Ainsworth, Fanny Graves, Fidelia S. Thatcher, and on. By March 1, Adams had received 181 petitions with 16,740 signatures, and he continued testing the House members with his parliamentary skill.

Adams probed the members' defense of the Gag Rule. He presented a petition of "nine ladies of Fredericksburg, Virginia," who called for the prohibition of slave trade in the District of Columbia, and was defending their right to petition and their reputations when John Mercer Patton of Virginia claimed that the women were free Negroes or mulattoes, and "infamous." With the House in uproar, Adams also prepared to present a now-famous petition by slaves, written in a neat hand (probably that of the master) and signed with wiggily signatures, or X's. Before he could read the petition, however, Adams was attacked. Was he suggesting that slaves had a right to petition Congress? "I object!" bellowed Jacob Lawler of Alabama. "I want it to appear in the [House] Journal that I objected!" Charles Eaton Haynes of Georgia also raised his voice in protest, and Waddy Thompson, Jr., of South Carolina accused Adams of inciting the slaves to rebellion. Others shouted that Adams was a pawn of "incendiary fanatics," that he was offending the South, that he was threatening the Union. Another called for censure. "Expel him! Expel him!" someone shouted. Adams told the Speaker that he had merely raised a parliamentary question about the slave petition: Was it in order? He had neither presented it nor said that it was, in fact, from slaves. He then announced that the petition was indeed from slaves — twenty-two of them — but against abolition!

The House exploded again with shouts. Its members quickly passed three resolutions, the first two of which declared any member who presented petitions from slaves to the House disrespectful of the "feelings" of the House and the "rights" of Southern states, and "unfriendly to the Union"; they stated that slaves had no right to make such petitions, only the citizens of the United States. (Even that right was superseded by the Gag

Rule, underscoring once more the similarity of free people and slaves.) The third resolution made it appear that Adams had apologized to the House for his efforts on behalf of the petitioners.* Adams, of course, had done no such thing, and was not likely to. He demanded to speak in his own defense, and his speech was the most stinging he ever made. He cracked his verbal whip at the slaveholders, and accused the House members of denying the right of petition for political reasons, an act "no despot, of any age or clime, has ever denied . . . to the poorest or the meanest of human creatures. . . . When the principle is once begun of limiting the right of petition, where would it stop? . . . The honourable gentleman makes it a crime because I presented a petition which he affirms to be from colored women, which women were of infamous character, as the honorable gentleman says — prostitutes, I think the gentleman said."

"I did not say they were prostitutes," Patton called from his seat. "They are free mulattoes."

Adams ignored him and addressed the chair. "The word 'woman' is an expression much dearer to my heart than that of 'lady.' I thought the honorable gentleman had said they were 'infamous.' I shall forever entertain the proposition that the sacred right of petition, of begging for mercy, does not depend on character any more than it does on condition. It is a right that cannot be denied to the humblest, to the most wretched."

Adams's statement for the rights of all people was lost on Patton, who was far more concerned with his own reputation. "I have not said," he blubbered, "that I know these women."

Adams turned to him: "I am glad to hear the honorable gentleman disclaim any knowledge of them, for I had been going to ask, if they were infamous women, then who is it that had made them infamous? Not their color, I believe, but their masters! I have heard it said in proof of that fact, and I am inclined to believe it is the case, that in the South there existed great resemblances between the progeny of the colored people and the white men who claim possession of them. Thus, perhaps, the

---

* The third resolution did not pass, and censure of Adams for the time was removed. But two days later the House voted overwhelmingly for the second proposition, that slaves had no right to petition.

charge of infamous might be retorted on those who made it, as originating from themselves!''

The House exploded with shouts and accusations. The *Register of Debates* records: "Great agitation in the House!''

As an old man, Adams could have measured out his days sitting quietly at his desk in the House. But he chose to take the most volatile issue of his time — slavery — and force his fellow House members to consider it from every aspect: as a threat to the Union, as a catalyst to war with Mexico, as a divisive issue splitting the Congress, as an instrument for denying the American people a basic right. Adams could have stopped there. But in 1837, he extended the issue of slavery, with all its terrible ramifications, to the issue of freedom for all people: to women's rights as well. Why?

John Quincy was also at this time sorting through his parents' correspondence and papers. He was putting together his family's history, and it gave him a great sense of setting the Adams name properly before the American people, of setting the record straight. History, the Adamses felt, would show that their sacrifices had been warranted. Unappreciated during their lifetimes, they would be revered by future generations. And with this rectifying, Adams also became aware of how strong a woman his mother had been. Abigail fervently opposed slavery. "I wish most sincerely there was not a slave in the province," she had written John. "It always seemed a most iniquitous scheme to me to fight ourselves for what we are robbing the Negroes of, who have as good a right to freedom as we have!" Abigail also sought, as we shall see, equality for women, and demanded that her husband include that equality in the Declaration of Independence, warning him to "Remember the ladies." John Quincy, by championing the rights of all human beings, championed the demands of his mother; by defending the rights of women he honored her memory.

John Quincy was also listening, perhaps for the first time, to his wife. He, at seventy, and she, sixty-two, had together survived life's calamities: long separations, voyages, dark winters of despair, births and deaths of their children. Louisa's opinions about slavery remained cautious; for someone born in England she had absorbed much of her Maryland relatives' feelings. She understood what was right, but she also feared what might occur. Yet on the rights of women, Louisa was growing as bold as her husband on petitions. As they shared this struggle together, working closely on the petitions that flooded their home, and combating the hatred toward John Quincy, Louisa shared as well her doubts and opinions. Whether he agreed with her, or she changed with him, her private observations soon were echoed in his public positions. John Quincy Adams, then, was reacting not only to his conscience, but also to the two most powerful women in his life: his mother and his wife.

6

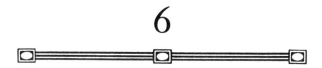

DURING THESE YEARS, Louisa Adams read and listened, and explored her own feelings about slavery, the abolitionists, and about women. The inner turmoil this caused her cannot be overstated. Ill much of their first two years in Washington, confined, recovering from the shock of the death of her second son, Louisa entered a period of religious and personal self-examination. In 1835, after John's death, she started each day with a series of long prayers, and then spent much time reading her Bible. Louisa compared the lives of the Apostles and interpreted the writings of St. Paul. She undertook a long religious poem, two lines of which contained this self-analysis: "She lived in error, faulty every day / Imploring God to guide her on her way." She prayed for her own death, but was ironically kept vigorously alive by her increasing bitterness against "all the varied forms of grasping, sordid, useless ambition." She again, as she had in 1825–28, worried about her sanity. Louisa confessed: "I love to lose myself in the ecstacy of wild thought and ramble into the regions of futurity. Perhaps this is insanity." Louisa was so troubled by her life and questioning that she rode into Boston and saw Dr. Harriot Kezia Hunt. Little is known of Dr. Hunt's impact upon Louisa, but we know that this radical woman physician was "a zealous little creature" and a "very peculiar individual," who treated neurasthenic women. Most of all, Dr. Hunt was one of the outspoken "emancipation ladies" of the age, a leader of the cause of women's suffrage, and an ardent feminist. That Louisa sought her out indicated both Louisa's concern about her own mental health, and its connection with her search for answers about slavery, abolition, and women.

Louisa's religion holds the prism through which we may view these other concerns. She was part of the religious revivalism sweeping the nation, but her exploration centered upon the relationship between men and women rather than between men and God. John Quincy's "deep interest" in the issues surrounding slavery took Louisa, by 1837, into a study of them as well. As she handled the flow of petitions that poured in, she had to have been, as we are even today, deeply moved by the strong feelings and outrage of the women petitioners. Louisa also read several newspapers, and the Adams family papers include copies of Garrison's *The Liberator*, an abolitionist publication. Louisa read abolitionist pamphlets, and her library included several volumes on women's rights, booklets from the Grimké sisters, and Wollstonecraft's *Vindication of the Rights of Women*. Perhaps most important, however, in 1836 Louisa had read for the first time Abigail Adams's letters to her husband, and in them she found articulation of the message she sought.

In 1832, Louisa undertook a detailed analysis of the Old Testament history. Her feelings of not being well-educated and her sense of inferiority threatened to halt the project several times. During her work, she scribbled a note: "To reason soundly requires great power of mind, deep research, strength for analysis, and close investigation, things altogether impossible to my weak nature or my limited capacity." Still, she overcame her doubts, and wrote a sixty-page analysis. The work made her study the Bible harder than she ever had, and look deeply into herself. She felt an uneasiness with her searching: "In all I see or hear," she wrote to herself, "I am constantly seeking for some standard by which to correct my own judgments, and while I ponder with admiration on the ingenuity of man, there is something wanting to afford me satisfaction."

Louisa's doubts centered on the questions of equality, and the Biblical treatment of women. Were women closer to God than men? In the Garden of Eden, Louisa wrote, "Women and man were co-equal, and this is proved by their perfect equality after Eve had tasted the forbidden fruit, and when she had *attained* the *knowledge* which had been forbidden, for had she not shared the apple with him, he might have remained happy in Paradise, and she *alone* would have reaped the punishment of her fault, and by her disobedience to God have been closest to inferiority." Further, Louisa asked, "If woman is to be considered inferior to man, why was she made the Mother of Men after her Sin? That the race might depreciate?" Moreover, the Messiah was "born of *woman*" and was not this fact "worthy to prove the equality of woman with man!"

From these religious origins, Louisa's questioning broadened into observation of life around her. Woman, she said, was at first the object of her husband's eye, but after bearing his children, she became a "secondary object" and as the number of children increased, she faded "into a mere automaton used as occasion requires and at other times remains an unwelcome burthen." Was this what the Bible taught, that women were inferior to men, that they were men's servants? "Woman, made to Cook his Dinner, wash his Clothes, gratify his sensual appetites, and thank him, and love him for the permission to drudge through life, at the mercy of his caprices — Is this the interpretation intended by the Creator? The Father of all mercy?" Louisa wrote that women must be alert, that the world places all weakness and frailty on their side. "We know that the power, the property and the law are all on the other, as well as publick opinion; which created by man is always in favour of himself."

Coming at this same time, and not incidental to her questioning and condemnation, was a rediscovery for Louisa Adams. John Quincy was sorting his father's papers, and Charles compiling his grandmother's letters for a book. Louisa Adams had the chance to read Abigail Adams's letters to her husband written in the 1770s during his absences at the Continental Congresses. Abigail's letters conveyed the certainty of her importance to her husband, and her respected place in family and community. This was not a limited role, a confinement as guardian of some confected morality, but a valued position as "farmeress," mother, teacher, employer, revolutionary that gave Abigail Adams a clear sense of herself as a person. Louisa found Abigail's letters "full of energy, buoyant and elastic," and said: "We are struck by the vast and varied powers of her mind, the full benevolence of an excellent heart and the strength of her reasoning capacity." She was also impressed with Abigail's message.

While John Adams was in Philadelphia in 1776, working on a draft of the Declaration of Independence, Abigail had made a declaration of her own. She longed to hear, she wrote him, that the Continental Congress had declared independence, and Abigail wanted women to gain their independence with men. "Do not put such unlimited power into the hands of the Husbands," she wrote. "Remember all Men would be tyrants if they could. If particular care and attention is not paid to the Ladies, we are determined to foment a Rebellion, and will not hold ourselves bound by any laws in which we have no voice, or Representation." It was this cry, Louisa knew, that was now being made by the female abolitionists: Were they not fomenting a rebellion? Abigail's voice, coming sixty-one years later, carried the same themes of oppression and second-class status:

> That your Sex are Naturally Tyrannical is a Truth so thoroughly established as to admit of no dispute, but such of you as wish to be happy willingly give up the harsh title of Master for the more tender and endearing one of Friend. Why then, not put it out of the power of the vicious and the Lawless to use us with cruelty and indignity with impunity. Men of Sense in all Ages abhor those customs which treat us only as the vassals of your Sex. Regard us then as Beings placed by providence under your protection and in immitation of the Supreem Being make use of that power only for our happiness.

John Adams mulled this over in Philadelphia, and wrote a reply to Abigail shortly after receiving her letter. As for her "extraordinary" idea to make men and women equal under the new Declaration of Independence, "I cannot but laugh," he said. The struggle in Philadelphia had already made children and apprentices disobedient, schools and colleges "turbulent," and Negroes "insolent to their Masters." And now women growing restless and discontent? Adams was clearly amused. "We know better than to repeal our Masculine systems. Although they are in full Force, you know they are little more than Theory. We dare not exert our Power in its full Latitude. We are obliged to go fair, and softly, and in Practice you know We are the subjects." He begged not to be subjected to "the Despotism of the Peticoat."

Abigail, however, disliked her husband's reply. She wrote back: "I can not say that I think you very generous to the Ladies, for whilst you are proclaiming peace and good will to Men, Emancipating all Nations, you insist upon retaining an absolute power over Wives." Abigail threatened her husband; repressed women, she said, would rebel. "We have it in Our power not only to free ourselves but to subdue our Masters, and without violence throw both your natural and legal authority at our feet." Abigail sought to translate her social and familial power in Massachusetts to political power — for all women. Her role, and that of other women, in constructing this new nation, writing its laws, shaping its destiny was, she feared, going to be small and oblique. She also saw, long before other, younger women articulated it, the growing oppression of her sex, and she sought to avoid it by creating a truly new nation built on equality. Abigail believed that women, without a voice in making the laws that controlled them, would rebel. The American Revolution, Abigail Adams knew, was then being fought to free a people from laws they had not written, and was a struggle that promised freedom only to a white, male minority. Seven decades later, with Abigail Adams's admonition to her husband unheeded, American women of the 1830s and 1840s would have to struggle for, declare, and write their own Declaration of Independence.

Abigail's letters spoke, as well, to Louisa. They articulated many of her own feelings about equality, about the laws men wrote to govern women, and the sense of unfairness and outrage and rebellion that Louisa felt in 1837. Abigail's letters were the stimulus for Louisa's understanding of herself and the plight of women. Louisa thought that her mother-in-law's letters must be printed, "allowed to shine," because they would attract and stir the "hearts of many a timid female" too reluctant to find her own words. She was certain that Abigail could act as surrogate, articulating for these women and convincing men of women's own "clear, full and vigorous" minds.

But the moment was gone when, as Abigail Adams had wished, women might have achieved equality with men in a single document. By 1837, Louisa Adams knew, the goal would come — if it ever did — in small steps: with the realization of their servitude, the declaration of their demands, the pieces of social, economic, and political power gained slowly and painfully. Opposing them now were not only men, but also the majority of American women, who, like Mary Hellen Adams and Abby Brooks Adams, felt content in their subservient status. The door, which had stood so widely open, was now bolted shut: A few women had only begun searching for the key. Abigail Adams's letters, Louisa said, were "treasures," documents of a lost opportunity, and guideposts to the awakening.

7

THE ABOLITIONIST WHIRLIGIG swirled around Louisa Adams, and touched her life directly and intimately. She may have been too old to shape these events herself, but she was too sensitive not to be changed by them. Like other women, Louisa was searching for her role.

In May 1837, two weeks after the Anti-Slavery Convention

of American Women, two sisters, Angelina and Sarah Grimké, set out on a nine-month speaking tour of New England, sponsored by the Female Anti-Slavery Society. The sisters were daughters of a South Carolina slaveowner, and could recite the horrors of slavery from first-hand observation. In the next nine months, by February 1838, the Grimké sisters would speak in the cause of anti-slavery before more than forty thousand men and women in sixty-seven towns. Their presence would cause a furor: Few women ever spoke in public, and never about such radical ideas. The Grimkés addressed audiences integrated not only with men and women together, but also with free blacks. Moreover, they demanded, along with the freedom of the slaves, the "simple equality" of the sexes, the freedom and rights of women.

As John Quincy Adams set forth that spring on his annual migration to the Old House, the Grimké sisters also left New York City to stir the New England abolitionists, and their opponents. The Adamses and Grimkés would soon meet and form a mutually beneficial bond. Angelina and later her husband, Theodore Weld, would draw close to John Quincy; Sarah Grimké would correspond with Louisa Adams, and together they would develop and share ideas about women's rights that would open the door to Louisa's freedom. Louisa and Sarah would discover in their Protestant religion the roots of equality, and Sarah would articulate the feelings of American women like Louisa Adams when she said: "I ask no favor for my sex. I surrender not our claim to equality. All I ask our brethren is that they will take their heels from our necks and permit us to stand upright on that ground which God designed us to occupy."

Angelina and Sarah Grimké were the first female abolitionist agents in the United States. They faced widespread hostility and censure. The young abolitionist movement was embattled everywhere. Rioters in 1834 had attacked abolitionists and blacks in New York and Philadelphia. Abolitionist men who spoke in public had been heckled, stoned, beaten, tarred and feathered. The press distorted abolitionist views, or lied about them — hence the need for abolitionist newspapers — and encouraged hecklers, who interrupted almost every meeting with catcalls, or threw eggs, vegetables, rocks and bricks. But the abolitionists believed that they were doing God's work, and met violence with their own nonviolent resistance.

The Grimkés spoke in small parlor meetings, and in huge public gatherings of the Boston Female Anti-Slavery Society in Washington Hall, where Angelina addressed more than four hundred women. Sarah and Angelina spoke before the first anti-slavery meeting ever held in Brookline, and at crowded gatherings in Ipswich, Essex, and Byfield. In Amesbury, Angelina — called "Devilina" by her enemies — debated two male dissenters, the first debate ever held in public between a male and a female platform speaker.

The Grimkés soon had New England in an uproar. Here was a direct confrontation between the Quakerism of Philadelphia — to which the sisters had converted — and the Puritans of Boston. The Congregationalists had already refused to read notices of abolitionist meetings from their pulpits, and on July 28, 1837, with the Grimké tour whirling about the state, the Rev. Nehemiah Adams — whose friendliness to Southern viewpoints earned him the sobriquet "Southside Adams" to distinguish him from JQA — issued a pastoral letter to the Congregational Churches. Among other things, the Rev. Adams directed the churches not to allow "strangers speaking on subjects the ministers do not agree with" to enter their sanctuaries, and warned against dangers to the "female character" of the good church ladies from other women who "intinerate" as "public lecturers and teachers."

And what were these dangers to the good women of Massachusetts? Angelina, small and delicate in her simple Quaker dress, spoke out: "We have given great offense on account of our womanhood, which seems to be as objectionable as our abolitionism. The whole land seems aroused to discussion on the province of women, and I am glad of it. We are willing to bear the brunt of the storm, if we can only be the means of making a break in that wall of public opinion which lies right in the way of woman's right, true dignity, honor and usefulness." Sarah, in speeches and writing, attacked the Biblical argument (as Louisa did) that woman's inferiority was God-given, and claimed that woman was created by God as man's companion, in all respects his equal. She decried the marriage-centered education given to women, demanded equal pay for equal work, and drew the parallel between women and slaves. Sarah urged women to abandon all frivolity, love of fashion, the false protection of chivalry, and instead become conscious of their own dignity and worth as people. The equality would be total: "Whatsoever it is morally right for a man to do," Sarah argued, "it is morally right for a woman to do."

The pastoral letter, and Sarah's and Angelina's rousing speeches, spurred the tour. Some women walked six to eight miles to hear the sisters. In July, fifteen hundred women crowded into the Lowell City Hall, and several hundred more had to be turned away. At Brockton, Brookline, Charlestown, and Cambridgeport overflow crowds greeted them. In Bolton, even when notices of their meetings were torn down, three hundred people heard them speak, and in Worcester a thousand came to listen while hundreds more men and women stood outside, some on ladders or on wagons looking in the windows. In Woonsocket Falls, as Sarah was speaking, the beams holding the gallery cracked, and a carpenter warned the women sitting there that the building was dangerously unsound and might collapse. But when the organizers asked for volunteers to leave, not a woman stirred, and they stayed until Sarah had finished her speech.

At meeting after meeting, the Grimkés spoke freely, articulating ideas that had been taking shape in their writing or lectures, or during the tour. Women must begin making changes themselves. They must cast off their restraint, their embarrassment in the company of men. They must look to themselves for solutions to their own problems. They must read, pray, speak, act to overthrow slavery. Men might tell women that they should not concern themselves with political issues. But women must remember, Angelina said, that "the denial of our duty to act in this case is a denial of our right to act; and if we have no right to act, then may *we* well be termed 'the white slaves of the North,' for like our brethren in bonds, we must seal our lips in silence and despair." Sarah and Angelina urged white women to reach out to black women slaves. "They are our countrywomen

— *they are our sisters;* and to us as women, they have a right to look for sympathy with their sorrows, and effort and prayer for their rescue."

On a warm and promising June day, as their campaign surged forward in Massachusetts, Angelina and Sarah Grimké, escorted by William Lloyd Garrison, rode a carriage from Boston to Quincy to visit John Quincy Adams. They and other abolitionists had been pleased with Adams's vigorous defense of the right to petition, and his persistence in opposing the Gag Rule, but they (and other abolitionists) were equally displeased with Adams's refusal to embrace their position without reservation. In private, more and more, John Quincy associated with the anti-slavery proponents: William Ellery Channing, who considered slavery a great moral evil; William Slade of Vermont, and abolitionists John Greenleaf Whittier, Joshua Leavitt, James and Lucretia Mott. Adams even called himself "a fellow sufferer in the same holy cause," and accepted their praise for his defense of fundamental American freedoms. But he continued to oppose abolition of slavery in the District of Columbia as impractical, and the abolitionists remained ambivalent about the courage of this old man. The American Anti-Slavery Society had adopted a resolution thanking Adams for defending "so wisely and so well" the right of women to be heard by Congress, but then qualified the praise with a scold for opposing abolition in the District and thereby not sustaining "the cause of Freedom and of God." It was this troublesome dichotomy that the Grimké sisters and Garrison rode out to Quincy to discuss. But the dichotomy — support for the rights of men and women to petition, but opposition to freedom of slave men and women near his Washington home — told much about Adams's position.

Adams greeted the Grimkés and Garrison warmly as their carriage pulled up before the Old House, and showed them into the parlor; Louisa was still in Washington, temporarily unable to travel when the banks suspended all specie payment during the Panic of 1837. The Grimkés, Garrison, and Adams conversed in firm and gentle tones, and their discussion centered on John Quincy's unwillingness to speak publicly in support of abolition of slavery in the District or the abolition movement. His reasons, noted in his diary, were that his principles and personality made "it necessary for me to be more circumspect in my conduct than belongs to my nature." Garrison couldn't understand this equivocating. Either Adams was for abolition, or against it. Angelina grew disgusted, and said that Adams had "no idea of the power of moral right, the supremacy of the laws of God over those of men." John Quincy knew well the laws of God. It was the vagaries of men that troubled him. The discussion soon stalemated, and Sarah later wrote that they "came away sick at heart of political morality." How could this man who so resolutely defended the right to petition oppose abolition in the District because it wasn't practical? Angelina got mad. Bluntly, she asked John Quincy "whether women could do anything in the abolition of slavery." Adams never hesitated, and replied enigmatically: "If it is abolished, *they* must do it." The Grimkés and Garrison departed unhappy with Adams's stubbornness. Sarah wrote the next day, thanking him for his efforts and concern for the rights of women, but regretting his continued opposition to abolishing slavery in Washington. That posture, Sarah thought, was "a surrender of moral principle to political expediency."

The Grimkés' tour of New England was more measurably successful. Their appearances stimulated the formation of women's anti-slavery societies in West Amesbury, Holliston, Andover, West Newberry, and Brookline, and at six meetings in Boston some 154 women enlisted. What had started as a series of lectures ended as a crusade. The Grimkés won the right for respectable women to speak in public. They challenged men to reconsider their attitudes toward women. They even prompted a public meeting in the Boston Lyceum in January 1838, where four men debated the question "Would the condition of women and society be improved by placing the two sexes on an equality in respect to civil rights and duties?" The conclusion was no, of course, but the debate was heated and, most important, the question raised in public.

The climax of the Grimké crusade came on February 21, 1838, when Angelina spoke before the Massachusetts State Legislature on behalf of abolition. She and Sarah, who was ill and couldn't speak, marched through a jeering mob of men to the

State House in Boston behind a phalanx of anti-slavery women. Safely inside the full hall, Angelina laid down the themes then arousing abolitionist women:

> I stand before you as a citizen, on behalf of the 20,000 women of Massachusetts whose names are enrolled on petitions which have been submitted to the Legislature. . . . These petitions relate to the great and solemn subject of slavery. . . . And because it is a political subject, it has often tauntingly been said, that women had nothing to do with it. Are we aliens because we are women? Are we bereft of citizenship because we are mothers, wives and daughters of a mighty people? Have women *no* country — *no* interests staked in public weal — no liabilities in common peril — no partnership in a nation's guilt and shame? . . . I hold, Mr. Chairman, that American women have to do with this subject, not only because it is moral and religious, but because it is *political*, inasmuch as we are citizens of this republic and as such our honor, happiness, and well-being are bound up in its politics, government and laws.

In daring and startling words, Angelina said that women's influence now came only as courtesans and mistresses. "This domination of women must be resigned — the sooner the better; in that age which is approaching she should be something more — she should be a citizen."

For the first time in America's history, a woman stood in a legislative hall and argued for the rights of women. As Sarah listened to her sister from the unprecedented vantage point of the Speaker's chair, she looked out across the legislature and thought: "We Abolition Women are turning the world upside down."

8

LOUISA ADAMS closely followed the Grimkés' tour, read
their books and pamphlets, and found connections
among her own thinking, Abigail's writings, and Sarah Grimké's
speeches on women's equality. Louisa was reading widely, writing, searching. Her attitudes about slavery began to change as the
questioning and focus became more humanized. By 1837, Louisa
thought that her feelings were more like those of her father and
mother, who had been shocked by seeing slaves and slave-trading
in Washington. Louisa now felt a "dislike of a system, to give
it no harsher name, harassing, distressing and degrading to the
finer feelings of the heart."

Perhaps more than any other one thing — although these
events cannot be separated in their impact on her — Louisa's
reading first widened her perception. After finishing the *Report
on Slavery*, she wrote Charles that "It is a powerful composition;
strong in its language, powerful in religious exhortation, and
incontrovertible in its religious argument. The doctrine is in-
trinsically sound. It is lofty! It is strictly just!" By 1838, Louisa
was regularly reading the Grimkés' writings, the radical *Liberator*, and other publications, and concluded: "Of Slavery I
have a most decided horror: therefore I have no prejudice in
favor of Slaveholders." But, she went on, "We ought to reflect
on their situation; on the efforts of education; and of habit; on
the nature of their property; and also on the difficulties of Climate, ere an unfortunate, uneducated, unprepared race, untaught
of *right* or *wrong*, and whose worst passions have probably been
kept in a state of excitement, should be let loose upon the world
without means to provide for themselves or their families and
without the knowledge of the religion which teaches and pre-
scribes our moral duties."

Horrified by slavery, but arguing for gradual emancipation,
Louisa wrote Charles an account of a newspaper article that

disturbed her. The incident and her reaction demonstrate Louisa's ambivalence between what she knew was right and what society told her was right. A slave family — father, mother, and three children — had been divided and sold, with the mother and children taken across the Potomac to Alexandria, and placed in a one-room shack before being separated and shipped to new owners. There, the desperate mother, to keep her children from being taken from her, strangled one to death and was strangling the second when the children's screams brought men running to the building. The story aroused strong feelings in Washington, and townspeople raised money to purchase them all, and free them; the Adamses contributed fifty dollars. Soon after the macabre incident, the freed woman came to Louisa to thank her. Louisa expected the black woman to be wearing mourning clothes for the death of her child, and when she appeared in a bright dress and a bonnet with yellow ribbons, Louisa Adams refused to see her, and had her sent away. As upset as Louisa was by the mother's preference of death over separation from her children — a theme, not incidentally, that stirred a response deep within Louisa herself — her code of proper etiquette was stronger. Louisa was truly horrified by slavery and this incident, but she could not completely overcome her social conditioning.

The incident illustrated Louisa's entrapment between her growing awareness of slavery's horror and her persistent, but changing, social attitudes. Louisa was a victim of her years, her social status, and her upbringing. She was offended, as with the black woman, by improper dress, or by bold women who allowed ankles to show during vigorous dances, or by young women who asked men to dance. Traveling to Quincy on the steamboat, Louisa observed younger women helping themselves to brandy and water in the salon, and a woman who, after dining "amply" upon the steamboat fare, "very coolly walked into the Ladies Cabin and called for a Bottle of Cider which she as coolly drank and paid for." Louisa found such freedoms unsettling, but to her credit she didn't reject them. She found some women's "easy assurance" radical, but like masculine intelligence in other women, also attractive. Louisa recognized that there was a "new world . . . rising around me."

But as conservative as Louisa Adams was in her social attitudes, she was radical in her politics. Most American women were wary of the female abolitionists; much of the opposition to women's rights came from women, who feared a loss of special status in equality. These women agreed with Catherine Beecher, who rapped the female abolitionists for shaking "this nation like an earthquake," and told them that "Heaven has appointed to the one sex the superior, to the other the subordinate station." Louisa, however, admired educated women and their strength. She agreed with Angelina Grimké that women had to overcome the "silly ineptitudes" employed by man "ever since he laid down the whip as a means to make woman his subject. He respects her body but the war he has waged against her mind, her heart and her soul has been no less destructive to her as a moral being."

Louisa made the distinction between social and political freedom. This woman, who read widely and spoke her mind on politics, who knew some of the greatest politicians of this period, who had waged a political campaign, was now involved every day with abolitionists and their petitions, and the basic issues they represented. "The abolitionist excitement was tremendous," Louisa wrote Charles after a debate in the House. "The platoons came so swift and thick while I was present, instead of dampening my spirit they seemed to produce a contrary effect, and inspired a degree of ardor to my hotspur head, full equal in force and energy to their own." It was "lucky," Louisa said, that she had no chance to jump to her feet and speak, for she would have overpowered even the Southerners in the House with her thundering "for the *privilege of speech*, the ne plus Ultra of womans rights." Drawn in, Louisa closely followed the accounts of the Grimkés' tour. She bought their pamphlets, and wrote Charles that she was "delighted" with Sarah Grimké's *Letters On the Equality of the Sexes and the Condition of Women*, "but I suppose these letters will not suit your Lordly Sex." Louisa lectured her son on equality and women's rights. "Where I see such Women as your Grandmother go through years of exertion, of suffering, and of privation," she wrote, "with all the activity, judgment, skill and fortitude, which any man could display; *I cannot believe that there is any inferiority in the Sexes*, as far as mind and intellect are concerned, and man is aware of the fact

[373]

— for he knows that all the solid and great virtues are exacted from those they choose to deem the weakest [italics added]."

Louisa's entire life now focused on the issues of slavery and women's rights. Her reading, thinking, letters, religious study, and her work at home reading, recording, and filing petitions for her husband all touched these issues. Not surprisingly, on January 11, 1838, Louisa wrote Sarah Grimké, the sister who was most outspoken about the rights of women and equality. Louisa knew, from her reading, that many of the things Sarah Grimké was saying in public Louisa was considering in private. "My dear Madame," Louisa began, "Although I have not the happiness of a personal acquaintance with you, the pleasure which I derive from the perusal of your two *Letters on the Province of Women*, induces me to address you." Louisa wished to share an idea that, if elucidated by a mind like Sarah's, "would yield at least an argument in our favour."

Louisa set forth her idea of women's rights based on her reading of the Bible: that God created woman and man together, and when he "breathed the breath of life into the nostrils of the creatures of his own hand," he did so equally. "We no where see any evidence of inferiority in the female," she told Sarah Grimké, and cited Biblical references in support. "Man may submit woman for his own purposes," Louisa continued. "He cannot *degrade* her in the sight of *God*, so long as she acts up to those great *duties* which her Nature and her Constitution enforce, and which enjoins the highest virtues that combine society and the relations of daughter, Wife and Mother: from whence originate all the great characteristics which ennoble man from the Cradle to the tomb."

Sarah sent Louisa a book, and wrote from Brookline, where she and Angelina were speaking on their tour. In Quaker fashion, she addressed Louisa as "Dear Sister," and wrote in a neat, small hand with strong, determined letters. She thanked Louisa for her "valuable & interesting" letter, and thought her ideas on the creation of Adam and Eve "one of the strongest arguments in favor of the equality of the sexes which has yet been suggested." Sarah agreed on every point, and Louisa must have read her letter with increasing excitement. Sarah wrote: "Our first parents I believe were created equal in every respect, if I may so speak, they were the halves which constituted a perfect whole." She believed, as Louisa did, that they were endowed with the same physical beauty, mental and spiritual powers; that what was morally right for man, was morally right for woman. They even agreed that society, by treating woman as inferior and confining them, was causing much of women's sicknesses. "I have no object to a convenient division of labor between the sexes," Sarah wrote, "but I believe that the sedentary occupations of a large number of women in civilized countries is unnatural & that from this cause arises much of the mental imbecility."

Although they never met, Sarah Grimké had a profound effect upon Louisa Adams. During their correspondence she sent Louisa materials about slavery, including the booklet *Emancipation in the West Indies*, by James A. Thome and Horace Kimball, and asked Louisa to read it "prayerfully & attentively," for the end of slavery was certain, she said; "Its death warrant is signed." Sarah also asked Louisa her opinion about a pamphlet of her recent writings; "I am in search of Truth," she wrote, "I think I love no opinions because they are mine." Louisa protested that her education was inadequate to comprehend all that Sarah taught, and she poured out her heart. Her female education, Louisa wrote, made her feel inferior to her husband and other men. Her mind had been wasted with "amusement in the lighter branches of literature, rather than in those solid works which tend to mend the heart, and strengthen and improve the mind." Sarah replied sympathetically: "How often we thus find woman suffering all her life from the defects of that system of education which has been adopted & which can hardly fail to nurture in us a desire for trifling pursuits — we have aimed to be the idol of man's worship rather than the companion of his heart, the sharer & aider of his intellectual pursuits."

Sarah gently led Louisa along a path. Step by step, she was elevating her vision, encouraging her examination of her fears and prejudices. Sarah and Angelina were working on *American Slavery as It Is*, an anti-slavery pamphlet published in 1839,* and

---

* *American Slavery As It Is: Testimony of a Thousand Witnesses*, a devastating indictment of Southern slavery, sold more copies than any other anti-slavery pamphlet ever written—a hundred thousand in 1839 alone.

Sarah asked Louisa to do some work on it. She wanted Louisa to find historical evidence "if there is any" of the "danger of Immediate Emancipation." Sarah's request directed Louisa to ask others, including her husband, about slavery, and most important, to examine the institution and her own fears of it. Sarah's request also guided Louisa toward understanding her own disgust, voiced in one letter, over the "profligacy of the free negroes." Sarah asked Louisa whether her opinion was formed on "actual & extensive knowledge or whether it is the result of hearsay evidence." Louisa did her homework, and sent Sarah replies containing a detailed report upon the facts of emancipation elsewhere in the world, and sketchy observations of freed slaves in Washington. Sarah urged Louisa to study slavery and emancipation in the Bible, where she would find "indignation & wrath against the oppressor & the imperative command to cease from wickedness." If slavery is a crime against God and man, Sarah reasoned, what other remedy could there be but "immediately to cease the commission of the crime."

Sarah educated not only by letter, but also by example. Louisa followed her new friend in newspaper accounts, which she carefully saved, and which are now part of the Adams Papers. Sarah wrote from Massachusetts, and from Philadelphia, where she attended Angelina's wedding to Theodore Weld, the Women's Convention, and The Free Produce Convention. Louisa clearly realized that she was corresponding with a woman on the front line of an exciting, and dangerous, movement. Events in Philadelphia underscored that. After the Welds' wedding on May 14, 1838, the Anti-Slavery Convention of Women opened in Pennsylvania Hall. This hall was the largest of its kind in Philadelphia, and symbolized the right to free speech, and defiance of those who intimidated abolitionists. Philadelphia reformers built the hall for forty thousand dollars, and it contained stores and committee rooms on the first floor, a large hall and gallery on the second and third floors. For its dedication ceremonies on May 14, brave and cheering greetings were read from a handful of prominent Americans, including John Quincy Adams.

The hall was booked during its first week of use for the Women's Convention and reform meetings. But threatening posters appeared around Philadelphia, and rumors spread that the abolitionists were promoting "amalgamation" of the races. By Wednesday, with the hall filled with three thousand men and women, an angry mob broke down the front doors, then shattered the windows with bricks as Angelina Grimké spoke. When the women met the next morning, the mob returned. Appeals to the mayor of Philadelphia and the sheriff for protection brought replies that the abolitionists should prevent blacks from attending the evening meeting. The women rejected the request, and instead ended their daytime meetings by marching arm-in-arm with black women, a tactic used during the Boston riot of 1835, and passed safely through the mob despite curses and stones, which injured one of them. That evening the mob returned again; they set fire to the hall, which was fortunately empty, and then battled police sent to disband them. When the fire department arrived, its men sprayed water on neighboring rooftops, but made no attempt to save Pennsylvania Hall. Before midnight, the entire building, the abolitionists' shelter, had burned to the ground, amid cheers. But riot and fire did not stop anti-slavery women: Friday morning they marched together, arm-in-arm, to a nearby schoolroom and continued their convention.

These attacks upon the abolitionists renewed Louisa's fears for her husband's safety. John Quincy sometimes walked home alone at night from the House, and he constantly received threatening letters: One named the hour and day he would be murdered, another included a drawing of him with a bullet in his head. The burning of Pennsylvania Hall fed Louisa's fears; Sarah tried to calm her, and take her farther along the path. "Dear Sister," she wrote after the fire, "Philad. is deeply imbued with the spirit of slavery, her interests are interwoven with the South, she has locked hands with the oppressor, she is rioting in the blood-bought luxurious [sic] of slavery." When this stronghold of oppression was attacked, Sarah said, Satan's helpers came forward. "The burning of Pennsylvania Hall only proves," she wrote, "that the spirit of slavery reigns triumphant in a nominally free city & calls for greater efforts on the part of the friends of liberty to resist its encroachments." Sarah asked Louisa to study these events more closely. "I cannot help thinking that more reflection will induce thee to alter thy opinion & to perceive that *nothing* threatens our country with 'domestic convulsion' but the continuence of slavery. . . . Where can the record be found of a nation suffering loss by giving freedom to its slaves."

Sarah pushed Louisa onward, challenging her to see the correctness of immediate emancipation, and the prejudices of her own perceptions. But most important, Sarah led Louisa to make the connection between slavery and women's rights. You live in Washington, she wrote, where slaves are jailed and auctioned. "In view of the unnumbered wrongs inflicted on a million of our country-women by the ruthless tyrants of the South," Sarah asked, have you visited any black slave women in jail? Have you, Sarah prodded, "listened to the tale of sorrow which many a female slave can tell of the wild passions of unbridled masters?" Have you

> cried with the widow torn from her husband, the mother sold from her children, the thousands of slavery's victims who pass through Washington & moisten the soil with their blood & their tears. . . . Can we feel the wrongs of women & not deplore a system which degrades her to the level of a beast. Can we feel as we should feel for these unhappy women & not solemnly query in the presence of our God: Lord, what will thou have me to do in the great work of rooting out slavery from our land.

Sarah's challenge, we now know, reached deep inside Louisa Adams. From this moment until her death, she sought to answer it, somehow, in her own way. Was she, as one of "the white slaves of the North," any different from the black female slaves of the South? Sarah's request for witness, and her prayer to God for guidance, became the substances that bonded all of Louisa's own searchings and questionings. But it was one thing to raise the hypothetical issue of male and female equality, which Louisa was doing, and quite another to stride down to the Washington jail, as Sarah wished. Louisa, sixty-three years old and a woman of the upper class, was not going to march into the filth of the slave pens to talk and weep with her black sisters. "I have informed Miss Grimké," Louisa wrote Charles, "that I am not of her way of thinking on the subject, but we are quite correspondent." Sarah Grimké's challenge would have to root and sprout slowly, like a spring bulb that survives beneath the frozen winter soil, and blossom in Louisa's own special way and time.

On her own, Louisa was defining herself as a woman. She was moving, now with Sarah's help, toward an answer to that basic, Adams-like question: What is my purpose in life? Reminders of this question, and Sarah's challenge, were everywhere: in the petitions, in the chained slaves struggling through Washington, even on stationery popular among women abolitionists, which reached Louisa and remains in her papers today. Printed on the stationery was the figure of a black woman, on her knees, her wrists in manacles with heavy chains hanging from them, her hands clasped pleadingly above her chest, her face lifted heavenward. The figure was encased in an oval, and around the upper half were the haunting words: "Am I not a woman and a sister?"

9

WHILE LOUISA AND SARAH continued their correspondence, John Quincy relentlessly pursued the fundamental right of petition, and grew to understand, as Louisa did, the broader issue of equality. There was something lovable and brave in this old man with the wheezing voice, teary eye, and acid tongue, and while the abolitionists remained convinced that Adams did not go far enough in his commitment to freedom, American women of a wider political spectrum embraced the old man and cheered his defiance. On August 2, 1838, for example, Adams addressed a gathering of perhaps five hundred women in Tranquility Grove, in Hingham, Massachusetts. He made clear his awakening to the issue of women's rights: He called these women of Hingham his constituents, "for I consider the

Ladies of this Congressional district as much my constituents as their relatives by whose votes I was elected." Women, it was said, have no political rights, Adams told them, and their petitions are treated by Congress as if they had no rights at all, as if women did not exist. "But all history refutes this position," Adams said, echoing Angelina and Sarah Grimké. "You have political rights." He had spent fifteen days speaking before Congress, and would continue to speak, on "the great question of human rights — the right of petition — the right of women to be heard by the government." John Quincy's speech was short, but daring. By calling these women his constituents, and supporting their political rights, he was embracing, gently, the themes of Angelina's speech to the Massachusetts Legislature, and the correspondence between Sarah and Louisa.

No woman missed the nuance of Adams's speech, or his public position. Just before his brief address in the grove, Adams received a letter of thanks from a woman in Hingham for his "just, generous and Christian defence of the character and claims of my sex." Lydia Maria Child sent John Quincy a short address she wrote for the Anti-Slavery Convention in Philadelphia, and added: "I am not willing to die without saying how deeply, how sincerely, how fervently I thank you for the magnanimous course you have pursued in Congress. . . . The full and deep meaning of the present time is rarely understood by men." Adams himself clearly defined his position when he wrote in September of his continuing struggle to defend "the rights and honour of my countrywomen." These were the same rights and honor Louisa, and Abigail, had long championed.

As the petitions came "flocking in faster than ever" to their home, Louisa (and Mary) continued to read, record, and file them for John Quincy's presentation. The tiring work made them all ill and cranky. Louisa's face swelled and the inflammation was so great that she feared it might break the skin. John Quincy rose at three every morning, sorted petitions until eight, breakfasted on boiled milk and stewed peaches, and went to the House for twelve to sixteen hours. The name of no other member of the House appears more frequently in the list of proceedings, yet getting himself to his desk and sustaining the battle took dedication, courage, and obstinancy. Nothing went well or easily. During these crucial years, John Quincy Adams was seventy to seventy-five years old; "I am with all parties the *venerable* gentleman from Massachusetts," he said. "I now and then sport a Resolution which makes them bristle up." How he and Louisa sustained their spirits is a lesson in courage.

In the middle of the debates on slavery and petitions, with threats from all sides, and few supporters, the Adamses' finances collapsed.* By 1839, Louisa and John Quincy had borrowed five thousand dollars from Antoine Guista, and the notes (with interest) were overdue. Adams desperately wrote Charles begging him to sell some property and send three thousand dollars. Once, returning to Washington from Quincy, Adams was so short of cash that he had to borrow ten dollars from his niece Elizabeth Adams to get home. Inflation also eroded their small income. Food and clothing costs rose precipitously in the late 1830s, and during the battles in the House, John Quincy was dunned by creditors for overdue bills for coal, firewood, stair carpeting, servants' wages, even the pew rental in St. John's Church. To help cut back, he walked to Congress throughout the winter of 1839. "The terrible idea of the quarter of a dollar for a hack," Louisa said, "induces him to risk his bones, and no persuasion can induce him to spare himself." Louisa tried to persuade him to retire, but John Quincy gloried in the agitation he caused in the House, and the public acclaim. His vitality was intertwined with his work; his strength, his ego, were in his politics. To remove him would be to cut him from his source of life. Even in 1840, when Adams tripped on some newly laid matting on the House floor and dislocated his shoulder, he disobeyed doctor's orders and returned to his desk the next morning, feeble and shaking but determined. Louisa found it "utterly impossible to keep him quiet," and he continued climbing chairs and hauling down heavy books and papers for his speeches. Adams understood his need to stay in the struggle: "More than sixty years of incessant active intercourse with the world has made political movement to me as much a necessary of life as atmospheric air,"

---

* Even the kitchen and porch of their Washington home came clattering down, victim of rotten beams and thunderstorms.

he wrote in his diary. "This is the weakness of my nature, which I have intellect enough to perceive, but not energy to control. And thus while a remnant of physical power is left to me to write and speak, the world will retire from me before I shall retire from the world."

Adams, so beaten just thirteen years ago, now thrived. In 1841, he even let the abolitionists convince him to join in their defense of thirty-nine slaves who had revolted at sea on the *Amistad*. When their case reached the U.S. Supreme Court, Adams was seventy-four, and making his final appearance as a lawyer. He argued for two days before the Court: because the men had been found in a state of freedom (after their revolt), they should be set free and not returned to their captors. If they were not set free, Adams said, could any human being of this nation be certain of the blessing of freedom? When the Court ruled in Adams's favor, he was filled with unfettered joy, and wrote to his abolitionist friends: "The captives are free! 'Not unto us! Not unto us!' but thanks, thanks, in the name of humanity and justice to *you*." Broke as he was, Adams never submitted a bill to the abolitionists for his legal work.*

Adams soon needed the abolitionists to help him. In 1842, in a bitter fight on the House floor, the slaveowners and sympathizers sought to censure and expel Adams from Congress. Not content with trying to silence the old man, House members now wished to be rid of him entirely. The "Days of Storms and Earthquakes," as Louisa described them, began on New Year's Day, 1842. The Adamses' F Street house was filled with more than five hundred people, and the throng was so thick that Louisa ordered the front doors closed until the crowd thinned. Several abolitionists mingled in, wary of the opposition Congressmen and keeping to themselves. They were in Washington as a lobbying force to bind together a small band of Congressmen willing to oppose slavery. This little nettle of zealot Whigs** resolved to

---

* For an excellent and detailed account of the *Amistad* case, see Samuel Flagg Bemis, *John Quincy Adams and the Union*. New York: Knopf, 1956, pp. 384–415.

** Among these Congressmen were Joshua R. Giddings of Ohio, a man close to John Quincy Adams and beloved by him; William Slade

attack the Gag Rule with petitions, resolutions, and speeches. To solidify their work, the abolitionists had brought in Theodore Weld, Angelina Grimké's husband, for research and ghostwriting. The Whig insurgents arranged for Weld's access to the Library of Congress, and provided room, stationery, and incidentals.

Weld had arrived December 30, and his desk in the alcove of the Library of Congress was already piled high with books and newspapers, to which he added materials put together by Angelina and Sarah. Weld moved into comfortable chambers at Mrs. Spriggs' boardinghouse, directly in front of the Capitol. "I have a pleasant room on the second floor," he wrote Angelina, "With a good bed, plenty of covering, a bureau, table, chairs, closets, and cloathes press, a good fire place, and plenty of dry wood to burn in it." Mrs. Spriggs' was perfect for all of Weld's needs. The Library of Congress was a block in one direction, the Capitol less than that in the other, and the railing of Capitol Park fifty feet from the front door. Every morning before breakfast, Weld, a firm believer in exercise, entered the park, where he took deep breaths, flapped his arms, and for more than an hour ran and hopped and jumped along the crisscrossing gravel paths. When he returned, Mrs. Spriggs set before him a deep bowl of milk, into which he crumbled Graham bread. Weld was a Grahamite, a practice he had started after Angelina and Sarah had attended a course of lectures in Boston by Sylvester Graham. The Grimké sisters were convinced that Graham's largely vegetarian diet was the perfect way to health, and also freed women from the toils of the kitchen. So, Theodore Weld ate breakfasts of raw apples, cold water, and Graham bread crumbled in milk; lunches of stewed beans; dinners of pears, rice, and molasses. He and Angelina and Sarah never used tea, coffee, sugar, or spices because of their boycott of slave-grown produce, and they eschewed butter, fish, and meat from Graham principles. Almonds, figs, raisins complemented Weld's meals, or pies without shortening, potatoes, cornbread with fresh fruit. In a

---

of Vermont; Seth M. Gates of New York; and Sherlock J. Andrews of Ohio. Giddings, Gates, and Andrews had another thing in common: They had been personally converted to abolition by Theodore Weld.

time of over-eating and over-drinking, when the better part of a woman's life was spent cooking and serving huge meals, Weld's messmates at Mrs. Spriggs' thought him strange to scorn juicy roasts, rich gravies, thick butter and cream, aromatic teas and coffee. But Weld stuck to his vegetarian habits, crumbling his Graham bread into his bowl to make mush, content in the knowledge that he supported a diet that simplified housekeeping, improved nutrition, and furthered the cause of Sylvester Graham, whose flour, bread, and crackers survive to this day. And for abolitionists on a low budget, Graham's diet had another advantage: It was cheap.

Appreciative of life's simplicities, Weld approved of the Adamses' house and style that New Year's Day, especially compared to the "pomp and tinsel" of the White House, which he had just left. At the Adamses', Weld "found him and his wife living in a plain style house," he wrote Angelina and Sarah, "plainly furnished, and themselves plainly dressed — the old gentleman very plainly." When he was introduced, John Quincy said, "Is this Mr. Theodore Weld? I know you well, Sir, by your writings." Adams took Weld by the hand, and led him across the room to meet Louisa. "In so doing," Weld wrote, "I was glad to hear him call her '*my dear*,' as I think you told me they lived unhappily together."

Weld was attracted to Adams. A week later, he returned for dinner. "It was a genuine abolition gathering," he wrote enthusiastically, "and the old patriarch talked with as much energy and zeal as a Methodist at a camp meeting. Remarkable man!" The Adamses were less smitten, and John Quincy, the devoted imbiber, dismissed his guests as "Rechabites who drink no wine." Louisa thought "the dinner was stupid beyond conception." She was the only woman present — Mary and Elizabeth stayed upstairs — "and the guests were all Teatollers and Mr. Weld . . . a grahamite. . . . The conversation was cold and uninteresting."

Weld's admiration, however was boundless. He watched John Quincy Adams on the floor of the House, where he launched an attack over shouts of "Order!" and "Silence him!" Adams spoke with a "voice like a trumpet, till slaveholding, slave trading, and slave breeding absolutely quailed and howled under his dissecting knife." Weld, from his seat in the gallery, cheered the old man while slaveholders tried to silence him with points of order "and, by every now and then screaming at the top of their voices: 'That is false.' 'I *demand* Mr. Speaker that you *put him down.*' 'I demand that you shut the mouth of that old harlequin.'" The scene below him was one of agitation and hatred, and Weld reported that Adams swung his verbal cleaver without mercy, and rejoiced to hear it thud "into the very bones" of the slave-holders' arguments. At least half a dozen slave-holding members left their seats to gather about Adams and glare at him, and the old man glowered back. When they interrupted him, John Quincy shouted, "I see where the shoe pinches, Mr. Speaker, it will pinch *more* yet," or, "I'll deal out to the gentlemen a diet that they'll find it hard to digest." Weld was amazed and impressed by the cantankerous old man.

But Whig leaders of the House had decided to get Adams; if they could crush him, no one would rise to challenge their power. In late January, Adams, as he always did, presented anti-slavery petitions, proceeding as far as he could until the Speaker applied the Gag Rule. But on January 25, Adams read a petition from forty-six citizens of Haverhill, Massachusetts, asking Congress to immediately adopt "measures peaceably to dissolve the Union of these United States." The petition sent the House members into waves of shouting and protest that lasted for several tumultuous minutes. Finally, Thomas Walker Gilmer of Virginia rose and submitted the following resolution: "Resolved, That in presenting to the consideration of this House a petition for the dissolution of the Union the member from Massachusetts has justly incurred the censure of this House." Here was their chance: Censure would rid them of Adams once and for all.

The Southerners rose to speak one after another, and the nastiest was Henry Wise. The galleries had filled with spectators, and many Senators also crowded the lobby and aisles. Wise played to them as well as the House members. Tall and lean, a Virginia aristocrat and slaveowner, Wise strutted with an excitable and high-strung manner, and orated in a flowing style that might sear marble. When Wise spoke, said one observer, he could "vomit fire" like a dragon. The Virginian started by denouncing Adams as a "white-haired hypocrite" whose policy was "not yet, not yet, wait a little longer, keep up the excitement, agitate-agitate, keep the slaves in this District like mice in a receiver to make experiments with, make a further experiment in religious zeal, try how foreign influence will work, hold on to the bone of contention, agitate-agitate." Wise went on, describing slavery as "friendly to equality. Break down slavery," he said, "and you would with the same blow destroy the great democratic principle of equality among men." Here, the Clerk noted laughter from "one portion of the House." Wise went on speaking for almost two hours, and closed with a vicious attack upon Adams. "That one should so have outlived his fame! . . . To think of the veneration, the honor, the reverence with which this person might have been loved and cherished." But Adams, Wise said, ranked with Benedict Arnold and Aaron Burr. "The gentleman is politically dead; dead as Burr — dead as Arnold."

Adams, of course, was very much alive, and barely able to control his temper against Wise's "filthy invective." House members continued insulting JQA, calling for his expulsion; the slaveholders thought they had Adams in their grasp, and held a meeting that evening to plan their strategy. Rep. Joshua Giddings of Ohio, a close Adams friend, tried to organize the Northern Whigs, but they preferred to let the old man twist in the wind. Joshua Leavitt and Theodore Weld formed a committee of two to offer what help they could, and when they called at Adams's home that night, he heard them with tears in his eyes. He had expected to fight alone. He directed Weld and Leavitt to check certain arguments, and to have books and documents supporting them on his desk in the morning.

So began John Quincy Adams's defense. Where Marshall and Wise and the others had taken the better part of three days to attack him, John Quincy would occupy, with interruptions, six days. As Louisa observed, his earnestness in the cause might "break his health, although it will never tame his spirit." That autumn, Adams had left Quincy for the opening session of Congress complaining of boils, pimples, a catarrhal cough. His head had felt puffy, he said, as though stung by bees. He obtained relief only by shifting his attention from the pain in one spot to another in his body. He ached, he groaned, but as the session got underway he felt better, and with the battle in full cry, Adams now seemed in perfect health. Weld was astonished, and had to work hard staying ahead of the old statesman's demands for documents, papers, books, research, and advice. Weld and Adams worked together on his defense, and Weld kept the old warrior supplied with facts, facts, facts. He spent long evenings at the F Street house, and the two men became intimate friends. Sometimes John Quincy stopped the feverish work to describe his boyhood or college years, which Weld would later retell to his grandchildren.

Adams turned his own defense into a defense of human freedom. In his speeches before the House there remains today the sharp, poignant feeling of John Quincy's drawing upon the stored strength of years of self-discipline, of early rising, fortitude, exercise, reading of Bible and Cicero; a sense of his drawing at last upon his intellectual and physical storehouses. This was the center of the struggle he had spent his life preparing for, and he was ready. Adams carefully laid out his reply, with Wise sometimes interrupting, by first detailing the violations of the Southerners: attempting to destroy the right of *habeas corpus*, trial by jury, freedom of the mails, of the press, of petition, of free speech itself. He accused Southerners of enslaving Northern black citizens. He reminded Wise, who had spoken of assassins, of his role in the Cilley-Graves duel that killed a member of the House. Through it all, Adams was interrupted by threats and questions of order, which only made him tougher. "The Old Nestor," Weld gloated, "has cast all their counsels headlong, turned all their guns against themselves, and smitten the whole host with dismay and discomfiture." Adams's stamina amazed Weld. He wrote Angelina:

> Last Friday, after he had been sitting in the house from 12 o'clock till 6, and for nearly half that time engaged in speaking with great energy against his ferocious assailants, I called at his house in the evening, and he came to meet me as fresh and elastic as a boy. I told him I was afraid he had tired himself out. "No, not at all," said he, "I am all ready for another heat." He then began and went through with the *main points*

which he designed to push in his speech the next day, and with as much rapidity and energy of utterance and gesture as though he had been addressing the house. I tried to stop him, telling him he would need all his strength for the next day, but it was all in vain. He went on for an hour, or very nearly that, in a voice loud enough to be heard by a large audience. Wonderful man!

Adams stood before the House for a week, and during the sparring and slugging found sleep difficult; no one dared tell him to slow down. "When they talk about his old age and venerableness and nearness to the grave," Ralph Waldo Emerson wrote about Adams, "he knows better. He is like one of those old cardinals, who, as quick as he is chosen Pope, throws away his crutches and his crookedness, and is as straight as a boy. He is an old roué, who cannot live on slops, but must have sulphuric acid in his tea." After the sixth day of speaking, while still in full tongue, Adams informed the House leaders that he would need at least another week to complete his arguments. But he offered to sit down if anyone made a motion to table the question of censure, never to be taken up again. John Minor Botts, a Virginia Whig, jumped to his feet and so moved, and his motion rapidly passed 106 to 93. Adams had won. But he was not finished with them yet. Before adjournment that same day, the old curmudgen presented two hundred petitions, and after they were tabled one by one under the Gag Rule, Adams went home in high spirits. He was scarcely able to crawl up to his chamber, but he did "with the sound of 'Io Triumphe' ringing in my ear."

"Well we have triumphed," Weld wrote Angelina, "the *north* for once triumphed." At first he was ecstatic, and thought the victory a major one marking slavery's downfall. But when the debates and noise settled, Weld saw the long, dark path ahead. "That slavery has *begun* to fall is plain," he wrote, "but that its fall will be resisted by those who cling to it, with energy and desperation and fury as only fiends can summon when they know their hour has come, the end will be slow. Woe to abolitionists if they dream that their work is well nigh done."

Both Weld and Adams knew that what appeared to be a slowly emerging victory was in truth the first seam in the Union.

John Quincy's goal of staving off the inevitable struggle was being achieved, but the debates over petitions and censure made all too clear the bitter thread running through the nation that within fifteen years would start pulling the fabric of these United States apart. Adams now turned his attention to overcoming the Gag Rule, to the annexation of Texas and war with Mexico. For the first time in his career, he also enjoyed the public acclaim he had found so elusive.

10

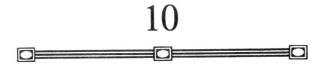

WHEN THE HOUSE debates grew dull, John Quincy Adams slipped out and sat for his portrait to various artists, proclaiming the work "hideous" or falling asleep, and he sat also for the new daguerreotype photographs at Plumbe's Gallery on Pennsylvania Avenue, or at Matthew Brady's. The severity of his expression had changed, replaced by a sadness, by watery eyes, a lined and puffy face, the whole countenance drooping and conveying the impression of a sliding toward death. This was a resigned, more gentle old man, his eyebrows arched in question as though always inquiring about his beloved Union. By his seventy-seventh year, still battling the Gag Rule, slavery, and United States policy toward Texas and Mexico, Adams basked in the love and awe of his grandchildren, and a public adulation unequaled at any other time in his life.

The compound in Quincy swarmed with Adams grandchildren. Every summer, Louisa traveled north with Mary and her daughters, and Looly and Fanny joined the growing number of children produced by Charles and Abby. Louisa preferred the role of indulgent grandmother, but found herself instead the compound's disciplinarian, while John Quincy, unlike his role as father, often seemed a soft-headed old grandpapa who loved getting letters from his grandchildren and replied with uncharacteristic gossip. The only dark cloud passed in 1839, when the Adamses' hearts were broken one more time: Fanny suddenly became ill with a painful inflammation of the bladder and bowels, a rapid pulse and high fever — perhaps appendicitis — and, just eight years old, died. The Adams house in Washington again grew "painfully gloomy," and Looly stayed out of school for the entire winter.

In Quincy, Charles had built a home on the hill above the Old House, and he and Abby and their large family spent summers there away from the heat of Boston. Charles was a somber man, without color or imagination. "He studied the classics and read *Clarissa Harlowe* to his young wife," said their son Charles 2d, "who evidently was bored to extinction." Charles and Abby opened the doors of their new home on the hill, and their kids tumbled into all kinds of mischief. The paths along the gentle slope to the Old House filled with grandchildren (some in soggy diapers whose downward momentum was barely controlled), who visited the grandfather they always called "the President" and the grandmother they addressed as "Madame."

"Summer was drunken," said Henry. He tagged along after Charles and John and Louisa, and they in turn were sometimes tailed by Mary and Brooks and even little Arthur. They swarmed over the farm, swam in the sea below the town, marched through the woods and forded streams, and watched the Plymouth stagecoaches raise roostertails along the dusty road connecting Quincy with Boston and the world beyond. Summer intoxicated them all. The best days flowed in with the August heat, when grandparents and father (and sometimes mother) took naps. Then these scions filled their hours in the hayfields around the old house listening to cicadas and arguing about how long it would be until the first frost, or stalking the President and Madame's cows. This game soon evolved to discovering a variety of good uses for the discs of cow manure that dotted the fields. These patties, left several days in the hot August sun, firmed into plate-size missiles whose use tested the collective ingenuity of these offspring of two U.S. Presidents. During slow

August afternoons, Henry, Charles, John, and Louisa 2d could be seen fanned out like scavengers searching for the perfectly dried cow patty. Fresh ones proved too flimsy, dried ones simply crumbled, but the patty that had baked beneath the August sun to the right moment — and not before or beyond — became, in the minds and hands of the Adams grandchildren, a thing of beautiful possibilities. Properly thrown, it would spin like a discus, to great admiration, before striking an object — a cow or younger brother — and bursting apart. Best of all, Louisa could be sent creeping into the old house — she could be quiet and was unlikely to be intercepted by a suspicious adult — to liberate a small portion of gunpowder from the President's supply. Then, the proper cow patty would be propped up with a stick, gunpowder packed underneath, a candle wick placed as a fuse, and, after everyone had sprinted a safe distance, ignited with a rewarding ka-BLOOOOOOM that sent grass, dirt, and cow dung across John Quincy Adams's fields.

John Quincy never complained, perhaps because he loved his grandchildren and, from the death of his own sons, had learned that it was no small thing when they loved him. He was the centrifugal force of the Old House. His grandchildren remember Adams sitting, forever writing in his study, or strolling his land, deep in thought. He tolerated no laxity in himself or his heirs. One day, Henry, who stood at the head of his class, started arguing with his mother against going to school. Abby insisted that the boy go; Henry stubbornly said he would not. Suddenly, the old President emerged from his study, determination in his eye, and without saying a word gently but firmly took Henry's hand. Silently, grandfather and grandson went out the front door of the Old House, down to the gate, on to the road. John Quincy walked Henry the mile to school, took him through the front door, to his desk, saw him in it, and turned and walked back home to his study. Not a word passed between them, and none was needed.

Henry especially loved the President's study, with its window seats where the youngsters sat and read while the old man wrote, or dozed. Henry hung about the library, handling John Quincy's cherished books hauled from his diplomatic and political posts, deranging the papers, pulling open and ransacking the drawers of the desk. Henry searched the old purses and pocketbooks for foreign coins, drew the sword cane, and snapped the traveling pistols. He burrowed into every corner, and even penetrated the old President's dressing closet "where a row of tumblers," Henry wrote, "inverted on the shelf, covered caterpillars which were supposed to become moths or butterflies, but never did."

Charles and Abby found their own children trying. Charles was a good and fair parent, but an uncontrolled hypochondriac, who every time one of his children took sick also thought he had the same disease. Before middle age, Charles was an amateur expert on dysentery, croup, whooping cough, scarlet fever. Abby proved a more sensible, but less durable, parent. She was vulnerable, weak, entirely dependent on Charles and her father, who all his life gave Abby cash for herself, her house, furniture, and schooling for his grandchildren. Abby accepted without complaint her subservient role, but by 1843, under the weight of childrearing and childbearing, Abby was suffering from "nervous depression," mysterious headaches and stomach disorders, deafness, and an incessant ringing in her ears. In July, her physician advised Abby to take a long voyage "for a change of air and Scene, as a remedy of her complaints." John Quincy saw clearly what was troubling his favorite daughter-in-law. "I believe the chief if not the only cause of her complaint," he wrote Louisa, "was the care of five small children at once, and all at home." Abby agreed to take a holiday, with her father and oldest son. Charles would stay with the rest of their family at the house in Quincy, "quiet as oysters." But to everyone's surprise, old John Quincy decided at the last minute to come along, and what started as a restful excursion to the spas for Abby soon became a major journey of acclaim for John Quincy Adams.

Abby's trip disintegrated almost from the start: She felt "dreadfully homesick," and asked for a lock of Arthur's hair. Worse, delegations of admirers waylaid her father-in-law at their hotels and stopped their stagecoaches. At first, the old man declined all invitations to speak or visit, but at Saratoga Springs, John Quincy basked in the adulation of hundreds of women admirers, and when he departed that famous spa the women filled the balconies of the old mansions and hotels, and "waved their hands and handkerchiefs," Abby wrote. Everywhere they stopped, admirers fired cannon celebrating the old man's arrival; they mobbed him when he went for walks, and begged him to change his itinerary and speak to them. Adams tried to resist, but the roar of the crowd stirred his political juices; the adulation soothed the painful years of his Presidency and the abuse from the House.

Adams received a delegation in Burlington, Vermont. He promised to oblige the ladies of Rochester, who asked his support "in our efforts to gild the cloud of sorrow that hangs over the pathway of the Orphan." Entering Montreal, Canada, Adams found men, women, and children waving little American flags along his route. When the Adams entourage (for that was what it was now) sailed down the St. Lawrence River, the people on shore fired cannon salutes. In Niagara Falls, a large crowd welcomed him in the rain, and Adams went out in an open carriage to an Indian meeting where he made a speech, although he complained that the rain suppressed all his ideas. A few days later, the good people of Buffalo sailed a Great Lakes steamer to fetch Adams, and he, now dragging Abby and her father and son like excess baggage, flourished on the lovely sail upon a steamer filled with admiring women, and reached Buffalo where, Abby wrote Charles, "he was received with five thousand cheers and all honors, everybody came to see him." John Quincy "requested" Abby to accompany him to a party, and they stayed an hour for a supper of ices, fruit, and cakes before returning to the steamer and Niagara Falls. The next morning they departed for Rochester "where," said Abby, "we arrived at two to go through the same thing, your father consenting to all things."

Abby and her father tried to quit the tour. John Quincy could not turn down any invitation, and he had worn them out, she said, "and I am so cross I can't speak to him." When Adams promised that he would not stop at one town, precisely as he spoke the promise a woman rushed up and urged him to attend a reception there, and he said yes. Abby turned on her heels and gathered her son and father; they had piled their luggage on the railroad cars when John Quincy promised reform. The luggage was removed, and Brooks even consented to dine with Adams that evening. But when invitations from Auburn and Syracuse arrived, John Quincy said yes to both. Abby was "cross as a bear." It did no good. At every stop, Adams got out, and the people cheered and fired cannon. In Utica, men took the horses from the Adams carriage, and pulled it themselves. At Auburn, several hundred free blacks marched with torches to escort the old man. Abby thought the procession was fifty miles long, and perhaps it was, stretching from town to town. Adams paraded from nine to eleven, then rode the train to Syracuse where he paraded until five, and then took the train on to Attica for a third celebration. "As to the P.," Abby told Charles, "he will stop wherever he is asked . . . I fear for your father, I should think it would kill him but he holds out. These demonstrations of respect from all parties are very affecting, but your father sadly wants resolution to say no, to this, as to delivering Lectures." A delegation sent from Cincinnati intercepted John Quincy and asked that he go to Ohio, and Adams consented and planned the trip for November.

Abby rebelled. At one time, "all jammed and dirty and cross" in a carriage, expecting to be taken to their hotel, Abby and her father and JQA arrived instead at the governor's home. Adams was surprised and delighted, but Abby and her father refused to get out. When John Quincy demanded that they pay their respects, Abby refused, and told him through clenched teeth: "I shall not do it, Sir." She didn't, and they continued to their hotel, to "a silent supper," and to bed. Abby and her father and son refused now to ride in the same train compartment with John Quincy, and went on to Saratoga Springs ahead of him for a fortnight. "I fear if I don't rest longer than today here I shall be worse than when I left home," she wrote, "this journey is so hard. . . . Some days I feel finely, others my head is pretty bad, just as I was but stronger."

On his own, Adams slowed not a step. As his train churned across New York State, he wrote in his diary: "Crowds of people were assembled along the track, received me with three cheers, and manifested a desire to hear and see me." Their acclaim for him revived Adams's drooping spirits. His popularity reached a level never before or since equalled by any member of his family. But while John Quincy drew sustenance from this journey, Abby benefitted not at all: After returning home, she remained in poor health.

In October 1843, John Quincy Adams, drawn again by the adoring American people, traveled to Cincinnati for the laying of a cornerstone at that city's observatory. Adams was seventy-six, but he rode the railcars and steamers through the approaching cold of winter with boyish vigor, walked torchlight parades and made late-night speeches, and spoke to every crowd along the Ohio Canal. The cheering welcomed him to Jefferson, Springfield, Dayton, Lebanon; in Columbus he declared that the subject of astronomy was "one of the most important that can engage the attention of the human race" — a thought first articulated during his Presidency. When he finally reached Cincinnati, he rode under a wide banner across Sixth Street that said "John Quincy Adams, the Defender of the Rights of Man." Adams, however, did not overlook the women: After one speech, a "very pretty" lady kissed him on the cheek, and he promptly "returned the salute on the lip," he said, "and kissed every woman that followed, at which some made faces, but none refused." Adams spent a week in Cincinnati, speaking in the rain to a plain of umbrellas at the laying of the cornerstone, and again that evening to two thousand at a temperance tea given by the ladies of the city. He returned to his hotel through a double line of torchlights held by his admirers. Adams's learned speech on astronomy was twenty-five thousand words long, and its scholarship equalled his work on weights and measures — "a gem," Brooks Adams later called it.

John Quincy returned home from Ohio exhausted "beyond description," Louisa said. Even the old man himself admitted: "I came home half dead — but am getting better." The doctor ordered him to bed, and Louisa felt compelled to use her "smart tone" to make JQA obey, "as you know what a rebellious subject he is on such occasions." Within a few weeks, Adams had recovered health and vigor, and Louisa reported him "already inclined to *rebel* — God help us." When Congress opened December 4, Adams immediately presented petitions against slavery and started arguments opposing the annexation of Texas. He had drawn deeply from a summer and autumn of public acclaim, and enjoyed reserves of strength and vitality.

Abby Brooks Adams, however, continued with headaches and nervous depression. Worse, in November 1843 she suffered a miscarriage. Louisa sympathized with her daughter-in-law. "I have been used to such accidents myself," she said, as indeed Louisa had.

11

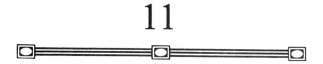

ACCLAIM AND VICTORY filled John Quincy Adams's old age. Only a year after his trips through New York and Ohio, at the opening session of the Twenty-eighth Congress in December 1844, Adams saw the Gag Rule defeated forever. The victory was almost anticlimactic to the battle, for Adams and the Whig anti-slavery insurgents had issued a signed appeal to the people of the United States for petitions against the Rule, and the flood kept the issue aboil as the anti-slavery forces flexed their growing political muscle. On December 3, 1844, Adams introduced a resolution to rescind the Gag Rule, as he had at each opening session of Congress. With little debate, and to his surprise, the House voted 105 to 80 to adopt his resolution, and the Gag Rule quietly ended. He had worn them down, and won, but it was a lull before the storms of the coming decade. The right of petition was re-established, and Adams had achieved a major step along the path toward human freedom. "Blessed, ever blessed, be the name of God," he wrote in his diary.

John Quincy turned his attention to the issues of Texas

annexation and the Mexican War, which he rightly saw as tied closely to the spread of slavery. Adams spent his seventy-ninth birthday at his desk in the House listening in sweltering heat to debates on the war. Letters from Robert Buchanan, written on captured papers engraved with the national arms of Mexico, gave Louisa and John Quincy fresh details of the battles. Louisa said that because of Robert they were always "glad to hear good news from the Rio Grande," but the war upset John Quincy and "he thinks the Country on the road to ruin." It didn't ease his conviction when Robert, sent with thirty men to capture Mexican cannon, was struck in the chest by grape-shot, fired through the chaparral; the charge luckily was spent and did little injury to him. "Your Father seems quite broken hearted at the present state of the Political World," Louisa wrote Charles, "and we hardly know what to make of him. — He is more impracticable than ever and cannot bear to be asked a question on any subject. — He seldom speaks to the family, and on the subject of the War is almost *savage*."

John Quincy Adams went every day to the House to join the debates. Louisa, more and more a nurse to him, thought her husband "totally unfit to go to Congress": his memory troubled him, his voice was weaker, he was absent-minded "and often neither seems to hear or see." Charles, during a visit, wrote Abby that "The P. looks feeble." Yet John Quincy remained outspokenly opposed to slavery, to the Mexican War, and could not be kept home and quiet; he continued arguing in Congress, which produced, said Louisa, "a thundering sensation." His grandson Charles observed that his grandfather never ceased in his commitment; he was "an old man absorbed in work and public life. . . . A very old-looking gentleman, with a bald head and white fringe of hair — writing, writing — with a perpetual ink-stain on the forefinger and thumb of the right hand."

Two days before his eightieth birthday, John Quincy Adams impulsively turned during a walk and made his way across the lower Tiber Creek bridge toward his favorite swimming rocks. The morning was already rising hot and still, the temperature at 84° F., and as John Quincy approached his favorite swimming spot he started peeling off his clothes. Some young men already churned the Potomac, their clothing scattered on his favorite rock, and one whispered, "There's John Quincy Adams." The river was warm and sluggish, streaked with patches of early sunlight, and Adam tossed aside his clothes and waded slowly in — the tide was low — before stroking out to deeper water. He swam for half an hour, savoring the cool and refreshing feeling, before wading back to his rock, drying himself in the hot sunlight "like the old pelican he was," dressing, and walking home. He returned two more mornings, despite temperatures in the low seventies that caused him to shiver as he tried to dry in the sun, and he noted with some sadness that the walk to and from his F Street home now took him half an hour each way, when as Secretary of State he had covered the distance in just eighteen minutes. Louisa soon put a stop to these shenanigans. "In his present weak state," she wrote Abby, "he frightens me almost out of my life." Even though she claimed that John Quincy "listens to no one," these were the last swims he took in the Potomac. From this July on, the old man bathed in his bedchamber at sunrise. There was no comparison: The tub was small and cramped, the water either too hot to be refreshing, or too cold. He rubbed his old body with a horsehair strap and a coarse mitten to give it the glow it had during his Potomac River outings, but it wasn't the same.

In November 1846, Adams accepted unanimous nomination by the Whigs in his Congressional district, and while he regarded himself as a man of the whole country and not one party, he was still pleased to be known as a Conscience Whig, as a man opposed to slavery and the war with Mexico. Adams did not campaign, or make the usual report to constituents. He did not have to, and his fellow citizens returned him to Congress with a majority of sixteen hundred votes. It was his last election.

Victorious, John Quincy Adams left the Old House and spent the rest of the month with Charles and Abby in Boston, an annual custom. Louisa went on to Washington with two servants, Mary, and Mary Louisa. On November 20, the old man got up as usual between four and five, bathed in his room with strap and mitten, and after breakfast started out for a morning walk with a friend, Dr. George Parkman, to visit the new Harvard medical college. Suddenly, he seemed to trip, his knees weakening; with the help of Dr. Parkman he staggered back to Charles's house. Adams had suffered a light cerebral hemorrhage, or stroke. While in no pain, he realized that he had little strength, or power of thought. "From that hour," he later wrote, "I date my decrease, and consider myself for every useful purpose to myself or my fellow-creatures, dead."

Louisa hurried from Washington to Boston in just thirty-six hours by rail and steamer.* "He is severely stricken," she wrote Mary. His right arm to the shoulder and right leg from the foot to the knee were numb, and his speech so slurred that only Abby could understand him. Any agitation was painful, and excitement made him so nervous "that he drewls like a baby." By January, he could get down to Charles's study, and go outside for brief carriage rides. Adams carefully wrote his last will, which he did not discuss with Louisa, listing thirty-three detailed articles on ten pages of foolscap, and the care and precision showed that he was not as "dead" as he had proclaimed. He divided the bulk of his estate, after debts, between Louisa, Mary Hellen Adams and her daughter Mary Louisa, and his only surviving son, Charles. He left small portions to other grandchildren, nephews, and nieces, an annuity to Louisa Catherine Smith, his cousin, and scattered his tokens and mementoes. To Charles, he offered the same opportunity his father had given him: to take full title to the Old House and its property by paying twenty thousand dollars into the estate.

John Quincy, Louisa, and Charles left for Washington on February 7. When Adams walked into the House, its members stood and applauded the old man they had tried to silence. The House proceedings halted while members helped Adams to his desk. Here was a statesman of the age, a patriarch who had known Washington, Jefferson, Lafayette, the Founding Fathers, a living link between the nation's beginning and its coming of age. Adams attended every House session. He responded to roll calls, and pressed for peace along the Rio Grande. But he rose and spoke only once: against a proposal to give the owners of the *Amistad* a fifty-thousand-dollar indemnity.

* Louisa sailed up Long Island Sound on the steamer *Atlantic*. Twenty-four hours later, on its return to New York City, the steamer went aground in a storm and broke up with heavy loss of life.

Louisa worried that John Quincy might not get safely to and from Congress. He was weak, and his mind wandered so much that he forgot to change his shirts, and wore over them only his old brown coat with its frayed buttons. He left his winter cap on his bald head into late May. Louisa and John Quincy both anticipated "that *melancholy* thing that some persons so fearfully dread . . . the fated hour must come." They quietly celebrated their fiftieth wedding anniversary during the summer of 1847, in Quincy, and returned to Washington and opened the F Street house "to the multitudes." The Adamses' New Year's party in 1848 seemed as full as those they celebrated when JQA was Secretary of State. Louisa even sent out word that she would receive visits on Saturday evenings; no entertainment, she warned, her singing and piano-playing days now behind her, but "a little Cake and Lemonade."

A new generation of Adams ladies and gentlemen filled their F Street home so full that this winter one young visitor actually had to be turned away for lack of a bed. The young Adams ladies sang and danced for the guests, and two of the young gentlemen, said Louisa, "Screamed" Swiss mountain songs, accompanied by guitar "tuned to the highest pitch of discord." Adams himself ventured out for an evening, and returned from a dinner party in a gleeful mood. Louisa thought he came home appearing "as if he had been ten years younger and looking his *best* looks." And that's the way she wished to remember him.

On Monday, February 21, 1848, John Quincy Adams rose at his usual hour, read his Bible, breakfasted, and later rode his carriage through the cold winter morning to Capitol Hill. He arrived early at his desk, and spoke with several members sitting near him. During the opening proceedings, perhaps bored, John Quincy wrote several stanzas of poetry to the Muse of History, whose marble form rode her wheeled and winged chariot over the door to the Hall of Representatives. The day's business started about noon, and the House had under consideration a resolution calling for the awarding of medals and the thanks of Congress to various American generals who had fought in the 1847 campaigns against Mexico. The Speaker called for ayes and nays on the question of interrupting the House calendar to accept such a resolution, and when he called Adams's name the old man who thought the Mexican war "most unrighteous" stood and loudly replied with a firm and clear "No!" against the motion — which nonetheless carried the House overwhelmingly.

Adams did not know that President James K. Polk had received a treaty of peace, signed at Guadalupe Hidalgo, outside Mexico City, on February 2; the news reached the White House on February 18. The President would forward the treaty to the Senate on the twenty-second. The expansion of the United States, its Manifest Destiny, which John Quincy Adams had worked for, was now reality. Four weeks earlier, one of Johann A. Sutter's workmen had discovered gold particles in the tailings from his millrace in the newly ceded territory of California, and a rush to that land was on. The country had reached its continental limits. It would now turn to its sectional differences.

After his ringing "No!" Adams sat quietly at his desk, while the House clerk read the resolutions. An abolitionist reporter at the press table fifteen feet away noticed a deep color tinging Adams's temples. John Quincy tried to speak, and started to rise, clutching at the corner of his desk for support, then slumped over the left arm of his chair and fell to the floor. "Look to Mr. Adams!" someone shouted, and House members rushed to him. The chamber filled with the whisper "Mr. Adams is dying, Mr. Adams is dying." Members carried him out of the hall on a sofa to the Speaker's office, where only physicians and close friends were allowed near him. Adams could speak a little, and had no pain. He revived enough to ask for Henry Clay, who arrived weeping and spent an hour holding John Quincy's hand. That evening, the old statesman murmured his last words: "This is the end of earth, but I am composed."*

For more than two days, John Quincy Adams lay dying. The House, the Senate, the entire U.S. government adjourned business, and waited and prayed. It was fitting that this man, who so valued duty to his country, would fall while working at his desk in Congress. Adams had sacrificed everything to his nation. Diplomat, Senator, Secretary of State, President, Representative, healer of the wound of war, John Quincy had per-

---

* Another report recorded his saying, "This is the last of earth—I am content."

formed sweeping, bold acts for his beloved country. But it would fall to Louisa to touch the heart of one of its people.

Louisa Adams arrived at two-fifteen with her friend Mary Elizabeth Cutts. Louisa bent down to her husband's face, but John Quincy did not recognize her. Four physicians now gathered around Adams, and the gentlemen friends of the family insisted that Louisa and Miss Cutts return home. They did, and Louisa fainted when leaving the Capitol for her carriage. But she returned the next day, and stayed by her dying husband's side. One of the committee rooms was prepared for her, and she passed the night in the Capitol reclining on a sofa, but getting little rest.

When Adams had collapsed on Monday at one o'clock, John G. Palfrey, a Boston Unitarian minister, member of the House, and close friend, had sent a messenger immediately to the Washington telegraph office. New lines between Washington, Baltimore, Philadelphia, New York, and Boston had only recently opened, and often failed, and Palfrey kept a young man standing by during the next two days getting messages through whenever he could. His first, sent to Charles Francis Adams from the Speaker's office at one-thirty, clicked later that afternoon into the Boston Magnetic Telegraph on Court Square at the rear of City Hall, near Charles's law office: "Dear Adams: Your father fainted half an hour ago. . . ." Palfrey described in detail John Quincy Adams's last hours, first to Charles who rushed from Boston, and then to Abby, who stayed behind. "Oh how I long to take my old place by your Father's bed," Abby wrote Charles, "and resume my former duties and comfort your mother. It seems wrong for me to be absent. . . . How I dearly love them both."

Palfrey told of how the doctors rubbed brandy over John Quincy's feet, and applied suction cups to his temples. He reported Adams's pulse at a hundred beats a minute, although fluctuating, and his hands warm and perspiring freely. Several times on the twenty-second, and on the twenty-third, when John Quincy's pulse and breath stopped, only to return even stronger, Palfrey thought the old man would die. On the evening of the twenty-fourth, when Palfrey briefly left his place in the Capitol, a messenger hurriedly called him back, and when he reached the Speaker's room he found it crowded, but still. From the foot of the bed, Palfrey heard no breathing. John Quincy Adams had died at seventeen minutes past seven — "making the time of his illness," Palfrey noted, "fifty-four hours, or two days and a quarter exactly." Adams would have liked the preciseness of that. Louisa learned the news almost as soon as Palfrey. She remained in the F Street house, and found security with her friends, Mary, and the younger Adamses. Palfrey visited, and found her "comfortable and calm," and that evening Louisa slept well.

The nation Adams loved and served fell to mourning. While his body lay in the committee room downstairs, where medical attendants prepared it for burial, the House met in an "impressive" scene, and delegates from Massachusetts, Ohio, and even South Carolina gave eulogies. The House members unanimously agreed that one member from every state and territory of the Union would escort Adams's body home to Quincy. President Polk directed that all executive offices in Washington be closed for two days, and the Secretary of War ordered the national flag flown at half-staff, army officers to wear crepe, and the colors of the American regiments placed in mourning. At dawn on every military post, thirteen guns were fired, and in Washington every half hour from sunrise to sunset a single cannon boomed in mournful solitude for the old gentleman, followed at sunset by "a national salute of 29 guns."

On February 26, from the hour John Quincy loved most, when dawn first touched the sky, the rumble of cannon filled every minute until his funeral procession started at noon. Adams's silver-mounted coffin, decorated with the spread and defiant American eagle, covered with evergreen boughs and early spring flowers, had lain in state for two days in the House. At ten minutes before noon, the Speaker called the House of Representatives to order, and as the bell on Capitol Hill tolled, walking to its slow rhythm, the President, Vice President, the Justices of the Supreme Court, diplomats, army and navy officers, Senators, Charles Francis Adams, Mary Hellen Adams, and, finally, Louisa Catherine Adams, entered and seated themselves. The service marked the first of dozens that took place over the next month. Not since Washington's death had there been such a public mourning, and not until the death of Abraham Lincoln, then an obscure House member, would there be such an enormous funereal procession and outpouring. Within a week, the Congressional Committee of Escort took John Quincy home, by funeral train and steamboat, for burial. Flags along the route flew at half-staff, and people lined the tracks with their heads bowed. In Boston, a huge crowd met the train, and the coffin was placed on a carriage pulled by six black horses trimmed in crepe, with heavy black plumes on their heads. The procession made its way to Faneuil Hall through streets thronged with mourners. After several days, the coffin was taken to Quincy, and as the body entered the town, small cannon were fired from the top of Penn's Hill, where John Quincy as a boy had watched with his mother the battles of the Revolutionary War. The procession paused at the Old House, and at the church; neighbors carried the coffin into the Stone Temple, the family tomb, and put John Quincy Adams to rest beside his mother, father, sister, and his son George. And as the citizens, dignitaries, and Congressmen filed past the vault, one of the members of the Committee of Escort stepped forward, and with trembling voice said in the soft tones of the South:

"Goodbye, Old Man."

12

LOUISA PULLED IN the edges of her life. She found comfort with her sister Carolina Frye and with Mary. She recounted to all who would listen how "remarkably cheerful" John Quincy had been the morning before he collapsed, and how eagerly he had wanted to get to the Capitol and the politics he loved. Louisa remembered her husband's last words, the "placid expression" on his face, the "sweet serenity" that showed "a mind at Peace with God, and with all mankind." For a year, as she had with the deaths of George and John, Louisa Adams eased her pain with the therapy of poetry. But the blow this time struck especially hard: "Thy fist has gone forth O Lord my God," she said, "and I am left a helpless widow. . . ." Louisa complained repeatedly of a "dreadful fluttering at my heart," which caused her pain and made her anxious.

Although ill almost continuously after John Quincy's death, Louisa lived comfortably for the first time since her marriage. She rented out a house in Washington, which John Quincy had purchased from her sister Harriet Boyd for three-thousand-dollars. In 1843, Thomas Baker Johnson, Louisa's brother, had died after a long illness, and left her ten-thousand-dollars in her own name. From her accounts, placed in Charles's care, by 1849 Louisa earned five-hundred-dollars in interest every quarter. She never could spend all the money and she was, Charles assured her, well off. Louisa paid her debts, refurbished the parlor at F Street, bought new horses for her carriage. She entertained again, and on New Year's Day, 1849, received two-hundred guests, mostly Congressmen and diplomats. She still followed politics, and President Zachary Taylor, Vice President Millard Fillmore, and Henry Clay sometimes dropped by for free-wheeling discussions about slavery.

In April 1849, with spring "bursting on us in all its natural beauty," Louisa suffered a stroke. She could not stand alone, and never did so again. She could not use her right hand or arm, and wrote with difficulty, her handwriting rising and falling across the page like topographical lines on a map measuring the hills and valleys of her life. She had to learn to feed herself with her left hand. Louisa grew deaf, and her eyesight dimmed. She felt that she had aged from "one stage of existence to another," much as John Quincy had after his stroke. She spent the next three years in "quiet and contented infirmity."

Charles traveled to Washington every six months at the end of this decade; the trip took less than forty-four hours from his breakfast table in Quincy to his mother's bedside on F Street in Washington. The death of his father had changed him. He wrote Louisa that "the first feeling of standing alone, and having others looking to me for guidance is novel and startling. It lays a weight of responsibility for action upon me which I never felt before." In 1840, Charles had been elected to the Massachusetts legislature, and he had served three years in the State House and two in the Senate. He had established the *Boston Whig*, a newspaper opposing slavery, and in 1848, the "conscience" Whigs opposing Taylor's re-election had nominated Van Buren for President and Charles Francis Adams for Vice President. Defeated, Charles still made regular trips to Washington to confer with Free Soil Congressmen, and to visit his mother. Louisa cherished the companionship and attention of this lucky son "whom I never deserted"; she still felt guilty about leaving George and John, "a penance which I trust God in His mercy will pardon and accept."

In June 1850, Charles brought Henry with him to see Washington for the first time. Henry was twelve, and looked to Louisa exactly as Charles had when they were in Russia, which made her partial to this grandson. Henry would grow up to be the family historian, and his eye was already keen. He found Washington foreign: the rich mud and spring flowers, the broken streets and scattered buildings, the quarter-built Washington Monument, the horses grazing the President's lawn, "the want of barriers, of pavements, of forms; the looseness, the laziness; the indolent Southern drawl; the pigs in the streets; the negro babies and their mothers with bandanas; the freedom, openness, swagger, of nature and man. . . ." This was not New England; not neat, cleaned up, squared and correct, but more like his grandmother, relaxed, flowing, warm, Southern.

Before 1848, Henry had remembered her sitting in her paneled room, at breakfast, with her heavy silver teapot, sugar bowl, and cream jug, "thoroughly weary of being beaten about a stormy world." Louisa had seemed to this grandson "singularly peaceful, a vision of silver gray, presiding over her old President and her Queene Anne mahogany; an exotic, like her Sèvres china; an object of deference to every one." Now, she found comfort among her family members, in the heat of Washington, which she called "mild," in the shadows of her F Street home beneath the catalpa trees planted by her husband. She appeared, to Henry, not to belong to New England at all, "but to Washington or to Europe, like her furniture, and writing-desk with little glass doors above and little eighteenth-century volumes in old bindings, labelled 'Peregrine Pickle' or 'Tom Jones' or 'Hannah More.' " She had lived, he sensed, a life "of severe stages, and little pure satisfaction," and survived a marriage of more than fifty-one years to a formidable, demanding New England man. But she had more than survived; Louisa had persevered (that good Adams word) and overcome, and was now hardly more Bostonian that she had been over five decades earlier, on her wedding day in the shadow of the Tower of London. Henry later speculated that Louisa had bequeathed to him, along with his "quarter taint of Maryland blood," the impulses of rebellion against New England sobrieties. Louisa brought into this tight New England family — a family that liked the neatness of seeing things in white or black, right or wrong, light or dark hues — a regard for tone, for shadow.

During her last years, that complexity had deepened. As she aged, Louisa Adams lost sight of, but not her interest in, the women's movement. In 1840, the World Anti-Slavery Convention in London had banished all women to the galleries, even the several dozen American women who had sailed more than three thousand miles were refused seating because of their sex. Rejected, these American women, who included Lucretia Mott and Elizabeth Cady Stanton, returned to the United States determined to assert their rights along with those of the black slave. In 1848, Mott and Stanton organized the first United States Women's Rights Convention. They assembled more than a hundred American women in Seneca Falls, New York, and wrote the Seneca Falls Declaration of Independence, drafted by Mrs. Stanton, which began: "We hold these truths to be self-evident; that all men and women are created equal. . . ." There followed demands for political, religious, social, and economic equality. Mrs. Stanton, however, went further, and introduced over the objections of the others a resolution calling for women to enjoy "the sacred right" to vote. These women, the most outspoken feminists in America, were shocked. The idea of voting rights was so bizarre that Mrs. Stanton's father thought his daughter had lost her mind, and rushed to Seneca Falls to determine if she was rational. Her motion lost, and in the end the reaction by men and women around the country to the Convention was one of derision. Abigail Adams's declaration would have to wait another century.

But Louisa Adams was not content to let the abolitionist women turn the world upside-down. The effect of Louisa's life on those around her was diffuse; the growing good of the world is partly dependent upon unhistoric acts. Louisa was too old, too timid, to join the Stantons and Motts and Grimkés. She was more representative of the majority of American women of her time, who preferred the safer, middle, less earthshaking path. Intimidated by her husband and sons into torpidity, she stood on the edge. She thought her life wasted, worthless. Men were placed on earth for a purpose, she believed, which they discovered and acted upon. As late as 1840, however, Louisa had felt directionless, without meaning. That year she began her autobiography, which she titled *Adventures of a Nobody*. Louisa considered herself of no significance. Intelligent, loving, politically astute, she felt pushed aside; in her own mind, she remained hardly more a servant girl. But there was also inside her something that wouldn't surrender, a combative desire accelerated by her correspondence with Sarah Grimké, to find some small way to give meaning to her life as a woman. Louisa Adams thought about it, prayed for it, and when at last the idea came, it arrived with the suddenness and the power of a true and good act.

In 1846, Louisa hired a cook named Julia, and that summer planned to take her to Quincy. But Julia was a slave, and Louisa found that she could not take her north without posting a large bond against Julia's escaping. Instead, Louisa hired a cook in Boston. In 1847, Louisa again planned a trip to Quincy when "the smiles of Summer" beckoned, and again wished to take Julia with her. But Julia's owner refused. For one thing, Julia, by working as a cook, had already purchased almost half the cost of her freedom — that is, half her value on the Washington slave market. She needed $200 more, "and that must not be risked," said Louisa with irony. "The fear of the *abolitionists* has seized her Mistress and she will not permit her to go where she would become Free."

Louisa considered Julia "an excellent servant," and worried that she might be sold "to a Brute, a Virginia Slaveholder." And here Louisa's act took root. "I wish," she wrote Abby, "I could raise the sum wanted to release her from her bondage." Julia's price had been $400, but by this time the slave had earned another $75 toward her freedom, and paid it. Louisa now needed only $125. Her income from her brother's will gave her more than enough money; Johnson Hellen, Louisa's nephew, held Julia's slave papers. Louise wrote Abby: "If I could be put into a way of raising a subscription for this purpose, I should be *very* happy. Perhaps you could suggest some means. – I should be almost as glad as if I was buying my own freedom."

In a sense, Louisa was. While John Quincy Adams had negotiated great treaties, expanded the nation sea to sea, brought armies to peace, and stood alone as an old man against the slaveholders, raising the awful questions that cut through the tissue and sinew of mid-nineteenth-century America, he had never reached out to one frightened, lonely, caged human being. Louisa Adams did. She bought the title to an enslaved black woman; set Julia free. In so doing, Louisa, who had been imprisoned as a woman, freed part of herself. She created her own special reply to Sarah Grimké's challenge, and to the haunting question, "Am I not a woman and a sister?"

During the winter of 1852, Louisa Adams fell gravely ill. A victim of strokes and a weakening heart, she couldn't sleep or defeat the pain that raged within her; her hands and arms puffed up "like cushions." Only heavy doses of opiates gave her comfort. Elizabeth wrote Abby that Louisa was "truly in a deplorable state. She says often that she wants to die, that the worse she is the better it will be for her soon. – It will indeed be a happy exchange." But Louisa tenaciously grasped the slender stalk of life. On her deathbed, huddled beneath a blanket of opium, her mind drifted. She asked every day if Clay were dead. She dreamed that Charles had come from Quincy, but was ill and walking with a cane. She asked about Mary, Elizabeth, Abby, Looly.

Louisa loved spring best of all the seasons. Not long before his own death, John Quincy had written to her while he was alone in May in New England, and reminded her of those spring-time days of their youth, when they had been in love and read the incomparable words of the coming of this season, from the Song of Solomon. Louisa had remembered, and had written back that she welcomed the end of life's struggles, ambitions, toils, and the "blessed promise held forth to us, in the prospect of that eternal Spring which shall know no change, but which shall endure for ever and forever." Now for twelve weeks, from mid-winter, Louisa rallied and sank, rallied and sank, spirited and stubborn to the end. She seemed to be waiting, and only when April flowered to May with its eternal promise of warmth and bud and song did she let go. Surrounded by the blossoms John Quincy had planted around their F Street home, Louisa lay in pain, waiting, comforted by her family and the words of Solomon's ancient song

> My beloved spake, and said unto me, Rise up, my love,
>   my fair one, and come away.
> For, lo, the winter is past, the rain is over and gone;
> The flowers appear on the earth; the time of the singing
>   of birds is come, and the voice of the turtle
>   is heard in our land;
> The fig tree putteth forth her green figs, and the vines
>   with the tender grape give a good smell.
> Arise, my love, my fair one, and come away.

On May 14, Mary Louisa Adams sent a telegram to Charles: "Grandma is worse come immediately." But Charles, as with his father's stroke four years earlier, could not reach Washington in time.

Louisa Catherine Adams, her life's promise fulfilled, died at noon, May 15, 1852.

Chapter Notes

The intention here is to give the reader an indication of the sources used in writing this book, but not to footnote every paragraph. The major body of the research comes from the Adams Papers. Quotations from the Adams Papers are from the microfilm edition, by permission of the Massachusetts Historical Society (abbreviated APM here). Titles of works not given in full here can be found in the bibliography. To save space, the names of principal Adams family members have been abbreviated as follows:

JA — John Adams
AA — Abigail Adams
JQA — John Quincy Adams
LCA — Louisa Catherine Adams
TBA — Thomas Boylston Adams
GWA — George Washington
    Adams

JA2 — John Adams 2d
CFA — Charles Francis Adams
LCA2 — Louisa Catherine Adams
    2d
CFA2 — Charles Francis Adams
    2d
Mrs. JA2 — Mary Hellen Adams
ABA — Abigail Brooks Adams

Abbreviated, also, are frequently used sources, such as Louisa Adams's *Record of a Life* (Reel 265), listed here as *Record*, and *Adventures of a Nobody* (Reel 269), listed as *Adventures*. Page numbers of dates for these documents are given when available. John Adams's *Diary and Autobiography* is abbreviated *D & A*. The listing of sources is generally in the order in which they appear.

Sources identified in this form — "LCA to CFA April 30, 1828 (APM)" — are letters from the Adams Papers and available on microfilm in selected libraries.

I. LONDON, 1797

Chapter 1

Most of the details about LCA come from Royall, *Sketches*, p. 203; LCA to Thomas J. Hellen, March 4, 1820; LCA to CFA, April 30, 1828 (APM); LCA to GWA, June 25, 1825 (APM); "hanging and marriage," LCA to CFA, Sept. 3, 1850 (APM); *Record* (APM) and *Adventures* (APM); *The Selected Letters of Henry Adams*, Newton Arvin, ed. (New York: Farrar, Straus and Young Inc, 1951).

The details about John Quincy come from many sources, including his *Diary*, *D & A*, vol. I, p. 15ff.; Bemis, *Foundations*. The wedding details may be found in "American Ties with All Hallows Church, London," *Maryland Historical Society*, Sept. 1947, pp. 214–17.

Chapter 2

The history of the Johnsons is scattered, but pieces may be found in *D & A*, vol. II, pp. 127–50 and 299–300; III, p. 330; IV, p. 49; Edward S. Delaplaine, *The Life of Thomas Johnson* (New York: The Grafton Press, 1927); *Maryland, A History 1632–1974*, Richard Walsh and William Lloyd Fox, eds. (Baltimore: Maryland Historical Society, 1974); LCA to Miss Mease, Oct. 6, 1832 (APM); LCA to CFA, July 5, 1828 (APM); *Archives of Maryland*, pp. 7, 13, 45, 47, 79, 140, 225; LCA to ABA March 2, 1834 (APM); *D & A*, vol. II, p. 382.

Chapter 3

The history of the Adamses is found among many sources. Some of the best are Bemis, *Foundations;* Shepherd, *The Adams Chronicles; Adams Family Correspondence* (AFC), vol. I, pp. 117, 145, 252, 285–6, 384; AA to JA Aug. 28, 1774 (APM); JQA to JA Oct. 13, 1774 (APM). Correspondence between JA, AA, and JQA included *New Letters*, p. 211; *AFC*, vol. II, p. 66, 255, 261, 271, 307; *Familiar Letters of Abigail Adams*, pp. 63–4, 137–8, 120–21, 128–9, 142, 144.

Smallpox inoculation details are found in *D & A*, vol. II, p. 253; *AFC*, vol. II, pp. 55, 57, 66; *New Letters*, p. 50; *Public Health in Boston*, pp. 84, 134–5; *Story of Medicine*, pp. 223–9.

Chapter 4

Much of Louisa's history in England comes from *Record, Adventures;* LCA to ABA March 2, 1834 (APM); *D & A*, vol. II, pp. 299–300, 357, 358–9, 363; vol. III, p. 240; vol. IV, pp. 49, 249.

The history of women may be found, among other works, in Ryan, *Womanhood in America;* Smith, *Daughters of the Promised Land; The Lady's Monthly Museum*, II, 1799, p. 36; Stone, *Family, Sex and Marriage in England*, pp. 357, 359.

Chapter 5

Abigail Adams's letters on John Quincy's trip are found in *New Letters*, p. 135; AA to John Thaxter, Feb. 15, 1778 (APM); *Letters* of AA, p. 95ff.

JQA as teacher of French, JQA's *Life in a New England Town* (*LNET*), p. 7.

Letters between Abigail and John Quincy: *Letters* of AA, pp. 114, 115, 423; AA to JQA, Jan. 12, 1780, March 20, 1780 and Nov 20, 1783 (APM).

JQA at Harvard: Mary Cranch to AA, May 7, 1786 (APM); JQA to AA, Aug. 1 and Oct. 12, 1787 (APM); AA to March Cranch, July 16, 1787 (APM); JQA to Abigail Adams Smith, Jan. 17, 1787 (APM); *LNET*, p. 7; *Letters* of AA, p. 231. Scene at breakfast, *Letters* of AA, p. 268.

Chapter 6

Accounts of LCA's education come from *Record; D & A*, vol. III, p. 149. The source for women's social roles is Stone, *Family, Sex and Marriage*, p. 536. LCA's style of living is detailed in LCA to ABA, March 2, 1834 (APM).

Chapter 7

JQA's life in Newburyport: JQA to CFA Nov 7, 1827 (Parsons on Bacon) (APM); *LNET*, pp. 23, 42, 43, 71, 87–8; Marlowe, *Coaching Roads*, pp. 162, 175, 178–9.

Mary Frazier: *LNET*, pp. 78–80; JQA *Diary*, Dec. 8, 1787 and Jan. 26, 1788 (APM).

JQA's low spirits: JA to JQA, Jan. 23, 1788 (APM); JQA *Diary*, Dec. 8, 1787 (APM); *LNET*, pp. 23, 42, 46, 62, 63, 65, 68, 71, 95, 132. Depression at Braintree, *New Letters*, p. 70; JQA *Diary*, March 13, 1791.

JQA is no "saint": see *Journals* for the years 1788 and 1789 (APM).

Poetry: *LNET*, p. 88ff. *The Herald of Freedom*, Feb. 10, 1789 and March 10, 1789.

JQA and AA exchange of letters on Mary Frazier: AA to JQA, August 1790, Reel 374; JA to JQA Sept. 1790; AA to JQA Sept. 1790; JQA to AA Aug. 29, 1790; AA to JQA Nov. 1790; JQA to AA Nov. 20 and Dec. 14, 1790; Aunt Eliza to JQA June 9, 1794; James Bridges to JQA Sept. 28, 1790 (all APM). See also JQA *Memoirs*, vol. IV, pp. 357–60.

JQA's memory of Mary Frazier: *Memoirs*, vol. IV, pp. 357–60; *LNET*, pp. 169–70; *Recollections of Samuel Brech, 1771–1802*, H. E. Scudder, ed. (London: Sampson Low, Marston, Searle and Rivington, 1877).

JQA as Boston lawyer: APM, Reels 21 and 25.

Melancholy and depression in Boston: JQA *Diary*, July 19 and 20, 1792. Walks on the mall are from JQA *Diary* entries noted in text; see also APM Reels 22 and 25. Franklin's quote, *Autobiography and Selected Writings of Benjamin Franklin*, Dixon Wecter and Lazar Zuff, eds. (New York: 1969), p. 179.

JQA's "passion": James Bridges to JQA, June 28, 1789 (APM); J. Putnam to JQA, Oct. 3, 1789 (APM).

JQA's appointment: JQA to AA, Nov. 14, 1794 (APM); *New Let-*

ters, p. 83; JQA *Diary*, June 3, 6, 28 and 30, 1794; JA to JQA, May 29, 1794.

Gift of money from JA: JQA to Charles Adams, Nov. 20, 1794; East, *The Critical Years*, p. 242 (footnote).

Chapter 8

Description of the Johnson home is found in *Record.*

JQA on women and marriage: *LNET*, p. 79; JA to JQA, Aug. 25, 1795 (APM); JQA to AA, Aug. 16, 1796 (APM); "blunted sensations," JQA to AA, Nov. 7, 1795 (APM).

Louisa's comments on her engagement are from *Record* and *Adventures;* LCA to JQA, Aug. 13, and Dec. 30, 1796 (APM); JQA to LCA, Nov. 12, 1796 (APM). Abigail's doubts: AA to JQA, Aug. 10, 1796 (APM).

Chapter 9

Women in colonial New England: Ryan, *Womanhood in America,* pp. 99, 110; Smith, *Daughters,* pp. 53–4, 59, 60; Julia Cherry Spruill, *Women's Life and Work in the Southern Colonies* (Chapel Hill, N.C.: Russell, 1969), p. 127; Anon. *Reflections on Courtship and Marriage* (London: 1779), p. 22.

John Adams's "Itches, Aches, Agues. . . ." JA to Abigail Smith, Feb. 14, 1763 (APM); courtship letters in *Adams Family Correspondence,* vol. I, pp. 1–12, 15–19, 22–51.

Chapter 10

Courtship by mail: LCA to JQA, Sept. 13, 1796 (APM); JQA to LCA, Dec. 13, 1796 and Jan. 7, 1787 (APM); LCA to JQA, Jan. 31, 1797 (APM).

JQA to Joshua Johnson on ship, May 12, 1797 (APM).

LCA on "forcing" herself on him: LCA to JQA, Jan. 31, 1797 (APM).

Johnson's finances in *Record* and *Adventure.*

JQA's "choice": JQA to LCA, May 12, 1787, and his reply to LCA, May 26, 1797 (APM).

Chapter 11

Letters on Berlin post: JA to JQA, June 2, 1797 (APM); JQA to JA, July 22, 1797 (APM).

Honeymoon: Stone, *Family, Sex and Marriage,* pp. 335–6; JQA and LCA to AA and JA, July 28, 1797 (APM), AA to Mary Cranch, Dec. 12, 1797 (APM); AA to JQA, Oct. 3, 1797 (APM); JA to JQA, Oct. 25, 1797 (APM).

Johnson financial collapse: *Adventures; Record;* Joshua Johnson to JQA, Sept. 12, 1797, and JQA's reply, October 1797, Reel 386 (both APM); LCA, in *A. S. Colvin's Weekly Messenger* (Washington, D.C.), Saturday, June 2, 1827, Reel 269 (APM).

II. BERLIN/WASHINGTON 1797–1809

Chapter 1

Louisa's journey in *Record*, pp. 62–4; JQA to AA, Dec. 28, 1797 (APM); TBA on LCA's miscarriage, *New Letters*, p. 158 (April 21, 1798); Smith, *Daughters*, p. 131.

JQA's role in Berlin: Bemis, *Foundations*, pp. 91, 94. LCA's observations of Berlin in *Record* and *Adventure*.

Chapter 2

Rouge incident: *Adventures; Record*, pp. 70–71.

Details on Charles Adams's life: Reels 366 and 367 (APM); *New Letters*, pp. 211, 255, 261–2 (death), 269; death, *Letters* of AA, p. 270.

William Stephens Smith: *New Letters*, pp. 209, 263; *Letters* of AA, p. 283.

Chapter 3

LCA's pregnancy: *Adventures;* LCA to ABA, Dec. 18, 1833 (APM). JQA, "the pleasing punishment": JQA to LCA, May 21, 1804. Töplitz in *Adventures*.

Women and birth control: Ryan, *Womanhood*, p. 164; Stone, *Family, Sex and Marriage*, pp. 77, 87, 486, 142 (footnote); G. J. Barker-Benfield, "The Spermatic Economy," in *The American Family in Socio-Historical Perspective*, Michael Gordon, ed. (New York: 1973); Charles Rosenberg, "Sexuality, Class and Role in 19th Century America," *American Quarterly*, May 1973, pp. 131–53.

Birth: JQA to AA, April 14, 1801; JQA to TBA, April 21 and July 21, 1801 (APM).

Chapter 4

Account of visit to Washington: *Adventures;* LCA to JQA, Oct. 4, 1801 (APM); JQA to LCA, Sept. 23, 1801 (APM); LCA to JQA Sept. 16 and Oct. 4, 1801.

Roads: Marlowe, *Coaching Roads*, pp. 2, 52, 55, 120; Langdon, *Everyday Things*, pp. 25, 32.

Dickens: *American Notes*, chapter XIV, pp. 22–3.

Adamses' trip north: *Adventures;* JQA to AA, Nov. 10, 1801 (APM); AA to TBA, Dec. 27, 1801 (APM).

Louisa in Washington: *Record; Adventures;* childrearing and birth of JA2 in *Adventures*.

Chapter 5

Plumer quote: William Plumer to William W. Plumer, Jr., April 8, 1806; Papers of William Plumer, Letterbook (Library of Congress).

Washington: Green, *Washington Village and Capital*, pp. 23 ("ruins"), 28, 38–9, 41, 49.

Jefferson and LCA: Green, *Washington Village and Capital*, p. 47; *Adventures*.

Abigail's concern for her son — all APM: AA to JQA, Feb. 9, 1806; AA to JQA, March 24, 1806; "cracker in his pocket," AA to LCA, Dec. 8, 1804; AA to JQA, Dec. 18, 1804.

Separation of family: *Adventures;* JQA to LCA, Aug. 12, 1804 (APM); LCA to JQA, April 11 and May 29, 1804 (APM); LCA to JQA, Sept. 4, 14, 23 and Oct. 1, 1804 (APM); "true to my fears" sons left behind, *Adventures;* LCA to AA, Nov. 12 and Dec. 5, 1805 (APM); AA to LCA, Dec. 17 and 19, 1805, and Jan. 12 and Feb. 15, 1806 (APM); LCA to AA, Jan. 6, 1806 (APM); AA to LCA, Jan. 19, 1806 (APM).

Louisa's pregnancy: LCA to JQA, May 18, June 2 and 24, 1806 (APM); *Adventures; A.S. Colvin's Weekly Messenger.*

Traveling expenses: Reel 208, by date.

Charles Francis Adams's birth: *Adventures* (including kidnapping); JQA *Diary,* Aug. 18, 1807; LCA to Catherine Nuth Johnson, August 18 and 20, 1807.

Adamses to Russia: *Adventures;* Bemis, *Foundations,* pp. 151–3.

III. ST. PETERSBURG/LONDON 1809–1817

Chapter 1

The voyage and thoughts of home: Bemis, *Foundations,* pp. 153–5; JQA *in Russia,* pp. 3–6, Reel 208 (APM); JQA to AA, Aug. 9, 1809 (APM); William Gray to JQA, Aug. 4, 1809 (APM); Kirker, *Bulfinch's Boston,* p. 11; JQA *Diary,* March 25, 1829; AA to JQA and LCA, Aug. 5, 1809 (APM); AA to Caroline Smith, Aug. 12, 1809 (APM); JQA to AA, Aug. 9, 1809 (APM); "pikes and swords," JQA *in Russia,* pp. 19, 43, 45 (APM); JQA to TBA, Sept. 24, 1809 (APM).

Chapter 2

The Adamses in St. Petersburg: *Adventures;* LCA to AA, Oct. 23, 1810 (APM); "paces," JQA *Diary,* Dec. 3, 1809, and Feb. 22 and 23, 1811; JQA *in Russia,* p. 50 (APM); JQA *Diary,* March 20, 1812; LCA to AA, Oct. 28, 1809 (APM); JQA to AA, May 2, 1811 (APM); JQA *Diary,* Dec. 4, 1809, and May 23, Sept. 12, and Nov. 13, 1810; JQA to AA, Sept. 12, 1810 (APM); Czar's pears, JQA *Diary,* May 23, 1810.

Adams and Rumyantsev: wig, Reel 208 (APM); "wig and all . . . ," *Adventures;* JQA *Diary,* Feb. 8 and Oct. 24, 1810; Bemis, *Foundations,* p. 160; Grimsted, *Foreign Ministers,* p. 173; Consul Harris, Bemis, *Foundations* pp. 159 (footnote), 160, 169 (footnote); JQA *Diary,* Jan. 4, 1812.

French, American, Russian history: Bemis, *Foundations,* pp. 166–72; JQA *Diary,* Feb. 27, 1810; Shepherd, *The Adams Chronicles,* pp. 229–32, 234, 236–7.

Diplomatic corps: *Adventures;* JQA to AA, March 19, 1811 (APM); JQA *in Russia,* p. 248; JQA *Diary,* July 16, 1810, Feb. 8, 1811 (Count Julien), Aug. 5, 1812; JQA to AA, March 10, 1811 (Caulaincourt) (APM).

Chapter 3

Czar Alexander: JQA *Diary,* Nov. 4, 1809, May 17, 1811; *Adventures;* "darling," JQA to LCA, July 2, 1814 (APM); Bemis, *Founda-*

tions, pp. 161–3; JQA *in Russia*, pp. 52, 54, 94; Grimsted, *Foreign Ministers*, p. 35; Czarina and mistresses, JQA *Diary*, Jan. 8, 1810.

Bribes and cash gifts: Grimsted, *Foreign Ministers*, pp. 20, 27, 29; Crankshaw, *Shadow*, p. 23; newspapers, Reel 208 (APM); codes, Grimsted, *Foreign Ministers*, p. 17; *Adventures*; society, Reel 264 (APM); "waltzing machines," LCA to CFA, Feb. 4, 1838 (APM).

Chapter 4

Russian society: JQA *Diary*, Nov. 14 and 27, and Dec. 24, 1809, Jan. 18, 1810, and Jan. 12, 1811; LCA to AA, Jan. 7, 1810 (APM); *Adventures*; psychological darkness, JQA *Diary*, Nov. 19 and 30, and Dec. 21, 1809, Dec. 26, 1810, and Feb. 17, 1811; JQA to AA, Nov. 16, 1810 (APM).

CFA at children's ball: LCA to AA, Nov. 16, 1810 (APM); *Adventures*; LCA to AA, June 2, and Nov. 16, 1810 (APM); JQA *Diary*, Dec. 14, 1809; LCA to ABA, Sept. 25, 1828.

Summer carriage procession: JQA *Diary*, Aug. 3 and 4, 1811, Sept. 24, 1810.

Ostentation on the banks of the Neva: *Adventures*; JQA *Diary*, July 26, 1810; *An Account of the Receipts and Expenditures of the United States for the Year 1810* (Washington, D.C.: A & G Way, Printers, 1812); Bemis, *Foundations*, p. 164.

Adams's expenses: JQA *Diary*, Nov. 28, 1809; Reels 208 and 210 (APM); LCA to AA, Feb. 8, 1810 (APM); *Adventures*, April 1, 1810; JQA to AA, Feb. 8, 1810 (APM); LCA to AA, May 13, 1810 (APM); LCA to AA, Jan. 7, 1810 (APM).

Servants: JQA to AA, Nov. 16, 1810 (APM); JQA *in Russia*, pp. 193–4; JQA to AA, Feb. 8, 1810 (APM).

Chapter 5

The Czar walking: JQA *Diary*, April 24, 1811, May 12 and 19, 1810, Feb. 2, 1810, and other entries.

Russian women: JQA *Diary*, Feb. 18, 1811, and July 16, 1810; LCA to AA, Jan. 7, 1810 (APM).

Catherine Johnson: JQA to LCA, Aug. 24, 1828 (APM); CFA to ABA, Sept. 15, 1828 (APM).

Alexander's interest in Catherine: LCA to AA, June 2, 1810 (APM); *Adventures*, Dec. 29, 1810; LCA to AA, June 2, 1810 (APM); CFA *Diary*, vol. I, p. 3.

Political results of JQA's friendship with Czar: JQA *Diary*, Dec. 26, 1810, and Dec. 29, 1809; Bemis, *Foundations*, pp. 166–75; Caulaincourt quote, JQA *Memoirs*, vol. II, p. 226.

Chapter 6

War statistics: Bemis, *Foundations*, p. 178; JQA Diary, Feb. 1, 1811.

Excursion to Crestoffsky is found in JQA *Diary*, June 26, 1811; *Adventures*, June 10, 1811.

Birth of LCA 2: *Adventures*; JQA to AA, Aug. 12, 1811 (APM); JQA to AA, Sept. 10, 1811 (APM); JQA *in Russia*, p. 305.

Nabby Adams Smith's death: AA to JQA, July 1813 (APM).

JQA on LCA: *Diary*, July 26, 1811.

Czar and Adams on walks: JQA *Diary*, March 3, 1812, and Oct. 17, Oct. 25, Nov. 20 and Nov. 19, 1811.

LCA on LCA2: *Adventures*, Nov. 19, 1811; LCA to JA, Dec. 13, 1811 (APM).

Chapter 7

Alexander's conversation with JQA: JQA *Diary*, March 19, 1812.

Details of Easter Week: soldiers, JQA *Diary*, April 14, 1811; JQA *Diary*, April 15, 22, and 29, 1810, and April 13, 1811; JQA to AA, May 2, 1811 (APM).

Chapter 8

"Fatten the corn," JQA to JA, June 12, 1812 (APM).

Death of LCA2: *Adventures;* LCA to CFA, May 4, 1846 (APM); Reel 264, Oct. 22 and 23, Nov. 6, and Dec. 29, 1812, Dec. 5, 1813, and Aug. 14, 1813 (APM).

JQA and his sons: JQA to AA, Feb. 17, 1810 (APM); JQA *in Russia*, pp. 9, 10, 13, 16, 17.

Sampling of best of nasty letters to GWA: JQA to GWA, Sept. 3, 1810, May 10, and Aug. 15, 1811 (APM); Bible, *Letters* of AA, pp. 430–68. George's early life appears on Reel 287 (APM).

CFA's life in Russia: LCA to AA, June 2, 1810 (APM); Duberman, *Charles Francis Adams*, pp. 7–11; JQA *Diary*, May 31, 1812; LCA to CFA, Feb. 4, 1838 (APM); JQA to AA, May 28, 1811 (APM). CFA's conversation with Tzar: JQA *Diary*, Nov. 19, 1811; LCA to JQA, Jan. 3, 1815.

War: JQA *Diary*, Sept. 25, 1812; JQA to JA, Oct. 24, 1812 (APM); JQA to TBA, Sept. 29, 1812 (APM); JQA *Diary*, Oct. 24, 1812, and May 11, 1813; Russian generals, JQA to AA, Dec. 31, 1812 (APM); spoils, JQA *Diary*, Oct. 28, and Nov. 25, 1812, May 11, 1813, Dec. 1, 1812; Rumyantsev, JQA *in Russia*, pp. 483, 525, and JQA *Diary*, Nov. 18, and Dec. 30, 1813, and Feb. 25, 1814; funerals, JQA *Diary*, June 23 and 25, 1813.

Alexander: JQA to LCA, July 2, 1814 (APM); Grimsted, *Foreign Ministers*, p. 38.

Chapter 9

Trip to Ghent: outfitting, Reels 208 and 210 (APM); JQA to LCA, May 3, 1814 (APM); JQA *Diary*, April 28, 1814, and following; sampling of letters, JQA to LCA, May 3, April 30, to CFA, May 31, June 20 and to LCA, June 29, 1814 (APM).

Treaty of Ghent: Shepherd, *The Adams Chronicles*, pp. 237, 239, 240–41; Bemis, *Foundations*, pp. 180–95; Adams in Ghent, JQA *Diary* entries June–December 1814; treaty signing and voyage, JQA *Diary*, Dec. 27, 1814, and JQA to LCA, Dec. 2, 17, and 30, 1814 (APM); letter to LCA "come and meet me," JQA to LCA, Dec. 27, 1814 (APM).

Louisa's trip: letters to JQA include Jan. 26 and 31 and Feb. 12, 1815 (departing) (APM); carriage provisions and costs, Reel 210 (APM); "Narrative of a Journey From Russia to France, 1815" Reel 268 (APM); LCA's expenses, Reel 21, and LCA to JQA, Jan. 31, 1815 (APM).

Chapter 10

The Adamses to England: Reel 208 (APM); Bemis, *Foundations*, pp. 221–3, 246; JQA to JA, May 29, 1816 (APM); LCA to AA, Sept. 11, 1816 (APM).

Family poetry: Reels 271 and 272 (APM); LCA to AA, Sept. 11, 1816 (APM).

Education of sons: LCA to JQA, Jan. 6, 1815 (APM); Reel 287, April 16, 1815 (APM); JQA to AA, March 25 and June 6, 1816 (APM).

George, Reel 287, April 16, 1815 (APM).

LCA's miscarriage: LCA to AA, Aug. 14, 1817 (APM).

IV. WASHINGTON 1817–1825

Chapter 1

Adamses in New York: Royall, *Sketches*, pp. 242–3; LCA to AA, Aug. 14, 1817 (APM); JQA *Diary*, Sept. 14, 1817; Thomas Moore, LCA to JQA, June 10, 1804 (APM); *Adventures;* LCA to Mrs. JA2, Feb. 19, 1832 (APM); LCA to CFA, Jan. 16, 1833.

Children to school: GWA to LCA, Sept. 30, 1817 (APM); JA to JQA, Dec. 7, 1818, Feb. 3, and May 21, 1819, and Sept. 8, 1820 (APM).

Chapter 2

Life in America: Hunt, *One Hundred Years Ago*, pp. 51–62; Royall, *Sketches*, pp. 308–9; Poore, *Perley's Reminiscences of Sixty Years in the National Metropolis*, pp. 31–9; Marshall's accident in Langdon, *Everyday Things*, p. 20.

State Department: Bemis, *Foundations*, pp. 225, 256, 259 (footnote); Shepherd, *The Adams Chronicles*, pp. 255, 263, 264; Treasury Department, Reel 482 (APM).

"That poison tobacco," LCA to Thomas J. Hellen, March 4, 1827.

Lottery: Reel 208 (APM); *National Intelligencer*, March 20, 1819.

Chapter 3

Intrigue of cabinet: JQA's *Memoirs*, vol. IV, p. 32; CFA *Diary*, vol. I, p. 31; Shepherd, *The Adams Chronicles*, pp. 256, 258.

Washington campaign: Young, *The Washington Community*, pp. 223, 224, 225, 226–7; Bemis, *Foundations*, pp. 273, 274; Green, *Washington Village and Capital*, p. 81.

Louisa's role: Reel 264, Feb. 19 and 21, and March 3, 1819 (APM); Reel 265, Dec. 15, 16, 20, 21, 22, 24, and 30, 1819, Jan. 5 and 6 and March 2 and 14, 1820 (APM).

Congressional Caucus: Bemis, *Union*, pp. 11–12.

Costs, Reel 208 (APM).

Englishman, 1812: Dangerfield, *Good Feelings*, p. 7; description of JQA, Green, *Washington Village and Capital*, pp. 108–9; "cankered with prejudice," Bemis, *Union*, p. 8; cold heart, JQA to Christopher Hughes, Sept. 26, 1833; "pumphandle handshake," *Boston Patriot*, Dec. 20, 1831, p. 2, col. 3.

Louisa: "timid," LCA to JQA, May 12, 1804; CFA on LCA, CFA *Diary*, vol. I, Sept. 23, 1824 (APM); Louisa "noticed": Reel 265, Jan. 29, 1820, Dec. 20, 1819, and March 13, 1820 (APM); "my campaign," Reel 265, Dec. 14, 1818 (APM).

Portrait: Oliver, *Portraits*, p. 102.

Chapter 4

Children must not be forgotten: JA to JQA, May 20, 1818 (APM).
"Iron Mask," CFA *Diary*, vol. I, Dec. 23, 1823.
Sons in college: CFA *Diary*, vol. I, p. 1; JQA *Diary*, Sept. 6, 1818; JA to JQA, May 20, 1818 (APM); GWA prize, JA to JQA, Sept. 8, 1820 (APM); "sugar plums," JQA to JA2, Nov. 17, 1817 (APM); "no satisfaction in seeing you," JQA to JA2, Dec. 15, 1821 (APM); JQA to JA2, May 6, 1822 (APM); CFA in LCA *Diary*, Feb. 8, 1821; JQA to CFA, Jan. 30, 1822 (APM); CFA *Diary*, May 10, 1824; JQA to JA2, May 6, 1822 (APM); LCA to CFA, May 6, 1822 (APM).
Johnson Hellen: CFA *Diary*, vol. I, p. 6; JA2 to Caleb Stark, Jr., Dec. 23, 1823; "moving in and out," JQA to LCA, Sept. 29, 1822; CFA *Diary*, vol. I, Sept. 26, 1823; "God bless him," JQA to LCA, July 15, 1822.
Thomas Hellen: LCA to Thomas J. Hellen, March 4, 1826 (APM); CFA *Diary*, Sept. 19, 1827; LCA to Thomas J. Hellen, May 31 and April 25, 1827 (APM); JQA to GWA, Nov. 12, 1827 (APM).
The ladies are found in Reel 265, Jan. 28 and Feb. 5, 1820 (APM).
LCA's headache: Reel 265, Jan. 7 and 10, 1820 (APM).
Fanny Johnson episode: Reel 265, Dec. 4, 6, 13, and 19, 1820, and Jan. 13, 14, 20, and 24, 1821; and March 10, 1821 (APM).

Chapter 5

Louisa's suffering: Reel 265, Feb. 15 and Dec. 20, 1819, and Jan. 11, 17, 19, and 20, 1820; erysipelas, CFA to ABA, Sept. 18, 1828, and Reel 265, March 23 and Dec. 3 and 13, 1821; unable to go out, Dec. 2, 1823 (all APM).
Dr. Physick: Hunt, *One Hundred Years Ago*, pp. 202–3, 206, 211; *National Intelligencer*, Saturday, March 25, 1820; Middleton, *Annals*, pp. 565–79, 581–2; Geoffrey Marks and William K. Beatty, *The Story of Medicine in America* (New York: Charles Scribner's Sons, 1973), pp. 167–9; Morton, *Pennsylvania Hospital*, pp. 451, 476–7, 497; LCA to JQA June 24, 1822 (APM); George W. Corner, *Two Centuries of Medicine: A History of the School of Medicine, University of Pennsylvania* (Philadelphia: J. B. Lippincott, 1865), pp. 53, 75; "Surgery at the New York Hospital One Hundred Years Ago," *Annals of Medical History*, Sept. 1929, vol. I, no. 5, pp. 490, 512.
Louisa on Dr. Physick: LCA to JQA, June 24 and 25, July 29, Aug. 15 and 30 and Sept. 12, 1822 (APM).
Thomas's diet: LCA to JQA, June 25, July 18 and 26, and Aug. 1, 1822 (APM).

Life in boardinghouse: (Miss Pardon) LCA to GWA, June 26, 1822; LCA to GWA, July 3, 1822; LCA to JQA, June 28, 1822 (all APM).

Louisa and politics: LCA to JQA, July 14, 15, 20, 22, 28, and 29, 1822; LCA to GWA, July 10, 1822; persuading JQA to travel to Philadelphia, LCA to JQA, June 28, 1822, LCA to GWA, July 9, 1822, JQA to LCA, July 10 and 15, 1822, LCA to JQA, July 26 and Oct. 2, 1822, and JQA to LCA, Oct. 7, 1822; "all crying me down," JQA to LCA, Oct. 7, 1822; "backbiters," JQA to LCA, Aug. 23, 1822; LCA to JQA, Aug. 31, 1822 (all APM).

Jonathan Russell: LCA to GWA, July 10, 1822; JQA to LCA, July 18 and 22, 1822; LCA to JQA, June 28 and July 22, 1822 (all APM); Dangerfield, *Good Feelings*, p. 7.

Chapter 6

Medical history: Hunt, *One Hundred Years Ago*, pp. 211–13; William G. Rothstein, *American Physicians in the Nineteenth Century* (Baltimore: Johns Hopkins University Press, 1972), p. 166; "chimera," Marks and Beatty, *Medicine in America*, p. 167.

Information on Dr. Physick's ophthamalic operation and instruments is found in Middleton, *Annals*, pp. 565–72; Morton, *Pennsylvania Hospital*, pp. 476–7, 497.

Thomas Johnson's operation: LCA to JQA, Aug. 6–7, 7–8, 17, 24–25, 27–28, and 31, 1822; Thomas "wasting away," LCA to JQA, Aug. 18, 1822 (all APM).

Louisa in Bordentown: LCA to JQA, Sept. 16–18, 19–20, and 28, 1822 (APM); Federal Writers Project, *New Jersey: A Guide to Its Present and Past* (New York: Viking, 1939), pp. 207–14.

Louisa's operation: Middleton, *Annals*, pp. 475, 573, 579; Morton, *Pennsylvania Hospital*, p. 451; Corner, *Two Centuries of Medicine* (see notes for Ch. Five, above), p. 53; William Brodenhamer, *A Theoretical and Practical Treatise on the Hemorrhoidal Disease* (New York: Wilkin Wood & Co., 1884), pp. 56–7; LCA to JQA, Oct. 2, 3, 5, and 6–7, 1822; Reel 208 (APM); *A Memoir of Philip Syng Physick*, J. Randolph, M.D.; Philadelphia: T. K. and P. G. Collins, 1839.

Chapter 7

LCA's health: Reel 265, Jan. 5 and 17, 1823 (APM).

Ingersoll quote, "$6,000": Meigs, *The Life of Charles Jared Ingersoll*, pp. 122–5; on Adams's house, p. 129.

Jackson Ball: Reel 265, Jan. 20, 1820, Dec. 20 and 27, 1823, and Jan. 2, 3, 6, and 8 and Feb. 28, 1824 (APM); CFA *Diary*, vol. I, pp. 32, 33, 34, 36; LCA to GWA, Jan. 1, 1824 (APM); poem, *Harper's Bazaar*, "Mrs. John Quincy Adams's Ball, 1824," March 1871, vol. 4, pp. 166–8; Mills, *Proceedings*, pp. 40–41; JQA *Diary*, pp. 313–14.

V. WASHINGTON 1825–1830

Chapter 1

Election of 1824: Dangerfield, *Awakening*, pp. 339, 343; Smith, *First Forty Years*, pp. 170–71, 175–6, 181, 186; Bemis, *Foundations*, p. 450; Bemis, *Union*, p. 47; Young, *Washington Community*, p. 188; Shepherd, *The Adams Chronicles*, pp. 280–282.

Chapter 2

The Adams Presidency: Bemis, *Union*, pp. 55–91; Mills, *Proceedings*, pp. 47, 48; JQA to GWA, March 12, 1828 (APM); Shepherd, *The Adams Chronicles*, pp. 283–314; CFA *Diary*, March 31, 1827; Oliver, *Portraits*, pp. 148–50; JQA to GWA, Jan. 8, 1828 (APM); LCA to CFA, Jan. 24, 1828 (APM); Young, *Washington Community*, pp. 188–9.

Chapter 3

Louisa in the White House: "prison," Reel 265, Feb. 19, 1823 (APM); LCA to CFA, Sept. 16, 1827 (APM); LCA to GWA, Nov. 6, 1825 (APM); CFA *Diary*, March 11, 1828; Louisa on herself, Reel 265, March 15, 1821 (APM); CFA *Diary*, vol. I, pp. 315, 332.

Catherine Beecher: Smith, *Daughters*, pp. 133–4.

Louisa confined to chambers: LCA to Thomas J. Hellen, March 4, 1826; LCA to GWA, March 6, 1826; confinement, JQA to GWA, Jan. 28, 1827; LCA to GWA, Jan. 19, 1827; "Lehigh Coal Catarrh," LCA to Mary Roberdeau, June 14, 1833; JQA to CFA, Nov. 16, 1833; LCA to CFA, Nov. 21 and 28, 1836; LCA to ABA, April 23, 1837; LCA to CFA, Feb. 11, 1838 (all APM).

Melancholia: Reel 265, Jan. 7, 1820.

Boredom and isolation: LCA to CFA, March 10, and July 10 and 16, and Sept. 23, 1828; "isolation an evil," LCA to CFA, July 25, 1828; CFA to LCA, Aug. 2 and March 15, 1828 (all APM).

JQA on LCA's health: JQA to LCA, July 24, 1834; Reel 265, Jan. 7, 1820 (both APM).

Chocolate: LCA to AA, Dec. 7, 1803; Reel 208; LCA to CFA, Feb. 1, 1819; CFA to LCA, Feb. 10–15, 1829 (all APM).

LCA's plays: Reel 273, July 11, 1826; Lord and Lady Sharply, Reel 274 (both APM).

Servant girl: Reel 271, LCA to GWA, Sept. 4, 1825; LCA to JQA, Aug. 8, 1822; "rights of women," LCA to JQA, Aug. 28–29, 1822 (all APM).

"The more I bear . . .": LCA to Mrs. JA2, Aug. 19, 1827; Adams men "peculiarly harsh," LCA to CFA, Aug. 19, 1827 (all APM).

Chapter 4

George Adams: Bemis, *Union*, p. 116; Harriet Welsh to LCA, Jan. 16, 1819 (APM); "quivering," CFA *Diary*, April 28, 1829; dream, GWA to Thomas O. Bracket, Sept. 25, 1817 (APM); "literary amateur," CFA *Diary*, p. xxvi; JQA poetry to GWA, Reel 271 (APM); JQA to GWA, Oct. 16, 1825 (APM); GWA *Diary*, Reel 287 (APM).

George and Mary: "capricious," CFA *Diary*, May 20, 1824; John Adams 2d, "hot headed," Reel 265, Nov. 15, 1820 (APM); John and horses, CFA *Diary*, Aug. 21, 1829; John "artful," CFA *Diary*, June 13, 1829.

George's engagement: CFA *Diary*, Jan. 5, and May 19, 20, and 30, 1824; Louisa breaks up, LCA to CFA, Sept. 9, 1826 (APM).

George on guard against "female fidelity": Reel 287 (APM).

Chapter 5

John Adams: Bemis, *Union*, pp. 108, 109–11; JQA *Memoirs*, vol. VII, pp. 129–33; GWA to JQA, July 5, 1826 (APM).

JA death: LCA to JQA, July 11, 1826 (APM); JQA *Memoirs*, vol. VII, p. 125; LCA to Harriet Welsh, July 1826 (APM); LCA to JQA, July 16, 1826 (APM).

JA's will: Bemis, *Union*, pp. 111–12; JQA to LCA, July 14, 1826 (APM); JQA *Memoirs*, vol. VII, pp. 147–9.

Jefferson's poverty: Young, *Washington Community*, pp. 58, 59; LCA to JQA, July 15 and 17, 1826 (APM); JQA to LCA, July 14, 1826 (APM); "God Forbid," LCA to JQA, July 18, 1826 (APM).

Louisa to the spas: LCA to JQA, July 20, 1826 (APM); Ryan, *Womanhood*, p. 134; Smith, *Daughters*, p. 132; CFA *Diary*, July 25 and 26 and Aug. 7, 9, 14–23, 23–27, 29, and 31, 1826; LCA to JQA, Aug. 3, 1826 (APM); LCA to JQA, Aug. 7, 1826 (APM); LCA to JQA, Aug. 21, 1826 (APM).

Louisa and George in Quincy: on land survey, JQA to LCA, Aug. 26, 1826; on "state of George's mind," LCA to CFA, Sept. 9, 1826 (both APM).

Adamses' therapies for George: LCA to GWA, Jan. 29, 1826; JQA to GWA, Feb. 24, March 25, and March 4, 1827, and Dec. 31, 1826; LCA to GWA, Oct. 29 and March 6, 1826; Harriet Welsh to CFA, May 11, 1827; LCA to Harriet Welsh, May 14, 1827; JQA to GWA, May 19, 1827 (with *National Intelligencer*); JQA to GWA, Nov. 18 and 28, and Dec. 14, and 19, 1827 (all APM).

Chapter 6

Charles's exchange with JA: JA to CFA, Dec. 3, 1825; CFA to JA, Nov. 19 and 22, 1825; JA to CFA, Dec. 3, 1825 (all APM).

Charles as a dandy: CFA to JA, Jan. 29 and Feb. 26, 1826 (APM).

Charles in New York City: CFA *Diary*, June 22–July 8, 1826.

Charles and Abigail Brooks: CFA *Diary*, Jan. 31, 1827.

Peter Brooks and JQA: Brooks to Edward Everett, Feb. 17, 1827, Everett Papers Mss., Mass. Historical Society; Brooks to JQA, Feb. 17, 1827 (APM); JQA description of CFA, JQA to Brooks, Feb. 23, 1827 (APM); consent, Brooks to Everett, March 2, 1827; Brooks to LCA, March 15, 1827 (APM).

"Future support": JQA to CFA, Sept. 15, 1826 (APM); "her fortune," CFA *Diary*, Jan. 31, 1827.

Charles's passion: CFA *Diary*, Feb. 8, Jan. 3, and May 8 and 20, 1824, and April 9, 1827; mistress, CFA *Diary*, April 24, 1827.

CFA on Abby Brooks: CFA *Diary*, Feb. 10 and 13 and Aug. 5, 1827, and Dec. 27 and Sept. 8, 1828.

Chapter 7

On JQA's health: JQA *Memoirs*, vol. VII, pp. 35–8, 302–3, 288, 311; "career closed," *Memoirs*, vol. VII, p. 273.

George's election: Bemis, *Union*, p. 129.

Charles on George's sickness: CFA *Diary*, June 28, 1827.

Louisa's trip to Quincy: LCA to JQA, July 3 and 11, 1827 (APM); campaign, LCA to JQA, July 16, 1827, and LCA to JA2, July 16, 1827; LCA to JQA, July 26, 1827 (all APM).

Louisa on George: LCA to JQA, July 6, 1827; LCA to JA2, July 16, 1827; JQA to GWA, July 15, 1827; LCA to CFA, July 17, 1827 (all APM).

In New York City: LCA to JQA, July 26, 1827 (APM); CFA *Diary*, Aug. 2, 1827.

George, "firm purpose": JQA to LCA, Sept. 4, 1827; LCA to GWA, Sept. 15, 1827 (APM).

Chapter 8

JQA in Boylston farm room: JQA to GWA, Oct. 8, 1827 (APM).

JQA, CFA correspondence: JQA to CFA, Oct. 10, Nov. 11, and Dec. 9, 16, and 24, 1827, and Jan. 13 and Feb. 10, 1828; CFA to JQA, Jan. 22 and 28 and Feb. 19, 1828; JQA to CFA, Nov. 25, 1827 (all APM).

Charles and money: CFA *Diary*, Aug. 18, 1828; CFA to JQA, Nov. 6 and 20, 1827 (APM); JQA to CFA, Nov. 11, 1827 (APM).

CFA's argment with JQA: CFA *Diary*, Aug. 22, 1828; JQA to CFA, July 3, 1828; CFA to LCA, Nov. 22, 1828; "fund," JQA to CFA, Dec. 9, 1827; CFA to LCA, Jan. 3, 1829 (letters all APM); CFA *Diary*, Dec. 4, 1829; CFA to Peter Brooks, Oct. 26, 1828 (APM); CFA *Diary*, Nov. 13, 1828; "rolling in wealth," CFA *Diary*, Nov. 13 and 15, 1828; "rankling sore," CFA *Diary*, Nov. 4, 1828; "penny turns everything," LCA to CFA, Feb. 15, 1828 (APM).

George's debt: JQA to GWA, Jan. 21, 1828, LCA to CFA, Feb. 12, 1828 (APM).

JQA in White House garden: JQA *Memoirs*, vol. VII, pp. 288–93, 488–91; JQA to GWA, April 8 and June 3, 1827; JQA to CFA, April 20 and July 9, 1828; JQA to GWA, July 10, 1828; "a planter," JQA to GWA, July 10, 1828 (letters all APM).

Chapter 9

"Woes," JQA to CFA, Dec. 18, 1830 (APM).

Billiards table: for best account, see Edwin A. Miles, "President Adams' Billiards Table," *The New England Quarterly*, 1972, 45, pp. 31–43.

Jarvis attack: for the best account see Samuel Flagg Bemis, "The Scuffle in the Rotunda," *Proceedings of the Massachusetts Historical Society*, 1953–1957, number 71, pp. 156–66. Also, LCA to CFA, April 15, 1828 (APM); CFA *Diary*, Nov. 8 and Dec. 5, 1827.

JA2 marriage: 'Jackson's March," LCA to CFA, Feb. 3, 1828; JQA to

CFA, Feb. 26, 1828; LCA to CFA, Feb. 20, 1828; JQA to GWA, Feb. 22, 1828; LCA to CFA, Feb. 12, 1828; JQA to CFA, Feb. 25, 1828; LCA to CFA, Feb. 26 and 28, 1828 (all APM).

Chapter 10

Adams earthquake: JQA to GWA, March 12, 1828 (APM); JQA *Memoirs*, vol. VII, p. 471.

Election of 1828: LCA to CFA, May 26 and Dec. 11, 1828; CFA to LCA, Nov. 15, 1828 (all APM); "year begins in gloom," JQA *Memoirs*, vol. VIII, p. 89; Dangerfield, *Awakening*, p. 424.

Meridian farm: LCA to CFA, Jan. 11 and March 8 and 30, 1828 (APM).

Servants: LCA to CFA, Feb. 1, 1829 (APM); Bemis, *Union*, p. 159; LCA to CFA, Nov. 15, 1829 (APM).

Thomas J. Hellen's marriage to Jane Winnull: CFA *Diary*, April 20 and 25, 1829; LCA to CFA, April 16, 1829 (APM).

Charles on George in Boston: CFA to LCA, Jan. 3 and 24, and March 7, 1829, and Nov. 15 and 22, and Dec. 6 and 13, 1828 (all APM); "live like a pig," CFA *Diary*, Feb. 20, 1829; CFA *Diary*, March 22, 1829; "alarm," CFA to LCA, March 28 and April 4, 1829 (APM).

"Escort home": LCA to GWA, April 8, 1829; CFA to LCA, April 11, 1829; LCA to CFA, April 13 and 16, 1829 (APM).

"Come on immediately," JQA to GWA, April 20, 1829 (APM).

George's life: CFA *Diary*, April 13 and 27, 1829, May–June 1829, and p. 382 (footnote); Bemis, *Union*, p. 80.

George's death: CFA *Diary*, May 2 and 4, 1829; JQA *Diary*, May 5, 6, and 7, 1829; Bemis, *Union*, pp. 179–81; *Columbian Centinel*, Sept. 6, 10, and 13, 1829; LCA to CFA, May 7, 1829 (APM); guilt, LCA to CFA, July 5, 1829 (APM); CFA to LCA, July 10, 1829 (APM); JQA *Diary*, May 6, 1829; JQA to CFA, May 3, 1829 (APM); "ministering angel," LCA to CFA, May 7, 1829 (APM); JQA *Diary*, May 16, 1829; sign, JQA *Diary*, May 4, 1829; GWA poem, *National Intelligencer*, May 21, 1829.

George's body and pocket contents: JQA to LCA, June 13 and 15, 1829 (APM); LCA to JQA, June 14, 1829 (APM); JQA *Diary*, June 13 and 14, 1829.

Chapter 11

Charles in Boston: "how unfit," CFA *Diary*, May 20, 1829; "begin anew," CFA *Diary*, May 12, 1829; "trust," CFA *Diary*, June 22, 1829; "pain my father" and "thoughtless moment," CFA *Diary*, May 13, 1829.

Blackmail: CFA *Diary*, May 28 and June 20, 1829; CFA to Miles Farmer, June 20 and July 16, 1829, Library of Congress; CFA *Diary*, Aug. 27 and Sept. 1, 1829; CFA to Farmer, June 20, 1829, Library of Congress; CFA to D. H. Storer, July 16, 1829, Library of Congress; Reel 297, CFA, "Accounts as Manager of JQA's Finances 1828–1846" (APM); CFA *Diary*, July 16, Aug. 5 and 10, May 13 and 28, and June 30, 1829; burn, CFA *Diary*, June 2, 1829.

VI. WASHINGTON 1830–1852

Chapter 1

Charles's marriage: LCA's "violent attack," CFA *Diary*, Aug. 18–23, 1829; "consummated" marriage, CFA to JA2, Sept. 21, 1829 (APM); Abby Brooks Adams's birth: LCA to CFA, Nov. 17, 1833 (APM); LCA to JQA, July 24, 1841 (APM).

JQA's election to House: Bemis, *Union*, p. 207; Shepherd, *The Adams Chronicles*, p. 317; Louisa's anger, LCA to JA2, Oct. 31 and Nov. 14, 1830 (APM); LCA to CFA, Dec. 5 and 9, 1830 (APM).

Chapter 2

House of Representatives: Royall, *Sketches*, pp. 135–6; Dickens, *American Notes*, p. 118.

JQA on slavery: JQA *Diary*, Jan. 10, 1820; JQA *Memoirs*, vol. IV, p. 521; Shepherd, *The Adams Chronicles*, p. 318.

Slavery in District of Columbia: Green, *Washington Village and Capital*, p. 54; *National Intelligencer*, March 28, 1820, March 17, 1818.

JQA and de Tocqueville: George Wilson Pierson, *Tocqueville and Beaumont in America* (New York: Oxford University Press, 1938), pp. 418–20.

Louisa: poem, LCA to CFA, March 14, 1831; LCA to ABA, Feb. 28, 1831 (both APM).

Chapter 3

Railroad accident: JQA to CFA, Nov. 8 and 10, 1833 (APM).

Thomas B. Adams: "blue devils," TBA to JQA, Dec. 15, 1803 (APM); wife, CFA *Diary*, June 2 and Sept. 5, 1824; drunkenness, CFA *Diary*, May 25 and 31, and June 2 and 4, 1824; LCA to Mrs. JA2, Sept. 5, 1831 (APM); LCA to CFA, March 17, 1832 (APM).

JA2: JQA's investments, CFA *Diary*, Sept. 4, 1829; JQA to CFA, April 16, 1829; LCA to JQA, Sept. 17, 1829; LCA to CFA, Dec. 7, 1833; death, JQA to JA2, July 23 and 26, 1834; LCA to JQA, "soups," Oct. 21, 1834; "affectionate Son," JQA to CFA, Oct. 23 and 28, 1834 (letters all APM).

Chapter 4

Abolitionists: JQA to CFA, Dec. 15, 1835 (APM).

House debate: JQA to CFA, Jan. 28, 1836; CFA on JQA to LCA, April 25, 1836; health, JQA to LCA, April 7 and 21, and May 23, 1832; "battle of the grugs," LCA to ABA, Feb. 8, 1831 (all APM).

House members "crucify" JQA: JQA *Diary*, Feb. 6, 1842.

"Northern men, southern principles": JQA to CFA, May 2, 1836 (APM).

Gag Rule: Bemis, *Union*, p. 337; "last stage of my life," JQA *Memoirs*, vol. IX, p. 298, and vol. X, pp. 199–200; "ruin as a Public Man," JQA to CFA, May 24, 1836 (APM).

Chapter 5

Women: Lerner, *Grimké Sisters*, pp. 2–3, 269, 270–71; Arthur Calhoun, *A Social History of the American Family*, three vols. (New York: Barnes & Noble, 1945), vol. II, "a woman is a nobody," p. 84; Smith, *Daughters*, pp. 104–11.

Petitions: Lerner, *Grimké Sisters*, p. 275; Reel 505 (APM); Bemis, *Union*, pp. 341–2; "exuberant in toil," LCA to CFA, Feb. 5, 1837; Shepherd, *The Adams Chronicles*, pp. 328, 330–31.

Abigail Adams on slavery: *Familiar Letters*, pp. 41–2, 148.

Chapter 6

Louisa's self-exploration: Reel 271, July 31 and Oct. 26, 1835; Reel 268, Sept. 1, 1836 and Feb. 12, 1837; Reel 271, June 3 and Aug. 24, 1832 (all APM).

Abigail's letters: "power in the hands of husbands," *Adams Family Correspondence (AFC)*, vol. I, AA to JA, March 31, 1776, p. 370; "your Sex are Naturally Tyrannical," *ibid.*; JA's reply, "I cannot but laugh," to AA, *AFC*, April 14, 1776, p. 382; "I cannot say that I think you very generous to the Ladies," AA to JA, *AFC*, May 7, 1776, p. 402.

Chapter 7

Grimké sisters: Sarah Grimké to LCA Feb. 6, 1838 (APM); Lerner, *Grimké Sisters*, pp. 129–30, 192.

Nehemiah Adams: in *Annual Report of Boston Female Anti-Slavery Society* (Boston, 1837), pp. 42–3; Stanton *et al.*, *History of Woman Suffrage*, vol. I, p. 81.

"The whole land seems aroused," and "morally right for a man," from Angelina and Sarah Grimké, *Letters on the Equality of the Sexes*, pp. 10, 116, 120, 122.

"They are our sisters": Angelina E. Grimké, *An Appeal to Women in the Nominally Free States: Issued by an Anti-Slavery Convention of American Women & Held by Adjornment from the 9th to the 12th of May, 1837*, first edition (New York: W. S. Door, 1837).

Visit to JQA: LCA to JQA, May 22, 1837 (APM); Lerner, *Grimké Sisters*, p. 167; Bemis, *Union*, p. 349; Sarah Grimké to JQA, June 8, 1837 (APM).

Climax of Grimké crusade: Lerner, *Grimké Sisters*, p. 7; Smith, *Daughters*, p. 125; *The Liberator*, March 2, 1838; see also *Weld–Grimké Letters*, vol. II, pp. 572–4.

Chapter 8

Louisa on slavery: LCA to CFA, Feb. 10, 1837; on *Report*, LCA to CFA, Feb. 7, 1838 (both APM).

Louisa on liberated women: LCA to CFA, Feb. 21, 1838; LCA to Mrs. JA2, May 2, 1831 (both APM).

Catherine Beecher: Ryan, *Womanhood*, p. 148; Catherine Beecher, "An Essay on Slavery and Abolitionism with reference to the Duty of American Females" (Boston, 1839), pp. 98–9, 136–7. See also Angelina

Grimké, "Letters to Catherine Beecher in Reply to an Essay on Slavery and Abolitionists" (Boston, 1839), pp. 7, 103, 107.

Louisa and petitions: LCA to CFA, Feb. 10 and 24, and Dec. 15, 26–28, 1837, and Jan. 26–28, 31, and June 26, 1838; "delighted" with Sarah Grimké's *Letters*, LCA to CFA, Feb. 7, 1838 (all APM).

Louisa's correspondence with Sarah Grimké: LCA to SG, Jan. 11, 1838; LCA to CFA, Feb. 14, 1838; SG to LCA, Feb. 6, 1838; LCA to CFA, March 1, 1838; SG to LCA, Feb. 25, April 13, and Nov. 12, 1838 (all APM).

Burning of Pennsylvania Hall: Lerner, *Grimké Sisters*, pp. 244–50; see also *Liberator* accounts in Adams Papers Mss., May 1838.

Threats: Reel 524, Dec. 12, 1842; LCA to CFA, March 8, 1837 (both APM).

Figure of woman slave: Reel 511 (APM).

Chapter 9

Hingham: Reel 510; *Hingham Patriot*, Aug. 4, 1838.

Adams debts: JQA to CFA, March 3, 1837; LCA to JQA, Oct. 1, 1837; LCA to CFA, April 26, 1837; porch and kitchen collapse, LCA to JQA, May 20, 1837; JQA to LCA, Oct. 25, 1837; "quarter for a hack," LCA to CFA, Dec. 23, 1839 (all APM).

Accident: JQA *Diary*, May 18–20, 1840; LCA to CFA, May 20 and 24, 1840 (APM).

"Retire from the world," JQA *Memoirs*, vol. X, p. 451.

The Amistad case is well covered in Bemis, *Union*, pp. 384–415.

Fight against censure: Lerner, *Grimké Sisters*, p. 265; Bemis, *Union*, p. 424; LCA to CFA, Jan. 9, 1842 (APM); Theodore Weld to JQA, March 11, 1842 (APM); LCA to CFA, Feb. 5, 1842 (APM); *Diary of Philip Hone*, Allan Nevins, ed. (New York: 1927), vol. II, pp. 547–8, 583, 581–2; JQA *Memoirs*, vol. XI, p. 75; JQA *Diary*, Aug. 3, 1844.

"Old roue," Ralph Waldo Emerson, *Journals*, Edward W. Emerson and Waldo E. Forbes, eds. (Boston and New York: 1909–1914), vol. VI, pp. 349–50.

Chapter 10

Grandchildren: Mary Louisa Adams to JQA, May 22, 1835 (APM); Fanny's death, LCA to ABA, Jan. 26, 1840 (APM); *The Education of Henry Adams* (New York: Random House, 1918), p. 22; JQA to LCA, June 7, 1845 (APM); LCA to JQA, Aug. 9, 1841 (APM).

Charles a hypochondriac: CFA to LCA, Dec. 22 and 26, 1841 (APM).

ABA: Peter Brooks to ABA, Jan. 11, 1842; CFA to LCA, Dec. 22, 1836, and March 15, 1838; JQA to LCA, cause of her complaints, July 8, 1843 (all APM).

Trip to New York State and Canada: LCA to CFA, July 14, 1843; ABA to CFA, July 16 and 23, 1843; "oysters," CFA to ABA, July 8, 1843; Saratoga women and JQA, ABA to CFA, July 16, 1843; ABA to CFA2, July 23, 1843; ABA to CFA, July 29, 1843; ABA to Henry Adams, Aug. 4, 1843; Reel 527, Sept. 1843 (all APM); Cincinnati, Shepherd, *The*

Adams Chronicles, pp. 338–9; LCA to CFA, Nov. 25 and 27, 1843 (APM); LCA to ABA, Nov. 20, 1843 (APM); LCA to CFA, Dec. 3, 1843 (APM).

Chapter 11

Gag Rule: JQA *Diary,* Dec. 3, 1844.

JQA: Texas, LCA to CFA, May 28, 1846 (APM); "feeble," CFA to ABA, June 6, 1846 (APM); "ink stain," Francis Russell, *Adams: An American Dynasty* (New York: American Heritage Publishing Co., 1976), pp. 229–30; swimming, Bemis, *Union,* p. 525; JQA *Memoirs,* vol. XII, p. 269; LCA to ABA, July 14, 1846 (APM); election, Reel 535, Nov. 19, 1846 (APM).

JQA stroke: Reel 535, Dec. 1846 (APM); JQA *Memoirs,* vol. XII, p. 279; LCA to Mrs. JA2, Dec. 11 and Nov. 28, 1846 (APM); LCA to ABA, Jan. 27–Feb. 4, 1848 (APM); LCA to Mrs. JA2, Dec. 30, 1846, and Jan. 2 and 13, 1847 (APM); will, Bemis, *Union,* p. 528 (footnote); LCA to Mrs. JA2, Jan. 19, 1847 (APM); return to Washington, Bemis, *Union,* p. 530; LCA to ABA, May 14, 1847 (APM).

JQA death: LCA to CFA, Jan. 2, 1848; younger generation, LCA to ABA, Jan. 17–23, 1848; LCA to CFA, Jan. 9, 1848 (all APM); Bemis, *Union,* p. 534; *Congressional Globe,* 30th Congress, 1st Session, 1847–8, Monday, Feb. 21, 1848, pp. 380–1; Palfrey to ABA, Feb. 22, 1848 (APM); Palfrey to CFA, Feb. 21, 1848 (APM); Palfrey to ABA, Feb. 24, 1848 (APM); Reel 537 (APM).

Chapter 12

LCA: loved the spring, "clouds of birds," LCA to CFA, March 8, 1838; Reel 270, March 18, 1849; money, LCA to JQA, March 24 and 31, and April 5, 1832; house for $3,000, JQA to LCA, June 15, 1837; Thomas J. Hellen's will, LCA to CFA, Dec. 2, 1843; "well off," CFA to LCA, Oct. 23, 1848; fixed up house, LCA to CFA, Nov. 15, 1848; guests, LCA to CFA, Jan. 2, 1848; stroke, LCA to ABA, March 11, 1849; LCA to CFA, Aug. 7, 1849 (all APM).

CFA: "feeling alone," CFA to LCA, Nov. 19, 1848 (APM); election, Duberman, *Charles Francis Adams,* p. 163.

Henry Adams: looked like Charles, LCA to CFA, June 18, 1841 (APM).

Louisa's guilt: LCA to CFA, April 21, 1846 (APM).

Henry's observations on Washington and Louisa: *The Education of Henry Adams,* pp. 45, 16–19.

Seneca Falls: Smith, *Daughters,* p. 113.

Julia: LCA to ABA, Aug. 7, 1846, May 14, 1847, and Jan. 27–Feb. 4, 1848 (all APM); Reel 301.

Solomon's Song: Reel 503; JQA to LCA, May 1, 1841; LCA to JQA, May 4, 1841 (all APM).

LCA death: "blessed promise," LCA to JQA, May 6, 1841; "wants to die," Elizabeth C. Adams to ABA, May 6, 1852; Mrs. JA2 to CFA, May 14, 1852 (all APM).

Selected Bibliography

In addition to original materials by Louisa Catherine Adams, which include her diaries and letters, and selected original materials by her husband, the following works were of value.

Adams, Abigail, *Letters of Mrs. Adams, the Wife of John Adams*. Introduction by Charles Francis Adams. Boston: Little, Brown, 1840.
————, *New Letters of Abigail Adams, 1788–1801*. Edited by Stewart Mitchell. Boston: Houghton Mifflin, 1947.
Adams, Charles Francis, *The Diary of Charles Francis Adams*. Six volumes. Vols. 1–2 edited by Aïda and David Donald; vols. 3–6 edited by Marc Friedlander and L. H. Butterfield. Cambridge, Mass.: Harvard University Press, 1964–1974.
Adams, Henry, *The Education of Henry Adams: An Autobiography* (1918). Boston: Houghton Mifflin, 1961.
Adams, John, *The Diary and Autobiography of John Adams* (1961). Edited by L. H. Butterfield and others. Four volumes. New York: Atheneum, 1964.
Adams, John Quincy. *The Diary of John Quincy Adams, 1794–1845*. Edited by Allan Nevins. New York: Ungar, 1951.
————, *John Quincy Adams in Russia*. Edited by Charles Francis Adams. New York: Praeger Publishers, 1970.
————, *Life in a New England Town, 1787, 1788. Diary of John Quincy Adams, While a Student in the Office of Theophilus Parsons at Newburyport*. Introduction by Charles Francis Adams, Jr. Boston: Little, Brown, 1903.
————, *Memoirs of John Quincy Adams, 1795–1848* (1874–1877). Edited by Charles Francis Adams. Twelve volumes. Freeport, N.Y.: Books for Libraries Press, 1969.

————, *The Writings of John Quincy Adams.* Edited by Worthington C. Ford. Seven volumes. New York: Macmillan, 1913–1917.

Adams, Louisa Catherine, "Narrative of a Journey from St. Petersburg to Paris." With a foreword by Brooks Adams. *Scribner's Magazine* (October 1903), 34:449–64.

Adams Family Correspondence. Edited by L. H. Butterfield and others. Four volumes. Cambridge, Mass.: Harvard University Press, 1963–1973.

Bemis, Samuel Flagg, *John Quincy Adams and the Foundations of American Foreign Policy.* New York: Knopf, 1949.

————, *John Quincy Adams and the Union.* New York: Knopf, 1956.

————, "The Scuffle in the Rotunda, A Footnote to the Presidency of John Quincy Adams and to the History of Dueling." *Proceedings of the Massachusetts Historical Society,* 1953–1957. 71:156–66.

Blake, John B., *Public Health in the Town of Boston, 1630–1822.* Cambridge, Mass.: Harvard University Press, 1952.

Boulding, Elise, *The Underside of History.* Boulder, Colo.: Westview Press, 1976.

Brodenhamer, William, *A Theoretical and Practical Treatise on the Hemorrhoidal Disease.* New York: Wilkin Wood & Co., 1884.

Butterfield, L. H., "Tending a Dragon Killer." *Proceedings of the American Philosophical Society* (April 1974), 118:165–78.

Connelly, Owen, *The Gentle Bonaparte: A Biography of Joseph, Napoleon's Older Brother.* New York: Macmillan, 1968.

Crankshaw, Edward, *The Shadow of the Winter Palace: Russia's Drift to Revolution, 1825–1917.* New York: Viking Press, 1976.

Dangerfield, George, *The Awakening of American Nationalism, 1815–1828.* New York: Harper & Row, 1965.

————, *The Era of Good Feelings.* New York: Harcourt, Brace, 1952.

Dickens, Charles, *American Notes and Pictures From Italy.* London: Oxford University Press, 1957.

Duberman, Martin B., *Charles Francis Adams, 1807–1886.* Boston: Houghton Mifflin, 1961.

East, Robert A., *John Quincy Adams: The Critical Years.* New York: Bookman Associates, 1962.

Green, Constance McLoughlin, *Washington Village and Capital, 1800–1878.* Princeton, N.J.: Princeton University Press, 1962.

Grimsted, Patricia Kennedy, *The Foreign Ministers of Alexander I.* Berkeley, Cal.: University of California Press, 1969.

Hunt, Gaillard, *Life in America One Hundred Years Ago.* New York: Harper & Brothers, 1914.

Kirker, Harold and James, *Bulfinch's Boston.* New York: Oxford University Press, 1964.

Langdon, William Chauncy, *Everyday Things in American Life, 1776–1876.* New York: Charles Scribner's Sons, 1941.

Lerner, Gerda, *The Grimké Sisters from South Carolina.* New York: Schocken Books, 1971.

"Letters of Hon. Elijah H. Mills." *Proceedings of the Massachusetts Historical Society,* 1881–1882. 19:14–50.

Marks, Geoffrey, and William K. Beatty, *The Story of Medicine in America.* New York: Charles Scribner's & Sons, 1973.

Marlowe, George Francis, *Coaching Roads of Old New England.* New York: The Macmillan Company, 1945.

McMaster, J. B., *History of the People of the United States, from the Revolution to the Civil War.* New York: Farrar, Straus, 1964.

Meigs, Wickin M., *The Life of Charles Jared Ingersoll.* Philadelphia and London: J. B. Lippincott, 1900.

Middleton, William S., M.D., "Philip Syng Physick, Father of American Surgery." *Annals of Medical History* (September 1929), I, 5:562–82.

Miles, Edwin A., "President Adams' Billiard Table." *The New England Quarterly* (1972), 45:31–43.

Morton, Thomas G., *The History of the Pennsylvania Hospital, 1751–1895.* Philadelphia: Times Printing House, 1895.

"Mrs. John Quincy Adams' Ball, 1824." *Harper's Bazaar* (March 18, 1871), 4:116–68.

Oliver, Andrew, *Portraits of John Quincy Adams and His Wife.* Cambridge, Mass.: Harvard University Press, 1970.

Poore, Benjamin Perley, *Perley's Reminiscences of Sixty Years in the National Metropolis,* Vol. 1. Philadelphia: Hubbard Brothers, 1886.

Recollections of Samuel Brech, 1771–1802. H. E. Scudder, ed. London: Sampson Low, Marston, Searle and Rivington, 1877.

Royall, Anne N., *Sketches of History, Life and Manners in the United States, – by a Traveler.* New Haven, Ct.: 1826.

Ryan, Mary P., *Womanhood in America.* New York: New Viewpoints, 1975.

Smelser, Marshall, *The Democratic Republic, 1801–1815.* New York: Harper & Row, 1968.

Smith, Mrs. Samuel Harrison, *The First Forty Years of Washington Society.* New York: Charles Scribner's Sons, 1906.

Smith, Page, *Daughters of the Promised Land.* Boston: Little, Brown, 1970.

Stanton, Elizabeth C., Susan B. Anthony, and Matilda J. Gage, *History of Woman Suffrage.* Six volumes. New York: Fowler and Wells, 1881–1922.

Stone, Lawrence, *The Family, Sex and Marriage in England 1500–1800.* London: Weidenfeld and Nicholson, 1977.

Young, James Sterling, *The Washington Community.* New York: Columbia University Press, 1966.

INDEX

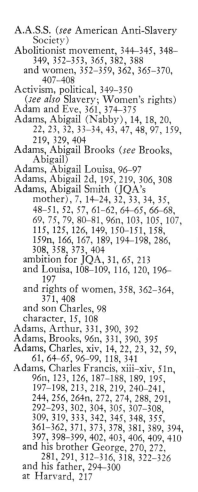

Adams, George Washington (*cont.*)
education, 164–166, 188, 198, 217, 269–270
fear of his father, 270, 273–274, 292, 316
JQA's expectations of and for, 111, 164, 166–167, 188, 257, 259, 264–270, 271, 274, 279–280, 282, 294–295, 296, 316, 318, 322
Louisa's "abandonment" of, 120, 126, 318, 329–330, 406
love of his grandfather, 273, 275–276, 280
outcast, unraveling, 269–276, 279–282, 290–293, 312–316
studies and practices law, 217, 241, 270–271
suicide, 316–322
farewell poem, 320
parents' remorse, 318–320
settling his affairs, 323–326
Adams, Georgiana Francis (Fanny), 308, 329, 331, 343, 389, 390
Adams, Hannah, 109–110
Adams, Henry, xiii–xiv, 96n, 331, 390–392, 406–407
Adams, Isaac Hull, 195, 219
Adams, John, xiii, xiv, 4, 7, 8, 9, 12, 13–17, 18, 22, 24, 32, 34, 45, 48–49, 52, 57, 64–65, 66–68, 69, 80, 96n, 97, 103–104, 107, 125, 126, 162, 167, 185, 188, 189, 190, 194–198, 215, 216, 252, 254, 269–270, 272, 283, 286, 309, 341, 404
ambition for JQA, 58–59, 65
and Declaration of Independence, 362–364
and education of his children, 15–16, 17
and grandson George, 273, 275–276, 280
and son Charles, 98–99
death, funeral, will, 275–278
in Europe, 31–32
liking for Louisa, 108–109, 120, 197, 276–277
President, 77–78, 82, 91, 92, 98, 104, 110, 259
Vice President, 46, 48, 58n
Adams, John Quincy, xiii–xiv, 12, 30, 37, 409, 410
age and infirmities, 345–346, 397–401
and education of his children, 111–112, 164–168, 188, 215–217
and his mother, 14–15, 33, 34, 35, 43, 49–51, 52, 57, 61–62, 64–65, 79, 109, 115, 126, 188, 358
and Johnson family, 60–65
and money, 52, 58, 73, 81–82, 95–99, 148–151, 204–205, 210–211, 277–279, 298–299, 333, 341, 343
impoverished, 312, 381
and parental authority, 42–52, 57, 58, 60, 61–62, 64–65, 78
and political compromise, 249–253, 368–369
and preservation of the Union, 336–337, 338, 339, 347–348, 385, 388–389
and Revolutionary War, 17–24, 125, 404
and women's rights, 379–380
appointed to Lisbon, 73, 75, 78
as a father, 6, 215–216, 260, 270, 274, 280–282, 290, 293, 294–302, 314
and George's death, 318–322

bathing, 4, 53, 173
becomes born-again Christian, 277
betrothal, 64, 66–67
birth, family, early life, 13–24, 196
calculating history, xiv
campaign against Jackson, 302–305, 306, 309–310
collapse, funeral, death, 401–404
continentalist, 203, 401
Conscience Whig, 398
diary, 4, 46, 49, 54–55, 60, 74, 80, 190, 206–207, 216, 244, 250, 252, 257, 270, 276, 290, 298, 309, 336, 381–382, 396
dominance of Louisa, 116–118, 119–120, 130, 163–164, 213–215, 267–268
drinking and knowledge of wines, 345n–346n
education, 15–17, 31–35, 68
exercise, 203–204, 397–398
flautist, 35, 185
gardening, arboriculture, 301, 410
good writer, xiv
grandfather, 390–392
gravity, 5, 72, 76, 94–95
hard, cold, precise, 4, 5, 61, 72–74, 82–83, 212, 260
harsh temper, 124, 227, 260, 346, 386
Harvard professor, 117
in House of Representatives, 331–339
and annexation of Texas, 396–397, 398, 399, 400–401
attempted expulsion, 382–389
fight against slavery, 335–339, 344–345, 346–349, 353–359, 368–369, 377, 379–389, 396, 397
law study, lawyer, 41, 43, 44, 45, 47, 52–53, 55, 57, 110
liking for winter, 3–4
"Lord Sharply," 266
love for Mary Frazier, 44–45, 46–52, 95
Macbeth policy, 226, 244, 333
mellowing, 124, 314, 315
Minister Resident to the Netherlands, 57–66, 72–76, 82, 126
minister to Berlin, 76–78, 87–104
and treaty with Prussia, 92, 102
minister to Great Britain, 185–189
minister to Russia, 119–120, 123–172
and Alexander I, 139–140, 142, 144–145, 149, 151–152, 156–157, 160, 168, 170
and American ships, 156
churchgoing, 132–133
nationalist, 203
non-party politics, 110, 112–113, 117, 119, 398
old Nestor and curmudgeon, 386–388
portraits, 187, 194, 214, 389
President, Presidency, 176, 189, 199, 218, 252–259, 284, 288, 291–292, 296, 300
campaigning for the office, 206–215, 219, 221, 226–227, 239–245, 249–253
lame duck, 259, 290
plans and miscalculations, 253–255
public acclaim, 389, 392–395, 396
reading Cicero, 6, 12, 103, 205, 329, 333, 387
reading the Bible, 6, 16, 19, 33, 127, 165, 166, 174, 190, 203, 205, 249–

[435]